CAMBRIDGE LIBRARY COLLECTION

Books of enduring scholarly value

Classics

From the Renaissance to the nineteenth century, Latin and Greek were compulsory subjects in almost all European universities, and most early modern scholars published their research and conducted international correspondence in Latin. Latin had continued in use in Western Europe long after the fall of the Roman empire as the lingua franca of the educated classes and of law, diplomacy, religion and university teaching. The flight of Greek scholars to the West after the fall of Constantinople in 1453 gave impetus to the study of ancient Greek literature and the Greek New Testament. Eventually, just as nineteenth-century reforms of university curricula were beginning to erode this ascendancy, developments in textual criticism and linguistic analysis, and new ways of studying ancient societies, especially archaeology, led to renewed enthusiasm for the Classics. This collection offers works of criticism, interpretation and synthesis by the outstanding scholars of the nineteenth century.

Aftermath

The Scottish social anthropologist Sir James Frazer (1854–1941) first published *The Golden Bough* in 1890. A seminal two-volume work (reissued in the Cambridge Library Collection), it revolutionised the study of ancient religion through comparative analysis of mythology, rituals and superstitions around the world. Following the completion in 1915 of the revised twelve-volume third edition (also available in this series), Frazer found that he had more to say and further evidence to present. Published in 1936, *Aftermath* was conceived as a supplement to *The Golden Bough*, offering his additional findings on such topics as magic, royal and priestly taboos, sacrifice, reincarnation, and all manner of supernatural beliefs spanning cultures, continents and millennia. Sealing Frazer's profound contribution to the study of religion and folklore, this work remains an important text for scholars of anthropology and the history of ideas.

D0916381

Cambridge University Press has long been a pioneer in the reissuing of out-of-print titles from its own backlist, producing digital reprints of books that are still sought after by scholars and students but could not be reprinted economically using traditional technology. The Cambridge Library Collection extends this activity to a wider range of books which are still of importance to researchers and professionals, either for the source material they contain, or as landmarks in the history of their academic discipline.

Drawing from the world-renowned collections in the Cambridge University Library and other partner libraries, and guided by the advice of experts in each subject area, Cambridge University Press is using state-of-the-art scanning machines in its own Printing House to capture the content of each book selected for inclusion. The files are processed to give a consistently clear, crisp image, and the books finished to the high quality standard for which the Press is recognised around the world. The latest print-on-demand technology ensures that the books will remain available indefinitely, and that orders for single or multiple copies can quickly be supplied.

The Cambridge Library Collection brings back to life books of enduring scholarly value (including out-of-copyright works originally issued by other publishers) across a wide range of disciplines in the humanities and social sciences and in science and technology.

Aftermath

A Supplement to The Golden Bough

JAMES GEORGE FRAZER

CAMBRIDGE
UNIVERSITY PRESS

CAMBRIDGE
UNIVERSITY PRESS

University Printing House, Cambridge, CB2 8BS, United Kingdom

Published in the United States of America by Cambridge University Press, New York

Cambridge University Press is part of the University of Cambridge.
It furthers the University's mission by disseminating knowledge in the pursuit of
education, learning and research at the highest international levels of excellence.

www.cambridge.org
Information on this title: www.cambridge.org/9781108057509

© in this compilation Cambridge University Press 2013

This edition first published 1936
This digitally printed version 2013

ISBN 978-1-108-05750-9 Paperback

AFTERMATH

MACMILLAN AND CO., Limited
LONDON · BOMBAY · CALCUTTA · MADRAS
MELBOURNE

THE MACMILLAN COMPANY
NEW YORK · BOSTON · CHICAGO
DALLAS · ATLANTA · SAN FRANCISCO

THE MACMILLAN COMPANY
OF CANADA, LIMITED
TORONTO

AFTERMATH

A SUPPLEMENT TO
THE GOLDEN BOUGH

BY

Sir JAMES GEORGE FRAZER
O.M., F.R.S., F.B.A.

Fellow of Trinity College, Cambridge ;
Associate Member of the "Institut de France"

MACMILLAN AND CO., LIMITED
ST. MARTIN'S STREET, LONDON
1936

O miseras hominum mentes, o pectora caeca!
Qualibus in tenebris vitae quantisque periclis
Degitur hoc aevi quodcumquest!

Lucretius, Book II, lines 14–16.

PREFACE

THIS book is in no sense an independent treatise ; it is simply, as the title purports, a supplement intended to provide some fresh information on certain subjects which I have discussed more at large in *The Golden Bough*. Much of the new matter which the volume contains has been gathered from works that have appeared since the third and last edition of *The Golden Bough* was completed by the publication of the index volume in 1915 ; but I have also drawn on earlier sources which had escaped me when I wrote the original work. In that work, as in all my other writings, I have sought to base my conclusions by strict induction on a broad and solid foundation of well-authenticated facts. In the present work I have extended and strengthened the foundation without remodelling the superstructure of theory, which on the whole I have seen no reason to change. But now, as always, I hold all my theories very lightly, and am ever ready to modify or abandon them in the light of new evidence. If my writings should survive the writer, they will do so, I believe, less for the sake of the theories which they propound than for the sake of the facts which they record. They will live, if they live at all, as a picture or moving panorama of the vanished life of primitive man all over the world, from the Tropics to the Poles, groping and stumbling through the mists of ignorance and superstition in the eternal search after goodness and truth. When I first put pen to paper to write *The Golden Bough* I had no conception of the magnitude of the voyage on which I was embarking; I thought only to explain a single rule of an ancient Italian priesthood. But insensibly I was led on, step by step, into surveying, as from some specular height, some Pisgah of the mind, a great part of the human race; I was beguiled, as by some subtle enchanter, into inditing what I cannot but regard as a dark, a tragic chronicle of human error and folly, of fruitless endeavour, wasted time, and blighted hopes. At the best the chronicle may serve as a warning, as a sort of Ariadne's thread, to help the forlorn wayfarer to shun some of the snares and pitfalls into which his fellows have fallen before him in the labyrinth of life. Such as it is, with all its shortcomings, I now submit *The Golden Bough* in its completed form to the judgment of my contemporaries, and perhaps of posterity.

J. G. FRAZER

13th August 1936

CONTENTS

Magic may be divided into Homoeopathic or Imitative and Contagious Magic. A belief in magic has greatly affected the lives of primitive people, leading to economic stagnation as well as to tragic loss of life.

A familiar example of homoeopathic or imitative magic consists in making and injuring a magical image of an enemy. Imitative magic is also employed to facilitate childbirth, as in the Malay States, to relieve pain, as in Celebes, India, and Wales, and to cause sickness or death, as in New Guinea.

Many acts are forbidden in primitive society lest they might, on the principles of homoeopathic magic, entail undesirable effects. Certain foods are also forbidden for the same reason.

A magical sympathy is often supposed to exist between people at a distance, such that the actions of the one directly affect the other. Thus rules of conduct are often imposed upon wives during their husbands' absence in hunting, fishing, or fighting. Infidelity to an absent spouse is particularly dreaded and avoided.

Homoeopathic magic is often employed at sowing and planting to promote the growth and quality of the crops.

A fruitful branch of magic consists in the employment of the relics of the dead. By sympathetic magic birth and death are often associated with the flow and ebb of the tides.

Contagious magic is founded on the belief that things once conjoined remain, even after being disjoined, in sympathetic relation. Contagious magic is supposed to exist between a man and his bodily relics, especially his hair, nails, navel-string, and afterbirth. This has led to many observances throughout the world. Clothing and bodily impressions are often employed in contagious magic.

vii

CONTENTS   ix

through his name. Similarly primitive people are often forbidden to mention or address their relatives by marriage by name. The names of the dead are also frequently forbidden to the living.

A common taboo prohibits the telling of fairy stories at certain times and seasons, particularly during the day.

Sometimes the names of sacred chiefs and gods are tabooed. The same interdiction is frequently laid on the names of common objects of daily life, especially the names of objects for which men are searching, or of animals for which they are hunting. Thus in Malay, Assam, and Africa.

A common taboo in Africa forbids people to step over things or persons lying on the ground, from a fear that this will affect the thing or person stepped over.

CHAPTER XXXIV.—THE GARDENS OF ADONIS Pp. 350-352

The ancient gardens of Adonis have their analogy in many tribes of modern India.

CHAPTER XXXV.—THE RITUAL OF ATTIS Pp. 353-354

The self-mutilation of male worshippers at the vernal festival of Cybele and Attis finds an analogy in modern Nigeria.

CHAPTER XXXVI.—ATTIS AS THE FATHER
GOD . . . . P. 355

The Manggerai of West Flores, in the Indian Archipelago, personify the Sky and Earth as husband and wife.

CHAPTER XXXVII.—ON HEAD-HUNTING . Pp. 356-357

Among the motives alleged by head-hunters for the practice of taking heads is a belief that they thereby promote the fertility of the earth and the growth of the crops. Thus in Assam, Formosa, Nigeria, and South America.

CHAPTER XXXVIII.—THE TEARS OF ISIS Pp. 358-359

In modern Egypt a night about midsummer is called the Night of the Drop, because at that time a certain marvellous drop is believed to initiate the swelling of the Nile.

CHAPTER XXXIX.—THE STAR OF ISIS . P. 360

The Bafeoti of Loango, like the ancient Egyptians, employ the star Sirius to correct their calendar of twelve lunar months.

CHAPTER XL.—FEASTS OF ALL SOULS . Pp. 361-364

The custom of holding an annual feast to welcome the returning souls of the dead is observed in the Trobriand Islands, in China, in Tibet, and in Piedmont.

CHAPTER XLI.—MOTHER-KIN AND MOTHER
GODDESSES . . . . . . P. 365

A system of pure gynocracy, in which men are ruled by women, is reported to exist among the Valovale of South Africa.

B

CHAPTER I

MAGIC

IN *The Golden Bough* I have attempted to indicate the great part which a belief in magic has played in the early history of human thought. The belief rests on two main logical fallacies ; first, that by imitating the desired effect you can produce it, and second, that things which have once been in contact can influence each other when they are separated, just as if the contact still persisted. The magic based on the first of these fallacies may be called Homoeopathic or Imitative Magic, and the magic based on the second of these principles may be called Contagious Magic. If this analysis is correct it follows that a belief in magic is wholly fallacious. All its pretensions are false, and only deceive the dupes who trust in them. Yet the belief in magic has been, and still is, enormous throughout the world, though it has always been most prevalent among backward or primitive peoples. The magician believes that by his acts and words, his magical rites and incantations, he can control the forces of Nature for his own benefit and the injury of his enemies. The effects of this belief have been disastrous. Among primitive peoples, especially in Africa, natural death has commonly, or even regularly, been ascribed to the effects of maleficent magic, and the death has been usually avenged by the murder of the imaginary but really innocent culprit.[1]

But the disastrous effects of a belief in magic are not confined to the destruction of human lives. Its baleful influence has extended to the economic sphere. Speaking of the Kafir tribes of South Africa, a good authority tells us that

[1] J. G. Frazer, *Belief in Immortality* (London, 1913), i. 33 *sqq.*

I

" so strong is this fear of being accused of getting rich by magic that many people purposely refrain from undue cultivation of their land, lest others should accuse them of using magical practices to increase the fertility of the soil."[1]

Among the Bangala, a tribe of the Upper Congo River, the disastrous influence of a belief in magic or witchcraft has been admirably recorded by an experienced missionary in the following striking passage. " In judging the conservatism of natives and the way in which they have from generation to generation simply followed in the footsteps of their predecessors one must not forget that they have been, and many tribes still are, bound fast by witchcraft, fetishism, and superstition, and any tendency to burst these more than iron bands has been suppressed by fear of being charged with witchcraft. Some twenty-five years ago I knew a blacksmith who made a good imitation, from old hoop iron, of a trade knife, and when the king heard of it he thought he was too clever and threatened him with a charge of witchcraft if he made any more like it. If the man who made our locomotives had lived here, in Africa, and had given play to his inventive genius, he would not have been honoured, but killed as a witch. The native had a deep-rooted feeling that anything out of the ordinary was due to witchcraft and treated it as such. Some years ago I knew a native medicine woman who was successful in treating certain native diseases, and as she became wealthy, the natives accused her of giving the sickness by witchcraft in order to cure it and be paid for it ; for they said, ' How can she cure it so easily unless she first gave it to them ? ' She had to abandon her practice or she would have been killed as a witch.

" The introduction of a new article of trade has always brought on the introducer a charge of witchcraft ; and there is a legend, that the man who discovered the way to tap palm trees for palm wine was charged as a witch and paid the penalty with his life. That, however, did not stop the trade in palm wine. Through this fear of being charged with witchcraft, the natives would never of themselves have made any progress in art, science, or civilization. This fear was so real and so widespread that it stultified and killed every tendency to change and progress. The reasons which have

[1] Dudley Kidd, *The Essential Kafir* (London, 1904), p. 147.

caused a lack of material progress are the same that held them fast to their religious beliefs until the white man arrived with his tools, his skill, his medicine, and his religious teaching. In their old state they maintained strict conservatism, which, however, was quickly broken down by contact with the white man, whom they are always ready to acknowledge their superior in all things and worthy of imitation wherever this is possible."[1]

The rooted suspicion of magic or witchcraft with which these African blacks regard every material improvement in the arts and crafts has had a close parallel in ancient Rome. Once on a time a certain C. Furius Cresimus, whose small farm produced heavier crops than the largest farms in the neighbourhood, was shrewdly suspected of drawing away the corn from other people's fields by enchantment. Being brought before the public assembly at Rome to stand his trial on this charge, he produced in the sight of the people his ploughshares, his mattocks, his sturdy hinds, his sleek oxen, and pointing to them said, " These are my enchantments, gentlemen. I regret that it is not in my power to lay before you my toils and moils and sweatings." He was unanimously acquitted.[2]

Perhaps the most familiar example of homoeopathic or imitative magic is the practice of making a magical image of the person whom the magician desires to injure. By cutting, stabbing, or otherwise injuring the image he believes that he inflicts a corresponding injury upon his enemy whom the image represents ; by burning or otherwise destroying the image he imagines that he kills his foe. Of this practice I have cited many examples in *The Golden Bough*.[3] Here I will give a few additional instances. Thus, for example, in Morocco magical images made for this maleficent purpose are either of paper or of more substantial material. Thus if the magician wishes to cause his enemy to suffer from headache he will fashion an image of him in dough and pierce the head of it with a nail before putting the image in the oven. But

---

[1] J. H. Weeks, " Anthropological Notes on the Bangala of the Upper Congo River," in *Journal of the Royal Anthropological Institute*, xxxix.

(1909), p. 108.
[2] Pliny, *Nat. Hist.*, xviii. 41 *sqq.*
[3] *The Magic Art and the Evolution of Kings*, i. 55 *sqq.*

before doing so he should insert a scrap of his victim's garment in the image. If he wishes his victim to break his arm or his leg he wrenches the corresponding limb from the image. If he desires to make his victim suffer perpetual pain he beats a metal effigy of him with a hammer on the anvil for a whole day, saying, "As this hammer does not cease to strike the anvil for a whole day, so may misfortune pursue So-and-so his whole life long." Paper images are similarly treated for a similar purpose by piercing them with nails or thorns, or by tearing off a limb. In order that the victim may suffer throughout his whole life, the magician finally buries the image in a graveyard, a slaughter-house, a furnace, or a well. If the effigy is buried in the bed of a river the victim will be continually shivering from cold : if it is buried in a furnace he will constantly be hot with anger. If the image has been simply buried in the earth, without being broken or pierced, the victim will simply waste away. When the image is a statuette it suffices that it should be made by a sorcerer who recites the appropriate incantation ; but if the image is of paper it should be made by a scribe who writes cabalistic phrases on the body and limbs.[1]

Among the Ibo and Ijaw of Southern Nigeria "a mud, or wax image is modelled in the rough semblance of the man whom it is desired to injure, and while incantations are made, this is damaged by being pierced with a nail or spear or it is decapitated."[2] In Loango the magician fashions an image of his victim out of a root, pith, or wood, and with the appropriate imprecations throws it into a river or the sea or the wilderness, holds it in the fire, or hangs it in the smoke. Just as the image rots, shrivels up, or is reduced to ashes, the victim suffers a corresponding fate.[3]

Among the Bangala of the Upper Congo if a man loses a relative or has an enemy he goes to a magician (*nganga ya likenge*), who calls up in his saucepan of water the spirits of various people whose images are visible in the water, and the client, who sits by watching the water, allows one reflection

[1] E. Mauchamp, *La Sorcellerie au Maroc* (Paris), pp. 293 *sq.*
[2] P. A. Talbot, *The Peoples of Southern Nigeria* (London, 1926), ii. 182.
[3] *Die Loango Expedition, 1873–1876*, von P. Güssfeldt, J. Falhrenstein, E. Pechuël-Loesche (Stuttgart, 1909), iii. 2. p. 337.

after another to pass until the reflection of his enemy is shown in the water. That reflection or *elimo* (soul) he pierces at once with a palm splinter as a substitute for a spear, and the one who owns that soul will sicken and die. Sometimes a piece of wood or plantain stalk was roughly carved to represent the enemy, and wherever it was stuck or cut the enemy would feel intense pain in the corresponding part of his body, and to stick it in a vital part meant death.[1]

Among the Bakongo of the Lower Congo " the most powerful and most feared of all the fetishes in the catalogue belongs to the medicine-man who has the *mbanzangola* fetish. It is a wooden image, and is always retained in the possession of the witch-doctor, as it is too powerful to pass into the hands of a layman. A private person can buy other fetishes, but no private individual can own a *mbanzangola* fetish. If a person desires to cause pain, disease, or death to another, he goes to a medicine-man of this fetish order, and, having paid a fee, he drives in a nail or knife where he wants his enemy to feel pain. A knife-stab in a vital part means a painful death to the man's enemy ; a nail in the shoulder, elbow, or knee means excruciating agony in one or other of those joints, and indicates that the man does not want to kill his enemy, but only wishes him to have rheumatism, abscesses, or such minor ailments. These fetish images are often stuck over with nails, knives, and other sharp instruments. This is probably the only fetish image in connection with which there is no ' white art ' practised—it is neither a protective fetish nor a curative one, but is always used to inflict pain. On the other hand, I have heard that the nails, etc., driven into this image are offerings for benefits received ; and it is possible that someone suffering from a pain in part of his body has driven in a nail in a corresponding part of the image, to pass on the pain to an enemy whom he may think sent it to him, hence he may regard such a nail as an offering for a benefit he hoped to receive." [2]

A Greek inscription of the fourth century B.C. from Cyrene in North Africa records an interesting instance of the burning

---

[1] J. H. Weeks, " Anthropological Notes on the Bangala of the Upper Congo River," in *Journal of the Royal Anthropological Institute*, vol xl.

(1910), 395.
[2] J. H. Weeks, *Among the Primitive Bakongo* (London 1914), 225 *sq.*

of wax images for the purpose of destroying the malefactors whom they represented. Cyrene was founded by Greek colonists from the island of Thera in the Aegean, and in founding it the Thereans passed a very stringent decree directed against all such recreants as either refused to sail with the colonists or having sailed with them should afterwards desert the colony and return to Thera. Waxen images of all such traitors were to be made and burned, no doubt for the purpose of bringing down destruction on their heads.[1]

In Egypt, which borders on Cyrene, similar magical practices were rife in antiquity. On the subject Dr. Wallis Budge writes as follows : " There were, however, in Egypt many men who professed the art of Black Magic, the object of which was to do harm. In their hands the powers of magic were generally misused, and disastrous results, if we may believe the papyri, were the consequence. One of the commonest ways of working evil was by means of the wax figure. A man employed a magician to make in wax a figure of his enemy, whose name was cut or written upon it, and then to work magic upon it by reciting spells over it. If the spells contained curses they were supposed to take effect upon the living man ; and if the figure were stabbed, or gashes made in it with a knife, the living man suffered terrible pain, or wounds appeared in his body. If the figure were destroyed by fire or by any other means, the death of the living man ensued. The Westcar Papyrus tells us that the wife of one Aba-aner committed adultery in his garden with one of his servants. When the news of this was brought to him, he made a model of a crocodile in wax, and told his servant to go and place it in the river at the spot where his guilty wife's paramour was in the habit of bathing. As soon as this man entered the water on the following day, the wax crocodile turned into a huge living crocodile, which quickly devoured him. The Rollin Papyrus states that certain evil men succeeded in stealing a book of magic from the Royal Library, and that by following the directions contained in it they

[1] A. D. Nock, " A Curse from Cyrene," in *Archiv für Religionswissenschaft*, vol. 24 (1926), p. 172, and Dr. Ferri, " Alcuni inscrizioni di Cirene," in *Abhandlungen der Königlichen Akademie der Wissenschaften zu Berlin*, v. (1925) 19 *sqq.*

succeeded in making wax figures, on which they worked magic
with the view of injuring or killing the king of Egypt.   This
was held to be treason in the first degree, and the malefactors
seem to have suffered the death penalty.   The use of the wax
figures was not disdained by the priests of Amen-Ra at Thebes,
for they regularly burnt a wax figure of the fiend Apep, who
daily endeavoured to prevent the sun from rising.   This
figure was in the form of a serpent of many folds, on which
the name Apep was written or cut.   A case made of papyrus
inscribed with spells containing curses was prepared, and, the
wax figure having been placed inside it, both case and figure
were cast into a fire made of a special kind of plant.   Whilst
they were burning the priest recited curses, and stamped upon
them with his left foot until they were rendered shapeless and
were finally destroyed.   This magical ceremony was believed
to be very helpful to Ra, the Sun-God, who uttered over the
real Apep spells which paralysed him, and then killed him by
the fiery darts of his rays, and consumed him."[1]

In Burma similar magical practices of the injury of a foe
are still in use, as we learn from a good observer, Mrs. Leslie
Milne, who writes as follows : " As in many other countries,
in former times and even at the present day, small figures of
men and women are made to represent an enemy, and are
subjected to the injury they would inflict on that person.   In
southern Italy a lemon is sometimes named after an enemy
and needles or splinters of wood are stuck into it with the idea
of harming the person that it represents.   I have never heard
of fruit being so treated among the Palaungs, nor have I
heard of the drowning of a figure as in Kashmir, or of the
melting of a wax image in front of the fire as was done in
Europe.   The figures are made of earth, and as that in the
Palaung hills is not very plastic, it is moistened and modelled
on a piece of board in the manner of a rough bas-relief.   As
the board is kept horizontal, the figure retains the shape.   One
that was made for me as a specimen, by a wise man, was ten
inches long.   I hoped to bring it home, but it fell to pieces on
the journey.   Incantations are said over these figures, and
splinters of bamboo are stuck into them, or a hand or foot is

[1] E. A. Wallis Budge, *Osiris and the Egyptian Resurrection* (London, 1911)
ii. 177 *sq.*

cut off. The name is sometimes scratched on the figure while it is still damp. This can only be done by those who can write : those who cannot, whisper over it the name of the enemy."[1]

In Annam a common form of maleficent magic is to sculpture or to fashion out of paper a representation of the person whom the magician wishes to injure. This effigy is cut with the stroke of a knife or a nail, and hidden in the woodwork of the house or under the threshold of the person whom the magician desires to injure. It is believed that the master of the house will suffer an injury corresponding to the wound inflicted on the effigy. In Tonquin a similar maleficent magic is practised on wooden figures which represent the foes of the magician. The persons represented are supposed to suffer injuries corresponding to those which have been inflicted on their images. If the image is decapitated, the man soon dies. Malevolent carpenters will sometimes introduce into the roof of the house they are building little figures of wood or paper, carrying in their hands a stick, a knife, or a bucket. In the first two cases the figure is supposed to create domestic strife or robbery by armed burglars. In the last case all the good luck of the household is thought to be drained away by the mysterious action of the bucket. Further, in the chimney of the kitchen they place two images which by the action of the draught of air with the smoke are made to turn on their axes. This is supposed to breed perpetual quarrels between the householder and his wife, who are apparently thought to turn from each other as the images turn in the chimney.[2]

The Sedang, a warlike branch of the primitive Moï race in Indo-China, on the borders of Annam and Laos, employ the magic of images to secure success in hunting or war. Before setting out for war or the chase they fashion an image of the men or animals which they wish to kill, moulding them either out of the sand by the river-bank or the earth of their cultivated fields. Having done so they pierce the image with their spear, saying : " May the man or the animal thus perish with the thrust of my spear this very evening." They are

---

[1] Mrs. Leslie Milne, *The Home of an Eastern Clan* (Oxford, 1924), p. 263.

[2] P. Giran, *Magie et Religion Annamites* (Paris, 1912), p. 88.

persuaded that by this ceremony they ensure the success of their enterprise.[1] Among the Man Coc, a mountain tribe of Tonquin, when a man wishes to avenge himself on an enemy for some minor offence without killing him, he fashions an image of his enemy out of paper, fastens it to a tree, and shoots it with an arrow or a gun. This is supposed to make the culprit fall ill ; but for more serious offences the procedure is different and more complicated. The injured man writes the name and village of his enemy on a piece of paper, which he gives to a he-goat to swallow. Then he hangs the goat from a tree, and inflicts upon it a severe beating, saying all the time, " I am sorry to inflict such a punishment upon you, but the cause is my enemy, who has done me grievous wrong. You will have to bear witness of this before the divinities to whom you are despatched. If you fail to discharge this duty, your soul will never be reincarnated, but will float for ever in the air." After that he releases the unfortunate goat and lets it wander and die of hunger in the forest. He awaits with confidence the result of the message which he has sent by the goat to the heavenly powers, convinced that he thus ensures the death of his enemy and all his children.[2] In this last ceremony the goat is probably a substitute for an image of the man's enemy.

In Japan the practice of attempting to injure an enemy by maltreating an effigy representing him is common, and takes a variety of forms. The common mode of carrying out the charm is to form a lay figure of straw, pierced with nails, and to bury it beneath the place where the person to be punished usually sleeps. To avenge the infidelity of a husband or lover a jealous woman "will take an image of the faithless one, or, as the case may be, of his frail companion, or of both, and nail it to a tree within the grounds of some shrine. At whatever part of the effigy the nail is driven, there will be injury inflicted on the original in the flesh, but if she should meet the ghost of an enormous bull and exhibit terror at the apparition the potency of the charm is lost, and can only be revived with incantation and imprecations on the offending pair. Another

[1] " L'Envoûtement par l'Image chez les Moï, Annam," in *L'Anthropologie*, xxiii. (1912) p. 245.

[2] E. Diguet, *Les Montagnards du Tonkin* (Paris, 1908), p. 117.

account says that at two o'clock in the morning the operator goes to the shrine of her patron god (usually the *Ujibami*) ; on her bosom a mirror is hung ; sometimes she wears a crown formed of an inverted iron tripod bearing three candles. She carries a straw effigy of the victim in her right hand and a hammer in her left. She nails the image to the sacred tree before the shrine, and while so engaged she adjures the gods to save their tree, impute the guilt of desecration to the traitor, and visit him with their deadly vengeance. She visits the tree each night until the victim has sickened and died. Two other very similar forms of this type were described to me at Yokohama. In one the operator goes at night to the sacred tree of a shrine near her home, and, stating her purpose and the number of times she intends to come, drives in a nail through the image ; she then pays the specified number of visits, on each occasion driving in a nail ; after a number of nails have been inserted blood will issue from the tree if the victim is to die. In the other, among the details mentioned were the holding of a lighted incense-stick, by the operator, in each corner of her mouth, and the necessity of the most complete secrecy if the operation were to succeed in its object." [1]

The same method of injuring an enemy by injuring a magical effigy of him is known and practised by the Malays. " To destroy an enemy, there is prescribed in Malay versions of Muslim treatises a world-wide method of sorcery. A cabalistic symbol is inscribed on wax. The wax is moulded in the form of a man. Then the eyes of the figure are pierced with a needle, or its belly stabbed, while a purely Arabic charm is recited to call down upon the victim the anger of Allah ! To rob an enemy of power to harm, it suffices to draw his portrait in the dust of cross-roads, grind one's heel on his navel, tread on his pictured heart, beat the face with a stick, and recite a short imprecation." [2]

Thus among the Looboos, a primitive tribe of Sumatra, who differ from their neighbours in culture, language, and appearance, images of persons are made and ill-treated in all sorts of ways in order that by this means the persons themselves

[1] W. L. Hildburgh, " Notes on Some Japanese Magical Methods for Injuring Persons," in *Man*, xv. (1915) p. 118.
[2] R. O. Winstedt, *Shaman, Saiva, and Sufi* (London, 1925), pp. 165 *sq.*

may sympathetically suffer corresponding injuries. Usually two images are made, one of clay and one of wood ; the one is buried under the house of the person who is to be injured ; on the other Spanish pepper is smeared on the part corresponding to the heart ; or nails are knocked into that part of the image ; sometimes the image is hung on a rope and swung to and fro, in order that the person represented may in like manner shake with fits. If a lover finds that his love is not returned, he may employ a sorcerer to injure the woman by means of an image. The sorcerer makes an image of the woman out of earth taken from a burial-ground and dresses it in white, just like a corpse in a shroud. Then he makes a mixture of things that cause itch, down from plants, etc., and strews it on the image. Then he gets a little earth from the place where the woman last made water, also some locks of her hair and parings of her nails, and some grains of rice which she left over at a meal. Of these ingredients a mixture is made and placed on the puppet.[1]

In our own country cases of a similar use of magical effigies for the injury of enemies are upon record. In the reign of Duffus, the son of Malcolm, the seventy-eighth King of Scotland, " amidst these confusions the King was seized with a new and unusual disease, and no evident cause appearing, when all remedies had been tried in vain, a rumour was spread abroad, by I know not whom, that he was bewitched : the suspicion of this witchcraft arose either from some indication of his disease, or else because his body wasted and pined away by continual sweating, and his strength was so much decayed, that the physicians who were sent for far and near, not knowing what to apply for his relief ; when no common causes of the disease discovered themselves, they even laid it to the charge of a secret one. And whilst all were intent on the King's malady, at last news were brought, that nightly assemblies and conspiracies were made against him at Forres, a town in Murray. The report was taken for truth, there being nothing to contradict it ; therefore some faithful messengers were sent to Donald, Governor of the Castle, in whom the King confided much, even in his greatest affairs,

[1] J. Kreemer, " De Loeboesin Mandailing," in *Bijdragen tot de Taal-, Landen Volkenkunde van Nederlandsch-Indië*, lxvi. (1912) p. 329.

to find out the truth of the matter. He, from a discovery
made by a certain harlot, whose mother was noted for a
witch, detected the whole conspiracy. For the young girl,
having blabbed out, a few days before, some words concerning the sickness and death of the king, being apprehended
and brought to the rack to be tortured, at the very first sight
of it she presently declared what was designed against the life
of the King. Upon this some soldiers were sent, who found
the maid's mother and some other gossips roasting the King's
picture, made in wax, by a soft fire. Their design was that
as the wax did leisurely melt, so the King, being dissolved into
a sweat, should pine away by degrees, and when the wax was
quite consumed, then, his breath failing him, he should
presently die. When this picture of wax was broken, and the
witches punished, in the same month (as some say) the King
was freed from his disease."[1]

In England, under the reign of Henry VI, in the year
1447, the duke of Gloucester " worsted in all court intrigues,
for which his temper was not suited ; but possessing in a high
degree the favour of the public, had already received from his
rivals a cruel mortification, which he had hitherto borne without violating public peace, but which it was impossible that a
person of his spirit and humanity could ever forgive. His
duchess, the daughter of Reginald, lord Cobham, had been
accused of the crime of witchcraft, and it was pretended that
there was found in her possession a waxen figure of the king,
which she and her associates, sir Roger Bolingbroke a priest,
and one Margery Jordan of Eye, melted in a magical manner
before a slow fire, with an intention of making Henry's force
and vigour melt away by like insensible degrees. The accusa-
tion was well calculated to affect the weak and credulous mind
of the king, and to gain belief in an ignorant age ; and
the duchess was brought to trial with her confederates. The
nature of this crime, so opposite to all common sense, seems
always to exempt the accusers from observing the rules of common sense in their evidence ; the prisoners were pronounced
guilty ; the duchess was condemned to do public penance and
to suffer perpetual imprisonment ; the others were executed."[2]

---

[1] G. Buchanan, *History of Scotland*
(Edinburgh, 1751), i. 223.

[2] D. Hume, *The History of England* (Edinburgh, 1818), iii. 171.

But homoeopathic or imitative magic by means of an
image has.not always been used for the maleficent purpose
of injuring or killing a foe. Occasionally it has been employed
for the benevolent purpose of enabling the practitioner to be
born again to a higher form of life. On one occasion it was
so employed by the Rajah of Travancore in Southern India,
as we learn from the following passage of a contemporary
English writer. "Among the natives of Malabar every
man is confined to his own caste, follows the profession of his
ancestors, is married in childhood to his equal, and never
rises higher than the limited sphere in which he was born :
there may be exceptions, but they are very uncommon. One
indeed of an extraordinary nature occurred during my residence in Travancore : the reigning sovereign, who was of an
inferior caste of Brahmins, advanced himself into a higher,
by purifications, gifts, and ceremonies, part of which consisted in his majesty passing through the body of a cow,
of the size of life, and made of pure gold : this was the last
stage of purification ; and when performed, the cow was
divided among the Brahmins." The same writer adds in a
footnote : " Orme ascribes a different cause for the king of
Travancore's regeneration to that given to me by his subjects,
who, perhaps, were withheld by fear from assigning the true
reason. ' The king of Travancore has conquered, or carried
war into all the countries which lay round his dominions, and
lives in continual exercise of his arms. To atone for the blood
which he has spilt, the Brahmins persuaded him that it was
necessary that he should be born anew : this ceremony consisted in putting the prince into the body of a golden cow of
immense value ; where, after he had lain the time prescribed, he came out regenerated, and freed from all the
crimes of his former life. The cow was afterwards cut up, and
divided among the seers who had invented this extraordinary
method for the remission of his sins.' " [1]

Further, homoeopathic or imitative magic by means of an
image may be resorted to with the kindly object of facilitating
a woman's childbirth. Thus in Perak, one of the Malay
States, during the seventh month of a woman's pregnancy,
" a palm-blossom is swathed to represent a baby with a child's

[1] J. Forbes, *Oriental Memoirs* (London, 1813), i. 377.

brooch on the bosom. This doll, adorned with flowers, is laid on a tray and the tray placed in a cradle made of three, five, or seven layers of cloth according to the rank of the prospective parents. Midwife and magician sprinkle rice-paste on doll and cradle. The midwife rocks the cradle, crooning baby songs. Then she gives the doll to the future mother and father and all their relatives to dandle. Finally the doll is put back into the cradle and left there till the next day, when it is broken up and thrown into water."[1]

Again, homoeopathic or imitative magic has very often been employed for the benevolent purpose of relieving pain and healing the sick. Thus the Toradyas of Central Celebes employ rings of red stones to staunch the bleeding of wounds of all sorts.[2] The same principle of homoeopathic magic is employed by the Brahuis of Baluchistan to save the wheat crop when it is attacked by red rust. The remedy is thus described by Mr. Denys Bray, our best authority on the Brahuis. " At least once every five years a disease, variously known as *surkhi* or *ratti*, ' red rust,' attacks the wheat in Kalat, and the more thickly-growing and well-watered the crop, the severer the attack. It comes with the *nambi*, the moist south wind, which carries it rapidly from field to field ; but it soon disappears if the wind veers round to the north. If the *gorich* or north-wind doesn't blow, they get Sayyids to read charms over some earth and throw it on the fields. But if this fails, the Brahuis are not yet at their wits' end. They get hold of a boy seven years old, bathe him, and deck him out in red clothes, and make him drive a red kid through the fields attacked by the red rust. The kid is then slaughtered, and the meat distributed in the name of God. A most effective remedy this, they tell me."[3] And just as red stones are supposed to arrest the flow of red blood by homoeopathic magic so yellow objects are often employed as a cure for yellow jaundice. Thus among the Mehtars, the caste of sweepers and scavengers in the Central Provinces of India, when a child suffers from jaundice they get the flesh of a yellow snake which

---

[1] R. O. Winstedt, *Shaman, Saiva, and Sufi*, p. 118.
[2] N. Adriani and A. C. Kruijt, *De Bare'e-sprekende Toradja's van* *Midden-Celebes* (Batavia, 1912), 350.
[3] *Census of India*, 1911 : vol. iv., Baluchistan, by Denis Bray, p. 68.

appears in the rains, and of the *rohu* fish, which has yellowish scales, and hang them to its neck ; or they catch a small frog alive, tie it up in a yellow cloth, and hang it to the child's neck by a blue thread till it dies.[1] In Wales the old cure for jaundice was to put a gold coin at the bottom of a pewter mug, fill it with clear mead, and ask the patient to look into it without drinking any. This was to be done while repeating the Lord's Prayer nine times over without a mistake.[2] However, Welsh opinion seems to hesitate between regarding yellow objects as a cure or as a cause of jaundice and other ailments, as we learn from the following passage : " Yellow was considered very bad for the ' sterricks ' (hysteria), and country folk said that if you gazed too long upon a ' yellow rag ' you would become ' silly and moon-struck.' The plague was often called the yellow sickness or the yellow complaint. At the same time, a person suffering from jaundice was advised to wear a yellow ribbon or woollen rag around his throat. But in some parts of Wales it was asserted that yellow worn on any part of the body would induce or ' conjure ' the jaundice. If a yellow-hammer could be caught and held before the face of a person afflicted with jaundice, a cure might be expected. A piece of amber or a topaz put in a drinking goblet or cup, and the latter filled with mead, was a cure for jaundice. The skin of a lizard or viper placed under the pillow served the same purpose." [3] And in Wales, as yellow objects have been used as a cure for jaundice, so on the same principle of homoeopathic magic, red objects have been employed as a cure for scarlet fever and other maladies. So " in 1859 a doctor of the old school ordered a patient suffering from scarlet fever to be dressed in red night and day clothing. Red curtains were suspended from the window-pole and the old-fashioned, four-posted bedstead was draped with red material. Smallpox patients were also enveloped in red, and red blinds or curtains were drawn across the windows. At the first approach of scarlet fever or smallpox the person was subjected to red treatment. There was an old superstition

---

[1] R. V. Russell, *Tribes and Castes of the Central Provinces of India* (London, 1916), iv. 224.
[2] M. Trevelyan, *Folk-Lore and Folk-Stories of Wales* (London, 1909), p. 228.

[3] M. Trevelyan, *op. cit.* p. 312.

that if scarlet fever or smallpox were epidemic, red flannel worn around the neck, or next to the skin on any part of the body, warded away the disease. Even in the present day the peasantry of Wales cling very closely to the old superstition about a bit of red flannel as a preventive against fever, smallpox, and rheumatism." [1]

Further, homoeopathic or imitative magic is employed by the Looboos of Sumatra to impart virulence to the poison with which they smear their arrows. The poison is made from the sap of various plants. The mode of preparing the poison is kept secret by the priest or sorcerer, for many magical ceremonies are observed in the preparation of it. It may not be made in the house, but out in the forest. The priest or sorcerer is assisted by a number of persons, each of whom has his appointed task, the general intention of the ceremonies being to represent dramatically the desired effect of the poison. Thus one man will climb a tree and pretend to fall down from it ; another makes as if he must vomit violently ; while another lies naked on the ground and mimics the motions of a man in convulsions. The poison is very strong, and causes severe vomiting. [2]

Similarly, on the principles of homoeopathic or imitative magic, among the Kai of Northern New Guinea a sorcerer imagines that he can cause sickness or death by mimicking in his own person the sufferings and death of his victim. [3]

Among the natives of the Bathurst and Melville Islands, off the northern coast of Australia, the faces of boys at initiation are rubbed with the tendrils or " whiskers " of yams, for the purpose of promoting, on the principles of homoeopathic magic, the growth of whiskers on the faces of the novices. [4]

In primitive society many acts are forbidden, in other words, are tabooed, because it is believed that if they were committed they would, on the principles of homoeopathic magic, entail certain undesirable results. Of such taboos I have given many examples elsewhere. [5] Here I will add

[1] M. Trevelyan, *op. cit.* p. 311.
[2] J. Kreemer, *op. cit.* p. 308.
[3] Ch. Keysser in R. Neuhauss, *Deutsch Neu-Guinea* (Berlin, 1911), iii. p. 137.

[4] Baldwin Spencer, *Native Tribes of the Northern Territory of Australia* (London, 1914), p. 99.
[5] *The Magic Art and the Evolution of Kings*, i. 111 *sqq.*

some fresh examples.   Thus among the Birhors, a primitive tribe of Chota Nagpur in India, " a Birhor woman, like a Santal woman, must abstain from eating such fruits of the *tarop* (*Buchania latifolia*) or the *terel* (*Diospyrus tomentosa*) tree as may grow together in one accrescent calyx.   If she infringes this taboo, she will give birth to twins.   A woman must not comb her hair at sunset.   Should she do so her hair will fall on *Singbonga*'s rice, as that is the time when *Singbonga* (identified with the sun) retires to eat.   A pregnant woman must not step over a *sagar* or block-wheel cart. Should she do so, her child's throat will emit a creaking sound like that of a *sagar*.   A pregnant woman must not step over a dog.   Should she do so, her child's belly will make a rumbling noise like that of a dog.   A pregnant woman must not eat the flesh of deer, of hare or porcupine, or other animals with hair on their bodies, nor even look at them when brought home by a hunting party. Should she do so, she will give birth to children with hairy bodies."[1]

Again, the Chadar, a small caste of weavers and village watchmen in the Central Provinces of India will not throw the first teeth of a child on to a tiled roof, because they believe that if this were done his next teeth would be wide and ugly like the tiles.[2]

Among the Looboos of Sumatra, while a birth is taking place no one should peep round the corner of the house-door ; else the child in the womb might miss its way and so retard the delivery.   For the same reason people entering the house must not stop on the threshold but must come straight in or go straight out.   All chests and boxes must be open, and the clothes and hair of the woman must hang loose.   Further, all efforts are made to get a brooding hen and to set it down before the woman, in order that by its contagious example the birth may be hastened.[3]   This last provision is, of course, not a taboo but a positive injunction of homoeopathic magic. Among the Toradyas of Central Celebes it is similarly a rule that any person entering the house of a pregnant woman should not stand on the threshold but pass straight in, any

[1] S. C. Roy, *The Birhors* (Ranchi, 1925), pp. 376 *sqq.*

[2] R. V. Russell, *op. cit.* i. 402.
[3] J. Kreemer, *op. cit.* p. 313.

delay on the threshold being no doubt supposed to retard the woman's delivery.[1]

In Africa, among the Boloki or Bangala of the Upper Congo, when a man is making a canoe, he must not drink water, or otherwise it is believed that the canoe would leak, in other words, would take water into its hull, just as he takes water into his body.[2] Among the Ibibios of Southern Nigeria, " old women may not touch soup made in deep pots, ' lest they receive too much nourishment therefrom, which will cause them to live beyond the allotted span.' Neither may their chop (food) be cooked upon logs in which the least trace of sap remains, lest this should act as a rejuvenating influence. Only quite dry and sapless branches may be used for them. This taboo is most carefully kept. Many an aged crone sits shivering, at night-time, in a far corner rather than venture to warm her withered limbs near the glow of a fire nourished by partially dried logs, while all who hold by old custom would rather starve to death than eat food prepared over such fires. The reason is somewhat pathetic. They fear that, should the taboo be broken, their mothers and grandmothers, instead of welcoming them near the door of the ghost town, will drive them away with harsh words on arriving, and force them to dwell lonely and kinless amid outcast wraiths." [3]

In Wales a woman should never spin or knit in or near a field, for the witches will tangle the yarn.[4] This rule is an example of a taboo based on the principle of homoeopathic or imitative magic, the winding of the woman's threads being supposed to entail the winding of the corn-stalks by the witches. A similar taboo was observed, no doubt for a similar reason, by women in ancient Italy.[5]

Further, in primitive society many foods are forbidden, in other words tabooed, on the principle of homoeopathic magic. Thus among the Suk, a tribe of Kenya, in East Africa, a woman may not eat the flesh of a cow that has died in calf,

[1] Adriani and Kruijt, *op. cit.* ii. pp. 43 *sq.*

[2] J. H. Weeks, *Among Congo Cannibals* (London, 1913), p. 298.

[3] P. A. Talbot, *Life in Southern Nigeria* (London, 1923), p. 224.

Cf. *id.*, *The Peoples of Southern Nigeria*, iii. 743.

[4] M. Trevelyan, *op. cit.* p. 209.

[5] *The Magic Art and the Evolution of Kings*, i. 113, citing Pliny, *Nat. Hist.* xxviii. 28.

lest she herself should die in pregnancy.[1] Among the Lobango, a tribe to the west of Lake Tanganyika, the flesh of the parrot may be eaten only by very old men, for they say that if young men ate of it their children would have the waddling gait of the bird.[2]

The Toradyas of Bada in Central Celebes commonly eat the larvae of beetles, but a pregnant woman may not eat of this food, because they find that the insect swells through eating the pith of the tree, and they fear that if the woman partook of it the foetus in her womb would swell in like manner, and so impede her delivery.[3] Again, among the Kai of Northern New Guinea, many different kinds of food are forbidden to children on the ground of homoeopathic magic. Thus it is thought that if they ate of the flesh of the white cockatoo they would be cowardly like the bird. Further, if they ate the flesh of the cuckoo, a girl would afterwards give birth to children one after the other in unbroken succession, and a boy would be reduced to marrying a widow. Again if children ate the flesh of cassowaries or kangaroos they would get long necks and thick bellies like those of the bird and animal, and the girls would have no breasts, to the swelling of which they passionately look forward. If, at the season of puberty, a girl were to eat of mussels and crabs, her breasts would remain undeveloped like these crustacea in their shells.[4] Again the fruit of the *make* tree is thought to render the eater cowardly, hence it may only be eaten by women, but is always forbidden to men, and its wood may not be used to kindle a fire in which a spear is tempered, lest it should infect with its cowardice the spear and hence the warrior who used it. The reason for this taboo appears to be that the wood of the tree is eaten by the larvae of a species of beetle, which is presumably taxed with cowardice by the natives.[5]

The savage commonly believes that there exists between persons at a distance from each other a magic sympathy such that the actions of the one directly affect the other, however far

---

[1] M. W. H. Beech, *The Suk* (Oxford, 1911), p. 10.
[2] D. Livingstone, *Last Journals* (London, 1874), ii. 145.
[3] A. C. Kruijt, " Het landschap Bada in Midden-Celebes," in *Tijdschrift van het Nederlandsch Aardrijkskundig Genootschap* xxvi.(1909) p. 349.
[4] R. Neuhauss, *op. cit.* iii. 34 *sq.*
[5] R. Neuhauss, *op. cit.* iii. p. 104.

he or she may be away.   Such a magic sympathy, for example, is usually believed to exist between husband and wife when the husband is away hunting or at war and his wife remains at home.   In such cases during the absence of the husband the wife is commonly bound to observe certain rules of conduct, to do certain things or to abstain from doing others. She does certain things which are thought to promote the safety and success of her absent spouse : she refrains from doing other things which, if she did them, might endanger the success or the life of her distant husband.   Elsewhere I have given examples of this primitive form of a belief in telepathy.[1]   I will now adduce some fresh examples.

Thus among the Banyankole, a tribe in the south of Uganda, " when a man was out hunting, his wife refrained from sexual intercourse with other men, and she had to be careful not to kill anything ; even vermin, if caught, must be thrown away and not killed.   She might let no man pass behind her back, but warned him to keep in front of her. Should she neglect any of these precautions, her husband's chances of obtaining game in the hunt would be ruined." [2] Among the Thonga or Ronga of south-eastern Africa the rule of continence is also binding on a woman during her husband's absence at the chase.   On this subject M. Junod, our great authority on the tribe, writes as follows : " Old Makhani assured me that incontinence on the part of the wife at home would have as a consequence that the husband would be attacked and killed by wild beasts far away in the desert. These women must moreover observe certain rules in their everyday life.   They must smear the floor of their huts only early in the morning or late in the evening, viz. at the time of day when their husbands are not busy hunting ; then all will go well with them.   Thus the behaviour of the wife has its effect on the husband's fate.   Sometimes she will take a plate, fill it with attractive food, call her children, and distribute it to them, in order that her husband, when passing through the villages in the far-distant country, may be well treated by the inhabitants of the land.   Should a death occur in the hunter's village during his absence, it is very

[1] *The Magic Art and the Evolution of Kings*, i. 119 *sqq*.

[2] J. Roscoe, *The Banyankole* (Cambridge, 1923), p. 163.

dangerous for him. It was for this reason that Makhani was attacked by a buffalo which injured his skull. Those at home must expose themselves to vapour baths in the early morning and late in the evening, as in the case of smearing the hut."[1] In the same tribe, when a man is away hunting a hippopotamus, his wife at home is bound to observe certain rules of conduct for the purpose of ensuring his success and safety in the chase. " As soon as the assagai is thrown, somebody runs to the hunter's village to inform his wife. The woman must at once shut herself up in the hut and remain perfectly quiet. She lights a pipe and keeps it burning the whole time. A little child brings her her pipe (Ronga women are great pipe smokers). She must neither eat nor drink ; or, if she is very thirsty, the child will bring her some water. In any case, she must not crush her mealies ; she must not go out of the hut except to satisfy her natural wants. Why ? Because if she were to move to and fro in the village, this would induce the hippopotamus to rush wildly upon her husband and possibly kill him. Moreover, the fact that she remains confined within the circular walls of the hut will have as a consequence that the wild beast will be in some sort imprisoned in a small space ; it will not be able to run far away and escape."[2]

Among the Tumbuka of Central Africa, when the hunters were going forth to kill an elephant, after all preparations had been made, and sacrifices had been offered to the spirits of the dead, " the chief hunter charged the villagers who remained that there must be no quarrelling or immorality indulged in within the village. None were to leave their homes to visit other places, but all were to remain quiet and law-abiding lest the game disappear, or turn in anger and rend the hunters. As he left the village he blew a loud blast on a little horn he carried, and shouted back to the people, ' Let those who have gone before, go in peace ; but let him that utters my name die.' The curse was to prevent any talk about the projected hunt lest the game hear about it and hide away."[3] Among the Baya, a tribe of equatorial Africa

[1] H. A. Junod, *The Life of a South African Tribe*, 2nd edit. (London, 1927) ii. 62.

[2] Junod, *op. cit.* ii. 69.
[3] D. Fraser, *Winning a Primitive People* (London, 1914), p. 136.

on the eastern borders of what used to be the Cameroons, hunters observed a period of continence of three days before going forth to the chase lest they should be killed by the animals. If a wife does not accompany her husband on the expedition she is bound to remain in her hut the whole time of his absence. Above all she must practise strict continence. If a village has hunted several times without success the hunters accuse their wives of infidelity, and a hunter is called in to exorcise them. If the ill-luck persists, the women are subjected to the poison-ordeal in order to determine the culprit who by incontinence has brought misfortune on the village.[1]

Among the Wandamba of East Africa, in the Tanganyika Territory, the principle of magical telepathy is also employed to bring down the elephants which they hunt. "When following a herd containing a large bull they rub some of his excrement into one or two of their cicatrices, which they open slightly for the purpose, and pour some of the original medicine into his footprints, thereby causing him to travel slowly and lag behind apart from the rest of the herd. An elephant or any other animal may also be called back out of a herd by taking a piece of grass, leaf, or twig which he has chewed and expectorated, and placing it on a lonely grave, whereupon the desired animal may shortly be encountered alone and deprived of life like the occupant of the grave ; part of the leaf or grass should also be mixed with the original medicine and rubbed on the gun and in one of the cuts. Another device sometimes employed in order to procure a copious blood spoor after wounding is to stick a fruit of the *mtonga* tree on the end of a gun, roast it in fire, and then pour the juice down the barrel of the gun and rub it into one of the cuts on the hunter's arm ; and it is always a wise precaution to rub in a little more medicine on viewing the quarry and before approaching to close quarters." In this tribe moreover, elephant hunters are bound to practise the strictest continence during the hunt, and their wives at home must observe the same rule.[2] Among the Hehe, another tribe of Tanganyika, while the hunters are

---

[1] A. Poupon, "Étude ethnographique des Baya de la circonscription du M'bimon," in *L'Anthropologie*, xxvi. (1915) pp. 107 *sq.*

[2] A. G. O. Hodgson, " Some Notes on the Hunting Customs of the Wandamba of the Ulanga Valley, Tanganyika Territory," in *Journal of the Royal Anthropological Institute*, lvi. (1926) pp. 62 *sq.*

out to kill elephants, the people at home may not beat each
other nor break firewood nor cut their hair, for they say that
were they to do so their actions would harm the absent
hunters.[1] Among the Wachamba, a tribe of Usambara in
Central Africa, while a hunter is away in the forest his wife at
home is bound to observe all the magical restrictions which
are incumbent also upon him. She remains alone for weeks,
and, following the directions of a medicine-man, abstains from
doing certain things which, according to the sage, might
bring harm upon her distant spouse. Thus she may not cut
anything in the house, nor place her bed in the sun, nor shut
her house-door, nor flirt with other men or have intercourse
with a stranger. She is forbidden to receive visits from men
in her hut. Only her closest relations may feed with her. If
she does not observe these restrictions, it is believed that her
husband will fall ill or perish in the forest.[2]

Speaking of the Bantu tribes of Central Africa in general,
a writer who lived twenty-nine years among them tells us that
" hunter's taboos affect also the hunter's wife, and the laws
pertaining to success in the chase are numerous and intricate.
Inviolate faithfulness of husband and wife during the former's
absence in the hunting field is one of the first and most important laws for hunters if they are to have luck. If a woman
is unfaithful during her hunter husband's absence, the hunter
is exposed to failure, danger from wild animals, and even
death. If the elephant charges and the hunter is killed, the
woman is tried for murder on the ground of concealed adultery
and breaking the taboo, and is at once executed." [3]

Similar practices based on the principle of magical telepathy or action at a distance are reported from other parts of
the world. Thus among the Oraons of Chota Nagpur in
India, while the men are absent from the village on the
Summer Hunt, not only the hunters themselves, but their
wives at home, are bound to observe strict sexual continence.
" It is believed that if this taboo is disregarded by any Oraon,
male or female, his or her fellow-villagers, or at any rate the

---

[1] O. Dempwolff, " Beiträge zur
Volksbeschreibung der Hehe," in
Baessler Archiv, iv. (1914) pp. 160 *sq.*
[2] A. Karasek, " Beitrage zur Kennt-
nis der Waschambaa," in *Baessler-
Archiv*, iii. (1913) p. 88.
[3] D. Campbell, *In the Heart of
Bantuland* (London, 1922), p. 94.

members of his or her family who have joined the hunt, are sure to have ill-success at the hunt. Another taboo which the stay-at-home Oraons of such villages have to observe is that they must not kill, beat, or even purchase any eatable fowl or animal so long as the hunters are away from home. An interesting feature of this Summer Hunt is that so long as the men are out hunting, the Oraon women of the village behave like men. Several of them dress like men, go about with men's *lathis* or sticks in their hands, and use the jargon of the males. As for example, they say to each other, *gucha ho becha ho* (come along, let us dance)—as men say while talking to each other, instead of *guchae bechae ho*, as women ordinarily say to each other. The women also pose as men before strangers coming to or passing through the village, and realise drink-money from them by threatening to poke them with their *lathis*. Oraon women of such villages are by common consent allowed at this period perfect liberty to behave in this way, and even alien landlords and police-officers submit to their demands for drink-money. The utmost license of speech is also permitted to these women, and they may with impunity abuse any man they meet in the filthiest language they choose. During these days the women also set up an *akhra* or dancing-ground for themselves in the village. This *akhra* is called the *chot* or minor *akhra*, and here the women dance and sing till a late hour of the night in the manner of young men. If during these days any Oraon woman refuses to join the dances at the *Chot akhra*, the other women pour water over her head, poke her with their *lathis*, and finally drag her by force to the dancing-ground. The idea seems to be that to omit the village dances during these nights bodes ill for the village—and perhaps for the hunters too. Two motives appear to lie at the root of this custom—first, an anxiety to let the outside world know that everything is going on as before in the village so that the enemies may not know that the fighting people of the village are away ; and, secondly and principally, the superstition that if the people in the village are merry, the hunters also will, by sympathetic magic, have cause to be merry. After they have finished their dances at the *akhra*, the women approach the houses of such men as have not joined the hunting-party, poke their *lathis* at the doors of their huts, taunt the men (except, of course, old men and young children) as womenly cowards and abuse them in the filthiest language they can think of. Before proceeding to the *akhra* they generally drive away these stay-at-home men temporarily from the village, unless they have themselves already taken care to keep themselves out of their way." [1]

Among the Moï, a primitive people of Indo-China, "hunting rites are numerous and for the most part rest on the same conception which we have noticed before in relation to other rites, namely the belief in the power of imitative or sympathetic magic. Thus a hunter never eats the flesh of the hare or deer for fear of becoming as timorous as these creatures. This species of food is only permitted to old men, women, and children. If a wild-boar hunt is in progress the hunters taking part must abstain from fat and oil. Without this precaution the animal would undoubtedly slip through the meshes of their nets and escape its pursuers. When the Laotians slaughter elephants for the sake of their ivory the women are absolutely forbidden to cut their hair or nails, otherwise the monsters would infallibly break the stakes of the palisade in which they are entrapped." [2] Among the Chams, another people of Indo-China, " the women who remain behind in the village are strictly forbidden to quarrel among themselves while their husbands are away looking for eaglewood. A breach of this regulation would mean that the men would run grave risk of being attacked by tigers or bitten by serpents." [3]

Among the Kiwai of British New Guinea a man may not go out hunting while his wife is in childbed or menstruating, for it is believed that were he to do so he would be killed by a pig or a shark, or meet with some other calamity. The blood flowing from his wound is associated by sympathetic magic with that of his wife. If a woman has intercourse with another man while her husband is away hunting, it is believed that the absent spouse will meet with nothing but ill-luck. [4]

---

[1] S. C. Roy, *The Oraons of Chota Nagpur* (Ranchi, 1915), pp. 231 *sqq.*
[2] C. Baudesson, *Indo-China and its Primitive Inhabitants* (London), p. 135.
[3] *Ibid.* p. 305.
[4] G. Landtman, *The Kiwai Papuans of British New Guinea* (London, 1927), pp. 114 *sq.*

The same people hunt dugong by harpooning them in the sea, and during their absence the people at home have to observe certain precautions for ensuring the success of the harpooners at sea. These have been described by Professor Landtman as follows : " When, after a successful expedition to the reefs, a dugong is being cut up, the harpooner secures the skin of its face, including the nostrils and the neck. The piece of skin is stretched between splints of bamboo and dried. Part of the windpipe is fastened at the mouth, and at the lower end of the skin a bunch of magical herbs. The skin is hung on a stick by a string passed through the nostrils. Before leaving for the reefs the owner obtains a little of the *manababa* plant from his wife (she has held it for a while in her vulva), and some of it he chews and spits upon the skin. The rest is kept in the hole of the harpoon-shaft, and part of the same medicine he will later on chew and blow out upon the first pole (*masi*) to be used for the harpooning platform. The skin is called *momoro wodi* (" dugong nose "). Sometimes several skins are hung up outside the same longhouse by different people. The lower jaw of a dugong recently caught is hooked on to each skin. The skin is supposed to bring success to the harpooners. No one at home goes near it. It would be very bad if one of the children should happen to touch the skin and cause it to move : ' suppose push him like that, face he go other way—dugong he go too, clear out.' During the night the harpooner's wife watches the skin from the door in the moonlight. If the thing stirs of its own accord, she will rejoice, for it means that her husband is at the very moment spearing a dugong. The wind is supposed not to be able to move the skin, on account of the shortness of the string with which it is attached. It is important that the stick on which it hangs should lean over a little in the direction of the reefs, indicating the spot towards which the dugong should betake themselves. Hunting in the bush or by canoe under sail— that is nothing (it is not so difficult), say the natives. If the game is not to be found in one place, the hunters are at liberty to look for it anywhere else they choose. Not so the harpooner on the platform. He remains stationary, and it is the dugong which must be induced to go to him. Hence the many rigorous observances required in that kind of hunting.

While the harpooners are out on the reefs, the people at home
must observe certain very strict rules of conduct in order not
to jeopardize the others' luck, but also to assist them in a
positive way.   The dugong will be frightened away if firewood is cut or coconuts are broken close to the house (particularly in the evening, when the harpooners have mounted
the platform).   That kind of work must be performed some
distance off in the bush.   No drum must be heard in the
village, nor any noise ; the people at home must keep just as
quiet as the crews waiting in the canoes.   Sometimes all the
young people are sent away from the village, so as not to
' move ' the house by any chance.   They go and camp at
some suitable place, while only the old people remain at home.
On the other hand, it is regarded as a lucky sign if a baby
cries during such a night.   This means that a dugong is just
being speared.   The people seem to think that the spirit of
the dugong comes to the child, and the pricking of the animal's
whiskers on its face and body makes the baby cry.   No
women must quarrel while their husbands are harpooning,
for the spirits of the women too are thought to participate in
the fight, causing a noise which will be heard by the dugong.
The worst is if a man ' steals ' the wife of a harpooner at home,
for it is from her body that the husband has obtained the
medicines essential for success.   ' Suppose man he humbug
that room (where the medicines come from) he shut him door
belong dugong, all same shut him door.'   While the harpooner is away, his wife will in the daytime wear her grass
skirt very loosely tied on, and for the night she takes it off
entirely and sleeps nude.   Sometimes in the night she lies
down naked on her back at the door through which her
husband has passed out, holding her feet widely apart, one
at each doorpost.   This causes the dugong to come.   Some
women refrain from lighting a fire while their husbands are
away harpooning, lest they should burn their hand—a bad
thing, for it is with that hand that they have passed the valuable medicines to the men.   All the harpooners recognize the
important services rendered them by their wives, and for this
reason they take care to let their relatives by marriage have a
share in the dugong meat.   During the absence of the harpooners on the reefs some old man at home may assist them

by means of a certain rite, which he performs on the village beach. He walks along the water's edge by himself in the night chewing some *manababa*, which he spits into the water, uttering certain incantations. Providing himself with a bough of the *warakara* tree, he steps out into the sea and repeatedly makes a sweeping gesture with the bough in the water towards himself, after which he throws the bough on to the beach and leaves it there. At the same time he calls on all the dugong to come to the harpooners, and names all the islands whence the animals should muster at the reef where the harpooners are waiting. He also asks certain spirits to bring the dugong there." [1]

In Samoa "when a boat belonging to any family was fishing for *bonito* or sharks it was forbidden to mention the names of the fishermen by the people on shore, as if they were talked about they would get no fish. I do not know whether the people believed that the *aitus* or spirits would hear the conversation and report it. If any person came to the house of a family from which some of the members had gone on a fishing expedition and were to ask where they were, they would be told that they were ' looking aside ' (*faasangaese*). It was also forbidden to untie any bundles of native cloth or mats in the house, or to lift up the nut blinds nearest to the sea whilst the boats were out. It was also forbidden to wash a *bonito* on the beach on such occasions ; whilst the fact of the chief being angry, or one of the men's wives being sulky or scolding in his absence, was quite sufficient to account for the fishing party being unsuccessful." [2]

Even in England there may be found traces of this primitive belief, that the good luck of fishermen at sea can through sympathetic magic be directly influenced by the conduct of their wives at home. At Flamborough in Yorkshire, " we have the custom of *Raising Herrings*. It is believed that a good fishing season will surely follow this ceremony. When the men are at sea, the wives and other women disguise themselves in various ways, often in the garments of their male relations, and with music and laughter go about the village

[1] Landtman, *op. cit.* pp. 137 *sqq.*
[2] G. Brown, *Melanesians and Polynesians* (London, 1910), p. 249.

visiting the houses of their neighbours, and receiving alms or God-speed." [1]

Savages commonly suppose that a magical sympathy or telepathy exists between absent men and their families, especially their wives, at home, not only in seasons of hunting and fishing, but also in times of war, and among them accordingly wives at home are bound to observe at such times certain rules of conduct for the purpose of ensuring the safety and victory of the absent warriors. Thus, among the Banyoro, a large and important tribe of Uganda, in time of war it was incumbent upon all wives who were left behind to live chaste lives, to make offerings to the gods, and to abstain from cutting their hair, and to put away all vessels used by their husbands until they returned. Should a wife shave her head during her husband's absence on an expedition and he be wounded or killed, she would be blamed as the cause, and the heir to the property would send her back to her relatives and claim the original marriage fee ; and she would find it difficult to obtain a husband in the future. Should a warrior strike his foot against a tree root or against a stone, he would attribute the cause of the accident to his wife who, he would say, was going about visiting and enjoying herself, instead of making offerings to the gods to protect him. [2]

Among the Baganda, the most important tribe of Uganda, when a man was setting forth to war his wife would accompany him for about a mile. " There the wife would kneel down by the roadside to bid her husband farewell ; she would hand him his weapons, and they would exchange necklaces, and take leave of each other, the wife committing her husband to the care of the gods. She would stand and watch her husband out of sight, and then pluck some grass from the roadside at the spot where they had taken leave of each other; this she would carry back with her to her house, and put it under the grass with which the house was carpeted, near the main post, and there it would be kept until her husband returned. The necklace would be placed with the fetishes,

[1] *County Folk-Lore*, vi., *East Riding of Yorkshire* (London 1912), p. 25, quoting A. H. Armytage in *Flamborough, Village and Headland* (Saffron Walden, 1880), p. 143.

[2] J. Roscoe, *The Northern Bantu* (Cambridge, 1915), p. 82.

and each day she would offer a little beer to them and pray, saying, ' My husband is at war, take care of him.' The warrior's friend, who had care of his wife, would tell her from time to time what offerings she should bring, that he might take them to the priest, and obtain the latter's inter- cession on behalf of the warrior. If a wife was negligent in these duties, or if she allowed any other man to make love to her, and was unfaithful, it was believed that her husband would fall, or at least be wounded in battle, because the gods resented her behaviour, and withdrew their favour and protection from him. . . . Should the wife be a woman who never menstruated, the husband, when taking leave of her, would scratch her with his spear, sufficiently to draw blood, and this would ensure his safe return. From the time that the warrior left his wife, he observed the rule of chastity until after the first battle was fought, or at least until the army had taken some spoil ; negligence in this respect would be fraught with grave disaster to his home and his children, or his wife would die, and the expedition would also be a failure."[1] In this account, which I have borrowed from Canon Roscoe's classic work on the Baganda, the prayers and offerings of the wife to the gods for her absent husband are purely religious, not magical. Here, as in so many cases, magic is reinforced by religion. Otherwise the relations between the Baganda husband and wife, particularly in the matter of mutual conjugal fidelity, are strictly magical, based on the principle of telepathy. With regard to mutual conjugal fidelity Canon Roscoe tells us elsewhere that " when a warrior returned home, his principal wife went out to meet him, relieved him of his weapons, and gave him a gourd of water ; some of this water he drank before entering his house. If his wife had been unfaithful during his absence at the war, the water was supposed to cause him to fall ill, and so the wife's unfaithfulness was discovered. Accordingly, if the husband fell ill, the wife was promptly put into the stocks and tried ; if she then confessed her guilt, and named the man with whom she had done wrong, the latter was heavily fined, or even put to death." With regard to the conduct of persons at home in time of war, Canon Roscoe tells us further

[1] J. Roscoe, *The Baganda* (London, 1915), p. 352.

that " during the time that a punitive expedition was away,
no one who was left behind was allowed to kill a sheep, but
only goats or cows might be killed. The penalty for killing
a sheep was confiscation of the man's property ; the reason
given for this custom is that those left behind were looked
upon as women, and that accordingly the meat of the sheep
was taboo to them. No man was allowed to enter the house
of a woman whose husband was absent, if the wife was sitting
in the doorway ; nor might a wife touch any man's clothing,
for, if she did so, it would bring misfortune on her husband's
weapons and might even cost him his life. The gods were
thought to be very particular about women observing the
taboos during their husbands' absence, and having nothing to
do with men. A man's principal wife was responsible to him
for the conduct of his other wives ; he tested her chastity on
his return home, by the water test described above, and if she
was found faithful, her word was accepted for the conduct of
the others." [1]

Among the Agni, a tribe of the Ivory Coast in West Africa,
when the men of a village have gone forth to war, leaving only
the aged and infirm men and the women and children behind,
all the women in the village paint their faces, breasts, and limbs
with white clay dipped in water. The paintings consist in
bands, either vertical or horizontal, and in diverse drawings
which seem to be left to individual tastes. Especially the clay
is smeared round both eyes. Thus decorated the women
assemble in the central place of the village, either of their
own accord or at the order of the old men who are left at
home. They take each a stick, which is called a gun, and
fall into line at the order of the oldest wife of the chief of the
village. Thus decorated and armed they execute a series of
very animated dances, running from one end of the village to
the other. The woman who commands them incites them
continually to fresh efforts, singing very licentious and filthy
songs, directed in abuse of the chief of the enemy, and in
praise of their own chief and his warriors. These refrains are
repeated by the dancers without the accompaniment of any
musical instrument. The wife of the chief and the old men
take particular care that the women do not pronounce the

[1] J. Roscoe, *The Baganda*, pp. 362 *sqq.*

name of any who are not directly concerned in the war.
The dances consist of rapid marches, analogous in cadence
and rhythm to the war dances of the men. The ceremony
ends with a rush of the women to the gate of the village from
which the men went forth to war. There they brandish their
spears and make derisory gestures in the direction of the chief
of the enemy and addressed to him. After that the dancers
resume their domestic duties, having laid down their sticks
but retaining their body-paintings, which they do not remove
until after the return of the warriors to the village. Afterwards, whenever their domestic duties permit of it, and
especially when they hear the shots of the warriors in the
distance, they resume their dances and songs. All the time
that these ceremonies last the women are supposed to be
transformed into men. Each of them is called by the name
of her husband, her brother, or her son, and the sticks
which they carry are called rifles. When the dancers are
tired, they sit on the earth, and converse among themselves
in the manner of men, addressing one another in salutations
otherwise reserved for the male sex. The wife of the chief
brings a jar of water, which, for the occasion, is thought to
be palm-wine. One of the women supports the jar on her
left thigh, and from it pours the water into a goblet, which she
holds in her right hand. From the goblet she first pours water
on the ground as a libation to Mother Earth and the spirits of
the dead buried in the village. Then she fills the goblet a
second time and passes it to the wife of the chief, who in her
turn pours some drops as a libation on the ground, then drinks
the rest of the water in the manner of men, allowing some of
the liquid to drip at each extremity of the mouth and imitating
the grimace which men make at drinking strong liquor.
Afterwards each of the women receives the goblet and drinks
the water in the same manner. When all have drunk, the
woman who has been pouring out spills what remains of the
water on the earth, and addressing the wife of the chief, says,
" Father so-and-so, I thank you." It is notable that except
in these circumstances the women never drink in this manner,
which is absolutely special to men. After drinking, the
women talk among themselves, continually addressing each
other in the names of men, each of them recounting their

supposed warlike exploits, telling, for example, how many prisoners they made, and giving the most precise details of their imaginary prowess. Then at the order of the chief's wife the dances and songs begin again, to last the whole day and a good part of the night, with the exception of intervals just noted and such as were consecrated to domestic work. During these last intervals, the comedy of sexual inversion ceases, and women resume their ordinary names. This custom constitutes for the women at once an amusement and a duty. On the one hand, the women take the greatest pleasure in this sort of comedy, and in the songs and talk which it authorizes : it suffices to observe the happy expression which they wear during the ceremony and the zest with which they afterwards recount its incidents. The occasions of it are not very frequent. On the other hand, the ceremony is obligatory. Whenever the women show any slackness or reluctance to begin the dances, they are urged on to them by the old men, " The men are fighting ; you must perform the ceremony." If they hear rifle-shots, the old men call to the women to dance faster and to sing more loudly. If the warriors, on returning from battle, learn that the women have not devoted all the time at their disposal to performing the ceremony, they reproach and abuse them. And if they return defeated, they do not hesitate to allege that the defeat is due to the failure of the women to perform the ceremony at the moment of battle. This custom is based on the belief that victory will fall to the side of those whose wives danced and sang the most, and above all danced and sang at the very moment of battle. That is why the dances are redoubled when the rifle-shots are heard. And that is why, when the fighting takes place at too great a distance for the sound of it to be heard in the village, it is necessary for the dancing and singing to continue all day long, with the briefest possible intervals, in order to ensure that the actual moment of combat should not coincide with a cessation of the dances and songs.[1] It might be difficult to find a stronger proof of savage faith in the telepathy of war. These savages apparently think that victory in battle depends more upon the women at

---

[1] M. Delafosse, " Coutumes observées par les femmes en temps de guerre," in *Revue d'Ethnographie et de Sociologie*, iv. (1913) pp. 266 *sq.*

home than upon the men in the field.

Among the Efiks of Southern Nigeria, " as night fell on the day when Efik warriors left the town, the wives who remained behind used to go to their sleeping-rooms and there don the garments of their absent lords. With this clothing the head wife also took the name of her husband, and while the ceremony lasted might call herself, or be addressed, by no other. Once clad in this strange attire, the women sallied forth to visit the chief compounds of the town, drinking palm wine, laughing and jesting at each. No matter how heavy and anxious might be the hearts beneath this manly guise, they dared not show the least anxiety, but must appear happy and brave, that by sympathetic magic the courage of their absent husbands should be upheld. The ceremony was called ' Ikom Be,' and it was most strictly forbidden that any man should witness it ; for this also was among the women's mysteries, and destruction would have fallen upon the race should any male have profaned the rites by his presence. All night long the women danced round the town to prove their courage and endurance. Only after dawnbreak might they creep back to rest, and even then tears were forbidden lest indulgence in such weakness might magically affect their absent lords—turning to water their hearts within their breasts and causing their strength to melt away." [1] Another account of the Efik customs runs thus : " Among the Efik during the absence of the fighting men, the women used to march about the town making a martial display with swords and guns, singing boastful war songs and keeping up their spirits gener- ally, so that the souls of their warriors in the field might be sympathetically encouraged. Each wore the clothing of her absent lord and also took his name, and might be addressed by no other during the ceremony, which was called Ikom Be, and might not be witnessed by any male or destruction would fall upon the town." [2] The analogy of this Efik custom to the custom of the Agni on the Ivory Coast described above is close and obvious.

Among the Ijaw of Southern Nigeria, while the men were

[1] D. A. Talbot, *Women's Mysteries of a Primitive People* (London, 1915), pp. 191 *sq.*

[2] P. A. Talbot, *The Peoples of Southern Nigeria*, iii. 846.

away at the war, the women at home had to keep up a bold and happy appearance, and had to offer sacrifices to the fetishes.   Every day they spread the tables with the favourite dishes of their absent husbands so that the souls of the warriors might not be driven by hunger to partake of the ensnaring feasts of the enemy's magician.[1]   Among the Ibo of the same region a wife had to remain strictly chaste during the absence of her husband at the war.   Her infidelity might affect the war medicines of her husband, and cause him to be wounded or killed.[2]

Among the Bantu people of Southern Nigeria, while the men were away at the war their wives at home were forbidden to wash, and they remained very quiet and anxious, and held no festivities of any kind.   If any of them during this time had illicit intercourse, it was believed that her husband would surely be killed, and if any of them had previously sinned in this way and had not confessed her fault before his departure, it was believed that he would incur great danger and would hear a shot whistle by his ears.   If he, after all, returned in safety, he would sell his faithless wife into another country.[3]

Among the Bangala of the Upper Congo, "when men went to fight distant towns their wives were expected not to commit adultery with such men as were left in the town, or their husbands would receive spear wounds from the enemy. The sisters of the fighters would take every precaution to guard against the adultery of their brothers' wives while they were on the expedition."[4]   Among the Ila-speaking tribes of Northern Rhodesia " the women were instructed to remain chaste while their husbands were away fighting, lest harm should befall them.   They were also forbidden to throw anything at one another, for fear lest their relations should be speared, or to imitate any kind of blow.   They were also forbidden to dance, the period until the safe return of the warriors was assured being one rather for mourning than for rejoicing."[5]

[1] P. A. Talbot, *op. cit.* iii. 835.
[2] P. A. Talbot, *op. cit.* iii. 842.
[3] P. A. Talbot, *op. cit.* iii. 856.
[4] J. H. Weeks, *Among Congo Cannibals*, p. 224 : *id.* in *Journal o*

the *Royal Anthropological Institute*, xl. (1910) p. 413.
   [5] E. W. Smith and A. M. Dale, *The Ila-speaking Peoples of Northern Rhodesia* (London, 1920), i. 176.

Among the Thonga or Ronga of South-east Africa in time
of war " the whole clan is subjected to many taboos. Those
who remain at home must keep quiet. No noise must be
heard in the villages. The women must not close the doors
of the huts. It is taboo : their husbands might meet with
' bitterness ' (*shibiti*). They might lack strength to run
away. Fires must be lit in the huts in the evening in order
that the warriors might ' have light ' where they are. It is
taboo to omit this precaution. Work in the fields must be
more or less suspended ; women may attend to it in the morning only, before the heat of the day, while the air is still fresh.
' Then, if the warrior has stepped on a thorn, the thorn will
be cool ; if he has knocked against a stump, the stump will
be quiet and not hurt him.' (Mboza). Old men who remain
at home must keep watch, and if they see a messenger coming
they follow him to the chief. Should he bring bad news,
they do not inform the women, as it is taboo to mourn over
warriors before the return of the army. A fine is imposed
upon those who contravene this law. It is taboo also to have
sexual relations as long as the army is on the warpath. This
would cause thorns to hurt the warriors, and they would be
defeated." [1]

Among the Khetran Baloch of Baluchistan in olden days
the women were strictly forbidden to grind corn on their
handmills when the men were out on a raid, because they
believed that the noise of the grinding would cause confusion
in the ranks of the raiders. [2] Among the Dusuns of the
Tuaran and Tempassuk districts of British North Borneo,
" when their men are on the warpath their women must not
weave cloth or their husbands will be unable to escape from
the enemy, because they would become uncertain in which
direction to run. In the weaving of cloth the backwards and
forwards movement of the shuttle represents the uncertain
movements of a man running first to one side and then to
another, in order to escape from an enemy. Women may not
eat from the winnowing basket ; for the edges of it represent
mountains, over which their men would not be able to climb.

---

[1] H. A. Junod, *The Life of a South
African Tribe* (London, 2nd edit.
1927), i. 470.

[2] Denys Bray, *Ethnographic Survey of Baluchistan* (Bombay, 1913),
i. 63.

The women must not sit sprawling about, or with their legs crossed, else their husbands will not have strength for anything.   On the other hand it is lucky for the women to keep walking about, for then the men will have strength to walk far." [1]

Among the Toradyas of Central Celebes, while the men are away on a raid certain taboos must be observed by the friends of the absent warriors.   The house must be kept clean. The sleeping-mat of the absent man may not be rolled up, but must be hung over a stick.   The wife and the nearest relatives may not leave the house by night.   Many sticks are burned to make a light during the whole night.   No cooking-pot may be lent out.   The wife may not wash her hair, nor seek for lice upon her head.   She may not dance or pay visits. The origin of these taboos lies in the belief that the soul of the absent warrior can suddenly return to the house.   In such a case he must find everything in order.   He must not see anything to make him uneasy or restless, since the body of the warrior is affected by all the emotions of his soul, and he might thereby be made unfit before the battle.   There were also other taboos which aimed at a sympathetic effect.   Thus the wife may not leave off her bark-cape (*baadje*), her head-dress, or her head-band in her sleep, so that her husband in the battle should not lose his head-dress, whereby his long hair would fall over his face and blind him.   During his absence she might not sew or handle anything in which there were thorns, nor pleat mats with *pandanus* leaves, whose edges were beset with thorns.   For if she did so her husband, on the day when he came face to face with the enemy, would feel pain in the soles of his feet.   In order that this should not happen the wife, every evening and morning, strewed the floor of her house with certain leaves, lest the soul of her husband should come to grief in this way.   The wives also continually carry about small branches of the waro-waro, a plant whose pods are very light and easily wafted by the wind. The waro-waro is the symbol of agility, and the carrying of it by their wives at home, must, by sympathetic magic, make the warriors agile in their movements.   The names of the absent

---

[1] I. H. N. Evans, " Notes on the Religion, Beliefs, etc., of the Dusuns, British North Borneo," in *Journal of* *the Royal Anthropological Institute,* xlii. (1912) p. 392 *sq.*

men may never be mentioned by those who remain at home : a mention of his name would lure the soul of the absent warrior back to the house, leaving his body without strength for the fight. Similar rules are observed by any young girl who has given her bark-cape or her head-dress to a young man who has gone off to war.[1]

Among the Kiwai of British New Guinea it is deemed very important that the people who remain at home while their friends are absent on a raid should observe certain rules of conduct, for their conduct is believed materially to affect the raiders and the expedition. " In the absence of the warriors the few old women who are associated with every man's house must keep some fires burning in the house in order to keep it warm, or defeat is sure to follow. The whole village must be kept quiet, for otherwise the enemy will be warned pre-maturely (as if hearing the noise) and run away. Therefore the women at home do only the most necessary work. They also have to restrict themselves to certain kinds of food. Fish and turtle are forbidden on account of the shyness of these animals, but dugong may be eaten, for they do not flee away so easily. Coconuts must not be husked or broken near the house, only in the bush, in order to avoid noise. A woman must not even wail if she feels sad, thinking of her absent husband." It is particularly disastrous if any man seduces the wife of an absent warrior during the raid, for in that case the husband would not succeed in killing any enemy, but might very likely be killed himself.[2] In the Loyalty Islands, to the east of New Caledonia, " a woman whose husband or son was absent in war would place a piece of coral to represent the warrior on a mat before her, and move it about with her right hand to represent his movements in the fight. Then with her left hand she would brush away imagi-nary obstacles and evils. The warrior was thus thought to be protected by the charm performed at home." [3]

Further, homoeopathic magic is often resorted to at sowing and planting for the purpose of promoting the growth and

---

[1] N. Adriani and A. C. Kruijt, *op. cit.* i. 235.

[2] G. Landtman, *op. cit.* p. 157.

[3] S. H. Ray, " The People and Language of Lifu, Loyalty Islands," in *Journal of the Royal Anthropological Institute*, xlvii. (1917) p. 297.

quality of the crops. Thus, for example, among the Chams
of Indo-China, when the flax is being gathered in it is proper
to pretend to be drunk, for the plant is thereby encouraged to
preserve its inebriating qualities.[1] The Toradyas of Central
Celebes prefer that a coconut-palm should be planted by an
old woman who has many children and grandchildren,
because they believe that a tree planted by so fruitful a woman
will bear a plentiful crop of coconuts.[2] The Berbers of
Morocco, at sowing wheat, observe customs which are similarly
based on homoeopathic magic. At Ait Hassan it is a woman
who scatters the first handful of seed. At Addar this duty is
confided to the girl who has the longest hair, for it is believed
that the wheat which grows from such grains will be as long
as the girl's hair. In the same order of ideas, at Nedroma
they think they can make a prodigious crop rise from the
earth by inviting the tallest worker to stretch himself at full
length in the first furrow. Then, in the place which he
occupied, they bury figs and an onion. Indeed, to bury in
the first furrow certain fruits of a particular structure, such as
figs, pomegranates, and locust-beans, is a usage frequently
observed. At Chenoua the peasant buries two pomegranates
in his field of cereals, and two locust-beans in his field of broad
beans. In Kabylie pomegranates, nuts, and acorns buried
under the same conditions serve to assure a heavy crop.[3] The
multitude of seeds found in figs and pomegranates, and presumably in the other plants employed for this purpose has
probably suggested their use in these fertility charms.

The homoeopathic magic of plants wears another and less
agreeable aspect in the Marshall Islands of the Pacific, where
they think that if a man eats a bread-fruit or pandanus fruit
which has fallen from a tree and burst, he will himself fall
from a tree and burst in like manner.[4]

A fruitful branch of homoeopathic magic consists in the
employment of the flesh, bones, or other bodily relics of the
dead as vehicles of magical force.[5] Thus among the Thonga

[1] H. Baudesson, *Indo-China and its
Primitive People*, p. 263.
[2] Adriani and Kruijt, *op. cit.* i.
267 *sq.*
[3] E. Laoust, *Mots et choses berbères* (Paris, 1920), p. 312.

[4] P. A. Erdland, *Die Marshall-
Insulaner* (Munster i. W., 1914),
p. 339.
[5] *The Golden Bough: The Magic
Art and the Evolution of Kings*, i.
147 *sqq.*

or Ronga of South-east Africa, when a battle had been fought with great slaughter, "magicians from all Zoutpansberg came and asked to buy parts of the slain in order to prepare their powerful charms. In fact, in their opinion, the flesh and blood of an enemy killed in battle is the most efficacious of all charms and makes a first-rate drug called *murumelo*. This medicine is also used for other purposes : with it the seeds are smeared in order to ensure a good harvest. When the mealies are two feet high, the magician ties together leaves on stems at the four corners of the field, after having treated them with the drug ; the blacksmiths from the Iron Mountains of Zoutpansberg buy it and mix it with their mineral ore, in order to strengthen the iron which they melt in their furnaces. Without this help they would obtain but slag. The hunters inoculate themselves in the following way with the powder obtained from the tendons and the bones : they make incisions in the skin of their wrists and elbows, draw a little blood, mix it with the drug, cook both in a pot, expose their arrows and assegais to the smoke, and rub the incisions with the powder. They will then be able to aim straight. The powder specially prepared from the tendons of slain enemies will be spread on the paths during future wars ; foes marching on it unknowingly will suddenly become unable to walk and will easily be killed. . . . The Nkuna magicians, in olden times, before they were influenced by their Pedi neighbours, used to dissect the tendons of the back (*riringa*) of the slain enemy, which they smeared with his medulla and hung to the shields of the warriors. Enemies seeing these shields would ' tjemeka nhlana '—' have their backs broken,' a figurative expression which means to be terror-stricken. A part of the body was also preserved and mixed with the war-medicine ; the idea which underlies this custom being evidently this : when you have eaten the flesh of your enemies, you have absorbed all their strength and they are unable to do you any further harm." [1]

Among the Wandamba of Tanganyika, when a man has been killed by an elephant and buried long enough to allow the bones to crumble, a medicine man comes to the grave and extracts from it part of the cranium, radius, and tibia, which

[1] H. A. Junod, *The Life of a South African Tribe*, i. 476 *sq.*

he puts in his medicine-bag.   When these are ground and cooked, and mixed with his original medicine, together with the parts taken from the dead elephant, they enhance still further the efficacy of the medicine.   Similar extracts from the bones of men who have been killed in battle or have died by drinking poison at a trial by ordeal are used for the same purpose, since, being parts of persons who have died violent deaths, they will hasten the violent death of the hunted animal.[1]

A Hausa charm to render a husband blind to his wife's infidelity is as follows :   take a certain kind of field-mouse, known to the Hausas as *Beran Benghazi*, and cut its throat. Then dry the body, taking care to save the blood with it, and pound it up with certain roots.   Obtain the right hand of a corpse, place the powder in couscous (?), and stir it with the dead hand, hiding it in your own.   At any time after the husband has eaten the couscous so doctored, he will be amenable to treatment, and all the wife has to do is place the dead hand under his pillow.   After this he will become so tractable that she will be able to talk to her lover in his presence, and he will even summon the lover to visit her at her request.   In both cases it is the corpse which exercises the soporific influence, for the husband is made as if to appear dead for the time.   The mouse (which moves in dark corners) and the roots (which never see the sun) cause the husband to be blind to the wife's misconduct even when he is awake.[2]

Among the Kpelle, a tribe of Liberia, warriors think that they become brave if they eat part of the corpse of a brave enemy, or drink the blood, or use his skull as a drinking-cup.[3]

In Java burglars strew earth from a grave in the houses which they intend to rob for the purpose of plunging the inmates into a slumber as deep as that of the dead.[4]   Among the Kiwai of British New Guinea, in order to destroy some other man's coconut tree, a sorcerer will proceed as follows. When somebody has died in the village the sorcerer provides

---

[1] A. G. O. Hodgson, " Some Notes on the Hunting Customs of the Wandamba," in *Journal of the Royal Anthropological Institute*, lvi. (1926) p. 64.

[2] A. J. N. Tremearne, *The Ban of the Bori* (London), pp. 165 *sq.*

[3] D. Westermann, *Die Kpelle* (Goettingen and Leipzig, 1921), p. 203.

[4] A. Bastian, *Die Völker des östlichen Asien* (Jena, 1869), vi. 170.

E

himself with a powerful poison by thrusting a small piece of the *tiroho* plant into the nose of the corpse, afterwards removing it and keeping it for future use. When the occasion offers itself, he sticks the *tiroho* into the trunk of a coconut tree belonging to his enemy, and pulls it out again. After that the tree will produce no more fruit, and all the young coconuts will die and fall off. The bane can be undone by the sorcerer if he washes the stick of *tiroho* in water, paints it red, and takes it home.[1] In New Britain a thief places bones on the breasts of sleepers in a house which he wishes to rob : the bones are thought to keep the sleepers slumbering soundly while the thief carries off the goods.[2]

Again, animals are a fertile source of homoeopathic magic, which seeks to employ their desirable properties for the use and benefit of mankind.[3] Thus, for example, the Kpelle, a tribe of Liberia, imagine that the flesh of the dwarf antelope imparts speed and cunning to the eater, and that the flesh of the leopard communicates strength and dexterity to him who partakes of it, and that the same desirable qualities are acquired by him who wears the teeth and claws of the leopard. The powdered shells of snails are supposed to heal sicknesses of various sorts, because the snail goes straight forward without turning on its tracks, and is in fact a good progressive animal, hence a patient who swallows a portion of its shell may be expected to make good progress towards recovery. The head and skin of a leopard are kept by a chief in his hut on account of the strength which is supposed to emanate from them.[4] Among the Banyankole, a tribe in the south of Uganda, when a child was slow of learning to speak, the parents would catch a bird called the *kanyonza* which was known for its chattering, and was said to be almost able to talk. The child's tongue was made to touch the bird, and it was believed that thereafter the child would be able to talk in a few days.[5] The following is a Hausa charm. If you

[1] G. Landtman, *The Kiwai Papuans of British New Guinea*, p. 99.

[2] B. Danks, " Some Notes on Savage Life in New Britain," in *Report of the Twelfth Meeting of the Australasian Association for the Advancement of Science* (Brisbane, 1910),

p. 456.

[3] *The Golden Bough : The Magic Art and the Evolution of Kings*, i. 150 *sqq.*

[4] D. Westermann, *op. cit.* p. 203.

[5] J. Roscoe, *The Banyankole*, p. 115.

suspect that any person is trying to wound or imprison you, get a piece of a skin of an electric eel and wear it on your person, for this will not only enable you to slip from the hands of anyone who tries to catch hold of you : it will also cause all blows of clubs or swords to slide off harmless.[1] Among the Ekoi of Southern Nigeria, when an infant is thought old enough, its wrist is cut and medicine rubbed in. The medicine which is intended to give strength is made from the index finger of the chimpanzee, and to impart quickness and activity fierce black ants are pounded up and used.[2]

The Pangwe or Fan, a tribe of West Africa, attribute to the swallow the peculiar power of evading its enemy, the hawk. Hence they think that if a man kills a swallow and carries it as a parcel on his person he will be sure to avoid the shots of the enemy.[3] The Bakongo of equatorial Africa employ frogs in composing the potion which warriors drink before going forth to battle, because they have noticed that when a frog's heart is extracted from its body it continues to pulsate for some time afterwards, and they hope that the frog medicine will communicate to them a corresponding tenacity of life.[4] In Loango men tie strips of antelope skins to their legs in order to give them the fleetness of the antelope.[5] The Ba-Ila of Northern Rhodesia compound medicines from various living creatures to assure the safety of their warriors in battle. They notice that a certain insect called Injelele darts rapidly over the surface of a pool or lake, so rapidly that you can hardly follow its motions. Accordingly, this insect is eaten with food to make the eater invisible in battle. Again, the skunk is a difficult creature to kill or catch, because when it is chased it jumps rapidly from side to side. Accordingly the Ba-Ila use it as a charm to ensure their safety in the fight. Some take the nose of the animal, others some of its hair, and put them in the medicine bag which they wear on their bodies. These are charms to secure that the spears of the enemy will fail to reach the wearer : that, indeed, he will be as hard to hit as the skunk. Similarly the quail, on account

---

[1] A. J. N. Tremearne, *The Ban of the Bori*, p. 172.

[2] P. A. Talbot, *The Peoples of Southern Nigeria*, ii. 372 sq.

[3] G. Tessmann, *Die Pangwe* (Ber-

lin, 1913), ii. 6.

[4] J. H. Weeks, *Among the Primitive Bakongo*, p. 192.

[5] *Die Loango-Expedition*, iii. 2, p. 351.

of its ability to hide, is eaten by a warrior to render him un-discoverable by the enemy.[1] And as people often eat the flesh of certain animals in order to acquire the qualities of these creatures, so in certain cases they avoid eating the flesh of others lest they should acquire certain undesirable qualities which are characteristic of these animals. Thus, for example, in Madagascar a pregnant woman is bound to abstain from eating a whole list of animals, which it is feared might influence for evil her unborn child. She may not eat water-scorpion or crabs, because otherwise her child would have deformed hands. She may not eat a certain bird of night (*tararaka*), because if she did so her child would have goggle-eyes like the bird. She may not eat *menamaso* (small wading birds), nor the feet of birds in general, and above all the feet of the goose and the duck, lest her child should have webbed feet and no calves. She may not eat red pepper, for otherwise her child would have red hair; nor mulberries or raspberries, lest he should have birth-marks of corre-sponding colour; nor the white of an egg, lest he should be an albino; nor the Madagascar sparrow, lest he should be quarrelsome like the bird; nor the ears of sheep, lest he should become timid like the sheep.[2] Among the domiciled Hindoos of Baluchistan " if a boy does not begin to talk freely within a reasonable time, he is given, in Barkhan, water out of which a sparrow has first drunk, and a piece of cake baked of dough which has first been rubbed over a kind of drum called *tabla*. In Lahri he is made to eat the head of a partridge roasted on embers, and in Bhag any food which has been touched by a sparrow or a parrot. These devices, of course, loosen his tongue and he becomes as chirpy as a sparrow or a partridge and as loud as a drum."[3]

During the time of harvest the Lakhers of North-Eastern India may not eat a bird or rat, because if they did so the spirit of the rat or bird would eat the paddy (rice in the fields). The reason why some of them sacrifice a mole instead of a hen is that the mole in burrowing throws up a large quantity

---

[1] E. W. Smith and A. M. Dale, *The Ila-speaking Peoples of Southern Rhodesia*, i. 263, ii. 360.

[2] A. and G. Grandidier, *Histoire physique, naturelle et politique de* *Madagascar*, vol. iv., *Ethnographie de Madagascar*, Part ii. (Paris, 1914) p. 250.

[3] Denys Bray, *Ethnographic Survey of Baluchistan*, ii. 51 *sq.*

of soil, and accordingly they hope that the paddy will bear a correspondingly large crop. Further, the porcupine is deemed to be a very propitious animal for the crops, as in burrowing he throws up a large quantity of earth, and accordingly at the harvest feast for the rice crop boys are given the flesh of porcupine to eat.[1]

The Toradyas of Central Celebes think that a sickness caused by a note of the woodpecker can be cured by a beak of the bird. When a man is suffering from a splinter of wood which has run into his body, the doctor will chew a piece of a tortoise's head and spit it on the suffering part of the patient's body, because they think that just as a tortoise withdraws and then protrudes its head, so the man's body will protrude and push out the intrusive splinter.[2]

The Kiwai of British New Guinea put the claw of a certain crayfish in a trap to enable the trap to catch many fish. This they do, because the crayfish turns its claws inwards in a peculiar fashion when walking, as if it were beckoning to some one. Hence its claw is supposed to beckon many fish to come into the trap.[3] Among these people, when a boy is being scarified, the head of a centipede is sometimes inserted into the wound, because these reptiles are almost as much dreaded as snakes. Hence the boy who has been inoculated with one of them is expected to become a great warrior.[4] When the first shoots of the yam crop come up through the soil, the natives of the Fly River, in British New Guinea, insert sticks in the ground for them to climb up. And in a hole close by the stick they insert certain pieces of the flying-fox which have previously been dried for the purpose. This they do because flying-foxes are extremely prolific ; hundreds of them may be seen hanging to a single tree at certain times of the year. And accordingly the natives imagine that by thus associating the yams with flying-foxes they will render the shoots of the yams equally prolific.[5] The Larrekiya youths of Northern Australia admire the musical chirping of a species of large grasshopper, and they eat the insect in order

[1] N. E. Parry, *The Lakhers* (London, 1932), pp. 437, 439.
[2] Adriani and Kruijt, *op. cit.* i. 409.
[3] G. Landtman, *The Kiwai Papu-* ans *of British New Guinea*, p. 170.
[4] G. Landtman, *op. cit.* p. 240.
[5] E. Baxter Riley, *Among Papuan Headhunters* (London, 1925), p. 98.

to acquire its vocal talent.[1] The Catios Indians of Columbia in South America give their boys the eyes of chameleons to eat, in order that the boys may ·be sly and circumspect like the animal. Also they give them to eat the eyes and the tail of the jaguar, that like the jaguar they may be strong in battle. Further, they give the youths to eat the eyes of certain birds which build very fine nests, in order that the young men may similarly build fine Indian huts.[2]

Further, inanimate objects also possess certain desirable qualities which primitive man attempts to appropriate by homoeopathic magic. Thus, in the opinion of the Malays of the Peninsula, " hard objects have strong soul-substance, of which magic makes good use. The sick are rubbed with bezoar-stones. A candle-nut, a stone, and an iron nail are employed both at the birth of a child and at the taking of the rice-baby.[3] The drinking of water in which iron has been put strengthens an oath, for the soul of the metal will destroy a perjurer. Applied to the wound, the blades of some daggers can extract the venom from a snake-bite, and the mere invocation of magnetic steel will help to join parted lovers."[4]

Before planting taro the Kai of Northern New Guinea place the shoots on a large and heavy block of stone in order that the crop of taro may in like manner be large and heavy,[5] and among them dancers possess certain round stones which roll easily on the ground. Before the men begin to dance each man chips off a small piece of this stone, takes it in his mouth with water, and then spits it out. By this ceremony he expects to acquire the mobility of the stone in the dance.[6] The Bukaua of Northern New Guinea employ stones shaped like taro tubers in the taro fields in order to promote by homoeopathic magic the growth of the taro crop. The stones are inserted in holes in the field, and they remain there until the harvest. At planting them the magician reinforces the effect of the magical stones by prayers which he addresses to

[1] H. Basedow, *The Australian Aboriginal* (Adelaide, 1925), p. 384.

[2] J. and M. Schilling, in *Archiv für Religionswissenschaft*, xxiii. (1925) p. 230.

[3] The rice-baby is an effigy made from the stalks of the rice on the harvest-field. Cf. *The Golden Bough :*

The Spirits of the Corn and of the Wild, i. 197 *sqq.*

[4] R. O. Winstedt, *Shaman, Saiva, and Sufi*, p. 74.

[5] R. Neuhauss, *Deutsch Neu-Guinea*, iii. 123.

[6] Neuhauss, *op. cit.* iii. 119.

the ancestral spirits, begging them to take care of the fields
and to ensure a good crop.[1] Further, among these Bukaua,
there are magicians who are believed to be able to cause
dearth by spoiling the taro crops through homoeopathic
magic. They have a great reputation and are much feared.
They work by means of stones which resemble the effects that
they desire to produce in the taro. For example, they employ
a stone which resembles a rotten fruit, which will cause the
plant to put forth many leaves but little or no fruit; or a round
stone with a long handle, which causes the seedling to put
out a long shoot but very small fruit; or a scraped stone of a
peculiar shape, which causes all the fruit to rot, so that in
digging up the plant nothing is found but foul matter adhering to the leaves; or a large stone with two small holes in it
resembling the holes made by beetles which have gnawed the
tubers, which is thought to cause the beetles to gnaw the real
tubers; or a small stone in order that the fruit itself may in
like manner be small.[2] Among objects possessed of magical
virtue the Kpelle of Liberia esteem stones very highly on
account of the endurance and strength which they are believed
to impart. Hence they make great use of them in magical
ceremonies for the benefit of the tribe or the town. In every
Kpelle village may be seen a stone hanging from a pole over
a path or buried in the ground. As the inhabitants of the
village in their daily avocations pass to and fro under or over
the stone they are supposed to acquire some portion of its
strength and stability.[3]

Among the natives of the Purari Delta in British New
Guinea we hear of a cure effected through homoeopathic
magic by the red glow of sunset. A native policeman was
suffering from a painful swelling in the groin. An old man
undertook to cure him. At sundown, while the sky was
aglow with red sunset light, the old man rubbed a red paste
on his hands, then facing westward he uttered a spell. Thereafter, still facing the western sky, he waved his arms before
him, then turning to the patient he rubbed the red paste over
his swelling. He explained in no uncertain terms that, as
the red of the sunset faded in a few moments, so he expected

[1] Neuhauss, *op. cit.* iii. 434.
[2] Neuhauss, *op. cit.* iii. 457.
[3] D. Westermann, *Die Kpelle*, p.
203.

the speedy and complete disappearance of the unfortunate policeman's swelling which had been smeared with the red paste. The result did not answer to his expectations.[1]

Men, both savage and civilized, are apt to associate by homoeopathic magic birth and death with the flow and ebb of the tides.[2] Thus in San Cristoval, one of the Solomon Islands, a woman of the noble Araha clan may not leave the house in her pregnancy. Pregnant women of other clans may leave their houses, but only at high tide, because they believe that it is only at high tide that women give birth to offspring successfully.[3] In Loango it is believed that people do not die when the tide is flowing, but only when it is ebbing.[4] Similarly the coast-dwellers of the North Andaman Islands believe that the soul of a dying man goes out with the ebbing tide.[5]

Thus far we have been dealing mainly with homoeopathic or imitative magic, which is based on the principle of resemblance, on the assumption that like things produce like effects. The other great branch of sympathetic magic, which I have called contagious magic, rests on the assumption that things which have once been conjoined remain ever after, even when disjoined from each other, in sympathetic relation, such that whatever is done to the one affects the other in like manner.[6] Thus for example contagious magic is supposed to exist between a man and the severed portions of his person, such as his teeth, hair, and nails, even when the teeth have been extracted and the hair and nails clipped. To take instances, among the Kai of Northern New Guinea a magician who desires to injure a person seeks to possess himself of some portion of his victim's person or of something which has been in contact with him, such as a hair of his body, a drop of his sweat, his spittle, or the remains of his food, or a shaving of wood. All these things must be taken quite fresh, as otherwise it would be uncertain whether the soul-

---

[1] F. E. Williams, *The Natives of the Purari Delta* (London, 1924), p. 231.

[2] *The Golden Bough: The Magic Art and the Evolution of Kings*, i. 166 *sqq.*

[3] C. E. Fox, *The Threshold of the Pacific* (London, 1924), p. 337.

[4] *Die Loango-Expedition*, iii. 2, p. 325.

[5] A. R. Brown, *The Andaman Islanders* (Cambridge, 1922), p. 175.

[6] Cf. *The Golden Bough: The Magic Art and the Evolution of Kings*, i. 174 *sqq.*

stuff of the man still remained in them.   In order to ensure
that the vital energy of the intended victim is still in the relic,
the object is inserted in a small bamboo tube and put by the
magician under his arm-pit to keep it warm.   Afterwards he
wraps the relic in a *Gama* leaf, in order that, just as *Gama*
leaves are devoured by caterpillars, so will the body of his
victim become the food of worms.   Afterwards he puts the
relic in a bamboo cane, and wraps it again in *Gama* leaves,
and ties them with the leaves of a certain climbing plant.
This climbing plant withers and decays very quickly, and so
shall the charmed man quickly lose his strength, and die.
Thus in these enchantments the magician employs both
contagious and homoeopathic magic for the destruction of his
victim.[1]

In New Britain much use is made of contagious magic for
the detriment or destruction of persons at whom the magician
has a grudge.   On this subject an experienced missionary
writes as follows: "Charms (*malira*) are many, and employed
for many purposes, such as to ensure love, to inflict disease,
and so on.   One consists in pricking the footprints of a person
with the barbed bone of a ray-fish.   This brings sickness or
evil on the person whose footprints have been so treated.
Sometimes they (the *malira* or charms) are made out of anything which has had connection or contact with a person, such
as remains of food of which she or he has partaken ; earth
from a footprint, excrement, spittle, hair, or clothing.   Any
of these things may be buried with incantation ceremonies,
and thus afflict the people concerned in various ways.   The
name of this custom is *puta* and the articles used *putaputana*.
This last kind of *malira* is much guarded against.   Expec-
toration is in the form of infinitesimal spray.   Stooling is
always in absolute secrecy, and with the greatest care.   When
shaving or cutting the hair, every scrap of hair is carefully
burnt, and the crumbs of one's food are also burnt.   Now all
these charms work by the power of the spirit world, and
through the spiritual connection of things and men, and day
and night people live and move and have their being in a
spiritualistic atmosphere.   They fear each other less as men
than they do as men possessed of a powerful *malira*.   To us

[1] R. Neuhauss, *Deutsch Neu-Guinea*, iii. 134 *sq.*

this is ridiculous, but not so to them."[1] Maori magicians
work harm on an enemy either by earth taken from his footprints or by a shred of his clothing, a lock of his hair, or his
spittle.   For this reason it is a rule with the Maoris when
they are travelling in the country of a hostile tribe not to walk
in the paths but to go as far as possible in the beds of streams
so as to leave behind them no footprints which a magician
might use to their bane.[2]

In Northern Australia, " in tribes inhabiting the country
around the Alligator Rivers a very favourite form of magic
is to get hold of some excrement, it does not matter how small
a piece, of a man or woman against whom you may have a
grudge, and whom you wish to injure.   All you have to do
is to get two or three friends to help you perform a rather
elaborate ceremony out in some quiet spot, where he cannot
see you, and you can easily compass his death.   The belief
has one beneficial result in that the camps of these natives are
much better from a sanitary point of view than in most Australian tribes, because everything is carefully buried lest
some enemy should be lurking about."[3]

Among personal relics which are the subjects of contagious
magic, extracted teeth occupy an important place.   Thus
among the Wajagga of Kilimanjaro in East Africa when a
child loses its milk-tooth it throws it on the roof of the hut
to the lizards playing there, saying, " Little lizard, you have
my tooth : send me a better one for it."   If the child does
not do this, it is thought that his second tooth will not come
quickly.[4]   In the Tigre tribes of Abyssinia, " if the milk-
teeth of little children break away, the parents say to every
one of them : ' Thou wert born in such and such a country,
and now that lies in this direction, turn thither and throw
thy toothlet ! '   And the little one takes a small piece of
quartz and another of charcoal with his toothlet.   Then he
turns in the direction in which they have told him and says,

[1] B. Danks, " Some Notes on
Savage Life in New Britain," in
*Report of the Twelfth Meeting of the
Australasian Association for the
Advancement of Science*, 1910, p.
455.
[2] E. Best, " Maori Religion," in
Report of the Twelfth Meeting of the
*Australasian Association for the
Advancement of Science*, 1910, p. 459.
[3] Baldwin Spencer, *Native Tribes
of Northern Australia*, p. 37. Cf.
id. pp. 257 *sqq.*
[4] B. Guttmann, *Dichten und Denken der Dschagganeger* (Leipzig, 1909),
p. 157.

MAGIC

' Howling hyena, this my pretty toothlet I give thee ; give
thou me thy ugly tooth.' And he throws his toothlet with
the other pieces. But later on when his man's incisors are
shed again or if they are broken by force, he gathers them and
also his molar teeth. Then when he is buried they are buried
with him, and his body is considered complete. But those
who do not know it do not pay attention to this nor gather
them."[1] In Marsa Matruh, the classical Paraetonium,
situated about 150 miles west of Alexandria on the Marmaric
coast, the population consists chiefly of Bedouins, with a
strong infusion of Berber blood. Among them, " in childhood, when a boy or girl loses his or her first teeth, the teeth,
as soon as they come out, are thrown into the air with the
exclamation, ' I have exchanged my tooth for thee, O star ! '
The explanation given for this practice is that there are from
time to time found in the fields white nodules of exceptionally
hard stone, which are believed to be fallen stars." The intention of the practice is no doubt to ensure by this means that
the next teeth of the child should be white and hard, like the
nodules of stone. A similar custom is practised by Algerian
children, who toss a lost tooth towards the sun, saying, " O
Sun, give me a new tooth ! "[2] Among the Sakalava, an
important tribe of Madagascar, when the first milk-tooth of a
child drops out, the child throws it on the roof of his parents'
house, saying, " I change this bad tooth for a good one."[3]
Among the Oraons of Chota Nagpur in India " children
besmear their own cast milk-teeth with cowdung and saliva,
and then throw these teeth on the roof of their own huts.
As they thus throw away the teeth, they call on the mice to
exchange their milk-white teeth with their own cast milk-
teeth, saying, ' May mine be new, and yours old.' "[4] Among
the Shans of Burma " when a child loses its first teeth it is
often teased by the big children, who call it ' Little Grandfather ' or ' Grandmother.' If an upper tooth comes out

[1] E. Littmann, *Publications of the Princeton Expedition to Abyssinia,* ii. (Leyden, 1910) p. 315.
[2] O. Bates, " Ethnographic Notes from Marsa Matruh," in *Journal of the Royal Asiatic Society,* 1915, pp. 724 *sq.*

[3] A. and G. Grandidier, *op. cit.* iv. 2, p. 292.
[4] S. C. Roy, " Magic and Witch-craft on the Chota Nagpur Plateau," in *Journal of the Royal Anthropological Institute,* xliv. (1914) p. 333.

it must be thrown on the roof of the house, and the child is
taught to say, ' Little mice, take away this old tooth and bring
me a new tooth.'   It is not an easy matter for a small arm to
throw so far, but there is always some kind big boy or man
who is willing to help.   The excitement is great when the
tooth falls short of the roof, or, when landing successfully, it
rolls down and falls to the ground.   It must at once be found
and thrown up again.   A lower tooth must be hidden among
the ashes of the hearth, while the same appeal to the little
mice is made." [1]   Among the Kiwai of British New Guinea
" the milk-teeth on falling out are sometimes buried—for
instance in a forefather's grave, just under the surface.   When
this is being done, the child is taught to call on the dead person
by name and say, ' I give you old tooth, you give me new one.'
In other cases the teeth are dropped into holes bored in the
beach by small reddish crabs (*siogoro* ; they look like spiders).
The child says, ' This teeth he no good, you give me good
teeth.'   Adults' teeth that have come out are thrown away
anywhere when no one is looking.   Teeth too can be used
for sorcery." [2]

Similar customs with regard to the cast milk-teeth are
known and practised in Europe.   In Swabia the first milk-
tooth cast by a child is dropped into a mouse-hole.   Then
the child gets a new one.   Others say that the child should
throw the tooth behind it, saying, " Mouse, thou hast an old
tooth, make me a new one."   Another version of this speech
at throwing away the tooth is, " Wolf, wolf, I give you here an
old tooth : give me a new one for it." [3]   In Masuren, a district
of Germany, a child throws its first cast tooth upon the stove,
saying, " Little mouse, little mouse, my dear little brother,
take my bone tooth and give me an iron one." [4]   In the North
Frisian Islands, " when a child's milk-tooth falls out, the
child should throw it into the clock or the chimney, saying,
' Little mouse, little mouse, I bring you a golden tooth.   Will
you bring me a tooth of bone in return ? '   Or, ' Little mouse,
little mouse, I bring you a tooth of bone.   If you bring me in

[1] Mrs. Leslie Milne, *The Shans at
Home* (London, 1910), pp. 40 *sq.*
[2] G. Landtman, *The Kiwai Papuans of British New Guinea*, p. 235.
[3] E. Meier, *Deutsche Sagen, Sitten,*

und Gebräuche aus Schwaben (Stuttgart, 1852), pp. 494 *sq.*

[4] M. Toeppen, *Aberglauben aus
Masuren* (Danzig, 1867), p. 83.

return a tooth of bone, I will bring you a silver tooth.' Or, ' Little mouse, little mouse, here is an old tooth. Give me a new one in return.' Or, ' Little mouse, there you have my old tooth ; bring me a new one instead.' " [1]

Again, among the personal relics which are the subjects of contagious magic the navel-string and afterbirth or placenta figure largely. [2] Thus among the Birhors of Chota Nagpur in India when a birth has taken place " the navel-string and the placenta are now taken up in a leaf-cup and buried just outside the threshold of the hut in a hole about a cubit deep. The Birhors assert that the reason why the afterbirth is thus buried and secreted is that should a dog or other animal eat it up the mother would sicken and die. If this hole is deep, the difference between the age of the present baby and its next brother or sister will be long, and if the hole be shallow, the difference will be short. The stump of the umbilical cord, when it dries up and falls off, is also buried just outside the threshold, but not so deep ; it is asserted that should it be eaten up by any animal, the child will sicken and die. If the stump of the navel-string is buried deep, the teeth of the baby, it is said, will be late in appearing ; but if the stump is buried just below the surface, the baby will teeth early." [3]

The Karwal of the United Provinces of India observe certain curious rites at a birth. A midwife of the caste attends. They bury the umbilical cord and placenta with a scorpion's sting, two and a half bits of donkey's dung, a porcupine's intestines, and some liquor. The scorpion's sting is supposed to render the babe immune, not from being bitten by, but from feeling, the bite of a scorpion. The dung is thought to prevent an excessive secretion of bile, the intestines of the porcupine to ward off colds, and the liquor is thrown in for luck. [4] Among the Kurmi, a caste of cultivators in the Central Provinces of India, " the part of the navel-

[1] C. Jensen, *Die nordfriesischen Inseln* (Hamburg, 1899), p. 248. In regard to these customs concerning first milk-teeth cast, cf. *The Golden Bough : The Magic Art and the Evolution of Kings*, i. 178 sqq.

[2] With what follows cf. *The Golden Bough : The Magic Art and the Evolution of Kings*, i. 182 sqq.

[3] S. C. Roy, *The Birhors*, pp. 223 sq.

[4] E. A. H. Blunt, in *Census of India*, 1911, vol. xv. Part i. p. 368.

string which falls off the child's body is believed to have the power of rendering barren women fertile, and is also intimately connected with the child's destiny. It is therefore carefully preserved and buried in some auspicious place, as by the bank of a river." [1] Among the Brahuis of Baluchistan, at child-birth " the navel is bound with a thread of blue cotton. But the cord that is severed is taken away and buried where no dog may hap upon it ; for should it, for lack of care, fall a prey to a dog or other beast, the babe grows restless and a lusty squaller." [2]

In Annam the navel-string and the afterbirth are reputed to possess particular virtues which according to their nature the people try either to appropriate or to guard themselves against. The navel-string should be kept for a year, and when it is dry they use it to calm the colics of the child. For this purpose they roast a part of it which they make the child swallow with some drink. When the part of the navel-string which remains attached to the child falls off, they gather it and hide it in some secret place until they can make use of it, or they hang it below the lamp to scare off evil spirits, or, again, they use it in the following manner : they take two pieces of brick reddened in the fire, and between them place the navel-string, which in a few moments is reduced to ashes : they gather the residue and use it as a medicine to cure the slight indispositions of the child. The afterbirth is also reputed to possess beneficent virtues or maleficent influences, which therefore they seek either to take advantage of or to avoid, according to the case. In Tonquin they generally bury the afterbirth, either before the door of the house, or in a certain place where they may go from time to time to see the state of the soil. If the soil grows hard, or if they have not buried the afterbirth at a depth of more than a metre, the infant will be subject to hiccup, and he will become subject to fits of vomit-ing if the soil should be too loose. At other times the after-birth is preserved with lime and a hundred needles in an earthen jar which is hung in a place exposed to the sun. This practice is intended to ensure the life of the child in cases where the parents are not able to rear the child them-

---

[1] R. V. Russell, *Tribes and Castes of the Central Provinces*, iv. 72.

[2] Denys Bray, *Life History of a Brahui* (London, 1913), p. 10.

selves, but are obliged to commit it to the care of strangers. Dumoutier reports almost the same custom. He adds that when the child reaches the age of ten the jar is taken down and thrown into the current of a river. Sometimes, but very rarely, the mother, to be certain of rearing her child, must eat a portion of the afterbirth.[1]

The people of Laos in Indo-China never consider the afterbirth as useless or throw it away in any corner : they believe that it remains in sympathetic connection with the individual, and according to its treatment will influence his lot in various ways. Attached to the highest branch of a tree in the courtyard, it becomes the prey of beneficent spirits, who will prepare for the child a happy life. Buried in the garden, it will secure the fidelity of the child to the house in which he was born : he will never leave it. Buried under the house-ladder it will, oddly enough, secure the child from pains in his stomach.[2]

Among the Looboos of Sumatra, the afterbirth is washed in water and put in a new rice-pot, which is then closed with a piece of white *kain* (?) and buried under the house. A stone is put over the spot to mark it. If the child cries, they think that ants have made their way into the rice-pot and are biting the afterbirth ; so they pour hot water on the ground over the buried pot in order to drive the ants away.[3] Among the Kooboos, a primitive aboriginal tribe of South-Eastern Sumatra, the natal fluid (*amnii liquor*), the navel-string, the afterbirth, and the blood, are regarded as in a way companions of the newly-born child, and above all a great vital power is ascribed to the navel-string and afterbirth ; because they are looked upon as brothers or sisters of the infant, and though their bodies have not come to perfection, yet their soul and spirit are just as normal as those of the child and indeed have reached a much higher stage of development. The navel-string and afterbirth visit the man who was born with them thrice a day and thrice by night till his death, or they hover near him. They are the good spirits, a sort of guardian angel

[1] P. Giran, *Magie et Religion Annamites* (Paris, 1912), pp. 110 *sq.*

[2] G. Maupetit, " Mœurs Lao-tennes," in *Bulletins et Mémoires de la* *Société d'Anthropologie de Paris*, vi. (Paris, 1912) p. 473.

[3] J. Kreemer, *op. cit.* p. 314.

of the man who came into the world with them and who lives on earth ; they are said to guard him from all evil. Hence it is that the Kooboo always thinks of his navel-string and after-birth before he goes to sleep, or to work, or undertakes a journey, and so on. Merely to think of them is enough ; there is no need to invoke them, or to ask them anything. By not thinking of them a man deprives himself of their good offices. Immediately after the birth, mother and child are washed and the afterbirth and navel-string are buried about a foot deep in the ground close by the spot in the forest where the birth took place, for Kooboo women are not allowed to bring forth in the village. Before they return to the house, this spot is subjected to a certain magical treatment (*gejampied*), for were this precaution omitted, then the navel-string and afterbirth, instead of being a good spirit for the newly-born child might become an evil spirit and visit him with all sorts of calamities out of spite for this neglect.[1]

Among the Dyaks of Borneo, when a father is removing the afterbirth to hang it on a tree either in the cemetery or on the site of a former house of the family, he is solemnly warned by his wife not to look to the right or the left, because were he to do so the new-born child would squint.[2] The assumption obviously is that by turning his eyes to right and left the father will, through contagious magic, cause the child to look askew. Among the Toradyas of Central Celebes in like manner the person who carries away the afterbirth may not look to the right or to the left, because otherwise the newly-born child will squint. The afterbirth is first washed in water, and then wrapped in leaves. It is then laid in a coco-nut shell or in an earthen cooking-pot, and to this some add spices. Sometimes the afterbirth is buried in the gutter out-side the house, so that, whenever it rains, it is continually washed. Or it is hung or laid in the branches of a tree. Generally the afterbirth of the first child is buried. If this child lives, the afterbirth of the second child is also buried.

---

[1] G. J. Van Dongen, " De Koeboes in de Onderafdeeling Koeboestreken der Residentie Palembang," in *Bij-dragen tot de Taal-, Land- en Volken-kunde van Nederlansch-Indië*, lxxxiii. (1910) pp. 228 *sq.*

[2] W. Howell, " Dyak Ceremonies in Pregnancy and Childbirth," in *Journal of the Straits Branch of the Royal Asiatic Society* (Dec. 1906), pp. 126, 128.

But if this child dies, the afterbirth of the second child is not
buried, but hung on a tree.   They say that, when the afterbirth of a child is hung on a tree and anything happens to it,
the child becomes noisy.   All this implies a vital connection
between a child and its afterbirth, but as to the nature of that
connection the Toradyas have no clear idea.[1]

Among the Kiwai of British New Guinea the afterbirth
is placed in a native receptacle (*baru*) and carried away and
buried secretly.   It is supposed to injure any one who might
tread upon the spot where it is buried, and if a sorcerer were
to get possession of it, he could, by means of it, work evil
magic on the mother, father, and child.   If the woman
entrusted with the disposal of the afterbirth were to bury
it very deep and to plant over it a tree of a certain species, the
mother would never bear another child.[2]   Among the Orokaiva of British New Guinea " the afterbirth is treated by
various alternative methods, some of which are thought to
affect the mother subsequently.   It may be placed in a small
receptacle built in a tree where it is left to decompose ; it
may be buried (if at the butt of a coconut tree the roots would
enclose or constrict it, and the result would be to render the
mother barren in future) ; I have been told that it may be
given to a sow to eat, ' when it is supposed to effect a transfer
of fecundity from the women to the pig.'   In some cases a
small enclosure is built underneath the house expressly to
prevent the pig gaining access to the afterbirth, which is
allowed to fall through the house floor ; and it is probably the
same notion at work : if the animal were to eat the afterbirth
it might have an adverse effect on the woman's fecundity." [3]
Among the Kai of Northern New Guinea, when the navel-
string falls off it is laid upon the branch of a fruit-tree.   The
child, especially if he is a boy, shall thereby become a good
climber.   As the natives have to obtain their fruit, especially
the bread-fruit, and birds and their eggs, from tall trees, it
is very important for these people to be good climbers.[4]
Among the natives about Cape King William, as the Germans

[1] Adriani and Kruijt, *op. cit.* ii.
48 *sq.*
[2] G. Landtman, *The Kiwai Papuans of British New Guinea*, p. 231.

[3] F. E. Williams, *Orokaiva Society*
(London, 1930), pp. 94 *sq.*

[4] Neuhauss, *op. cit.* iii. p. 27.

F

called it, in Northern New Guinea, when the navel-string falls
off, it is fixed to the edge of the net in which a child lies.   If
the child is of male sex, the navel-string, when the child
begins to walk, is loosened from the net and shot with an
arrow at a tree, so that it hangs from above.   Thereby the
boy will be able to climb trees in order later to take fruit from
them.   Otherwise the child when he grew up would be a
mere walker on earth, which would be hard for him.[1]   Similarly among the Yabim of Northern New Guinea, the navel-
string of a boy is put in a small netted pocket and hung on a
tree, because the boy must often climb trees in after-life.
For the navel-strings of girls no such custom is observed ;
but if the mother wishes no more children she throws the navel-
string into the sea.   Otherwise she places it under a large
stone.[2]   Among the Kulaman, a wild tribe of the Davao
district in Mindanao, one of the Philippine Islands, "the afterbirth is placed in the care of an old woman who carries it
directly to a sturdy molave tree (*Vitex littoralis Decne*) and
there attaches it to the branches ' so that the child may become strong like the tree.'   While on this mission the bearer
looks neither to the right nor to the left, nor does she hesitate,
for such actions on her part might influence the disposition
of the child or cause it to have physical deformities."[3]

In the Marshall Islands of the western Pacific the navel-
string of a boy is thrown into the sea in order that he may
become a good fisher : the navel-string of a girl is inserted
in a leafy *pandanus* tree, in order that she may be diligent in
plaiting *pandanus* fibre.[4]   In the Marquesas Islands, when a
birth had taken place, the afterbirth was hastily buried under
a frequented path in order that women passing over the spot
might acquire from the afterbirth the gift of fecundity.[5]

In the Kakadu tribe of Northern Australia the navel-string
" is cut off, by means of a mussel-shell, about two inches from
the abdomen.   It is dried and carried about, until the child
is about five years old, in one of the small bags that, in the
Kakadu and allied tribes, the native habitually wears sus-

[1] Neuhauss, *op. cit.* iii. 254.
[2] Neuhauss, *op. cit.* iii. 296.
[3] Fay-Cooper Cole, *The Wild Tribes of the Davao District, Mindanao* (Chicago, 1913), p. 156.
[4] P. A. Erdland, *Die Marshall-Insulaner* (Munster, 1914), pp. 125, 338.
[5] M. Radiguet, *Les Derniers Sauvages* (Paris, 1882), p. 173.

pended from a string round the neck. When once the child can move about freely it is merely thrown into a water pool, without any ceremony, but, up to that time it must be carefully preserved or else the child becomes very ill and probably dies. Should the child die before it is thrown away, it is burnt, but, on the other hand, if it be burnt while the child is still alive, either before or after such time as the child can walk about, the result again is serious illness and probably death. If the child dies while the mother is carrying the *Worlu* (navel-string), the death is attributed to the fact that the mother has broken one of the *kumali* (secret) rules ; she must, they say, have eaten forbidden food or washed in deep water, so that the child's spirit has gone from it. The father says to the mother, *Bialila niandida ; ameina jau ngeinyimma ; bialila warija*; 'the child (was) good; what kind of food (have) you (eaten); the child is dead.' He is very angry with the woman, and often punishes her severely." [1]

Speaking somewhat vaguely of the outlying tribes of Uganda on the backwaters of the Nile, a missionary tells us that " a matter of supreme importance is the safe disposal of the umbilical cord, which in the hands of evilly disposed persons may be a potent source of danger. If the cord is found and burnt by an enemy of the family, the child is bound to die, so the mother is careful to bury it in some obscure place away in the jungle ; for any one to be suspected of searching for the hiding-place is tantamount to being suspected of attempted murder. Then the father must be careful, according to belief in Patiko, on no account to cross a stream, or, indeed, any water, for some days after the birth of his child, or dire consequences will ensue." [2]

A curious branch of sympathetic magic consists in the treatment of wounds. Instead of applying treatment to the wound the surgeon, or rather the magician, applies it to the weapon which inflicted the wound, or to something else which represents it. Elsewhere I have given examples of this form of primitive surgery.[3] Here I will add a few more. Thus

---

[1] Baldwin Spencer, *Native Tribes of the Northern Territory of Australia*, p. 325.

[2] A. L. Kitching, *On the Back-*

waters of the *Nile* (London, 1912), p. 169.

[3] *The Golden Bough : The Magic Art and the Evolution of Kings*, i. 201 *sqq.*

the Kawars, a primitive hill tribe in the Central Provinces of India, " have the usual belief in imitative and sympathetic magic. If a person is wounded by an axe he throws it first into fire and then into cold water. By the first operation he thinks to dry up the wound and prevent its festering, and by the second to keep it cool." [1] In the Elgeyo tribe of Kenya, when a thorn has been extracted from a wounded foot it is carried along carefully until the next water is reached. There it is buried in the cool mud. This treatment of the thorn is supposed to keep the wounded foot cool and to prevent inflammation.[2] Among the Ibibio of Southern Nigeria, should a man be wounded in war despite all the magical safe-guards with which he has armed himself, the misfortune is attributed to a supposed breach of fetish law inadvertently committed or to the superior power of the enemy's magic. In such a case, instead of washing the wound with hot water as was the usual custom, the native doctor used to go into the forest and cut a stick the size of the gash. This sub-stitute was washed and tended as though it were the real wound, until by sympathetic magic the injured flesh grew whole.[3]

In the Kagoro tribe of Northern Nigeria, if a man is wounded by a spear or sword and the place refuses to heal, the weapon, if it can be obtained, is washed with water, which is drunk by the patient, who is then supposed to recover.[4]

The form of contagious magic which consists in applying medical treatment to the weapon which inflicted a wound instead of to the wound itself has been commonly practised, and doubtless is still practised here and there, by ignorant people in our own country. "The treatment of surgical cases in the North by no means corresponds to that pursued by the faculty. When a Northumbrian reaper is cut by his sickle, it is not uncommon to clean and polish the sickle. Lately, in the village of Stamfordham, a boy hurt his hand with a rusty

---

[1] R. V. Russell, *Tribes and Castes of the Central Provinces*, iii. 401.

[2] J. A. Massam, *The Cliff Dwellers of Kenya* (London, 1927), p. 226.

[3] P. A. Talbot, *Life in Southern*

Nigeria, p. 234; cf. *id.*, *The Peoples of Southern Nigeria*, iii. 823.

[4] A. J. N. Tremearne, " Notes on Some Nigerian Headhunters," in *Journal of the Royal Anthropological Institute*, xlii. (1912) p. 161.

nail. The nail was immediately taken to a blacksmith to file
off the rust, and was afterwards carefully rubbed every day,
before sunrise and after sunset, for a certain time ; and thus
the injured hand was perfectly healed. . . . This curious
mode of treatment still lingers here and there. Not long ago
it was practised on a hayfork in the neighbourhood of Win-
chester, and I lately heard a reference to it in Devonshire. A
young relation of mine, while riding in the green lanes of that
county, lamed his pony by its treading on a nail. He took
the poor creature to the village blacksmith, who immediately
asked for the nail, and, finding it had been left in the road,
said, as he shook his head, ' Ah, sir, if you had picked it up
and wiped it, and kept it warm and dry in your pocket, there'd
have been a better chance for your pony, poor thing ! ' . . .
Again, my Sussex informant writes : ' Several instances of
this old superstitious remedy have come under my observation, but the most remarkable one occurred in the house of an
acquaintance, one of whose men had fallen down upon a
sword-stick and inflicted an injury on his back which confined
him to his bed for several days. During the whole of this
time the sword-stick was hung up at his bed's head, and
polished night and day at stated intervals by a female hand.
It was also anxiously examined lest a single spot of rust should
be found on it, since that would have foretold the death of
the wounded man.' "[1]

A similar belief and practice in regard to the treatment of
wounds by contagious magic are reported from Lincolnshire.
" Perhaps the most extraordinary notion in connection with
iron is the firm belief that when it has inflicted any wound
there is some kind of sympathy between the injury and its
cause. Only a very short time before I left the Marsh a man
was badly cut by the knives of a reaper, and in spite of all that
medical skill could do he died the next day. But the true
reason for his death was thus accounted for by a Marshman,
' You see, he were nobutt one of them iggnerent Irishmen and
they knaws nowt ; if they hed but tekken the knife off and
seen to that, mebbe he wouldn't have died.' And when I

[1] W. Henderson, *Notes on the Folk-
lore of the Northern Counties* (London, 1879), pp. 157 *sq.* Cf. *County*
Folk-lore : Northumberland (London,
1904), p. 46.

myself had got a nasty cut in the face from a bolt which flew out of a bit of old shipwood I was chopping up, my own gardener, a particularly intelligent man, asked anxiously where the bolt was, and suggested that the wound would heal the quicker if all dirt and rust were carefully taken off its edges." [1]

From their close connection with the wearer's body articles of clothing are naturally supposed to be particularly subject to sympathetic or contagious magic ; indeed anything which has been in contact with the person may be dealt with by the magician on the same principle. Thus among the Baganda of Central Africa " women often fell ill, and in some instances died, because an enemy had contrived to obtain some of the weeds which they had handled when digging, or some of the earth which they had rubbed from their hoe, or a piece of string which they had used to tie the blade of their hoe to the handle, or again a shred of their barkcloth which they had thrown down. These fragments would then be used to work magic upon, and the spell would either cause the woman to fall sick, or in some cases would kill her." [2] Among the natives of the Central Provinces of India " magic spells are performed in various ways with or without the aid of a magician or witch. The idea that it is possible to transfer the fecundity of a fertile woman to a barren woman is at the root of a large number of the spells used. Thus any part of the body or any article of apparel of, or anything that has received the touch of, a woman who has had child (especially if it is associated with the time when she was in taboo) is efficacious and is eagerly sought after by a barren woman." [3] The Kai of Northern New Guinea believe that everything with which a man comes in contact retains something of his soul-stuff, by working on which a sorcerer may do the man himself grievous hurt. This is the great source of anxiety to the natives of New Guinea. Hence the native is at great pains to remove any traces of his presence from any object with which he has been in contact. If upon his way through the forest he leaves a lock of his hair or a thread of his girdle on a thorny bush, he

---

[1] Heanley, in *County Folk-lore : Lincolnshire* (London, 1908), p. 112.

[2] J. Roscoe, *The Baganda*, p. 344.

[3] J. T. Marten, in *Census of India,* 1911, vol. x. Part i. p. 153.

goes no further until he has removed every trace of it.   He
throws nothing away.   Even when he is a guest at a friendly
village he gathers the shells of the betel-nuts carefully in his
pouch which he always carries about with him ; or he throws
the remains in the fire.   Even the places where he sits retain
something of his soul-stuff, so on rising he is careful to efface
the traces of his person, either by stamping with his feet, or by
poking with his stick, or by sprinkling them with water from
a stream.   Or on the spot he places certain leaves which are
believed to possess the property of driving away his soul-stuff.
The soul-stuff is thought of itself soon to depart, but it is
desirable to hasten its departure, for once a magician gets
possession of the soul-stuff the original owner of it is often
supposed to be a doomed man.[1]

   Of the bodily impressions of which magicians avail themselves for the purpose of injuring through sympathetic or
contagious magic the persons who made the impressions, by
far the commonest appear to be footprints.   As, for example,
in the Kakadu tribe of Northern Australia, " still another
form of evil magic is associated with the mud that attaches
itself to the foot of a native walking through a swamp.   When
he comes on to dry ground he naturally scrapes the mud off,
generally using something such as a piece of paper bark to do
so.   If another man, who wishes to injure him, comes across
his tracks, he gathers up some of the mud or paper bark to
which it is attached.   He wraps it in some more paper bark
and ties it round with string.   In his camp, when it is quite
dry, he pounds it up until he can roll it into a ball, and then,
as in the previous case, places it in a hole that he makes at the
base of an ant-hill.   By and by the victim's foot breaks out
into sores which gradually spread all over it.   The toes drop
off, and the hands and feet decay.   No medicine-man can do
anything to counteract this form of magic.   It is a disease
which is every now and then met with among the Kakadu
natives, and is, superficially at least, suggestive of leprosy." [2]
Speaking of the Alligator district of Northern Australia, to
which the Kakadu tribe belongs, another writer describes the
magic of footprints as follows : " Upon other occasions in

[1] Neuhauss, *op. cit.* iii. 117.
[2] Baldwin Spencer, *Native Tribes*
of the Northern Territory of Aus-
tralasia, pp. 260 *sq.*

the same district, the footprint of a man who had been decreed
to die might be found upon a clay-flat or a river-bank. The
track must be intact ; if it be in the least degree imperfect it
is considered useless for the purpose. Taking for granted,
then, that it is clear and well-defined, the mould is cut out of
the clay *in toto* and buried in an ant-hill. There it is secreted
until such time as the spirit of the doomed man's father is
supposed to be in attendance at a ceremonial, when it is
fetched and broken over a blazing fire." This is supposed to
seal the doomed man's fate.[1]

In New Ireland a person who has been robbed looks for
the footprints of the thief, and if he finds them he takes them
up and performs ceremonies over them, which he supposes
will disable the malefactor, and so prevent him from doing
further mischief.[2]

In San Cristoval, one of the Solomon Islands, when a man
wishes to injure an enemy he will sometimes smear his own
foot with lime and then walk step by step in the foot-tracks of
his foe, believing that in this way he causes the man's death.
Or he takes the bone of a dead man, scrapes it, and sprinkles
the powder on the tracks of his enemy, at the same time driving
the bone into the footprints, as a man would drive a nail.
The death of the man whose footprints have thus been treated
is supposed to follow.[3] A similar form of magic dealing with
footprints is practised in other Solomon Islands. When a
man finds the footprints of his enemy he will take them up
and carry them home with him. This is supposed to cause his
enemy's feet and legs to break out into sores. Such sores are
common among natives of the Solomon Islands, and they are
often attributed to the magic of this use of his footprints by an
enemy. When a man suspects another of having thus bewitched him, he will get a friend or relative to go to the suspected magician and persuade him to throw away the earth
from the footprints. If after that the sores on the man's
legs and feet do not heal, his friends will make war on the
suspected magician.[4]

[1] H. Basedow, *The Australian
Aboriginal*, p. 175.
[2] P. F. Hees, " Ein Beitrag aus
den Sagen und Erzahlungen der
Nakanaı," in *Anthropos*, x.-xi. (1915–
1916) p. 48.
[3] C. E. Fox, *The Threshold of the
Pacific* (London, 1924), p. 262.
[4] R. Thurnwald, *Forschungen auf
den Salomo-Inseln* (Berlin, 1912), i. 443.

The Kiwai of British New Guinea seem to think it hopeless to pursue an enemy when he has got a good start, so all that they do is to shoot arrows into his footprints, or they have recourse to other forms of magic for his injury, which are supposed to act at a distance.[1] At Kerema in the Elema district on the south coast of British New Guinea we hear of a man who seriously believed that another native had killed his wife by collecting some sand out of her footprints, and had then placed the sand in a small bamboo with the requisite medicine.[2]

The Malays believe that a person's soul may be attacked through objects that have come into contact with its owner. " One way to abduct a girl's soul is to ' take sand or earth from her footprint or from her garden path or the front of her door or from her carriage wheels or her pony's hooves.' Frying the soul-substance in oil, one recites a charm :

> I am burning the liver, the heart, the lusts, and passions of my
> beloved,
> So that she is broken and hot with love,
> Madly in love with me, and restless,
> Burning as this sand burns." [3]

To bewitch an enemy, his horse or his ox, the Palaungs of Burma will take earth from his footprints or from the tracks of his animals, so that all the earth from the footprint is secured, whether broken or in one mass. This should be wrapped in large leaves and roasted over a slow fire.[4]

In Izumo, a district of Japan, if a house has been robbed in the night while the inmates are asleep, when they wake in the morning they will look for the footprints of the burglars, and if they find them they will burn mugwort in them. By this operation it is hoped or believed that the burglar's feet will be made so sore that he cannot run far, and that the police may easily overtake him.[5]

[1] G. Landtman, " The Magic of the Kiwai Papuans in Warfare," in *Journal of the Royal Anthropological Institute*, xlvi. (1916) p. 330.

[2] W. M. Strong, " Some Personal Experiences of British New Guinea," in *Journal of the Royal Anthropo-* *logical Institute*, xlix. (1919) p. 293.

[3] R. O. Winstedt, *Shaman, Saiva, and Sufi*, p. 67.

[4] Mrs. L. Milne, *The Home of an Eastern Clan*, p. 263.

[5] L. Hearn, *Glimpses of Unfamiliar Japan* (London, 1905), ii. 604.

Among the Angoni, Senga, and Tumbuka of Central Africa it is believed that if a man's footprints be stabbed or cupped by his enemy, in the morning he would be found in his hut bleeding from wounds, or blistered and dying.[1] Among the Wajagga of Mount Kilimanjaro in East Africa, when a blacksmith has been robbed he takes earth from the footprints of the thief, wraps them carefully in the skin of a banana and lays them on the coals of his smithy fire. He begins to blow up the fire with his bellows. He himself stands opposite and utters the curse-formula : " You, who have stolen such-and-such from me, may you swell up like a tree, and burst like a worm in the fire." If after that any one dies in the land with appearances of swelling, then they see in this the results of the curse. Thus it comes about that the smith can leave all his tools and implements openly about, because no one would dare to steal them.[2] Among the Teso people of Uganda one mode of injuring an enemy is to collect earth from his footprints and to mix it with medicine procured from some one skilled in such concoctions. The mixture is laid by in a potsherd, and then the feet of the unfortunate enemy will soon begin to swell mysteriously and the skin to peel off.[3] In Loango the footprints of an enemy are magically treated for his injury in various ways. Sometimes magical objects are deposited on them, sometimes a frog is made to jump in them, sometimes earth from the footprint is taken up and treated magically, sometimes it suffices to spit upon the footprints or obliterate them, and at the same time to think or to murmur a curse.[4]

Elsewhere I have attempted to show [5] that in the history of human thought the belief in magic has preceded religion or the worship of the gods ; but even when men have attained to a belief in the gods they still often think, as in ancient Egypt, that the gods can be influenced or controlled by the spells of the magicians. Thus with regard to the Oraons, a primitive people of India, we are told by a good

---

[1] D. Fraser, *Winning a Primitive People* (London, 1914), p. 142.

[2] B. Gutmann, " Der Schmied und seine Kunst," in *Zeitschrift für Ethnologie*, xliv. (1912) p. 85.

[3] A. L. Kitching, *On the Back-*

waters of the Nile, p. 238.

[4] *Die Loango-Expedition*, iii. 2, p. 339.

[5] *The Golden Bough : The Magic Art and the Evolution of Kings*, i. 220 *sqq.*

authority that " the Oraon's normal attitude towards his deities is that of a human being towards other human beings more crafty and powerful than himself ; and control through magic, and not propitiation by service, is the ideal method of dealing with his gods." [1]

[1] S. C. Roy, *The Oraons*, p. 225.

CHAPTER II

THE MAGICAL CONTROL OF THE WEATHER

In primitive society a most important function of magic is its use to control the weather for the good of the tribe by causing the rain to fall, the sun to shine, and the wind to blow in due season. On the proper discharge of this function it is believed that the prosperity and indeed the existence of the tribe is absolutely dependent. Accordingly the magicians who profess to discharge the office of weather-makers are extremely important personages, and sometimes, especially in Africa, they rise to the position of head-men or chiefs of the tribe. In any case, at this stage of development they are no longer private practitioners of magic, but public function-aries to whom the whole tribe looks for maintaining the food supply, and who may pay with their lives for any failure to exercise their craft to the satisfaction of the people. Else-where I have dealt at some length with the magical control of the weather : [1] here I must content myself with adducing some fresh evidence on the subject, beginning with the magical control of rain.

In San Cristoval, one of the Solomon Islands, " to get rain, fine weather, wind, calm, and so on, it is common to use sympathetic magic. Thus to get rain water is poured into a *teteu*, ' half of a coconut shell,' a charm is said, and the *teteu* is lifted up towards the sky ; or a coconut frond is taken and bent over to form an arch representing the whole sky clouded over, and then when you wish to stop the rain the frond is broken. So to get sunshiny weather take a fan and say a charm and wave the fan about, sweeping away the clouds, or

---

[1] *The Golden Bough : The Magic Art and the Evolution of Kings*, i. 244 *sqq.*

do the same merely with the hands. Or to get wind take a pandanus mat and tie it up." [1] The flapping of the mat with every breath of air is probably supposed to raise a wind. At Padada in Mindanao, when the people have planted the rice, the planters take their planting-sticks and place them on an offering of rice and pour water over them. In this way they think they secure a plentiful supply of rain for the rice crop by imitative magic. [2] When the Kiwai of British New Guinea find that the garden crops are withering and they wish to make rain, they concoct a magic medicine with the following ingredients : some sweet-smelling bark of the *sanea* tree, a wild juicy fruit of a certain tree, and a little of a certain swamp amphibian. All these are mixed in a vessel, and water both from a swamp and the sea, as well as sap from a tree, is poured on. Taking the vessel with its contents to the beach, the magician dips a pig's tail into it, and sprinkles the mixture into the air, thus imitating the fall of rain. He may also take some of it into his mouth and blow it out. He then utters a spell which is intended to cover the heaven with dark clouds, shutting out the light like the roof of a house. Two beings in the sky, called Deboa and Sura, are occasionally invoked to send down rain. In appealing to them the sorcerer takes water in his mouth and blows it upwards. [3] In this last ceremony imitative magic is supplemented by an appeal to heavenly beings ; here, as so often, magic is reinforced by religion.

The Bare'e-speaking Toradyas of Central Celebes employ the dry method of cultivating rice. Hence they are wholly dependent on rain and drought in the proper seasons for the prosperity of the crops. When rain is wanted, people go to a stream and splash or squirt water on each other, or they make a plumping sound on the water with the hands. To make rain they sometimes also have recourse to certain water-snails. These are hung by a string on a tree, and told that till rain falls they will not be put back in the water. So they appeal to the gods, who in pity send rain. [4] Here again once more we find magic reinforced by religion.

[1] C. E. Fox, *The Threshold of the Pacific*, p. 262.

[2] Fay-Cooper Cole, *The Wild Tribes of the Davao District, Mindanao*, p. 160.

[3] G. Landtman, *The Kiwai Papuans of British New Guinea*, p. 61.

[4] Adriani and Kruijt, *op. cit.* ii. 258.

The Lakhers of Assam are an agricultural people, and therefore need a regular fall of rain in order to ensure their subsistence. To procure rain they resort to a variety of charms, based on homoeopathic or imitative magic. Thus in Saiko a chosen man is sent out to fetch a stalk of wild cardamum (*Amomum dealbatum*). The cardamum stalk is planted in the village street, and the man who brought it rubs it up and down with his hand. When rubbed, the cardamum stalk makes a noise, "*Vut, vut, vut,*" which the Lakhers say resembles thunder, and while the man who is performing the ceremony is rubbing the stalk, another man pours a bamboo tube full of water over his back. The water resembles rain, and incidentally in running down the cardamum stalk it helps to increase the noise of the thunder. The day on which this ceremony is performed the whole village is taboo (*pana*). Another method used in Siaha and also in Saiko is as follows. An eel is caught and its head cut off and fixed to a pole planted on the roadside and pointed to the sky. Water is poured on to the eel, and also on to the person holding it up to the sky. As the eel lives in water it is believed that when it is killed its spirit becomes very thirsty, and if its head is pointed up to the sky in this way its spirit is sure to bring rain. On the day of the ceremony the village is taboo (*pana*). In Savang, if drought is threatened, the villagers go down to the Tisi River. There they find a stone with a large hole in its top which contains water, bale all the water out, and then sacrifice a fowl near the stone, and place the sacrificial parts of the fowl, that is, the tongue and the tail, in the hole. The fowl is then cooked, and a little of its liver and meat are placed inside the hole, and the rest of it is eaten. They think that the spirit who lives in the hollow stone will call down rain to fill its home with water again. Having eaten the chicken they all go home, and the rest of the day is taboo (*pana*). After a few days the stone is inspected, and if it has filled up with water and small fish are swimming about, the omen is favourable and good crops are expected ; if, however, the stone fails to fill up with water, it is believed that a drought will occur. In the Kawlchaw River there is a deep pool called Siataw, with overhanging precipices. The Lakhers believe that if fish are poisoned in this pool rain will fall, because the spirit of the pool is annoyed when the fish in his pool are poisoned.   Hence in times of drought the people of Saiko poison the pool in hopes of thereby procuring rain.[1]

The Ao, another agricultural tribe of Assam, in order to procure rain for their rice, practise various charms, some of which resemble those of the Lakhers.   " Usually either a stream is ' poisoned ' and fished with due rites, or sacrifices are offered to certain of the sacred stones which abound in Ao land.   The custom of poisoning a stream for rain is universal throughout the country.   Usually the water is first either exhorted or mocked.   For instance, Longmisa go down to a certain pool in the Dikhu with fish poison.   Arrived at the bank, all put leaf rain-shields over their heads as if rain were falling, and an old man, selected by a medicine-man as one whose action will be efficacious, first enters the water and pounds his bundle of poison and says : ' Is there no rain in the sky ?   Of course there is.   Let it rain and never stop till the river is big enough to carry away an old man.'   The pool is then fished in the ordinary way.   Changki are even ruder in their treatment of the water.   They go down to the Disoi and dam up one of the branches at a place where a little island divides it—a very common method of fishing among the Ao.   One of the elders says : ' You are so low we can bail you dry with our dao-holders (knife-sheaths).   We do not need bamboo dishes ' (such as ordinarily used to bail the water out of a dammed-up channel).   The elders then get into the water and splash it up-stream with their dao-holders.   Then the channel is bailed dry in the ordinary way and the trapped fish caught.   After this, for very shame, the heavens open and the stream comes down in flood.   Most Ao sacred stones are connected with the weather.   In fact they are as a rule too powerful rain-producers to be pleasant, and to meddle with or insult one entails a violent storm.   But some, by respect-ful sacrifices, can give rain in moderation.   Merangkong are so cautious that they operate at long range, and release a cock in the village street in honour of two stones away down in the valley at the junction of the Tsumak and Melak streams.   Mongsenyimti release a red cock with no white spots in honour of Shitilung (' elephant stone '), a particularly

[1] N. E. Parry, *The Lakhers* (London, 1932), pp. 452 *sqq.*

powerful stone just below the village. . . . Some rain ceremonies are nothing but very crude imitative magic. For instance, Changki, besides fishing in the Disoi, go to a boulder called Alungterungbaba and, rattling a stick about in a hole in the stone, make a noise which is supposed to resemble that of rain falling.   Another method, practised in Merangkong, is to lead water in bamboo aqueducts from certain streams to the village paths and sacrifice a cock with a prayer that rain may come." [1]   In this account, which I have borrowed from Mr. Mills' valuable monograph on the Ao, the sacrifices and prayers are religious, but the rest of the ceremony is magical.   As usual, primitive man does not hesitate to have recourse to religion when he thinks it will answer his purpose better than the old magical rites.   The same blending of religion with magic meets us in a ceremony which the Garos, another agricultural tribe of Assam, per- form for the purpose of procuring rain.   Among them " the rain god is invoked in cases of long-continued drought in the *Wachikrita* or *Salgurua* sacrifice.   The ceremony is a curious one and worth describing.   All the male members of the village repair to a big rock in the neighbourhood, each person holding a gourd of water in his hand.   The priest recites a prayer to implore the god to have mercy on them, sacrifices a goat, and smears its blood upon the rock.   The assembled persons then pour the contents of their gourds over the unfortunate priest to the accompaniment of the beating of drums and the blowing of wind instruments." [2]

The same instructive combination of religion with magic appears in the ceremonies which the Oraons, a primitive agricultural tribe of Chota Nagpur in India, observe for the purpose of procuring rain.   These have been well described by Mr. Sarat Chandra Roy as follows :   " A notable instance of imitative magic is the Oraon ceremony of rain-making. When rain is badly wanted in any part of the Oraon country, the Oraons of each village fix a day for the rain- making ceremony.   On the morning of the appointed day the women of the village, with the wife of the village priest or Pahan at their head, proceed to the village spring or tank,

---

[1] J. P. Mills, *The Ao Nagas* (Lon- don, 1926), pp. 131 *sq.*

[2] A. Playfair, *The Garos* (London, 1909), p. 88.

and there, after ablution, each woman fills her pitcher (*lota*) with water, and all proceed in a body to a sacred *pipar* tree (*Ficus religiosa*). Before these women have had their ablutions and are gone with their *lotas* towards the sacred *pipar*-tree, no one else that morning is allowed to touch the water of the tank or spring. On their arrival at the sacred tree, all the women simultaneously pour the water in their pitchers over the foot of the tree, saying, ' May rain fall on earth like this.' The wife of the village-priest now puts marks of vermilion, diluted in oil, on the trunk of the tree. After this the women depart, and the village priest or Pahan proceeds to sacrifice a red cock to the god Baranda at the spot. It is firmly believed by the Oraons that within a day or two after this ceremony rain is bound to fall. And in olden times, it is said, a heavy shower of rain would even overtake the women on their way home from the sacred tree. In this case, apparently, direct alliance, by sacrifice and by anointing the tree with vermilion, have been superimposed on what was once, perhaps, purely a ceremony of imitative magic. Such combination of imitative magic with prayer and sacrifice is a prominent feature in the chief religious festival of the Oraons. This festival, known as the *Khaddi* or *Sarhul*, is celebrated when the *sal*-flowers are in blossom in the month of April, shortly before the time for sowing paddy in their fields. Seasonable rain and plenty of it is a necessity to the agricul-turalist. And the Oraon is, above all, an agriculturalist. Naturally, therefore, he leaves no expedient untried to ensure plenty of rain. Thus, when on the occasion of the *Sarhul* festival, the village-priest or Pahan and his assistant, the Pujar, go in procession from house to house, the women pour large jarfuls (*gharas*) of water over the head, first of the priest, then of his assistant, and finally over the head of everyone and anyone ; and all the Oraons revel in water on that day and splash mud on each other so as to present the mud-besmeared appearance of persons sowing paddy-seeds in mud. By this they hope to have plenty of seasonable rain for their agricultural operations. A further custom observed on the same occasion, of all the Oraon families of a village heap-ing rice on the sacred winnowing-basket (*sup*) which the Pahan carries in procession, and the Pahan dropping rice

G

from his *sup* all along the route as he proceeds, and his assistant, the Pujar, continually dropping water from his *batari* or pitcher with a tube attached to it, all along the route, is another instance of imitative magic for securing plenty of rain and crops." [1]

With regard to the Birhors, a primitive jungle tribe of Chota Nagpur, we are informed that " as the Birhors, as a tribe, have not yet taken to agriculture, they scarcely feel the need for seasonal rains. Those few *Jaghi* families among them who have secured lands for cultivation have adopted from their *Munda* neighbours their magical rain-making ceremony, which is as follows : Early in the morning they go up the nearest hill and push down stones of all sizes which produce a rumbling noise in falling to the ground ; and this noise is at the same time intensified by beating a drum so as to produce a low heavy continued sound in imitation of the pattering of rain on the roofs of their huts." [2]

In the Thana District of the Bombay Presidency, in order to procure rain, stones are taken out of a pool and worshipped. They are then carried to every house in the village, and water is poured upon them by the inmates. Further, in the same district, as a charm for rain " the villagers go from house to house with boughs of the *Nim* tree (*Melia Azadirachta*) on their heads, and water is then poured upon them by the inmates. In the Deccan, boys cover their heads with twigs and leaves of the *Nim* and go round naked. Water is poured over their heads and thus rain is brought." [3]

The carrying of some symbol suggestive of rain or the fertility that comes with rain, and the drenching of the bearers with water, suggestive of a fall of rain, are features of ceremonies for the procuring of rain observed in Khandesh, the Deccan, and the Karnatak. Bhils of the Navapur Peta make an image of earth adorned with green plantain-leaves and flowers and place it on a board, which an unmarried girl carries through the village, accompanied by other women singing rain songs and praying for rain. At each house she

[1] S. C. Roy, " Magic and Witch-craft on the Chota Nagpur Plateau," in *Journal of the Royal Anthropological Institute*, xliv. (1914) p. 330.

[2] S. C. Roy, *The Birhors*, pp. 369 *sq.*
[3] R. E. Enthoven, *Folklore of Bombay* (Oxford, 1924), pp. 318, 323.

passes she receives grain and is drenched.   Pavra, Naira, and
Nahal Bhils perform Varhatya.   Boys and girls under nine
years of age go from house to house on four successive nights,
accompanied by men bearing torches which simulate lightning.   The girls, who are drenched at each house, sing :—

> Dondhya, Dondhya, give rain,
> Make rice and pulse grow.
> Make *jvari* and *bajri* grow.[1]

The Gonds, the principal Dravidian tribe of India, have a
peculiar ceremony for procuring rain by means of ploughing.
Two naked women go out and harness themselves to a plough
by night, while a third naked woman drives the plough and
pricks them with a goad.[2]   A similar mode of procuring rain
by a ceremony of ploughing is known to the Brahuis of
Baluchistan, among whom the rite is, or used to be, performed
by the chief himself.   On this subject Mr. Denys Bray writes
as follows :

" In the old days a halo of divinity surrounded the leaders
of the Brahui Confederacy.   Accredited with authority over
the forces of Nature, they were held directly accountable for
seasons good and bad.   When famine was sore in the land
the Brahui would look to the Khan (ruler) to exercise his
divine powers and bring down the rain for which the earth
cried out.   Then would the Khan doff his fine clothes for the
woollen overcoat of the peasant, and drive a yoke of oxen
across a rain-crop field.   Twice has my informant seen the
ruler of the country put hand to the plough to compel the rain
to fall ;   and so efficacious was the second ploughing that the
people began to fear another deluge.   But my informant is
now an old, old gentleman, and the ruler he saw ploughing
was Nasir Khan II, who has been dead these sixty years or
more. . . .   But happily for them, the Brahuis are not wholly
dependent on their chiefs.   When the flocks are dying for
want of rain, a sham-fight is arranged between the womenfolk
of two nomad encampments.   The opposing forces come
together in the afternoon at some lonely place, their head-

---

[1] J. Abbot, *The Keys of Power*
(London, 1932), p. 340. In this work
the author gives many more examples
of similar rain-making ceremonies

observed in India.

[2] R. V. Russell, *Tribes and Castes
of the Central Provinces*, iii. 106.

dress thrown back and girt round their waist.   Here, unseen
by the men, they belabour one another till the blood begins to
fall.   And with that they call a truce, for the falling of blood
will surely induce the falling of rain.   In some tribes the men
take matters into their own hands.   The men of one encampment march off to another in the neighbourhood, and there
make a great noise, and are soused with water for their pains.
Then they are given alms and sent about their business.   Both
customs are on the wane ; but it is safe to prophesy that the
women will be the last to abandon theirs.   Less obvious is the
idea underlying another old rain-making custom, now fast
degenerating into a game occasionally played by boys in Kalat
and other settled villages in times of drought.   One of the
boys acts as the *piraka*, dressed up like a little old man (for
this is what the word means), with a hoary beard of cotton-
wool on his chin, a felt cap on his head, a *zor* or felt coat on
his back, and a string of *Gungaru* or bells jingling about his
waist.   Round his neck his comrades put a rope and drag
him through the village.   And when they come to a door,
they stand and shout this Dehwari doggerel :

> *The buffoon !   The old mannikin !*
> *Down fell the grain-bin*
> *On top of poor granny !*

This is the signal for the goodman of the house to come out
with an offering of money or grain.   And the *piraka* shakes
himself and makes his bells jingle and bellows like a camel,
while the boys shout in chorus :

> *Good luck to the house of the giver !*
> *And a hole in the bin of the miser !*

And so they move on from house to house.   In the end their
collections are clubbed together, a pottage is prepared and
distributed among the people, and the game is closed with
prayers for rain.   I suppose the *piraka's* bellowing and the
jingling of the bells are imitative of thunder and the swish of
rain, but I can volunteer no explanation for his general get-
up, unless his snow-white is imitative of snow ; the game
at any rate is generally played in the uplands in the late
autumn." [1]

[1] D. Bray in *Census of India*, 1911, vol. iv. Part i. pp. 65 *sq.*

An instructive account of the rain-making ceremonies observed by the Bechuanas and other inhabitants of the arid Kalahari Desert in South-west Africa runs as follows : " Another of the witch-doctor's functions was rain-making. There were regular guilds of rainmakers.   In an arid country like South Africa, and especially in the Kalahari region, rainfall is the all-important subject.   If it is abundant, the crops will be abundant also, but if it is scanty, as last season's was (1921–22), there is sure to be a shortage of food.   Natives are improvident as a rule, and were more so in their heathen days than they are now, and the old Bechuanas were no exception to the rule.   In times of prolonged drought man and beast both suffer, and there is a famine, with the result that the stock die, and the natives are hard put to survive.   In the old days the chief was the great rainmaker of the tribe.   He was not only the temporal but the spiritual head of the tribe, and it was his duty to see that the fertilizing showers descended upon the land.   There is little doubt that the chieftainship evolved from the priesthood.   The highest compliment that the natives can pay to the memory of a departed chief is to say that he was a great rainmaker, and a man who was successful in this line was likely to become not only wealthy but powerful, and very likely eventually become chief.   Tradition bears this supposition out.   Many chiefs would not tolerate any rivals, no matter how successful they might be.   When there was a drought the chief, if he was not the rainmaker, used to send to the witch-doctor by night, and everything must be done secretly if it is to be successful.   The old Bechuanas would not tell folk-tales before sunset lest the clouds should fall on them.   The messenger must not look behind him, nor drink water, but when he gets near the rainmaker's abode he must bathe in a pure stream, because this will assist the rain to come.   The rainmaker uses his own spells to produce the rain.   He must smear himself with mud and pour out libations of beer and water to the ancestral spirits to send the rain.   Then the chief must sacrifice an ox of a peculiar colour, for a good deal depends on that.   If these ceremonies are not successful in drawing from the sky the fertilizing fluid, the rainmaker orders the chief and his people to go to the mountains or hills with their cattle.   They must drive these beasts to the highest points, and kill antelopes and monkeys, and throw stones into all the holes and gorges. From any-thing they kill they must remove the entrails and cast them into the streams and water-holes, as nothing must be brought back with the bodies. Women must also uproot plants and shrubs and cast them likewise into the streams and water-holes. It has already been suggested that some of the old Bechuanas used to offer human sacrifices in cases of extreme drought, but doubt was expressed as to the reality of this. At the same time a Christian native told me that when he was a small child he remembered seeing some little girl children being buried up to their necks in the earth, while the mothers kept up a terrible howling *pula, pula* (rain, rain) all the time. These children nearly died of thirst and exposure. He did not remember if there was plenty of rain afterwards. Some-times the contents of the gall bladder of the black sheep or goat was cut out and drunk by the rain-doctor, while he anointed his body with some of it mixed with medicines. The idea was that as it blackened his own body, so it would turn the clouds black and cause them to rain." [1]

Among the Bavenda, a tribe of the Northern Transvaal, there are professional rainmakers who resort to many different devices in order to produce the desired and needed rainfall. For example one rainmaker powders up some dried crab and *fukwe* bird, whose cry is regarded as the harbinger of rain, and mixes it with some refuse disgorged from the river when last in flood. He puts some of this mixture on to a small piece of broken pot over a fire which he lights on the veranda of his hut. As soon as the fumes from the potsherd begin to rise he goes into his hut, shuts the door and covers himself up with blankets. Before long he begins to sweat and he stays shut in his hut all day, completely enveloped in his blankets and sweating freely. Towards evening a small cloud is sup-posed to appear in the sky, drawn thither by the smoking powder, and presently the clouds are said to increase and rain to fall. The idea is that the powder goes up into the sky, and its constituents, all closely associated with water, there form rainclouds that turn into drops and fall, induced by the per-

[1] S. S. Dornan, *Pygmies and Bushmen of the Kalahari* (London, 1925), pp. 300 *sqq.*

spiration of the man in the hut.   Another rainmaker plays a
native horn and dances vigorously until he is bathed in sweat.
As the sweat drops from his body so it is believed that rain
will soon drop from the clouds.[1]

Among the Ila-speaking peoples of Northern Rhodesia
the rainmaker employs various charms based on the principle
of homoeopathic or imitative magic.   Thus, for example,
" taking a pot he puts into it some roots of the Mutimbavhulà
tree and some water.   Then holding a small forked stick
between the palms of his two hands he twirls it round in the
liquid, producing froth (*iovhu*).   Some of this froth he throws
in all directions, the idea being that it will collect the clouds.
Then another kind of medicine is burnt, and throws up a
dense smoke which is supposed to have some connection with
clouds.   The ashes are put into a pot of water, so that the
water becomes very black—another reference to black clouds.
Then he once again twirls his stick (*lupusho*) in this mixture—
to gather the clouds.   As the wind brings up clouds, so will
the movement of his stick.   All the time this is going on the
people are singing and invoking the praise names of Leza.
One refrain is :

> *Tuendele o muyoba, Leza, kowa !*
> Come to us with a continued rain, O Leza, fall !

When the operation is completed, the medicine is poured on
the ground, the pot is covered and left there by the little
huts." [2]   In this case the ritual of homoeopathic or imitative
magic is reinforced by the religious rite of a prayer addressed
to the supreme sky-god Leza, that he may come down to earth
in the form of rain.

Among the Ibo of Southern Nigeria a magician or doctor
attempts to make or stop rain by the use of certain stones.
If he wishes to bring rain, he takes the stone out near the
eaves of his house and makes a fire with grass and oil-bean
wood ; as the smoke rises the heavens are believed to grow
black with clouds.   If he wishes to stop the rain he waves a
broom towards the sky, takes the stone back into the house,
and covers it up, pulls away the first grass from the fire and

---

[1] H A. Stayt, *The Bavenda* (London, 1931), p. 312.

[2] E. W. Smith and A. M. Dale, *The Ila-Speaking Peoples of Southern Nigeria*, ii. 208 *sq.*

puts on another kind. Another method of these Ibo rain-makers is to offer a long prayer to a deity or spirit called Amade Awha, at the conclusion of which the rainmaker begins to weep. As his tears fall to the ground, so will the raindrops soon begin to drop from the clouds. Some chew certain leaves and spit them out, while others eject water in the direction in which it is wanted to come, no doubt in imitation of a shower.[1]

When the Berbers of North Africa desire to procure rain they take a large wooden ladle which is used for drawing water, dress it up as a bride, and carry it about in a procession, followed by women and children. From time to time the doll is sprinkled with water, and the procession collects contributions which are used afterwards to defray the expense of a feast held either in the bed of a stream, or on a threshing-floor, or on one of the mountain-tops where the ceremonial fires are kindled at the solstices. This ceremony for the procuring of rain is known and practised throughout North Africa, from the Atlantic to the Cyrenaica.[2]

In times of severe drought the Arabs of Marsa Matruh, the classical Paraetonium to the west of Alexandria, perform a rain-making ceremony as follows : " The owners of several fields club together and contribute each some article of clothing, in which a pole or stake is dressed to represent a woman. This wooden dummy is called *Zarafah*. The Arabs take then this *Zarafah* and carry it round their fields, shouting *ya zarafah haty er-rafa'ah-t*. The meaning of these words is somewhat obscure. . . . When the procession of the *Zarafah* is ended the dummy is stripped, the clothing and finery restored to the lenders, and the wooden stock is thrown away." [3]

Primitive peoples commonly believe that they can stop as well as produce a fall of rain by magic. In order to stop rainfall they often resort to the agency of fire, doubtless with the notion that the heat of the fire will dry up the water of the rain. Thus in Uganda, when the rain was very heavy and the lightning severe, the Baganda used to make fires which

---

[1] P. A. Talbot, *The Peoples of Southern Nigeria*, iii. 964.

[2] E. Laoust, *Mots et choses berbères*, p. 204.

[3] Oric Bates, " Ethnographic Notes from Marsa Matruh," in *Journal of the Royal Asiatic Society* for 1915, pp. 725 *sq.*

gave forth volumes of smoke, to keep the clouds from falling ; and they beat drums to let the god Gulu know where they were, that he might not hurt them with lightning.[1] The Berbers of Morocco similarly employ the agency of fire to stop the rain. Thus at Tachgagalt they think that to extinguish a firebrand with rain-water will suffice to dispel the rain and bring back fine weather. At Tanant this rite is performed by a young boy, born after the death of his father : he exposes himself to the driving rain with a firebrand in his hand, and he returns to shelter when the torch is extinct. At Amanouz people think that they can arrest the fall of rain by exposing to it a boulder or pebble which they have carefully passed over a fire.[2]

A similar mode of stopping the fall of rain is practised in Southern India. " When the tanks and rivers threaten to breach their banks, men stand naked on the bund, and beat drums ; and if too much rain falls naked men point fire-brands at the sky. Their nudity is supposed to shock the powers that bring the rain and arrest their further progress. According to Mr. Francis, when too much rain falls, the way to stop it is to send the eldest son to stand in it stark naked, with a torch in his hand." [3]   In Gujarat, to arrest the fall of rain, some people ask naked boys to throw burning coals into the rain water.[4] Sometimes it is prescribed that the burning coals which are thrown into the rain-water must first be passed between the legs of a person born in the month of *Phalgun* (February-March).[5] Among the Garos of Assam " when rain has been too constant and sunshine is desired, the *salaksoa* or ' burning of the sun' ceremony is observed. This ceremony is the reverse of that for rain, for whereas, in the latter, water is poured out to bring rain, in the former fires are lighted round about rocks to bring warmth and sunshine. In this, as in the rain ceremony, a goat or fowl is offered up." [6] Among the Palaungs of Burma " if too much rain has fallen, and there is no sign of fine weather, a calabash is filled with

[1] J. Roscoe, *The Baganda*, p. 315.
[2] E. Laoust, *Mots et choses berbères* (Paris, 1920), p. 250.
[3] E. Thurston, *Omens and Super-stitions of Southern India* (London, 1912), p. 309.

[4] R. E. Enthoven, *Folklore of Gujarat* (Supplement to *Indian Anti-quary*, xliii., 1914), p. 17.
[5] R. E. Enthoven, *Folklore of Bombay*, p. 117.
[6] A. Playfair, *The Garos*, p. 89.

water and corked with a loosely fitting piece of wood, wrapped round with leaves. It is then suspended over a fire, with the mouth downwards. A certain amount of water escapes and trickles out, dropping down into the fire : this is supposed to stop the rain. Before hanging up the calabash an incantation is said." [1] In Buin, one of the Solomon Islands, when people wish to make rain they throw the leaves of a certain species of tall palm into water, and when they wish to stop the fall of rain they throw the leaves of the same palm into a fire. [2]

Elsewhere I have dealt with the remarkable belief of some primitive peoples which associates twins with water and especially with rain. [3] The Bavenda of the Northern Transvaal think that if twins are not buried near water, the rain will not fall. [4] Speke was told by one of his men that in Nguru, one of the sister provinces to Unyanyembe, as soon as twins are born they are killed and thrown into water, lest drought and famine or floods should oppress the land. Further he was told that in the province of Unyanyembe, if a twin or twins die, for the same reason they are thrown into water. [5]

The magician who undertakes to make or stop rain often seeks, on the principle of homoeopathic magic, to assimilate himself to the phenomenon which he desires to produce. In short, if he wishes to make rain, he must himself be wet : if he wishes to make dry weather, he must himself be dry. [6] Thus among the Gagou, a tribe of the Ivory Coast in West Africa, when a magician is performing his ceremony for stopping the rain he must not himself touch water or drink it or bathe in it ; on the contrary when he is performing a ceremony to cause rain he must drink as much water as he can, and bathe in it incessantly. [7] Among the Ekoi of Southern Nigeria a certain chief was said to be able to produce rain by drinking water mixed with magic potions or to stop the

---

[1] Mrs. L. Milne, *The Home of an Eastern Clan*, p. 238.
[2] R. Thurnwald, *op. cit.* p. 449.
[3] See *The Golden Bough : The Magic Art and the Evolution of Kings*, i. 262 *sqq.* I there cited M. Henri Junod's work, *Les Baronga*. I may now refer to his later and fuller book, *The Life of a South African Tribe*, 2nd edit. (London, 1927). ii.

319 *sqq.*
[4] H. A. Stayt, *The Bavenda*, p. 310.
[5] J. H. Speke, *Journal of the Discovery of the Source of the Nile* (Everyman Library), p. 426.
[6] *The Golden Bough : The Magic Art*, etc. i. 269 *sq.*
[7] L. Tauxier, *Nègres Gouro et Gagou* (Paris, 1924), p. 144.

downpour by abstaining from taking water for two or three days at a time, but during this period he was not debarred from drinking palm wine.[1]   Among the Bakongo of the Lower Congo on the day when a magician is about to perform a ceremony for the stopping of rain he may not drink water nor wash himself.   But on the contrary when he desires to produce rain he takes certain leaves and puts them into a stream and then dives under the water.   When he returns to the surface the rain is supposed soon to fall.[2]   Among the Boloki, a tribe of the Upper Congo, " when a storm threatens to break during the funeral festivities of a man the people present will call the beloved child of the deceased and giving him (or her) a lighted ember from the hearth with a vine twined round it, will ask him to stop the rain.   The lad steps forward and waves the vine-encircled ember towards the horizon where the storm is rising, and says, ' Father, let us have fine weather during your funeral ceremonies.'   The son after this rite must not drink water—he may drink sugar-cane wine—nor put his feet in water for one day.   Should he not observe these prohibitions the rain will fall at once.   When it is desirable to have rain the native takes down from the shelf some sticks which have ' medicine ' bound round them and plunges them into water mixed with arrowroot leaves, and then the rain will soon begin to fall.   It is rarely that they have to resort to the rain-doctor to bring rain, as the rain falls with great regularity all the year round." [3]   The Lesa, a tribe of the Belgian Congo, possess a charm which is believed to prevent rain from falling.   It consists of a pot containing some gray matter and the skeleton of a serpent. Whoever employs this charm to prevent rain from falling must abstain from drinking water for nine days.   Otherwise the charm will be without effect.[4]   The Suk, a tribe of Kenya in East Africa, endeavour to procure rain by plunging a child of the Terit clan in a stream.[5]

Among the Bare'e-speaking Toradyas of Central Celebes

---

[1] P. A. Talbot, *In the Shadow of the Bush* (London, 1912), p. 71.

[2] J. H. Weeks, *Among the Primitive Bakongo*, p. 230.

[3] J. H. Weeks, *Among Congo Cannibals*, p. 281.

[4] N. Baeyens, *Les Lesa* (Bruxelles, 1914), p. 43.

[5] J. Barton, " Notes on the Suk Tribe of Kenia Colony," in *Journal of the Royal Anthropological Institute*, li. (1921) pp. 84, 90.

when the weather is dry and you wish it to remain so, you must not pronounce the word "rain", or the rain will think that it is called for and will come. Hence in Pakambia, where thunder-storms are very common, the word rain may not be pronounced throughout the year, and the term 'tree-blossoms' is substituted for it. Further, rain may not be mentioned during harvest-time, and a fire is kept burning in the rice-fields to prevent rain from falling. Drought may be confirmed by abstaining from bathing and drinking water. The rain-doctor (*sando*) who is to drive away rain must not come into contact with water; he does not bathe nor wash his hands; he drinks only palm-wine; and in crossing a brook he does not put his feet in the water. He builds a small hut in the rice-field, and in the hut he keeps a fire constantly burning. He also keeps by him a packet of leaves and bark of certain trees and plants, which have a power of driving away rain in virtue of their names. If the rain-doctor afterwards wishes to cause rain, he has only to sprinkle water on his fire and the rain pours down. To drive away rain, he blows lime towards it.[1] Among the Bukaua of Northern New Guinea, while a rain-maker is engaged in his professional duties he must rub his hair with black earth, put black spots on his face, and bathe every morning, stretching his arms out over the surface of the sea and calling for rain. It is believed that the sky will then darken, and the rain fall in torrents.[2] The Indians and Negroes of Guiana think that if during heavy rain you refrain from washing the inside of your pots the rain will stop; or at least to plunge the pots into the water would cause the rain to redouble.[3]

Sometimes rain-charms operate through the influence or spirits of the dead. Thus among the Bare'e-speaking Toradyas of Central Celebes, the rain-maker will sometimes sprinkle water on the grave of a chief, and pray to the dead man to send rain. Further he will hang a bamboo full of water over the grave so that the water drips on it constantly through a small hole in the bamboo.[4] Thus he combines the religious ritual of prayer with a ceremony of homoeopathic

[1] Adriani and Kruijt, *op. cit.* ii. 261 *sq*,
[2] Neuhauss, *op. cit.* iii. 456.
[3] J. Crevaux, *Voyage dans l'Améri-*

que du Sud (Paris, 1883), p. 276.
[4] Adriani and Kruijt, *op. cit.* ii. 259 *sq*.

or imitative magic, by dripping water in imitation of rain. Among the Palaungs of Burma " freshly picked tea leaves are sometimes offered at the end of the dry season to the spirit of a stream or spring, so that plentiful rains may fall on the tea gardens. If there has been a long period of drought, and the tea gardens are greatly suffering from want of rain, cooked rice is offered there to Ta Pan and Ya Pan (' Grandfather Pan ' and ' Grandmother Pan '), two spirits, husband and wife, who specially watch over the gardens. If this offering fails to bring rain, the Elders and other men in the village assemble on a moonlight night chosen by a wise man. They take charcoal—from any fire—grind it to powder, and blacken their faces with it. They do not wear the hair knotted as usual on the top of the head, but combed straight back over the shoulders. They go to a graveyard, strip themselves of all their garments, and streak their naked bodies with charcoal to imitate the stripes of a tiger. They then crawl three times round a newly-made grave, on their hands and knees, scratching the ground and growling like tigers. After they have finished crawling round the grave they take one of the poles from the bier on which a coffin has been carried to the graveyard (these biers are left upon the grave), and they carry the pole back to the village. When they arrive they ride astride on the pole as a child rides on a stick, and in this way they go from one end of the village to the other. When they reach the farther end they throw the pole into the jungle. No incantation is said with this performance. The wise man who described it to me said that he had seen the whole ceremony more than once. Sometimes they, at first, simply fetch the pole from a grave and lay it in a stream of water ; but if this does not bring the rain, the more elaborate performance takes place." [1] In this curious ceremony the simulation of tigers by the rain-makers at the grave may perhaps be intended to intimidate the dead man, and so induce him to comply with their wishes by sending the needed rain.

In some parts of Southern India it is believed that if the bodies of lepers are buried rain may not fall. Hence in cases of prolonged drought the corpses of such persons are some-

[1] Mrs. Leslie Milne, *The Home of an Eastern Clan*, pp. 237 *sq.*

times disinterred and thrown into a river or burned. " Some years ago a man who was supposed to be a leper died, and was buried. His skeleton was disinterred, put into a basket, and hung to a tree with a garland of flowers round its neck. The Superintendent of Police, coming across it, ordered it to be disposed of."[1]

Speaking of Persia, an Arab traveller of the tenth century, Ebn Haukal, says, " In the city of Sus (Susa) there is a river, and I have heard that, in the time of Abou Mousa Ashoari a coffin was found there : and the bones of Daniel the Prophet (to whom be peace!) were in that coffin. These the people held in great veneration and in time of distress or famine from droughts they brought them out and prayed for rain."[2] Another mediaeval Arab geographer has recorded that a certain prince, named Selman, who had been slain in battle with the Khazars, was placed in a coffin and deposited in their temple by the victorious Khazars. And afterwards in times of drought they used to bring forth the coffin and thus procure rain for their fields. In reference to this custom an Arab poet of Selman's tribe affirmed that the merits of Selman " obtain for the country a plentiful rain."[3]

Among the Bavenda, a tribe of the Northern Transvaal, prolonged drought is often ascribed to the anger of an ancestral spirit. When the identity of the offended spirit has been ascertained, all the people are summoned to do the sacred *tshikona* dance, either in a village within hearing distance of the grave, or in the forest near the grave. Meanwhile the chief, attended by his relatives, visits the grave and there performs a certain ceremony called *Phasi madi*, after which he deposits upon it the contents of the stomach of an ox. He beseeches the spirit to withdraw his anger and not to let the earth get hot and his descendants starve for want of water.[4] Near Timgad in Algeria, in a time of drought, a modern traveller found the Mohammedan peasants breaking into the grave of a holy man in order to pour water over his bones as a charm to procure rain. He was informed by a

[1] E Thurston, *Omens and Superstitions of Southern India*, p. 310.
[2] *The Oriental Geography of Ebn Haukal*, translated by Sir W. Ouseley

(London, 1800), p. 76.
[3] C. B. de Meynard, *Dictionnaire de la Perse* (Paris, 1861), p. 72.
[4] H. A. Stayt, *The Bavenda*, p. 310.

native that this mode of procuring rain in times of drought was often practised in the neighbourhood.[1]

Again, animals of various species are often employed in charms to make or stop rain.[2] Often it is prescribed that animals employed for this purpose must be black, doubtless with reference to the blackness of rainclouds. Thus among the Bagesu, a cannibal tribe inhabiting the slopes of the lofty Mount Elgon, in cases of prolonged drought " the rain-maker may consent to take the extreme measure of climbing the mountain and paying a visit to the deity on the top, a step which he asserts is fraught with danger and may cost him his life. A black ox is brought, and a quantity of beer, which are taken up the mountain by several village elders who accompany the rain-maker to a plateau near the mountain top. Here the ox is killed and eaten by the company, with the exception of one leg, at a sacred meal at which the blood is offered to the god. The leg is carried up the mountain to a priest who lives near a large pool in which is said to be a large snake which is the god. This pool is the spring which supplies many waterfalls upon the mountain. The priest takes the meat and hears the request of the rain-maker. The priest and rain-maker now make a trough of clay near the pool and pour the beer into it. The priest then stands near the trough and puts a long beer-tube into the spring in order to suck a little water through it. The snake resents this, for it guards the spring against any person drawing water from the pool. It is said to capture any man who rashly attempts to do so. When, therefore, the priest attempts to draw water, the snake darts forth and winds its deadly coils around him, but the odour of the beer saves him, for the reptile smells it, hastily uncoils itself, drinks the beer and is soon helplessly drunk. As soon as the men see it is helpless they break its fangs and proceed rapidly to fill a number of water-pots from the sacred spring, arranging them round the pool. The water thus drawn and set on the top of the mountain will without fail bring rain which will continue to fall daily until the priest takes steps to stop it by emptying the pots again.

[1] A. Wiedemann, in *Archiv für Religionswissenschaft*, vol. 14 (1911), p. 640.

[2] Cf. *The Golden Bough : The Magic Art and the Evolution of Kings*, i. 287 *sqq.*

The rain-maker descends the mountain with the elders who have waited for him on the upper plateau and in a short time rain begins to pour down. The rain-maker now waits, knowing that the people will soon come with offerings and requests to have the rain stopped. When the people have had enough rain and see that their crops will spoil for want of sunshine, they go in a body to the rain-maker to beg for sunshine. The rain-maker has now to make a second visit to the serpent-god with an offering of beer, and has to go with the priest through a similar performance to that above described in order to make the god drunk, after which he empties the pots and turns them bottom upwards to ensure sunshine. Thus the harvest is assured, the seasons are readjusted, and the year proceeds in its proper course."[1]

Among the Basoga of the Central District in Uganda, " there are very special ceremonies for rain-making. The chief of the district is responsible for the weather. He is believed to have power to send either rain or sunshine at will ; he can give or withhold as he pleases. Hence, when there is a prolonged drought and the crops are suffering, the people go in a body and beg rain from him, asking him to use his influence to make the rain fall. Should it come in a few days, they are happy ; but, should it still delay they reassemble and abuse the chief roundly for his callous behaviour, and demand that he shall exert himself and cease to be so idle. This generally has the effect of rousing the chief, who makes an effort to obtain the needed rain. He calls together the leading medicine-men of the district and commands them to bring the herbs needed for the great ceremony of rain-making. Three black animals are brought, a black cow, goat, and fowl ; these are killed, and their blood is caught in vessels. Fires are lighted in an open space near the chief's house and large pots are placed on them containing the blood of the animals, mixed with water and herbs, which is boiled until only a thick substance remains. As the steam rises, prayers are offered to the god of rain. The meat of these animals is eaten by the chief and the medicine-men. The medicine-men mix the blood and the herbs from the pots into two balls, one for the house of the chief and the other for the house of the

[1] J. Roscoe, *The Northern Bantu*, pp. 183 *sq.*

principal medicine-man. Each ball has a stick in it, and a medicine-man carries them and places one on each house. Each day these balls are taken and smeared with some of the fat taken from the animals sacrificed, until the rain comes. When rain comes and food is obtained, the people take pots of beer to the chief as a thank-offering, and a black ox to the medicine-man, in order that he may have fat for his fetishes."[1]

Among the Kikuyu, a tribe of Kenya, when the elders go to the sacred fig-tree to procure rain "they sacrifice a ram, preferably a black one. If, on the other hand, they pray for rain to cease, the sacrificial ram is preferably a white one, though a red one may be used. After the sacrifice, the intestines are taken and tied round the stem high up in the tree. The melted tail fat is then poured at the foot of the tree and a strip of the meat and fat are hung on a branch."[2] Among the Akamba, another tribe of Kenya, " a black goat should be sacrificed for rain ; a red one is, however, occasionally used. But whatever the colour of the animal sacrificed, it is very important that it should be entirely of one colour, and not spotted or parti-coloured. A parti-coloured animal would probably be considered as having some blemish."[3]

Among the Wagogo of Tanganyika when a rain-maker fails to produce rain by his ordinary methods he sacrifices a black ox, cuts up the hide into strips, and ties them about the arms of the people, as a mode of hastening the tardy rainfall.[4]

Among the Berbers of Morocco a very common ceremony for procuring rain is to lead a black cow round a village, an encampment, a mosque, or a chapel. It is especially practised by the pastoral tribes and nomads of the Middle Atlas. Among the Ait Immour young girls lead a black cow round the sanctuary of some holy man, singing the while. They then return to the mosque, where their procession disperses. Among the Ait Bou Zemmour an aged woman leads the animal by the ear three times round the little tent set up in the middle of the camp, which serves at once for the school and the

[1] J. Roscoe, *op. cit.* pp. 254 *sq.*
[2] C. W. Hobley, *Bantu Beliefs and Magic* (London, 1922), p. 60.
[3] *Id., loc. cit.*

[4] H. Claus, *Die Wagogo* (Baessler Archiv, Beiheft II, Leipzig and Berlin, 1911), p. 42.

H

mosque. The other women follow her. Among the Zemmout the custom is first of all to overturn the tent which serves as a mosque, then to lead the cow round the camp. The women remaining in their tents sprinkle with water the cow and the women who lead it. For this ceremony they generally choose a black cow, because black is the colour of the clouds that discharge rain.[1] In order to stop rain the women of Aith Ndhir take a dog and lead it round the encampment by a string which is wound round the body of the woman, and as they lead it they say, " Come, come, dog, thy mistress is overwhelmed by distress." Other Berbers employ a cat in ceremonies to stop rain, on account of the well-known aversion of cats to water. Thus at Tachgagalt an old woman attaches two black cats to her spindle, and with the cats as a team she ploughs the dunghill outside of her house. At Aith Sadden, when the rain falls too abundantly, a woman will tie up a cat and give it a sound beating, while she says, " Cat, cat, the rain will never fall."[2] Many other ceremonies observed by the Berbers for the procuring of rain by means of black cows are described by E. Westermarck. In these ceremonies, if the cow should urinate it is accepted as a sure sign that rain will fall soon. (See his volume, *Ritual and Belief in Morocco* (London, 1926, vol. ii. pp. 264 *sqq*.). In long-continued drought the Looboos of Sumatra try to make rain by bathing a cat.[3]

Again, frogs are often associated with rain-charms, in virtue, apparently, of their relation to water. Thus, for example, among the Bhatra, a primitive tribe of the Bastar State in the Central Provinces of India, when it is desired to bring on rain they perform a frog marriage, tying two frogs to a pestle and pouring oil and turmeric over them as in a real marriage. The children carry them round begging from door to door, and finally deposit them in water.[4] Similarly, among the Gonds, the principal Dravidian tribe of India, "when there is drought two boys put up a pestle across their shoulders, tie a living frog to it with a rag, and go from house to house

---

[1] E. Laoust, *Mots et choses berbères*, p. 245.
[2] E. Laoust, *op. cit.* p. 252.
[3] J. Kreemer, " De Looboes in Mandailing," in *Bijdragen tot de*

Taal-, Land- en Volkenkunde van Nederlandsch-Indië, lxvi. (1912) p. 327.
[4] R. V. Russell, *Tribes and Castes of the Central Provinces*, ii. 275.

accompanied by other boys and girls singing,

> *Brother Frog, give rain,*
> *Let the rice and kodon ripen,*
> *Let my marriage be held.*

The frog is considered to be able to produce rain because it lives in water and therefore has control over its element.   The boy's point in asking the frog to let his marriage be held is that if the rain failed and the crops withered, his parents would be unable to afford the expense."[1]   So in Southern India, to bring about rain, " Malas, the Telugu Pariahs, tie a live frog to a mortar, and put on the top thereof a mud figure representing the deity Gontiyalamma.   They then take these objects in procession, singing ' Mother frog, playing in water, pour rain by potsfull.'   The villagers of other castes then come and pour water over the Malas.   The Rev. S. Nicholson informs me that, to produce rain in the Telugu country, two boys capture a frog, and put it in a basket with some nim (margosa, *Melia Azadirachta*) leaves.   They tie the basket to the middle of a stick, which they support on their shoulders. In this manner they make a circuit of the village, visiting every house, singing the praises of the god of rain.   The greater the noise the captive animal makes the better the omen, and the more gain for the boys, for at every house they receive something in recognition of their endeavours to bring rain upon the village fields."[2]

A Chinese charm to produce rain when it is wanted in spring, summer, or autumn, is as follows.   They pierce a hole in the altar of the god of the soil, and connect the hole with the water channel at the back of the village.   By thus moistening the god of the soil they hope to incite him to produce a plentiful supply of the water which the ground sorely needs. Further, they arrange five frogs at haphazard on the altar of the god of the soil.   By their croaking the frogs are thought to call for rain, and so to stimulate the god to produce the needed downpour.[3]

Scattered about in the Caucasus are a number of communities of Mountain Jews, who differ essentially from

[1] R. V. Russell, *op. cit.* iii. 106.
[2] E. Thurston, *Omens and Superstitions of Southern India*, pp.

305 *sq.*
[3] E. Chavannes, *Le T'ai Chan* (Paris, 1910), pp. 495 *sq.*

European Jews in language, religion, and custom. These Jews are zealous adherents of the Talmud. In time of drought the whole village assembles in the churchyard, fasts the whole day, and prays to the god to send rain, while the children march round the churchyard several times and call upon Semirei, the god of rain. Meanwhile some women have caught frogs and clad them in little coats. That is a pious deed, and the frogs, who cannot live without water, join their supplication for rain with the prayers of the people.[1]

The Basoga of Uganda in Central Africa have, or rather formerly had, a remarkable way of producing rain by the sacrifice of a human victim. The custom has of course been abolished under English rule ; but it may be worth while to record it here, though it savours more of religion than of magic. The custom has been described by Canon Roscoe as follows : " Another way of obtaining rain is by offering a human sacrifice to the god Kahango. This god is said to live in a deep hole in a part of the country known as *The Pit of Kahango*, where a priest dwells. A man is chosen by divination, and is carried to the place of sacrifice. The victim is usually a cripple. He is laid near the edge of the pit on a bed of wild gourd creepers. The bearers are from a special clan who have this duty to perform. They also take with them an offering of a goat for a sacrifice and to supply the sacred meal with meat. As the victim is laid by the pit, the people say, ' You, Kahango, if it is you who are keeping off the rain, accept this sacrifice and let the rain come. If it is not you, then give this man strength to get up and walk back to us.' The people retire some distance away, and after a reasonable time has been given and the man has not come, they look to see whether he has been drawn into the pit or not. Should he be missing, they kill an ox and eat a meal near the pit. The people say that it is seldom a man returns : he usually falls into the pit. The rain, they assert, invariably comes after such an offering. When the first-fruits are ready, some are taken to the god and presented to the priest, and afterwards the food may be consumed by all the clans concerned."[2]

[1] C. Hahn, *Aus dem Kaukasus* (Leipzig, 1892), pp. 194 *sq.*

[2] J. Roscoe, *The Northern Bantu,* p. 255.

A much more innocent way of inducing or compelling the powers of Nature to produce rain is sometimes practised by the Looboos, a primitive people of Sumatra. They plant a banana stem in a stream. By thus imposing an obstacle to the flow of the current, they think that the stream will soon produce rain enough to swell its flow and so sweep away the obstacle.[1]

Chinese annals record that in the autumn of the year 669 B.C. there was a great excess of rain, and that to arrest it the people sacrificed a human victim near the altar of the god of the soil.[2] " Nearly every year petitions are incessantly put up to the rain-god to exert his powers on the parched earth, which cannot be planted until there is a rainfall. After prayers have been long continued with no result, it is common for the villagers to administer a little wholesome correction by dragging the image of the god of war out of his temple and setting him down in the hottest place to be found, that he may know what the condition of the atmosphere really is at first hand, and not by hearsay only."[3] A less drastic method of dealing with the image of the god Shiva in India is to drench the image with water for the purpose of procuring rain in time of drought. For the same purpose, naked boys carry a characteristic emblem of the god from door to door and are drenched with water by the inmates. This is supposed to bring about the needed fall of rain.[4]

Primitive man also believes that by his magic he can control the sun, causing the luminary in case of need to shine and hastening or delaying its going-down.[5] Thus when the weather has been unusually cold the Arunta of Central Australia will sometimes construct upon a selected ceremonial ground a large coloured design representing the sun. Radiating from a point upon a clear space, many lines are drawn with red and white vegetable down to represent the rays of the sun ; and these are intersected at different distances from the central point by a number of concentric circles which

[1] J. Kreemer, *op. cit.* p. 327.
[2] E. Chavannes, *op. cit.* p. 491.
[3] A. H. Smith, *Chinese Character-istics* (Edinburgh and London, 1900), p. 305.
[4] R. E. Enthoven, *The Folklore of* Bombay, pp. 317 *sq.*; *id., Folklore of Konkan* (Supplement to *Indian Antiquary*, xliii, 1914), p. 17.
[5] Cf. *The Golden Bough : The Magic Art*, etc., i. 311 *sqq.*

represent the fathers of the tribe.   The centre of the design is
occupied by a stick which is supposed to incorporate some
mystical and sun-creature known as *Knaninja Arrerreka*.[1]
By the construction of this effigy of the sun the Arunta no
doubt hope to increase the solar heat, and so to put an end to
the cold weather.   In San Cristoval, one of the Solomon
Islands, it is said that " a famous ancestor of the Mwara clan,
belated on his journey, took the leaf of a *tea*, a palm with red
fruit, and caught the sun in a noose, and now not only Mwara
clan men but others may do the same (may keep the sun from
setting) by tying a knot with a *tea* leaf round a tree by the
roadside.   One may see many such along the roads."[2]
The Kai of Northern New Guinea think that they can hasten
the setting of the sun by throwing charmed stones at the
luminary, and that they can delay its setting by binding it
with grass knots upon which they have whispered the name
of sun.   In the magic of the hunt they call to the sun to send
his rays through the thick covert of the tropical forest so that
the hunter may have light whereby to see his prey.[3]   In the
Loyalty Islands there used to be magicians whose special
business it was to control the sun, but they were not very
popular because the natives suffered much from the excessive
heat of the sun, and were apt to lay the blame for their sufferings at the door of the solar magicians.   They even insinuated
sometimes that one such magician was trying to cause a
famine in the land, so that many people would die of hunger
and thus there would be more human flesh for food.   It was
one of the prerogatives of this functionary to proclaim a
cannibal feast whenever he wished to do so.   He had, however, to observe certain rules and conditions which might be
supposed to militate against the too frequent repetition of such
orgies.   Thus, for example, he would be obliged to sacrifice
his own eldest son.   This, the first victim, he would be obliged
to have cut into a number of parts, corresponding to the
number of districts in his chief's dominion.   Each portion
would then be despatched by a special envoy accompanied by
the following message : ' This is part of the body of my own

---

[1] H. Basedow, *The Australian Aboriginal*, p. 265.

[2] C. E. Fox, *The Threshold of the Pacific*, p. 263.

[3] Neuhauss, *op. cit.* iii. 159.

son.' It was then held that the people were free to slay and eat each other.[1]

In Yap, one of the Micronesian Islands of the Pacific, there was a magician who professed to direct the motions of the sun by pointing the ray of a sword-fish at it. It was believed that in this way he could bring the sun down from heaven to earth, or cause the sun to deviate from his path to the north, south, east, or west by pointing with the ray to the direction in which he wished the sun to go. He performed any of these feats at the bidding of the chiefs.[2]

But the sun is not the only heavenly body which puny man attempts to coerce by his magic. At an eclipse of the moon the North Andaman Islanders attempt to frighten the luminary into showing her bright face again by lighting the end of a bamboo arrow-shaft and shooting it in a bow in the direction of the moon. Or they take plumes of shredded *Tetrathera* wood and blow them towards the moon.[3]

Once more primitive man seeks to control the wind by his magic so that it may blow or be still at his bidding. Among the Baganda of Central Africa when a new king was crowned he sent to his paternal grandmother's clan for a new fetish, *Nantaba*. The grandmother's relatives prepared a gourd for the ceremony and also selected a tree of a special sort for the fetish. When all was ready, four men were sent to the place with a present of cowry-shells and a white goat from the king. Bark cloths were spread round the tree to catch the chips as it was cut down ; as soon as it was felled, the king's grandmother hurried forward with the gourd, and, stooping down at the stump, held the gourd on it, with its mouth towards the quarter from which the wind came, so that the wind blew into it, making a mournful sound. She then placed some of the leaves of the tree in the neck of the gourd, and quickly covered it, while all the people shouted for joy that the wind had been captured. The gourd was stitched in a piece of goat-skin, and decorated with cowry-shells and beads, and called *Nantaba*. Thus adorned, the gourd was handed

[1] E. Hadfield, *Among the Natives of the Loyalty Group* (London, 1920), p. 112.

[2] P. S. Walleser, " Religiose Anschauungen und Gebrauche der Bewohner von Jap," in *Anthropos* viii. (1913) p. 1053.

[3] A. R. Brown, *The Andaman Islanders* (London, 1922) p. 144.

to one of the four messengers, who wrapped a bark-cloth round it and bound it to his person. He then carried it to the king, walking very slowly like a pregnant woman near the time of her delivery, and rested constantly. Indeed he was not allowed to walk more than two miles a day and was cared for like a delicate woman. On their return journey the messengers were not allowed to look on blood, and any meat which they ate was dried in the sun before it was cooked. When they arrived at the palace, a temple was built for the gourd, and one of the king's wives, *Kabeja*, was appointed caretaker of it. The gourd with the captured wind in it was thought to be a goddess endowed with powers of fecundity. Whenever the wind blew strongly, drums were beaten in the enclosure of the temple, to draw off the attention of the imprisoned wind-spirit, and prevent it from escaping. Offerings of beer were made, and requests for children were addressed to the spirit. During the king's life-time the fetish was honoured at Court, but when he died it was discarded, and the new king sent for a new fetish.[1]

When the natives of Loango are serving as sailors on European vessels and are overtaken by a great calm, if they wish to raise the wind they stroke the mast and rigging with their fingers, and whistle. They also shout lustily, clicking their tongues against the roof of their mouths, and crying, "Come, wind, come." They also invoke a fetish called Tiaba, which is specially made for overseas trade, saying, "Bring wind, Tiaba, bring good wind."[2]

When the Berbers of Morocco are about to winnow a heap of grain they plant a flag in the middle of the heap, because they think that the fluttering of the flag will raise a wind favourable to the operation of winnowing. The wind which they most desire to raise is the west wind, because it brings up clouds and rain. In the Ida Gounidif, if there is a dead calm when the winnowing is about to take place, the farmer informs his wife, who thereupon sweeps the ground about her mill with tufts of wool preserved for the purpose. After

[1] J. Roscoe, *The Baganda*, pp. 325 *sq.*

[2] *Die Loango Expedition*, iii. 2, p. 336.

plunging the tufts in water she fastens them to a wand of a
carob tree, which she sticks in the heap of grain which is to be
winnowed. By this ceremony she intends to bring up both
wind and rain.[1] The Berbers think that any light object
suspended in the air in swaying about with every breeze
possesses the magic power of calling up the wind. Hence
they will sometimes take the dried dung of an ass or a mule
and hang it by a thread to the central pole of the mill, or to a
stick inserted in the outside of the mill, and pointing towards
the west, or to the gate of the farm, or to an angle of
the terrace. Elsewhere a frog or a large black beetle is
suspended under similar conditions to a pole of the mill or to
the lower branch of a tree. They think that the wind is produced by the animal, which does not cease to move its legs to
and fro. The Ida Ouzzal provoke the west wind by hanging
a schoolboy's slate to the higher branch of a carob tree.
Under the influence of the sacred words inscribed on the slate
the leaves of the tree flutter and so call up the desired wind.
At Timgicht an amulet is inscribed by a *shereef* and fastened
to the highest branch of the tallest carob tree on the hills
which dominate the village. It is believed in the same way
that this will cause the leaves to flutter, and thus give birth to
a wind. According to a common Berber belief the wind
cannot blow if its progress is arrested by any obstacle. Hence
when wind is wanted they will sometimes undo the tresses of
their hair for the purpose of delivering the wind from the
barrier which might prevent it from rising. Among the O.
Yahya, when the time for winnowing has come but there is
no wind the farmer will tell his women-folk, " Unbind your
hair, for I am going to winnow." Among the Achtouken
young girls act in the same way for the same purpose : they
unloosen their tresses, and soak them with henna, then comb
them out, praying for a wind. Among the Ida Ou Brahim
when the desired wind obstinately refuses to rise they take a
boy, the last born of an old woman, dress him in a brown
garment, and lead him into the garden. From there they
conduct him to the heap of grain that is to be winnowed, and
having posted him with his face to the west, they tell him to
whistle. The boy complies, and whistles at first feebly, but

[1] E. Laoust, *Mots et choses berbères*, pp. 234 *sq.*

louder afterwards, and as the whistle increases in sound so the wind rises proportionately.[1]

Among the Birhors of the Chota Nagpur in India the members of the different clans are supposed to be endowed with various magical powers, differing according to the region from which the ancestors of the clan originally came. " Thus the *Here Hembrom* and the *Khudi Hembrom* clans are said to have powers over the weather. It is said that when high wind is approaching, if a man of either of these clans pours a jug of water on the *Than* (spirit-seat) or in front of the tribal encampment and bids the storm turn aside, the storm will immediately take a different direction, and even though it may blow hard on the country all around, the hill or jungle in which these clans may be encamping will remain quite calm and undisturbed. The reason why the men of these clans are said to be the *maliks* or masters of the storm is explained by saying that their *Buru-bongas* (mountain-gods) or *Ora-bongas* (home-gods) are situated to the north, which is the home of storms. Members of the *Jegseria Latha* clan, whose ancestral home and ' home-god ' (*Ora-bonga*) are further north than those of the *Here Hembrom* and *Khudi Hembrom* clans, are credited with the power of controlling monsoon rains and high winds in the same way. But with regard to this clan, it is also said that their special power over monsoon winds and rain is derived from the spirit known as *Bhir Dhir Pancho Panroa*, who is the guardian of the monsoon rains and who is specially propitiated by the men of this clan at their *thans* or spirit-seats. It is said that monsoon winds and rains will always abate their force when they approach a settlement of this clan." [2] When high winds blow or hailstorms occur Birhor women throw a husking pestle on the courtyard, and this is said to make the wind abate its violence and the hailstones to cease falling.[3]

In South China, " our boatmen, we noticed, whistled for wind in the same fashion as our sailors do. I have noticed this often in Burma, and fancy it is common to most countries." [4]

---

[1] E. Laoust, *op. cit.* pp. 393 *sq.*
[2] S. C. Roy, *The Birhors*, pp. 108 *sq.*

[3] S. C. Roy, *op. cit.* p. 368.
[4] A. R. Colquhoun, *Across Chryse* (London, 1883), p. 52.

The houses of the Kai people, in Northern New Guinea, are perched on trees, and so are particularly liable to suffer from the violence of high winds. They personify the storm wind, which they believe to come from some distant cave. To abate the violence of the storm they take the jaw-bone of a wild animal and lay it on the fire, with a request to the storm that he will take the jaw-bone and leave the house in peace. To protect themselves further against its violence they fasten a spike or spear to the outward wall of the house with its point turned in the direction of the wind, so that when the wind comes the spike or spear may wound him in the stomach, and so repel him from the house. Or at every gust of the wind they take a club or a stone axe and strike the balcony of the house, saying, " If you enter my house, I will beat your feet flat." [1]

Malay seamen seriously believe that they can cause the wind to blow by whistling. When the naturalist Hickson was approaching the coast of Celebes the wind suddenly failed, whereupon the native skipper whistled for it to come, first softly and then angrily.[2]

When Spencer and Gillen were crossing Australia they came among the Warramunga, a tribe inhabiting the very heart of the continent. " The day after we got there they were busy performing a wind ceremony, the object of which was to make the wind blow. There was no apparent need for the ceremony, as, at this time of the year, scarcely a day passes without a few strong gusts sweeping across the plains. However, they firmly believe that they can make it blow or make it stop, just as they like. At one time, when they were decorating themselves, the gusts were very unpleasant, and one of the other men told a wind-man to make it stop. Accordingly he shouted out to the wind, and, in a minute, there was a lull, and no one doubted but that this was due to the power of the wind-man. Next day it blew harder than ever, of course as a result of the ceremony, and we had a violent dust-storm—in fact a day hardly passed without one." [3]

The Caribs of the West Indies had various modes of

[1] Neuhauss, *op. cit.* iii. 157.

[2] S. J. Hickson, *A Naturalist in North Celebes* (London, 1889), p. 14.

[3] Baldwin Spencer and F. J. Gillen, *Across Australia* (London, 1912), ii. 366.

regulating the wind and the weather. When they saw a rain-cloud about to burst they whistled in the air and waved their hands in order to drive it away in another direction. In order to make the sea calm and lay a storm they chewed cassava root and spat it into the air and into the sea for the purpose of pacifying a certain spirit named Zemeen, who, they imagined was perhaps angry because he was hungry. If there was not a favourable wind an old man would strike the stern of the canoe with an arrow, after which the canoe would shoot ahead like an arrow.[1]

In Europe the custom of whistling to raise the wind is very common. Many examples of it are cited by Mr. R. Lasch in a learned article.[2]

---

[1] De la Borde, "Relation de l'origine . . . des Caraibes," in *Receuil de divers voyages faits en Afrique et en l'Amérique* (Paris, 1684), p. 29.

[2] R. Lasch, "Das Pfeifen und seine Beziehung zu Dämonenglauben und Zauberei," in *Archiv für Religions-wissenschaft*, vol. 18 (1915), pp. 589 *sqq.*

CHAPTER III

MAGICIANS AS KINGS

IN treating of the rise of magicians to political power as chiefs and kings I had occasion to notice the remarkable social system of the Australian aborigines, in which chiefs are conspicuous by their absence and their place of authority is taken on the whole by the old men of the tribe.[1] For this system of government by old men I coined the word *geronto-cracy*, which seems now to be generally accepted for this phase of social development. The system is found, though in a less marked degree, amongst other primitive peoples besides the Australian aborigines.

On the system as it existed in Australia in the first half of the nineteenth century I may cite the evidence of E. J. Eyre, who was intimately acquainted with the aborigines of Central Australia, and afterwards attained to notoriety as Governor of Jamaica. " There can hardly be said to be any form of government existing among a people who recognize no authority, and where every member of the community is at liberty to act as he likes, except in so far as he may be in-fluenced by the general opinion or wishes of the tribe, or by that feeling which prompts men, whether in civilised or savage communities to bend to the will of some one or two persons who may have taken a more prominent and leading part than the rest in the duties and avocations of life. Among none of the tribes yet known have chiefs ever been found to be acknowledged, though in all there are some men who take the lead, and whose opinions and wishes have great weight with the others. Other things being equal, a man's authority

[1] *The Golden Bough : The Magic Art and the Evolution of Kings,* i. 332 *sqq.*

and influence increase among his tribe in proportion to his years. To each stage of life through which he passes is given some additional knowledge or power, and he is privileged to carry an additional number of implements and weapons, as he advances in life. An old grey-headed man generally carries the principal implements and weapons, either for war or sorcery : many of the latter the women and children are never allowed to see, such as pieces of rock-crystal, by which the sorcerer can produce rain, cause blindness, or impart to the waters the power of destroying life, etc. ; the sacred dagger for causing the death of their enemies by enchantment ; the *moor-y-um-karr* or flat oval piece of wood which is whirled round the camp at nights, and many others of a similar nature. I have not, however, found that age is invariably productive of influence, unless the individual has previously signalized himself among his people, and taken up a commanding position when youth and strength enabled him to support his pretensions, and unless he be still in full possession of vigour of mind and energy of character, though no longer endowed with personal strength. The grey head usually appears to be treated with respect as long as the owner is no encumbrance to those around him, but the moment he becomes a drag every tie is broken and he is at once cast off to perish. Among many tribes with which I have been acquainted, I have often noticed that though the leading men were generally elderly men from forty-five to sixty years old, they were not always the oldest ; they were still in full vigour of body and mind, and men who could take a prominent part in acting as well as in counselling." [1]

Again, with regard to the Andrawilla tribe of East Central Australia, we read that " there is no form of government. The old men of the tribe possess a large amount of power over the younger members from the fact that they perform all the important tribal ceremonies. The old men are supposed to be able to make rain, and inflict and cure diseases, and drive away devils (*koochoo*)." [2]

---

[1] E. J. Eyre, *Journals of Expeditions of Discovery into Central Australia* (London, 1845), ii. 315 *sq.*
[2] F. H. Wells, in *Report of the Fifth* Meeting of the Australasian Association for the Advancement of Science, 1893, p. 518.

The same absence of effective chiefs and the same practical predominance of old men have been recorded among the aboriginal tribes of New Guinea. Thus with regard to the tribes inhabiting the western extremity of British New Guinea we are told that " unlike most native countries, there is not in Papua a village head-man or any one person who could be regarded as responsible for his tribe or village. It is true that throughout the country there are tribal chiefs, but in most cases their authority counts for little, or is obeyed in special cases only. The war chief may lead in time of war or the ceremonial chief at the time of festivals, but there is no person whose authority is implicitly obeyed in all circumstances. The government of a tribe, at least in the west, was carried on by a sort of council of old men who yarned over and came to some conclusion about knotty points, but it had no executive."[1] Similarly with regard to the Orokaiva, a tribe inhabiting the extreme east of British New Guinea, we are told that " there is no well-defined chieftainship among the Orokaiva, but merely a recognized ascendancy of the old men. The leader and ruler of any clan is the eldest of its men, provided he is not so old as to be incompetent, and provided always that his personality is equal to his position. It is consequently difficult to find a word which would correspond with our idea of ' chief,' and unsatisfactory to use the English word ' chief', as too pretentious for even the most important of clan leaders."[2]

Among these people, while there are no chiefs of the normal type, on the other hand magicians appear to have attained to a degree of social influence and authority which in time might develop into a regular chieftainship. Thus, for example, with regard to the natives of the Fly River in the western part of British New Guinea, we are told that " politically the sorcerers as a body, partly because they are among the elders of the village, and partly through the fear they impose, possess a deal of power. It is very largely on their advice that important tribal decisions are made. It is perhaps hardly necessary to say that every Papuan, no matter how civilized he is, believes firmly in sorcery and the

[1] W. N. Beaver, *Unexplored New Guinea* (London, 1920), p. 30.

[2] F. E. Williams, *Orokaiva Society* (London, 1930), p. 104.

power of the sorcerers." [1]   Again speaking of the Girara tribes, Mr. Beaver, a good observer, says " the chiefs of a village appear to have a little authority.   The late chief of Barimo, a man combining the dual functions of chief and sorcerer, was one of the few men I have seen implicitly obeyed by his people." [2]   Once more with regard to the bush people of western British New Guinea, Mr. Beaver tells us, " certain men are credited with supernatural powers either acquired or by inheritance, and the people are prepared to ascribe everything to them.   The coast folk invariably say the bush people are powerful sorcerers and the bush people accuse each other of the same thing.   Possibly and very often the sorcerer himself does nothing to shake this belief.   Why should he ?   It is a source of power and wealth to him, whether it be black or white magic.   When anyone dies from some unexplained cause, when a person dies from snake-bite (and in New Guinea no one except those killed in battle or the very aged die a natural death), when the crops fail, when there is too much rain or too little, it is all due to the sorcerer." [3]

Once more, with regard to the Kiwai of British New Guinea, another good authority informs us that " the sorcerer is found in every Kiwai village without exception.   His influence is great, and the whole community stands in awe of him.   He is a professor of magic and the natives have unbounded faith in his art and in the methods employed by him.   He professes to have the power to cause sickness and death.   He also claims to be able to counteract the evil forces he has set at work, and to restore a sick man to health." [4] Again the same writer observes that " if the sorcerer should be angry he will say to a man : ' This is your last day ; you will not see the sun rise tomorrow.'   It seems impossible to believe that such a curse pronounced upon a man will cause him to sicken and die, but so great is the fear of the sorcerer and his charms that unless the curse be counteracted the condemned man will die.   He gives up all hope and simply passes away." [5]   With regard to the Yabim, a tribe of Northern New Guinea, we learn that the chief, though not

[1] Beaver, *op. cit.* p. 135.
[2] Beaver, *op. cit.* p. 203.
[3] Beaver, *op. cit.* p. 97.

[4] E. Baxter Riley, *Among Papuan Headhunters* (London, 1925), p. 278.
[5] E. Baxter Riley, *op. cit.* p. 280.

necessarily a magician, is very often such.   He is chief and magician in one.[1]

In Kiriwina, one of the Trobriand Islands lying to the east of New Guinea, the functions of chief and magician appear to be similarly combined, as we learn from the following passage of the experienced missionary, Dr. George Brown. " The Rev. S. B. Fellows gave me the following account of the beliefs of the people of Kiriwina (Trobriands group) : The sorcerers, who are very numerous, are credited with the power of creating the wind and rain, of making the gardens to be either fruitful or barren, and of causing sickness which leads to death.   Their methods of operation are legion.   The great chief, who is also the principal sorcerer, claims the sole right to secure a bountiful harvest every year.   This function is considered of transcendent importance by the people." [2]

In Africa the political influence of the magician is very great.   His office is often exercised by the chief or king himself.   In that continent a special function which the magician is called upon to perform is that of procuring rain, and the rain-maker often rises to be the chief or king of his tribe. Elsewhere I have dealt at some length with this branch of the subject,[3] but here I will adduce some fresh evidence.   Thus with regard to the tribes inhabiting the valley of the Kasai, a tributary of the Congo, we are told that while the rule of the chiefs is absolute, a still greater influence is exercised over the people by the magicians or medicine-men.   Faith in the power of these men is deeply rooted in the negro mind.   The medicine-man concerns himself not only with the treatment of disease : he has medicines or charms against misfortune, wild animals, and enemies, and for good luck in hunting and in war, for the prosperity of the fields and so on.   In short he is credited with the power of determining the weal or woe of the people in every department of life.[4]   Speaking of the Akamba or Kamba tribe of Kenya, the missionary Krapf tells us that " wealth, a ready flow of language, an imposing personal appearance, and, above all, the reputations of being a

[1] R. Neuhauss, *Deutsch Neu-Guinea*, iii. 309.

[2] G. Brown, *Melanesians and Polynesians*, p. 236.

[3] *The Golden Bough : The Magic*

Art and the Evolution of Kings, i. 342 *sqq.*

[4] *Im Inneren Afrikas*, by H. Wissmann, L. Wolf, C. von Francois, H. Muller (Leipzig, 1888), pp. 141 *sqq.*

magician and rain-maker, are the surest means by which a Mkamba can attain power and importance and secure the obedience of his countrymen." [1] Among the Suk, another tribe of Kenya, there are two grades of chiefs, *Lemurok* or medicine-men and *Lekatuknok* or advisers. " These two grades exist side by side, but there is not a *Lemurok* in each section. Each section has its chief, but there are at present only two *Lemurok*. The powers of *Lemurok* are based on their knowledge of magic, and nothing of importance can be initiated without their advice. Thus, if it is proposed to make war, the first thing to be done is to consult the *Lemurok*, who, if they approve, will demoralize their opponents by magic. They do not fight themselves, but without their advice and spells nothing can be done. Again, if a man wishes to remove his cattle to some pasture, he must first consult the *Lemurok*, who know by their magic whether the place is fly-infected or suitable for cattle. They are also supposed to be able to foretell any cattle disease and are thus able to take precautionary measures." [2]

Among the Bakerewe, who inhabit the largest island in Lake Victoria Nyanza, the rain-makers enjoy a great reputation, for the making of rain is thought to be of the first importance by the people. Hence this office of rain-making is often reserved for the king : he is the great, the supreme, maker of rain for the country : and it is to him that his subjects address themselves as a last resort in times of drought. If he succeeds in his enchantments he soon becomes popular ; but if he fails he is universally despised and ruthlessly dethroned.[3] We have already seen that among the Basoga of the Central District, on the Northern shore of Lake Victoria Nyanza, the chief is regularly expected to make rain for his people, and was roundly abused by them if he failed to answer to their expectations.[4]

Among the Kuku, a tribe of the Upper White Nile, the most important personage is the Mata-lo-pion or the chief of water. He is credited with the power of making or stopping

---

[1] J. L. Krapf, *Travels and Missionary Labours in East Africa* (London, 1860), p. 355.

[2] M. W. H. Beech, *The Suk* (Oxford, 1911), pp. 36 *sq.*

[3] P. E. Hurel, " Religion et vie domestique des Bakerewe," in *Anthropos.* vi. (1911) p. 84.

[4] See above, p. 88.

the rain.   Special virtue is attributed to him, and his functions are hereditary.   He possesses a particular stone which is deposited permanently on the tomb of his father : it differs in no respect from the stones which the people generally use in grinding corn.   It is large, round, and slightly hollow at the centre on the upper part.   When the chief of water desires to make rain he pours water on the stone, and when he desires to stop the rain he removes the water from the hollow of the stone.   In both cases he begins by offering food and drink at the tomb of his father, then he addresses his shade and begs him to grant his prayer, thus reinforcing the magical rite by the religious rite of prayer.[1]

Again, speaking of the Bari, a tribe of the Upper White Nile in Uganda, the Italian explorer Casati says that " they have not many superstitious practices, but their respect and veneration for the dispensers of rain are greater than those felt for the chiefs of the country.   Exorcisms for rain are the source of great remuneration to those who practise them, but are often the cause of murder, especially when the forecast is not confirmed by facts." [2]   In this tribe the rain-maker operates by means of a stone over which he possesses an occult power that makes him, we are told, virtually the king of the tribe.[3]

Among the Mossi, a people of the Western Sudan, the power of making or stopping rain is attributed above all to the supreme ruler or king (*naba*), the master of the life and death of his subjects.   But indeed a similar faculty is ascribed by the people to every powerful man, and the missionary who reports the belief was himself invited to act as rain-maker. When the king wishes to make rain he brings out of his house a pitcher containing certain herbs which he fills with water to the brim.   If, on the other hand, he desires to stop the rain, he burns herbs of other sorts and the wind drifts the smoke in the direction in which he wishes the rain-clouds to depart. Or again he hangs the tail of a cow or a horse by a thread from a stick, and as the tail flaps in the breeze the wind drives away the clouds.   Hence when the rainy season is approach-

[1] J. Vanden Plas, *Les Kuku* (Bruxelles, 1910), p. 293.

[2] G. Casati, *Ten Years in Equatoria* (London, 1891), i. 304.

[3] As to the rain-makers of the Bari, see further C. G. Seligman and Brenda Z. Seligman, *Pagan Tribes of the Nilotic Sudan* (London, 1932), pp. 247 *sqq.*

ing he sends one of his people to the market-place to get nuts
of a certain sort from the women who have brought them
thither, for these nuts are necessary ingredients of the charms
which he concocts for the control of the rain.[1]

The Berbers of Morocco believe that the whole welfare
of the country depends upon a certain magical power (*baraka*)
which they attribute to the Sultan of Morocco. On this
subject Dr. Edward Westermarck tells us that " it is on the
Sultan's *baraka* that the welfare of the whole country depends.
When it is strong and unpolluted the crops are abundant,
the women give birth to good children, and the country is
prosperous in every respect ; in the summer of 1908 the
natives of Tangier attributed the exceptionally good sardine
fishery to Mulai Hafid's accession to the throne. On the
other hand, in the reign of his predecessor the deterioration
or loss of the Sultan's *baraka* showed itself in disturbances
and troubles, in drought and famine, and in the fruit falling
down from the trees before it was ripe. Nay, even in those
parts of Morocco which are not subject to the Sultan's worldly
rule, the people believe that their welfare, and especially the
crops, are dependent on his *baraka*."[2]

In Africa the rain-maker who fails to bring rain is often
punished for his failure. Elsewhere I have given examples
inflicted upon unsuccessful rain-makers.[3] Here I may give
a few others. Thus among the tribes inhabiting the eastern
shores of Lake Tanganyika the kings are credited with the
power of causing the rain to fall at the season when it is
needed for the digging of the earth and the sowing of the
seed. If the rain does not fall at the due time, or is too scanty,
the people lay the blame upon the king and tell him that he
does not know his business. After that, if the drought still
continues, the people take the matter into their own hand and
depose the sluggard king.[4] We have seen that the Bakerewe
depose their king in a similar case of prolonged drought.[5]
With regard to rain-makers among the Bagesu of Mount
Elgon in Kenya we are told by Canon Roscoe : " By con-

[1] P. E. Mangin, " Les Mossi," in
Anthropos, x.-xi. (1915–1916) p. 212.
[2] E. Westermarck, *The Moorish
Conception of Holiness* (*Baraka*) (Hel-
singfors, 1916), pp. 9 *sq*.

[3] *The Golden Bough : The Magic
Art*, etc., pp. 344 *sqq*., 352.
[4] Mgr. Lechaptois, *Aux Rives du
Tanganika* (Alger, 1913), p. 75.
[5] See above, p. 106.

stantly using their magical arts and seeking to influence others, and by their effort to regulate the supply of sunshine and rain, they have come to believe that they can bring about what is wanted, and the people have the utmost faith in their powers.   These men have not always the happiest existence. There are days which for them are decidedly unpleasant, anxious days, full of evil omens.   Rain does not always fall at the right moment, and crops suffer in consequence.   The people then betake themselves to the rain-maker, carrying offerings and making requests for immediate showers of rain. If the rain comes in a day or two, all is well ; but should weeks pass without a shower, then the crops wither up and the people become angry and remonstrate with the rain-maker for not exerting himself and giving them what they require. Should the rain still be delayed, they attack him, rob him, burn down his house, and roughly handle him, even to doing him bodily injury." [1]

The Ten'a Indians of the Yukon Valley in Alaska regard their shamans or magicians with great respect as supernatural beings, endowed with marvellous powers, in virtue of the familiar spirit (*een*) by which each of them is supposed to be attended.   The Indian is proud of his shaman and boasts of his achievements, yet at heart he hates him, for to him are attributed many of the accidents and misfortunes which befall the people.   For example, if a hunter has been out hunting and has failed to kill game he will impute his failure to the machinations of a shaman.   Or if a man is killed by accident, the people will think that some one of the victim's relatives is a shaman, who intended to kill another shaman, missed his aim in consequence of the other's familiar spirit, and involuntarily killed another in his stead.   Some years ago there lived on the Koyukuk river an unfortunate who was dumb, deaf, and blind : his condition was considered the natural and befitting punishment for his having taken back gifts which he had already bestowed on a shaman.   It is natural, therefore, that among these Indians the magicians or shamans should be more feared than loved.[2]   In South America the Kanamari

[1] J. Roscoe, *The Northern Bantu,* p. 182.

[2] F. J. Jetté, " On the Superstitions of the Ten'a Indians," in *Anthropos,* vi. (1911) pp. 718 *sq.*

Indians of the Amazon believed that neither sickness nor
death was due to natural causes, but was the result of magic
or witchcraft.   Hence the magicians, who could thus dispose
of the health and life of every individual, were greatly feared,
and enjoyed an authority at least equal to that of the chiefs.[1]
Similarly, in the opinion of the Jibaros, a tribe inhabiting the
upper waters of the Amazon, there is no such thing as natural
death.   Every disease, every death is considered as the result
of an evil spell cast by an enemy through the medium of a
sorcerer.   Every tribe thus possesses its sorcerer or *huishinu*,
and as he who can cause the disease can equally heal it this
person is at the same time the doctor ; in Jibaro the same
word designates the two functions.   These sorcerers have a
considerable power and influence on the life of the savages.
They are feared and receive attentions from everybody, they
are loaded with presents, but their situation is not exempt
from perils ; of all the individuals of a tribe the sorcerer stands
the greatest risk of perishing tragically, whether it be that a
neighbouring people accuses him of having caused by his
magic the death of one of their members, or whether it be that
in the tribe itself he has excited the suspicions of the sons of a
sick man whom he has not been able to cure, and who may be
a member of the sorcerer's own family.   The fame of certain
sorcerers extends sometimes beyond the limits of the group to
which they belong, and people do not hesitate to go and seek
them from a distance of eight or ten days' march to bring
them to the death-bed of a man of quality.   It does not appear
that this function is the privilege of certain families : it is
rather the most intelligent men who, attracted by the advan-
tages of the profession, gradually acquire by their skill and
astuteness a reputation in the little circle where they live.
Further, exorcism is always accompanied by the administra-
tion of infusions of medicinal plants or of secret remedies, and
the skilful sorcerers do not venture to treat a patient except
when the case seems to admit of cure.[2]

Elsewhere I have shown some grounds for thinking that
among the Malays the king or rajah may sometimes have been

[1] R. Verneau, " Étude ethnographique des Indiens de l'Amazone," in
L'Anthropologie, vol. 31 (1921), p. 266.

[2] Dr. Rivet, in *L'Anthropologie*,
xix. (1908) p. 239.

developed out of the magician.[1]   The same question has more
recently been discussed by a competent authority, who says :
" Are there traces of the magician in the Malay king ?
Among some, at least, of the Proto-Malay tribes of the
Peninsula the commoner chief or Batin is judge, priest, and
magician.   Between the old-world commoner chiefs of the
matriarchal tribes of Negri Sembilan and the Raja ruler there
are several ties.   Like the magician (and the European
district officer !) both can influence the weather, a wet season
will be ascribed to a cold constitution.   Both are chosen from
several branches of one family, theoretically from each branch
in rotation, actually from the branch that happens to possess
the candidate most suitable in years and character.   Both,
therefore, like the Malay magician, hold ' offices hereditary or
at least confined to the members of one family.'   Like the
Brahmin, the Malay ruler and the Malay magician have a
tabu language.   A king does not ' walk,' but ' has himself
carried ' ;   he does not ' bathe,' but is ' sprinkled like a flower ';
he does not ' live ' but ' resides ' ;   he does not ' feed ' but
' takes a repast ' ;   he does not ' die ' but ' is borne away.'   Of
the dozen or more words constituting this vocabulary half are
Malay, half Sanskrit.   Shaman and ruler both have felt the
influence of Hinduism.   Like the magician, the ruler has
wonder-working insignia of office.   The tambourine and
other appurtenances of the shaman will generate an evil spirit
if not bequeathed to a successor. . . . According to an old
account the State shaman of Perak was eligible for the Sul-
tanate, and the Raja Muda, or heir to the throne, could
become State shaman.   Modern man has forgotten that in
appropriating buffaloes with peculiar horns, albino children,
turtles' eggs, and other freaks of Nature, the Malay ruler
started not as a grasping tyrant but as a magician, competent
above all his people to face the dangers of the unusual and the
untried.   For under paganism, Hinduism, and Islam magician
and raja dead and alive have been credited with supernatural
powers."[2]

Among the tribes of south-west Madagascar the regalia of
the kings are regarded as deities and worshipped with prayer

---

[1] *The Golden Bough : The Magic
Art*, etc., i. 361.

[2] R. O. Winstedt, *Shaman, Saiva,
and Sufi*, pp. 49 *sqq.*

and sacrifice. They are lodged in a miniature house to the east of the palace. The little house is enclosed by a fence with two openings, one of them to the west for the entrance of worshippers and one to the east for the entry of the sacrificial animals. The regalia consist of the teeth of crocodiles. At his accession every king gets a new set of these teeth from a living crocodile, the largest teeth being chosen for the purpose. The crocodiles are supposed to devour only wicked persons, and to spare the lives of the good and innocent. In one case, at least, the crocodiles from which the teeth are taken live in a sacred lake.[1]

In the House of Commons under Elizabeth it was openly asserted " that absolute princes, such as the sovereigns of England, were a species of divinity." [2] A relic of this belief in the divinity of English kings and queens was the notion that they could heal scrofula by their touch. Hence the disease was known as " The King's Evil." On this subject the historian Hume, writing in the eighteenth century, observes : " Edward the Confessor was the first that touched for the king's evil : The opinion of his sanctity procured belief to this cure among the people : His successors regarded it as a part of their state and grandeur to uphold the same opinion. It has been continued down to our time ; and the practice has been first dropped by the present royal family, who observed that it could no longer give amusement even to the populace and was attended with ridicule in the eyes of all men of understanding." [3] But though the belief in power by kings to heal scrofula by their touch has long ceased to be held by our sovereigns themselves and by educated people in general, it seems to linger among the ignorant and superstitious, even in the twentieth century. On this subject Miss Sheila Macdonald, dealing with the folklore of Ross-shire, writes as follows : " An old shepherd of ours who suffered from scrofula or king's evil, often bewailed his inability to get within touching distance of Her late Gracious Majesty. He was convinced that by so doing his infirmity would at once be

---

[1] G. Julien, " Notes et observations sur les tribus sud-occidentals de Madagascar," in *Revue d'ethnographie et des traditions populaires,* vii. (1926) pp. 1 *sq.*

[2] D. Hume, *History of England,* vol. v. p. 441.

[3] D. Hume, *op. cit.* i. 178 *sq.*

cured. ' Ach no,' he would say mournfully, ' I must just be
content to try to get to Lochaber instead some day, and get
the *leighiche* (healer) there to cure me.' The said *leighiche*
is the seventh son of a seventh son, and as is well known, such
people are credited with being able to cure not only king's evil,
but many other specific diseases." [1] The belief that kings
had the power to heal scrofula by their touch has been by no
means confined to our English monarchs. It was claimed
and exercised by French kings from Philip I in the eleventh
century down to Louis XVI in the eighteenth. The
miraculous gift was exercised for example by Louis VI, who
reigned from 1108 to 1137. The sick flocked to him in crowds
to be touched, and the king himself performed the ceremony
with full confidence in its healing virtue. [2] In 1494 Charles
VIII of France touched for the king's evil at Naples. [3]

[1] S. Macdonald, " Old World Sur-
vivals in Ross-shire," in *Folk-Lore*,
xiv. (1904) p. 372.
[2] M. Bloch, *Les Rois Thauma-
turges* (Strasburg, 1924), pp. 31, 401.
This book, based on historical docu-
ments, is the fullest account of the
subject. A less full account is that of
Dr. Raymond Crawfurd, *The King's
Evil* (Oxford, 1911).
[3] W. Roscoe, *The Life of Leo the
Tenth* (London, 1846), i. 120.

CHAPTER IV

INCARNATE HUMAN GODS

CHIEFS and others who claim to be incarnate human gods abounded among the Polynesians of the Pacific Islands. On this subject we have the excellent evidence of the American ethnographer, Horatio Hale, who shared in the American expedition to the Pacific of 1838–1842, while the Polynesian system of religion and polity was still in full bloom. After arguing that the Polynesian system of taboo may have originated in the claims of some man either to communicate with divine powers or to be himself animated and pervaded by divine attributes, he proceeds as follows : " A strong argument in favour of this view of the origin of the tabu, is found in the fact that on nearly if not quite all the groups, there have been, at a very late period, men who have been regarded by the natives as partaking of the divine nature—in short, as earthly gods. At the Navigator Islands two such individuals, father and son, by name *Tamafainga*, had, for many years, down to the period of the first arrival of the missionaries, held the inhabitants in slavish awe, and ruled them by their will, by the dread of their supernatural power. At the Tonga Islands, though it is not known that any person is actually worshipped, as elsewhere, there are two high chiefs, whose official titles are *Tuitonga* and *Viati*, and a woman, called the *Tamaha*, who are believed to be descended from gods, and are treated with reverence on that account by all, not excepting the king, who regards them as his superiors in rank. In New Zealand the great warrior-chief, Hongi, claimed for himself the title of a god, and was so called by his followers. At the Society Islands, Tamatoa, the last heathen king of Raiatea, was worshipped as a divinity.   At the Marquesas there are, on every island, several men who are termed *atua*, or gods, who receive the same adoration, and are believed to possess the same attributes as other deities.   In the Sandwich Islands, that the reverence shown to some of the chiefs bordered on religious worship is evident from a passage in a speech of John Ii (formerly a priest and now one of the best informed of the native orators) delivered in 1841, and published in the Polynesian for May 1, of that year, in which he gives an account of some of their ancient superstitions.   He says, ' Here is another sort of tabu which I have seen, namely, that relating to high chiefs, and especially to the king.   They were called gods by some, because their houses were sacred, and everything that pertained to their persons.'   At Depeyster's Group, the westernmost cluster of Polynesia, we were visited by a chief who announced himself as the *atua* or god of the islands and was acknowledged as such by the other natives." [1]

But possession by divine spirit is by no means always permanent : very often it is merely temporary, as in the case of priests or others who profess to give oracular utterances through a divine spirit who has entered into their bodies and speaks through them.   In Fiji the priest used to give such oracles.   The procedure has been described by the missionary Thomas Williams, one of the earliest and best authorities on the Fijian religion.   He says : " One who intends to consult the oracle dresses and oils himself, and, accompanied by a few others, goes to the priest, who, we will suppose, has been previously informed of the intended visit, and is lying near the sacred corner, getting ready his response.   When the party enters he rises, and sits so that his back is near the white cloth by which the god visits him, while the others occupy the opposite side of the *bure* (temple).   The principal person presents a whale's tooth, states the purpose of the visit, and expresses a hope that the god will regard him with favour.   Sometimes there is placed before the priest a dish of scented oil, with which he anoints himself, and then receives the tooth, regarding it with deep and serious attention.   Unbroken

[1] H. Hale, *United States Explor-   Philology* (Philadelphia, 1846), pp.
ing Expedition, Ethnography and   19 *sq.*

silence follows.   The priest becomes absorbed in thought, and all eyes watch him with unblinking steadiness.   In a few minutes he trembles ; slight distortions are seen in his face, and twitching movements in his limbs.   These increase to a violent muscular action, which spreads until the whole frame is strongly convulsed, and the man shivers as with a strong ague fit.   In some instances this is accompanied with murmurs and sobs, the veins are greatly enlarged, and the circulation of the blood quickened.   The priest is now possessed by his god, and all his words and actions are considered as no longer his own, but those of the deity who has entered into him. Shrill cries of ' *Koi au !   Koi au !* ' fill the air, and the god is supposed thus to notify his approach.   While giving the answer, the priest's eyes stand out and roll as in a frenzy ; his voice is unnatural, his face pale, his lips livid, his breathing depressed, and his entire appearance like that of a furious madman.   The sweat runs from every pore, and tears start from his strained eyes, after which the symptoms gradually disappear.   The priest looks round with a vacant stare, and as the god says ' I depart,' announces his actual departure by violently flinging himself down on the mat, or by suddenly striking the ground with a club, when those at a distance are informed by blasts on the conch, or the firing of a musket, that the deity has returned into the world of spirits." [1]

Sometimes temporary incarnation or inspiration by a divine spirit is supposed to be produced by a draught of blood. Thus in the Mandaya tribe of the Davao district on Mindanao, one of the Philippine Islands, there is in each community one or more persons, generally women, who are known as *ballyan*.   These priestesses or mediums are versed in all the ceremonies and dances which their ancestors have found effectual in overcoming evil influences, and in retaining the favour of the spirits.   When the women are about to give an oracle they place the images of the gods, made of a certain kind of wood, upon a small altar.   A hog is brought. The chief priestess kills it with a dagger, and she and all the other women drink of the flowing blood, in order to attract

[1] T. Williams, *Fiji and the Fijians* (London, 1860), pp. 224 *sq.*   Cf. J. E. Erskine, *Journal of a Cruise among the*   *Islands of the Western Pacific* (London, 1853), p. 250, and L. Fison, *Tales of Old Fiji* (London, 1904), pp. 166 *sq.*

the prophetic spirit to themselves, and to give their auguries or the supposed utterances of their gods. Scarcely have they drunk the blood when they become as though possessed by an infernal spirit which agitates them and makes them tremble as does the person of a body with the ague or like one who shivers with the cold.[1]   In the Mundjhulas, a sub-division of the Gandmhali tribe in the Central Provinces in India there are certain devotees of the goddess Somlai in Sambalpur, on whom the inspiration of the goddess descends, making them shake and roll their heads. When they are in this state they are believed to drink the blood flowing from goats sacrificed in the temple.[2]

Sometimes the animal sacrificed to a deity is thought to show signs that the deity has accepted the sacrifice by bodily movements of shaking or quivering which resemble, though on a smaller scale, the convulsive movements of the inspired priest himself. Thus among the Cheremiss of Russia they take the destined victim to the sacred wood and there pour water over the animal's back, praying " Great God, accept this animal which we present to you : it is for you : preserve it from the touch of human hand and from all defilement. Accept it in good grace, with our love." If the animal trembles under the splash of the cold water, it is a sign that the god accepts it ; but if it remains impassive they repeat the trial seven times. If after seven trials it still remains impassive they reject it and take another victim.[3]

In Africa chiefs and kings have often claimed to be deities incarnate in their own person. Thus, for example, the Basango of the Zambesi " consider their chief as a deity, and fear to say aught wrong lest he should hear them : they fear both before him and when out of sight.[4]   In Urua, a country in the valley of the Lomami, a southern tributary of the Congo, " Kasongo, or the chief for the time being, arrogates to himself divine honours and power, and pretends to abstain from food for days without feeling its necessity ; and indeed

---

[1] Fay-Cooper Cole, *The Wild Tribes of the Davao District, Mindanao*, pp. 174 *sq.*

[2] R. V. Russell, *Tribes and Castes of the Central Provinces*, iii. 18.

[3] J. N. Smirnov and P. Boyer, *Les Populations finnoises des bassins de la Volga et de la Kama* (Paris, 1898), p. 175.

[4] D. Livingstone, *Last Journals*, ii. 77.

declares that as a god he is altogether above requiring food, and only eats, drinks, and smokes for the pleasure it affords him." [1]   The Bambala, a tribe of the Bushongo nation to the south of the Congo, have a king whom they regard as a god on earth, all-powerful to maintain the prosperity of the country and people.   On this subject the late eminent ethnographer, E. Torday, who discovered this divine king, writes as follows : " My long conversations with them made the political situation clearer than it had seemed at first.   Its intricacy had its source in the dual position of the Nyimi (king) as temporal and spiritual chief.   As the Prime Minister explained to me, to such people as the Bengongo and the Bangendi, the Nyimi was the King, the political chief of the country ; if they rebelled, theirs was a political crime.   But to the Bambala, the ruling tribe, he was also the head of the clan, the spiritual chief, the living representative of the founder, and, as such, sacred.   Hence their frenzied jealousy of his honour ;   an insult to him was an insult to all the members of the clan, dead, living, and not yet born.   They wanted him to defend this, their honour, at the risk of his life, at the risk of the nation's existence.   Nothing mattered so long as honour was satisfied.   There was not one amongst them who would not have freely given his life to save the head of the clan the slightest humiliation ;   as Chembe Kunji (god on earth) they loved him tenderly and resented the fact that he would not allow them to die for him. . . . In his own clan his position is really a more exalted one than that of the Mikado of Japan, for while in the latter country only part of the population professes the Shinto religion, the Bambala are all ancestor worshippers, and the Nyimi (king) is the living link that alone can join them through the chain of his one hundred and twenty predecessors to Bumba, the founder.   The spirit of Bumba lives in every one of them ;   it is the life of the living, the memory of the dead, the hope of future generations.   It is his spirit that makes the moon wane and increase, that makes the sun shine ;   it is his spirit that in the shape of rain quenches the thirst of the soil after the months of drought ;   it is his spirit that makes the seeds germinate and presides over the reproduction of all that lives.   This spirit is incarnated in

[1] V. L. Cameron, *Across Africa* (London, 1877), ii. 68.

the Chembe Kunji (god on earth) and Kwete (the king) is
Chembe Kunji ; any weakening of his power, every affront
to his dignity sends a tremor through all and everything that
shares his spirit and pushes it towards the abyss of annihila-
tion."[1]

Among the Barundi, a tribe of Ruanda to the west of Lake
Victoria Nyanza, each of the gods has his own form of worship
and his own priest or priestess, whom he possesses, and by
whose mouth he gives oracles.   The priesthood is generally
hereditary.   The High Priest Kiranga bears the name as
the living representative and seat of the great god Kiranga.
There are various ways in which a man or woman may become
Kiranga, for example by being struck, though not killed,
by lightning, the sign of the god's power.   In Ruanda the
inspired mediums are called Imandwa ; they may be men or
women.   Their ecstatic state is brought on by copious draughts
of beer, and in it they are not responsible for their actions,
while their words are received as oracular utterances of the
indwelling deity.[2]

Among the Basoga of Uganda a remarkable case of the
infant incarnation of a great god has been recorded by
Canon Roscoe as follows : " Mukama is the great creator
who made man and beast.   At one period he is said to have
lived in a deep hole on Mount Elgon, where, with his sons, he
worked iron and forged all the hoes which were introduced
into the land.   He is also the creator of all rivers, which are
said to have their source at his home.   Should a child be
born with teeth already cut, it is said to be an incarnation of
Mukama ; a hut is built for the child and a high fence built
around it, and the mother with her infant is placed there during
her seclusion.   When this period ends the child is shown to
relatives and friends.   A vessel of water is brought from Lake
Kyoga and also a reed from the papyrus-grass by the husband's
sister's son, who has to go secretly to the lake ; he must not
be seen by any person, neither as he goes nor as he returns.
He takes with him four water-berries, which he offers to the
spirit of the lake, as he draws the water.   Two houses are

[1] E. Torday, *On the Trail of the
Bushongo* (London, 1925), pp. 177 *sq.*,
and for an explanation of the title
Chembe Kunji see pp. 113-115.
    [2] H. Meyer, *Die Barundi* (Leipzig,
1916), p. 123.

built for the reception of the child when the period of seclusion ends ; one is intended for a sleeping-house and the other for a living-house. The mother with her child is conducted to this new home with great ceremony. In front walks the sister's son, carrying the papyrus-reed as a spear, and behind him follow a number of medicine-men. Next comes a woman carrying a native iron hoe which she brandishes as she walks. She utters a shrill cry as women do when in danger, in order to warn people of their approach. Behind this woman come members of the parents' clan, and, last of all, the parents with the child. The mother is escorted into the living-room, where a sacred meal is eaten, and after the meal the child is brought out and has its head shaved, the water brought from the lake being used to wet the head for shaving and to wash it after the shaving has taken place. After the ceremony of shaving is ended the father gives his shield to the child. The company remain three days with the mother and her child. On the third day the papyrus-reed is handed to the child, who is appointed governor over a portion of land. The mother remains with her child, her husband giving her up to this duty, and her clan presents him with another wife instead of the mother of Mukama. The child is now regarded as a god, and people come to him to make requests for any purpose. When he dies a medium is appointed to hold converse with him and to give his replies to suppliants."[1]

Among the Gouraghes, a tribe of Abyssinia, the King of the Sorcerers is called Yoe Demam. His function is hereditary. He wears a silver ring on his ankle as a token of his dignity. He does not cut his hair nor beard, and all who approach him kiss the earth before him. He never enters a house, and if a storm overtakes him on a journey he is content to seek shelter under a tree. He is considered as a god. His habitual residence is in the forest, where people come to worship him.[2]

In antiquity the kings of Mauretania in North Africa were worshipped as gods. This is mentioned by the African

---

[1] J. Roscoe, *The Northern Bantu*, pp. 248 *sq.*

[2] R. P. Azais, " Le Paganisme en pays Gouraghe," in *Revue d'ethnographie et des traditions populaires*, vii. (1926) p. 25.

church father, Tertullian, whose evidence on the subject is
confirmed by inscriptions.[1]   On this topic my learned friend
M. J. Toutain writes as follows : " The fathers of the African
church, and the Christian writers of Africa have affirmed
repeatedly that the inhabitants of Mauretania worshipped
their kings.   This statement is justified by several inscriptions, which prove that the affirmation is perfectly exact not
only for Mauretania, but also for Numidia.   The worship of
the kings of Numidia and Mauretania was continued under
the Roman Empire : this late survival of the worship is a
proof of the tolerance of the Roman governors of Africa.
From a bilingual inscription in Punic and Berber we learn
that there was a sanctuary of King Masinissa at Thugga.   It
was without doubt in honour of the same god that the stele
or tablet was engraved which was found at Abizar, in the
Great Kabyle, on which were the words TABLA DEO
MASIN. . . .   Among the successors of Masinissa, Gulussa,
and Hiemsal were also invoked by the Africans during the
first centuries of the Christian era.   The kings of Mauretania, Juba II and Ptolemy, received, during the same epoch,
divine honours.   It is true that the inscription of Caesarea,
upon which the name of the last king occurs, is formulated
in the Latin manner : *Genio regis Ptolemaei* ; but in this
formula we must trace the influence of Rome on a worship which in Africa was much older than the Roman
conquest." [2]

In Southern Nigeria, " throughout the land, as a general
rule, the king combines magico-religious with civil duties,
acts as the representative or priest of the town or clan in all
dealings with gods, jujus, and ancestors, and regulates all
religious ceremonies.   He is often regarded as semi-divine,
endowed with the spirit of his ancestors or the ancestral god,
is confined to his house on special occasions—chiefly, no
doubt, so that the sanctity in which he lives should not be
violated—and the prosperity of the countryside and the fertility of crops, animals, and men are thought to be linked
with his well-being and his performance of the proper magical
and other rites.   The power of bringing rain is often attri-

---

[1] Tertullian, *Apologeticus*, cap. 24.   *l'Empire romain*, iii. (Paris, 1920)
[2] J. Toutain, *Les Cultes païens dans*   p. 39.

buted to these chiefs."[1]   Among the Edo of Southern Nigeria
the king of Benin was worshipped as an incarnate deity.   On
this subject the Englishman, J. Adams, who travelled in
West Africa from 1786 to 1800, tells us that, " The king of
Benin is fetiche, and the principal object of adoration in his
dominions.   He occupies a higher post here than the Pope
does in Catholic Europe, for he is not only God's viceregent
upon earth, but a god himself, whose subjects both obey and
adore him as such."[2]   Again among the Ibo of Southern
Nigeria, many of the kings were never allowed to leave their
houses and were regarded as semi-divine.[3]

The Malay kings are believed to be an incarnation of
the Hindu god Shiva, and as such to possess the right of life
and death, not only over all their subjects, but over all living
creatures.[4]   In Central Celebes divinity was ascribed to
the Sultan (*Datoe*) of Loovoo.[5]

Among pretenders to divinity in Christian England was
James Naylor, a Quaker, in the time of the Protectorate.
Of him the historian Hume gives the following account :
" James Naylor was a quaker noted for blasphemy, or rather
madness, in the time of the protectorship.   He fancied that
he himself was transformed into Christ, and was become the
real saviour of the world ; and in consequence of this frenzy
he endeavoured to imitate many actions of the Messiah related
in the evangelists.   As he bore a resemblance to the common
pictures of Christ, he allowed his beard to grow in a like form ;
he raised a person from the dead ; he was ministered unto
by women ; he entered Bristol mounted on a horse, I suppose
from the difficulty in that place of finding an ass ; his disciples
spread their garments before him and cried, ' Hosannah to the
highest ; holy, holy, is the Lord God of Sabbaoth.'   When
carried before the magistrate he would give no other answer
to all questions than ' Thou hast said it.'   What is remarkable, the parliament thought that the matter deserved their
attention.   Near ten days they spent in inquiries and debates

[1] P. A. Talbot, *Peoples of Southern Nigeria*, iii. 563 *sq.*
[2] J. Adams, *Sketches taken during Ten Voyages to Africa* (London, N D.), p. 29.
[3] Talbot, *op. cit.* iii. 592.

[4] H. Kern, in *Bijdragen tot de Taal-, Land- en Volkenkunde van Nederlandsch-Indië*, lxvii. (1913) pp. 367 *sq.*
[5] Adriani and Kruijt, *op. cit.* i. 130 *sq.*

about him.   They condemned him to be pilloried, whipped, burned in the face, and to have his tongue bored through with a red-hot iron.   All these severities he bore with the usual patience.   So far his delusion supported him.   But the sequel spoiled all.   He was sent to Bridewell, confined to hard labour, fed on bread and water, and debarred from all his disciples, male and female.   His illusion dissipated, and after some time he was contented to come out an ordinary man, and to return to his usual occupations." [1]   With reference to the Albigenses Mr. E. G. A. Holmes of 3 Abbey Road, Whitby, Yorks, wrote to me, on 18th October, 1924, strongly denying the charge of mutual worship brought by the Catholic Church against the Albigenses or rather Catharists.   He refers me to Schmidt's " monumental work " on the subject. The reference seems to be to Charles Schmidt, *Histoire et Doctrine des Cathares ou Albigeios* (2 vols. Paris, 1848–49).

With regard to the divinity of the early Babylonian kings we are told that according to contemporary evidence each of the first five kings of the third dynasty of Ur was honoured as a divinity during the years of that dynasty.   That contemporary evidence is found on the cuneiform tablets from Lagash, Umma, Ur, Drehem, and Nippur.[2]

---

[1] D. Hume, *History of England*, vii. 336-337.
[2] T. Fish, " The Contemporary Cult of Kings of the Third Dynasty of Ur," in *Bulletin of the John Rylands Library*, vol. 12 (1928), p. 75 *sq.*

CHAPTER V

DEPARTMENTAL KINGS OF NATURE[1]

SOMETIMES the magician professes to control, not the whole range of Nature, but some one particular department of it, such as water or fire, of which he proclaims himself the king. Among the Kororofawa, a tribe of Northern Nigeria, one such magician bears the title of King-of-the-Water. In seasons of drought the chief priest (Akondu) calls the King-of-the-Water, who asks for his appropriate dedicatory offerings. These are a dog, a goat, a cow with a calf, and a hen with an egg. Then millet is brought from the king's house and presented to the King-of-the-Water, and the King-of-the-Water goes to his place of sacrifice near the water and remains there seven days. He then comes back and plants some of the corn and tells the people when rain will come. The King-of-the-Water has a sacred enclosure near a spring, which is surrounded by a wall and thus kept holy. There is a door in the wall. Inside this enclosure are three sacred trees, one called *noji*, another called *mariki*, and a third called *gieya*. They are close together, and a circular pit is dug in front of them. Each tree has two miniature huts built at its foot. A grass called *kalawali*, which appears to be a species of hemp, is planted within the enclosure, and grows to a good height. If a woman comes near this particular spring it turns to blood. If a man shaves his head and leaves the shavings on the ground, next morning his hair is seen in the pool. The only persons who are allowed to enter this enclosure are the King-of-the-Water and the one assistant that he has. The King-of-the-Water has not only power over

[1] Cf. *The Magic Art and the Evolution of Kings*, ii. 1-6.

the water, but over the animals in the water, such as crocodiles, and to him is due the first boat that was ever made.
He forbids a black pot, or decorated calabash, or decorated
water-gourd to be brought near his enclosure. If the King-
of-the-Water wishes, then water destroys the town. The
title of the King-of-the-Water is Kuzafi. It is said that, as a
general rule, the King-of-the-Water and the high priest work
very well together. There are sacred creatures in the pool
within the enclosure. They are freshwater crabs. One of
these is sometimes taken to people's houses for magical
purposes. It is stated that one use to which it is put is as
follows : A basin is taken and this freshwater crab is put
underneath it on the ground. The next day, on lifting up the
basin, it will be found that the crab has gone underground.
Then a bitter herb is taken, and certain roots. Four round
posts are put up round the pool and a sort of miniature fence
is made by twining the leaves between the posts ; a small
door is left. The whole thing is covered with a white cloth.
Having done this, the person who is performing the magical
ceremony says, " I wish to know whether I shall get my desire
or not." He then goes away and in the morning he will see
that if the crab is propitious he has swept the place clean.
If it is desired by means of this ceremony to kill a person,
four straws are taken, and one of them, representing the
enemy, is set upright, and the other three, the man himself,
his wife, and his son, are put lying down. Then the three are
taken away, and the crab comes and takes the other into his
hole. The enemy is thus disposed of.[1]

The once famous magicians, the King of Fire and the King
of Water in Cambodia, whose reputation extended all over
Indo-China, now exist in little more than name ; their power
and their fame are gone. The death-blow to their pretensions
was given by a French punitive expedition sent against the
King of Fire to avenge the assassination of the administrator
Odend'hal in April 1904. Their old glory is now only a
memory.[2]

[1] H. R Palmer, " Notes on the
Kororofawa and Jukon," in *Journal
of the African Society*, xi. (1911–
1912) p. 412.
    [2] H. Maitre, *Les Regions Moï* (Paris,
1909), p. 38.

CHAPTER VI

THE WORSHIP OF TREES

THE worship of trees is very widespread among the tribes of French or West Sudan. Thus, for example, among the Bobo, at the time of sowing, the chief of the village offers sacrifices in the field to any large trees that happen to be there. Each of these trees represents at once the Earth and the Forest, two great and powerful divinities which in the mind of the negro form a single great divinity. Thus the sacrifice is offered at the same time to the Earth and the Forest that they may be favourable to the sowing. The victim sacrificed on these occasions is a hen, or several hens. But these are not the only sacrifices offered by the Bobos to trees. At Kabourou there is a chief who owns a sacred tree, a wild fig. He alone has the right of making sacrifices to it. If another person wishes to make a sacrifice to it he can only do so by leave obtained from the chief. At Tone there are five large sacred trees in the village itself. After the harvest the chiefs of the village offer sacrifices to these trees, representing the Earth and the Forest, as a thank-offering for giving much millet, and for having warded off diseases, and so on. They offer hens to them. But contrary to the custom of many other tribes, the Bobos have no sacred woods or thickets.[1] Among the Menkieras, another tribe of the French Sudan, some people, but not all, offer sacrifices to trees. At Zinou and Bono the trees to which sacrifices are made are the *sounsoun, cailcedrats, karites*, and tamarinds, in which the spirit of the Forest is believed to reside.[2] On the day after a copious shower of rain

---

[1] L. Tauxier, *Le Noir du Soudan* (Paris, 1912), pp. 70 *sq.*   [2] L. Tauxier, *op. cit.* pp. 104 *sq.*

has fallen among the Nounoumas, another tribe of the French Sudan, the chief of the village takes a hen into his field.   If there is in the field a tamarind, a *karite*, or a *cailcedrat*, he pours the blood of the fowl over the tree.   But if there is no such tree he pours the blood of the fowl upon the earth.   The sacrifice is offered to the Earth and the Forest to procure a good crop.   They also invoke the Good God or Heaven.   In the mind of the negro the tree is, firstly, a child of the earth, since the Earth bears it upon its breast, and secondly a representative of the Forest, since the forest is formed of grass, plants, and trees.   Thus to offer a sacrifice to a tree is at the same time to offer it to the Earth and the Forest, the two great divinities of productivity.   That is why, when there is a tree in the field, they pour the blood of the hen upon it.   Three divinities are thus honoured by this sacrifice : the inferior divinity of the tree itself, and the more powerful divinities of the Earth and the Forest.   It is needless to explain why at time of sowing sacrifices are offered to the two latter divinities: it is the Earth which controls the growth of the grain, it is the Forest which is the divinity of vegetation in general.[1]   The Kassounas-Fras, another tribe of the French Sudan, also offer sacrifices to trees.   They have sacred trees, either at the gate of the village, or in the fields.   Each of these sacred trees has its master, whose leave must be obtained by any person who wishes to sacrifice to the trees.   They offer sacrifices every time that the diviner bids them do so.   The sacrifice consists of a hen, millet-meal, and sometimes a small pebble.   The Kassounas-Fras have also sacred woods.   It is the Chief of the Earth, assisted by the elders of the village, who offers sacrifices to the sacred wood each time that the diviner tells him to do so.   The sacrifice offered to the Sacred Wood is also offered to the Earth, of which the Sacred Wood is the child.   In these sacred woods there are small heaps of stones at which these sacrifices are offered.   At present one may walk in the sacred woods.   Formerly it was severely prohibited to do so.   But on no account may one cut wood there.[2]

The Nankanas, another tribe of the French Sudan, sacrifice to sacred trees, which may be at the gate of the village, or

[1] L. Tauxier, *op. cit.* pp. 190 *sq.*   [2] L. Tauxier, *op. cit.* p. 237.

in the fields, or in the forest. The sacred trees comprise tamarinds, wild fig trees, and various other species. The sacrifices are offered at the bidding of the priest or diviner. The Nankanas have also sacred woods or thickets. They offer sacrifices to them at sowing, at harvest, when rain does not fall, and whenever the diviner orders them to do so.[1] The Kassounas Bouras, another tribe of the French Sudan, similarly offer sacrifices to the trees of the field, of the forest, or of the village. They sacrifice hens to the trees, or even sheep and goats, whenever the diviner bids them do so. When the tree is in the ground of a private person it is the owner who offers the sacrifice of sheep or of goats. One who wishes to sacrifice to the tree goes to the tree with the owner of the ground. The offerer and the sacrificer share the flesh of the animal. But when the offering is a fowl, the offerer is free to sacrifice it himself. Everyone offers sacrifices to trees, but above all hunters perform this act of devotion, in order that they may have good luck in hunting. Again when they clear a patch in the forest, and are forced to burn down some trees, they offer sacrifices to the spirits of the trees, lest the spirits should be angry with them. The Kassounas Bouras have sacred groves or woods, not in every village but in many. In these sacred groves there is generally a large stone set at the foot of the tallest tree. All this, the grove, the tree, and the stone, represent the Earth, the sacred mother of all things. When the chief of the village visits the diviner to consult him, the diviner often counsels him to offer in the sacred grove, to the Earth, a certain sacrifice of a sheep or ox. The chief of the village gives to the Chief of the Earth an ox or a sheep, taken either from his own herds or from the herds of others. The Chief of the Earth then goes to the sacred grove to offer the sacrifice in the presence of the chief of the village and the elders. The flesh of the animal is for the Chief of the Earth and the elders. The chief of the village does not partake of it nor does the diviner. Private individuals may not themselves sacrifice in the sacred grove. They give that which they wish to sacrifice to the Chief of the Earth, who sacrifices it for them. It is, above all, the Chief of the Earth who eats the flesh of the victims offered in the sacred grove.

---

[1] L. Tauxier, *op. cit.* p. 271.

M. Tauxier reports a recent case of a childless chief, who engaged the Chief of the Earth to offer sacrifice for him in the
sacred grove.   The sacrifice was effectual, for the next year
four of the chief's wives were with child.[1]

The Mossi, another tribe of the French Sudan within the
bend of the Niger, worship certain species of trees, including
the tamarind and the baobab, as sources of fertility both human
and vegetable.   They sacrifice to the trees with prayers for
children, and if the prayer is answered the child is given the
name of the tree.   They are said sometimes to hang articles
of clothing on trees for the purpose of obtaining a good crop,
but the custom seems to be rare, for M. Tauxier, who reports
it, has not himself met with any instance ; but he adds that
among the Malinkee of Upper Guinea a traveller may notice
at every turn little baskets of offerings hung on trees or shrubs.[2]
The Koulango, another tribe of the same region, also sacrifice
to certain species of trees, including the baobab but not the
oil palm.   Such sacrifices are always offered at the bidding of
diviners, for example, when a person is ill, that the tree may
afford him healing.   They also offer to the trees, always by
order of the diviner, clothing, cowries, eggs, and so forth, and
very rarely a little silver or a little gold.   The Koulangos who
pass never touch these offerings, for they fear the vengeance
of the tree.   Almost every village possesses a guardian tree,
a custom general in the Sudan.   Each one makes offerings to
it, according to his circumstances, always after consultation
with the diviner and according to his directions.[3]

Among the Ibibios of Southern Nigeria, when a man is in
trouble he will sometimes go to a giant tree in the forest, and,
standing at the foot of it, will, with outstretched hands, pray
to the tree to the following effect : " You, O Tree, are a big
man, and heavy things seem but light to you.   I am but a
small being, poor and weak, and my trouble is too great for
me to bear.   Will not you, therefore, who are so strong, take
it from me ?   Since, to your strength, it would be as
nothing."   Then after sacrificing to the tree, the suppliant
goes away in peace, convinced that the burden of his sorrow

[1] L. Tauxier, op. cit. p. 324.
[2] L. Tauxier, Le Noir du Yatenga
(Paris, 1907), p. 374.

[3] L. Tauxier, Le Noir de Bondoukou (Paris, 1921), p. 174.

will be lifted from him.[1]   Near Ube, in Southern Nigeria,
there is a very tall tree, which is thought to be inhabited by
a spirit called *Ebiribong*.   At the time of planting the new
yams a great play is held at the foot of the tree in honour of
the spirit and a he-goat is sacrificed to him.[2]   In the land of
the Ibibios, when the palm-trees did not bear fruit, or bore it
only in insufficient quantity, the people used to be ordered to
search the countryside until a leper was found with face eaten
away with the ravages of the disease.   Him they dragged to
the nearest palm grove and bound by the waist and throat to
the tallest tree, his arms tied round the trunk as though
clasping it.   Through both feet were driven long hooked
pegs, sharply pointed, which pinned the victim to the ground.
There he was doomed to stay, suffering intolerable agonies
from wounds, hunger, and thirst, in the glare of a tropical sun,
until death released him from his sufferings.   The bodies of
such victims were never buried, but were left to decay on the
spot.   The natives averred that after this sacrifice there was
no dearth of fruit, for the Spirits of the Palms, pleased with
the offering, sent forth their rich, orange-hued clusters in such
profusion that " over the whole grove men cut till they were
tired." [3]

In Bengal the most sacred of all trees is the Pipal (*Ficus
religiosa*).   It is said that the trunk is the habitation of
Brahma, the twigs of Shiva, and the leaves of the other gods.
It is known as Basudeva and water is poured at its foot after
the morning bath, especially in the month of Baisak and when
people are in difficulties.   It is considered very meritorious
to plant these trees by the wayside and to consecrate them.
The *Bel* (*Aegle Marmelos*) is the sacred tree of Shiva ; its
leaves are indispensable in performing the worship of Shiva
and Sakti, and for this reason pious Hindoos of the Vaish-
nava sect will not so much as mention its name.   When the
tree dies, none but Brahmans may use its wood as fuel.   It
is believed to be a favourite tree with certain spirits, which
take up their abode in it.   The *Karam* tree (*Neuclia parvi-
folia*) is considered sacred in Chota Nagpur and its festival
is held by the Oraons with great rejoicings at the time of the

---

[1] P. A. Talbot, *Life in Southern
Nigeria* (London, 1923), p. 113.

[2] P. A. Talbot. *op. cit.* pp. 314 *sq.*

[3] P. A. Talbot, *op. cit.* p. 3.

harvest home.   A branch of the tree is fetched from the village
by the young men and women of the village, to the accompaniment of singing and dancing and the beating of *tom-
toms*.   It is stuck in the ground at some place within the
village and is decorated with lights and flowers.   The people
join in a general feast and, when they have eaten and drunk,
they spend the night in merriment and in dancing round the
branch.   Next morning at dawn it is thrown into the river,
and the spirit of evil is believed to be expelled with it.   The
aboriginal immigrants to Bogra from Chota Nagpur pay
similar veneration to the plantain tree after reaping the *aus*
crop.   Goats and pigs are sacrificed to it.   The bamboo is
worshipped before weddings, and after the ceremony the
bridal garland is thrown into a bamboo clump.[1]

   The worship of trees, especially the Pipal and Banyan, is
very popular in the Bombay Presidency.   The Pipal, which
here, as in Bengal, is the holiest of all trees, is said to be the
incarnation of a Brahman, and to cut it is thought to be as
great a sin as to murder a Brahman.   It is believed that the
family of one who cuts it becomes extinct.   Some people hold
that the spirits of the dead do not get water to drink in the
next world.   The water poured at the foot of the Pipal on
the 13th, 14th, and 15th day of the dark half of *Kartik*
(October-November) and *Shravan* (July-August) and on the
14th day of the bright half of *Chaitra* (March-April) is believed
to reach these spirits and quench their thirst.   There is a Pipal
tree in the village of Prachi near Prabhas in Kathiawar, vows
in honour of which are believed to procure offspring for childless persons.   In the Deccan and Konkan the Pipal tree is
held very sacred because it is believed that the god Brahma
resides in the roots, the god Vishnu in the trunk, and the god
Shiva on the top of this tree.   Persons who make a particular
vow or have a special object of which they desire the fulfilment
worship the Pipal tree and walk round it several times every
day.   The Banyan is worshipped by women on the full-
moon day of the month *Jyeshth* (May-June) and on the no-
moon day when it falls on a Monday.   On these occasions a
cotton thread is tied round the tree, and offerings of glass

[1] E. A. Gait, in *Census of India*, 1911, vol. vi. Part i. (Calcutta, 1912),
pp. 191 *sq.*

beads, coconuts, fruits, and so on, are made. At Malad in the Thana district the Pipal tree is worshipped daily by men and women of the Brahman caste. Women walk round this tree for a hundred and eight or more times daily. Some persons hold a thread ceremony for the Pipal trees in order to obtain a son, and worship the tree for a certain period. It is worshipped with fruit and copper coins. Wooden cradles are also offered to the tree.[1]

The Larka Kols, a primitive race of Chota Nagpur, believe that certain inferior spirits or divinities haunt the trees in and around villages, and on no account will they suffer the trees to be denuded of their branches, still less to be cut down. The English writer who reports this tells us that his own coolies, natives of Chota Nagpur, were driven from a grove where they had begun to cut wood by a party of exasperated villagers who alleged that the spirits (Bhongas), expelled from their habitation, would infallibly wreak their vengeance upon the villagers themselves.[2]

The Bhuiyas are a very important tribe in Chota Nagpur, Orissa, and Bengal. In the month of Kartik (October), or the next month, they bring from the forest a branch of the *karma* tree and worship it and perform the *karma* dance in front of it. They think that this worship and dance will cause the *karma* tree, the mango, the jack-fruit, and the mahua to bear a full crop of fruit.[3]

When the Bare'e-speaking Toradyas of Central Celebes go down to the seashore to make salt they set up in the ground a sacrificial stick with a certain leaf attached to it, and another stick, with betel attached to it, they set up in the sea. Further they lay a boiled egg and rice in the nearest tree as an offering to the spirits of the tree.[4] When these same Toradyas are out hunting and have killed a wild pig they make a slit in the trunk of a neighbouring tree, and insert in the slit a piece of the pig's liver, and in doing so they say to the spirit of the tree, " O thou, who hast had compassion upon us, accept the liver of this, thy domestic animal, and

[1] R. E. Enthoven, *Folk-Lore of Bombay*, pp. 117-126, who cites many more instances of this popular worship.

[2] W. Dunbar, " Some Observations on the Lurka Coles," in *Journal of the Royal Asiatic Society*, xviii. (1861) pp. 372 *sq.*

[3] R. V. Russell, *op. cit.* ii. 318.

[4] Adriani and Kruijt, *op. cit.* ii. 339.

eat it.   We ask no gift from thee, but grant that to-morrow
and all following days we kill more pigs, each of them as
large as yonder tree." [1]

Believing that trees are inhabited or animated by spirits,
or sylvan dieties, primitive man feels naturally great scruples
at felling a tree, for by doing so he renders the spirit homeless,
and may even inflict bodily injury upon him by the operation,
and he naturally fears the wrath of the aggrieved spirit.
Hence before they fell trees, primitive peoples are commonly
in the habit of performing certain ceremonies for the purpose
of appeasing the anger of the tree-spirit, and inducing him
to pardon the wrong they are doing him.

Thus the Baganda of Central Africa thought that all
large trees were the abode of spirits, which were friendly
disposed unless a person interfered with the tree.   No one
ventured to fell a large tree without first consulting one of the
gods.   An offering was made to the tree-spirit, and only after
the spirit had been thus propitiated did the man venture to
fell the tree.   But if he neglected to perform the offering it
was thought that the tree-spirit would cause illness in his
family.[2]   Among these Baganda " there was no question of
timber-rights, or of ownership over the forest, for all timber
was public property ;   but most people held the belief that
trees were possessed by spirits, and that the spirits needed to
be propitiated by an offering of a goat or of a fowl, with some
beer, and possibly a few cowry-shells.   The cowry-shells were
tied round the trunk of the tree, the beer was poured out at
the roots of it, and the animal, if it was killed, was killed in
such a manner that the blood ran to the roots ; the meat was
then cooked and eaten by the man who made the offering,
seated near the tree.   In some instances the goat was kept
alive and allowed to roam about at will in the garden in
which the tree grew." [3]   Among the Banyoro, another large
tribe of Uganda, before a tree was felled for the purpose of
making a royal canoe, the king used to send a man or an ox
to be offered to the tree-spirit.   The victim was killed beside
the tree, in a place where the blood ran on to the tree roots.
If an animal were offered, the flesh of the victim was cooked

[1] Adriani and Kruijt, *op. cit.* ii. 359.   [3] J. Roscoe, *op. cit.* p. 386.
[2] J. Roscoe, *The Baganda*, p. 317.

and eaten by the medicine-man and the workmen who were to fell the tree and build the canoe. The body of the human victim was left by the tree roots.[1]   Among the Basoga, another tribe of Uganda, " when a large tree is wanted for building or for a canoe, the man who is going to fell it takes a goat or a fowl for an offering, kills it by the roots of the tree, and pours out the blood by the roots. He cooks the meat and eats it with his companions who are going to work with him. After the meal he strikes one sharp cut into the tree with his axe, and waits until the sap begins to flow, when he stoops and drinks some of it from the incision and thus becomes a brother of the tree. He may then fell the tree and use its timber as he wishes without any danger to himself or to his family."[2]

The Wachagga or Wajagga of Mount Kilimanjaro observe a very extraordinary ceremony before felling a tree of a species called *Mringa*, for the purpose of converting the wood into bee-hives. The ceremony has been described by the Honourable Charles Dundas, to whom we owe a valuable account of the Wachagga. I will quote his description of the ceremony in full. " The tree in which the hive is hung is exhorted and threatened to secure its co-operation, and finally the collection of the honey is occasion for ceremony, prayer, and thanks. To give a characteristic example of these mystic performances, I may briefly describe the manner of felling a tree species called *Mringa*, which is commonly used for hive-making. This tree, which is always the private property of someone and may not be felled by him, is spoken of as ' man's sister,' and its felling is treated as a giving-away of a bride. The owner brings offerings of milk, beer, honey, Eleusine, and beans. These he formally presents to the tree as a dower on the occasion of its marriage and takes his leave after giving his blessing as to a daughter. On the following day the tree is felled, the owner leaves the village, and is represented by a relative delegated to ' hand over the sister.' The men who are about to fell the tree give him a calabash of beer, asking for his sister. Having drunk of this and poured the remainder in the stem, the relative now addresses the tree as

<hr/>

[1] J. Roscoe, *The Northern Bantu*, pp. 79 *sq*.

[2] J. Roscoe, *op. cit.* p. 249.

follows : ' My departing child, I have drunk of the beer, I
have received my gift for you.   I give you now to your lawful husband as you were informed of by your father yesterday.
You shall be a help to your husband, go cultivate and acquire
cattle and small stock.   Go and let yourself not become lean.
Cultivate for your father as he cultivated for you, so that you
grew up.   He led water to you and watered you, and now you
are grown.   Have fortune, my child.   Your face shines, it
shall be desired by all bees ; they shall come and yearn for
you.'   With these words he departs, and the felling com-
mences.   For this purpose two axes are used, one for the
initial stroke and the other for the actual work.   As they do
so they speak comforting words to the tree as to a girl who is
carried away from her home, reminding her that all is done
by her father's wish.   Now the tree is addressed as the enticer
of bees.   The first axe is laid on the tree by the leader, who
asks pardon for what he does, representing that poverty has
driven him thereto.   Next he implores the tree to bring him
good fortune and exhorts the bees of such and such strangers
to leave their home and come to his hive, adding not a few
unkindly wishes against the same bee-keepers.   Now the
place where the chopping is to start is smeared with *Kimomo*,
a concoction intended to attract the bees.   The stem is
marked with *Kimomo* into sections suitable for conversion
into hives.   This ritual is performed by each one of the group
in respect to one tree so that each has a prior claim to one of
the trees felled.   While they are busying themselves with the
fallen tree the owner makes his appearance, wailing his
regrets that he came too late to prevent the deed and exclaiming that his daughter has been robbed.   The others endeavour to soothe him, representing that it is all for his daughter's
best and appealing to him with outstretched hands, until he
finally consents to grasp them and be reconciled.   One or
two of the hives made from the tree are given to the owner." [1]

Before cutting down a large tree, the Palaungs of Burma
" offer a prayer to propitiate the spirit that may have made
its home in it ; this is only done if the tree is really large.
Spirits that are strong take possession of the large trees,
evicting any little spirits that may have made their homes

there ;   these may have to take up their abode in the smaller trees and bushes.   The weaker spirits appear to be harmless, and no one apologizes to them when their homes are cut down. If, however, a tree is large and straight, and will make a good post for a house, it is well to propitiate the spirit living in it. If this is not done, the spirit may follow the post to the new house, and bring trouble to the house-builder and his family. An offering of a handful of cooked rice is sometimes made, but the following prayer is usually considered to be enough.   The man repeating it squats down, with his hands palm to palm, and looking up at the tree he says, ' I wish to cut wood.   O spirit dwelling in this place please remove thyself.   I shall cut down this tree to make a post for my house.   Please do not blame me, O spirit.' " [1]   When the Kachins of Burma are about to fell a large tree out of which to fashion a coffin, five or six men go into the forest and choose a large tree, preferably a *latsai*, the wood of which was formerly reserved for chiefs but may now be used by commoners.   Before cutting it down they usually sacrifice a hen by dashing it against the trunk.   When the tree has been brought down they offer upon the stump the head of the victim and cook remains of it.   In default of a hen they present to the tree a little dry fish, always with the object of preventing the spirit of the tree from biting them, and also for the purpose of paying the spirit for the wood which they take for the coffin. [2]

A French officer engaged in surveying the country inhabited by the primitive Moïs of Indo-China witnessed one such ceremony of propitiation performed by the natives before felling a tree.   He says, " It sometimes happened in the course of our geodetical survey that we were compelled to cut down a tree which interrupted the field of view of our instruments. A most interesting scene preceded the act of destruction. The ' foreman ' of our Moï coolies approached the condemned tree and addressed it much as follows : ' Spirit who hast made thy home in this tree, we worship thee and are come to claim thy mercy.   The white mandarin, our relentless master, whose commands we cannot but obey, has bidden

---

[1] Mrs. L. Milne, *The Home of an Eastern Clan*, pp. 177 *sq.*

[2] P. C. Gilhodes, " Mort et funerailles chez les Katchins," in *Anthropos*, xii.-xiii. (1917–1918) p. 430.

us to cut down thy habitation, a task which fills us with sadness, and which we only carry out with regret.   I adjure thee
to depart at once from this place and seek a new dwelling-
place elsewhere, and I pray thee to forget the wrong we do
thee, for we are not our own masters.' "[1]

Among the Dyaks of the Dusun district in Southern
Borneo, when a coffin is to be made some male members of
the family go into the forest to find a suitable tree.   Having
found it they smear the trunk with a mixture of rice, fowl's
blood, and egg as a purchase-money for the wood paid to the
spirit of the tree, who flees from the felled tree and must be
propitiated.   At the beginning of the work a fire is lit to keep
off Apitau, a dangerous spirit of the forest.   Should the fire
go out during the work, the workmen will be smitten by the
forest spirit, and will fall ill in consequence.[2]   The Bare'e-
speaking Toradyas of Central Celebes believe that every large
tree is inhabited by a spirit ; hence before felling such a tree
they offer betel to the spirit of the tree, with a request that he
would depart and seek another home.[3]

With regard to the Kiwai of British New Guinea we are
told that " even nowadays, when provided with iron axes,
they show great reluctance in felling certain large trees, particularly if the tree stands by itself or is conspicuous in some
other way.   Such a tree is thought to be inhabited by one
of the *etengena*, a group of sylvan beings.   If it is necessary
to cut down some tree in which an *etengena* may dwell, the
being must be asked to remove to some other tree suggested
to it.   After a few days the man returns and prepares to
begin the cutting, but if his arms feel very heavy so that he
can hardly lift them, this is a sign that the *entengena* has not
yet moved from the tree and has passed into his arms to prevent
the felling of the tree."[4]

Among the Mailu Islanders of British New Guinea, when
a certain man named Veavo was about to cut down a
large tree to make a canoe, having put his mark upon the
tree, he " took care to count the number of its buttresses, and

[1] H. Baudesson, *Indo-China and its Primitive People*, p. 129.
[2] P. te Wechel, " Erinnerungen aus den Ost- und West-ländern," in *Internationales Archiv für Ethno-* graphie, xxi. (1913) p. 57.
[3] N. Adriani and A. C. Kruijt, *op. cit.* i. 276, ii. 352.
[4] G. Landtman, *The Kiwai Papuans of British New Guinea*, p. 65.

went back and told his friends or near relatives.   On a certain
day he set out with as many friends as there were buttresses,
and by the signs and certain marks he left along the track
found his way to the spot.   He first assigned to each man his
buttress to chop, and each man then, with his axe on his
shoulder ready, watched Veavo, the *gubina* (master or owner).
He held in his hand a small branch of *moda* covered with
leaves, and was chewing the usual ceremonial areca-nut,
betel-leaves, and lime, and his mouth was a mass of bright
brick-red saliva.   He spat this out over the branch in his
hand, and gently whisked it against the tree-trunk, addressing
the wood-sprites thus : ' The men have come together, be
favourable to us, do not split, and look upon us that the tree
may fall well.' Then the wood-sprites went away to make a new
village in the top branches of another *moda*, and the men
started upon the trunk with their axes, each at his own
buttress.   That day the tree was cut down, and the men
went back to their village to sleep, while the wood-sprites
settled down in their new quarters." [1]

The Namau tribes of British New Guinea " believed that
when a tree was felled its *imunu* (soul) was dispossessed, and
had to seek an abiding-place in another tree.   Its preference
was for a tree of the species from which it had been expelled,
but failing it there were alternative species in which it could
dwell temporarily.   As an illustration I was told that when
an *aravea* tree was felled its *imunu* entered a *laura*, a species
of the acacia group, and remained there until it could establish itself in another *aravea* tree." [2]   But the writer who has
recorded this belief of the Namau tribes does not tell us what
ceremonies these people observe at felling a tree and so dis-
possessing its spirit.

Among the Trobriand Islanders to the east of New Guinea,
when a canoe is to be made a tree is chosen for the purpose,
and the master of the canoe (*toliwaga*), " the builder, and a
few helpers repair to the spot, and a preliminary rite must be
performed before they begin to cut it down.   A small incision is made into the trunk, so that a particle of food, or a
bit of areca-nut can be put into it.   Giving this as an offering

[1] W. J. V. Saville, *In Unknown
New Guinea* (London, 1926), p. 122.

[2] J. H. Holmes, *In Primitive New
Guinea* (London, 1924), p. 154.

to the *tokway* (wood-sprite), the magician offers an incantation :—' Come down, O wood-sprites, O *Tokway*, dwellers in branches, come down ! Come down, dwellers in branch forks, in branch shoots ! Come down, come, eat ! Go to your coral outcrop over there ; crowd there, swarm there, be noisy there, scream there ! Step down from our tree, old men ! This is a canoe ill spoken of ; this is a canoe out of which you have been shamed ; this is a canoe out of which you have been expelled ! At sunrise and morning you help us in felling the canoe ; this our tree, old men, let it go and fall down.' This spell, given in free translation, which, however, follows the original very closely, word for word, is far clearer than the average sample of Trobriand magic. In the first part the *Tokway* is invoked under various names and invited to leave his abode, and to move to some other place, and there to be at his ease. In the second part the canoe is mentioned with several epithets, all of which denote an act of discourtesy or ill-omen. This is obviously done to compel the *Tokway* to leave the tree." [1]

The Mandaya, a tribe in the Davao district of Mindanao, one of the Philippine Islands, believe that certain trees are inhabited by malevolent spirits. The ground beneath these trees is generally free from undergrowth, and thus it is known that " a spirit who keeps his yard clean resides there." " In clearing ground for a new field it sometimes becomes necessary to cut down one of these trees, but before it is disturbed an offering of betel-nut, food, and a white chicken is carried to the plot. The throat of the fowl is cut and its blood is allowed to fall in the roots of the tree. Meanwhile one of the older men calls the attention of the spirits to the offerings and begs that they be accepted in payment for the dwelling that they are about to destroy. This food is never eaten, as is customary with offerings made to other spirits. After a lapse of two or three days it is thought that the occupant of the tree has had time to move and the plot is cleared." [2]

When a fruit-tree does not bear fruit primitive man often imagines that he can compel it to do so by threatening the

[1] B. Malinowski, *Argonauts of the Western Pacific* (London, 1922), pp. 126 *sq.*

[2] Fay-Cooper Cole, *Wild Tribes of the Davao District, Mindanao*, pp. 176 *sq.*

spirit of the tree to cut it down if it should remain persistently barren.   Elsewhere I have cited examples of this primitive form of horticulture in various parts of the world, including Europe.[1]   Here I will add a further example of it from Burma. " If a fruit-tree does not bear fruit, some quaint ceremonies are performed by the owner of the tree, in order to make it bear.   The Burmans hang bones on the branches or trunk of a barren fruit-tree, but the Palaungs take large bones and hammer them into the trunk, at the same time saying to it, ' If thou dost not bear much fruit, be afraid, for I shall come to kill thee.'   Another way is for the owner to ask a friend to climb to the top of the unfruitful tree, to speak for it.   The owner, waiting below, then takes a sword or a spear, and resting the point upon the tree, he asks, ' Wilt thou bear fruit ? '   The man in the tree, as a sort of godfather, answers for it, ' I shall bear fruit.'   The owner from below says, ' How much fruit ? '   The friend again answers for the tree, ' I shall bear very much fruit.'   The owner then threatens the tree, saying, ' If thou dost not bear fruit, I shall kill thee.'   The man in the tree answers, ' Do not say so, please, I shall certainly bear fruit.   Do not kill me and I shall be grateful.' "[2]

Sometimes primitive man believes that trees are tenanted by the spirits of the human dead.   Thus in the island of Formosa " a tree near the entrance to a village, usually selected on account of its large size, receives special homage from the various tribes of the Tsou group.   It is thought that the spirits of their ancestors take up their abode in these trees. Before sowing and after harvest, when they mow the grass, which is a ceremony performed once a year, and refill the bamboo water pipes, likewise an annual ceremony, the savages assemble under this tree, and sprinkling wine about the ground, they worship the spirit of their departed ancestors."[3] Again in Formosa " some of the Paiwan group believe that the spirits of their ancestors abide in a thick wood."[4]

Among the Ila-speaking people of Northern Rhodesia in

[1] *The Golden Bough : The Magic Art and the Evolution of Kings*, ii. pp. 20 *sq.*

[2] Mrs. L. Milne, *The Home of an Eastern Clan*, pp. 222 *sq.*

[3] J. M. Davidson, *The Island of Formosa, Past and Present* (London and New York, 1903), p. 570.

[4] J. M. Davidson, *op. cit.* p. 574.

every commune there is a grove consecrated to a demigod, that is, to the deified spirit of a dead man, whose name it bears, and who may be supposed to reside in the grove. Besides the principal grove each demigod has subsidiary groves or single large trees where he at times takes up residence. The origin of the groves may be the poles planted around the graves. In course of time they would grow up into large trees, decay, and be replaced by younger ones growing up around them. As it is taboo to meddle with the trees and the brushwood springing up under and around them, a dense impenetrable thicket is formed. Shimunenga's grove at Mala covers at least an acre of ground ; on its outskirts there stand several large wild fig trees, upon one of which in particular various skulls of cattle and animals hang bleaching—remains of past offerings. Only the priest ever enters this sacred grove, and he but once a year, when he has to cut his way in.[1]

Among the Siena, in the central district of the Ivory Coast, every village has a sacred grove, sometimes occupying an area larger than that of the village itself. These groves are kept very well, for in them the spirits of their ancestors, and the protective spirits of the village, are thought to reside. The talismans and other relics of their ancestors are kept in the clearing in the grove. Sometimes these groves survive the village to which they originally belonged.[2]

Here we may notice some other examples of sacred groves in Africa. Thus the Nounoumas of the French or Western Sudan have sacred groves in a large number of their villages. There is a particularly fine one at Leo. The inhabitants of the place offer a sacrifice to it every year after the harvest to thank the Earth (mother of the sacred wood) for having given a good crop.[3]

In Yatenga, a district of the French Sudan, there is a sacred grove for every village inhabited by the Mossi and Foulsa tribes. These sacred groves the people regard as their protectors and offer sacrifices to them in order to prevent

[1] E. W. Smith and A. M. Dale, *The Ila-Speaking Peoples of Northern Rhodesia*, ii. pp. 183 *sqq.*

[2] M. Delafosse, "Le Peuple Siéna ou Senoufo," in *Revue des Études* *Ethnographiques et Sociologiques*, ii. (1909) pp. 18 *sq.*

[3] L. Tauxier, *Le Noir du Soudan*, p. 191.

sickness from entering the village.   It is not permitted to take
wood or to cut trees in the sacred grove, nor to hunt nor to
kill beasts that live there, and above all the serpents.[1]   The
Mossi believe that the *tangande* or protector spirit of the
village takes the form of an animal, which dwells in the sacred
grove.   It may be in the shape of a crocodile, a boa, a panther,
a tortoise, a hind, a hare, and so on.   The particular animal
is sacred to all the villagers, and may not be killed by them
within the grove, though they may kill it elsewhere, even quite
close to the grove.   Nothing may be taken from the sacred
grove, everything there is sacred.   It is forbidden not only to
cut wood there, but even to gather wood that has fallen and
lies on the ground.   Still less is it lawful to set fire to the grass
in or near the grove, for a conflagration in the sacred grove
would be regarded as a catastrophe for which the people
would find no remedy.   No stranger is allowed to enter the
sacred grove, and if necessary force would be applied to
prevent the intrusion.   But if nevertheless a stranger should
succeed by sheer force in making his way into the grove,
expiatory sacrifices would be offered in the grove after his
departure to atone for the sacrilege.[2]

Near Idua Oronn in Southern Nigeria there is a sacred
grove whence no branch might be cut or leaf plucked on
penalty of death.   This was a place of refuge for escaped
slaves, and of sanctuary for those guilty of manslaughter.[3]

In the land of the Kikuyu, a tribe of Kenya, many of the
hills are crowned by sacred groves.   As no wood may be cut
in these groves for fear of bringing sickness on the land, the
trees of the grove are generally surrounded by a dense mass of
undergrowth.   At the top of the hill is a flat spot surrounded
by a thicket.   This is the place of sacrifice, and is called
athuru aliakuru.   When there is a famine or drought, it may
be decided that a sacrifice is necessary to remedy the evil.
Everyone must remain in their hut, with the exception of
fourteen old men.   These, the elected priests of the hill,
ascend with a sheep.   Goats are not acceptable to Ngai or
God on such an occasion.   On the top of the hill they light a

[1] L. Tauxier, *Le Noir du Yatenga*,
pp. 374 *sq.*
[2] P. E. Mangin, " Les Mossi," in

Anthropos, x-xi. (1915–1916) p. 193.
[3] P. A. Talbot, *Life in Southern
Nigeria*, p. 258.

fire, and kill the sheep by holding its mouth and nose till it dies of suffocation.   It is then skinned, and the skin is subsequently given to and worn by one of the old men's children. The sheep is then cooked, and a branch is plucked and dipped into the fat which is sprinkled on to the leaves of the surrounding trees.   The old men then eat some of the meat : should they not do this, the sacrifice is not acceptable.   The rest of the flesh is burned in the fire, and Ngai is thought to come and eat it afterwards.   It is said that no sooner is this sacrifice completed than thunder rolls up and hail rolls down with such force that the old men have to wrap their garments round their heads and run for their houses.   Water then bursts forth from the top of the hill and flows down the side.   If any of the trees in the grove are cut down, it is said that many people will die.   Chiefs and their wives are sometimes buried in these groves.   When war comes into the country, or after the war is over, to conclude the peace, a sacrifice of female goats is made on the *Kehalu*, in the sacred grove.[1]

Again in Ruanda, a district of Central Africa inhabited by the Barundi, there are many sacred groves.   These groves always mark the deserted homestead of a dead king, and may even grow out of his grave.   No one may touch or break a branch of a tree in these groves.   This respect for the groves is dictated not so much by piety towards the dead king, as by fear of the anger of his ghost.   All sorts of animals abound in the groves, and amongst them are snakes, in which the soul of the dead king is believed to be incarnate.   The priest of the district sometimes makes an offering to the spirit of the king by giving food and milk to the snakes.[2]

Speaking of the wild tribes of the Afghan frontier, Dr. Pennell observes " the frontier hills are often bare enough of fields or habitations, but one cannot go far without coming across some *zyarat* or holy shrine, where the faithful worship and make their vows.   It is very frequently situated on some mountain-top or inaccessible cliff, reminding one of the ' high places ' of the Israelites.   Round the grave are some stunted trees of tamarisk or ber (*Zisyphus jujuba*).   On the branches of these are hung innumerable bits of rag and pieces of

[1] C. H. Stigand, *The Land of Zinj* (London, 1913), pp. 241 *sqq*.   [2] H. Meyer, *Die Barundi*, p. 137

coloured cloth, because every votary who makes a petition at the shrine is bound to tie a piece of cloth on as the outward symbol of his vow. . . . One distinct advantage of these shrines is that it is a sin to cut wood from any of the trees surrounding them.   Thus it comes about that the shrines are the only green spots among the hills which the improvident vandalism of the tribes has denuded of all their trees and shrubs." [1]

Among the Oraons of Chota Nagpur in India every village has its sacred grove dedicated to the principal deity of the village.   In some villages the sacred grove has now shrunk to one or two ancient trees standing on a bit of fallow land.   But ancient custom forbids any one to cut trees or branches of trees standing in the grove.   When a tree or a branch dries up or falls down of itself, any one may take it on payment of a price to the representatives of the village community.   But no member of the pioneer families who originally cleared the site of the village and brought the land under cultivation is allowed to take or use the wood of the grove. [2]

Again among the Mundas, another primitive tribe of Chota Nagpur, " although the greater portion of the primeval forest, in clearings of which the Munda villages were originally established, have since disappeared under the axe or under the jara-fire,[3] many a Munda village still retains a portion or portions of the original forest to serve as Sarnas or sacred groves.   In some Mundari villages, only a small clump of ancient trees now represents the original forest and serves as the village-Sarna.   These Sarnas are the only temples the Mundas know.   Here the village gods reside, and are periodically worshipped and propitiated with sacrifices." [4]

Among the primitive Moïs of Indo-China every village has at least a patch of sacred grove, in which it is forbidden, under the severest penalties, to cut the smallest twig.   Any infraction of this rule exposes its author to severe reprisals, often entailing the death of the delinquent.   They believe

[1] T. L. Pennell, *Among the Wild Tribes of the Afghan Frontier* (London, 1909), pp. 33 *sq.*

[2] S. C. Roy, *The Oraons*, p. 172.

[3] " By the jara system, land is pre-

pared for cultivation by burning down portions of jungles."

[4] S. C. Roy, *The Mundas and their Country* (Ranchi, 1912), pp. 386 *sq.*

that the spirits inhabiting the profaned place would avenge themselves upon the village, causing all sorts of evil to fall upon it, for not having protected their retreat from sacrilegious hands.   When an epidemic or a case of death occurs of which the medicine-men cannot explain the origin, these sages attribute the calamity to a profanation of the sacred grove. The fear of being stricken to death by the spirits for such a profanation rouses the usually gentle and peaceful Moï to a fury in which he is capable of any violence.   Whenever such a profanation actually takes place, the medicine-man fixes a certain number of animals which are to be sacrificed for the purpose of appeasing the offended spirits.   And when the French Government undertakes some public work, such as the opening of a road or the construction of a canal, which involves the destruction of a sacred grove, the villagers offer important sacrifices before they allow the least morsel of the sacred wood to be cut.[1]

In San Cristoval, one of the Solomon Islands, there are sacred groves which are believed to be haunted by ghosts or spirits.   They are called " villages of the dead," and the people believe that if a man goes through one of them his soul will be left behind there.   Generally such a place is a thicket of a bamboo called 'au bungu, which is always sacred, and one large tree, usually a maranuri, a large tree with white flowers.   When one such sacred grove was cut down by a planter the awe-struck natives waited to see what would happen, as a consequence of such profanation.   In this particular grove near Hawaa a winged serpent was supposed to appear, changing from a man to a serpent and causing sores and illness to any who profaned the spot.   Sacrifices of pigs and pudding were offered here.   At other sacred groves, on the north coast of the island, passers-by used to lay down offerings of money.[2]

In the island of Yap, the inhabitants of which belong to the Micronesian family, there are sacred groves in which it is forbidden to cut wood.   It is thought that the spirit of the grove would visit with severe punishment any profane person

[1] J.   Canivey, " Notice   sur   les   moeurs et coutumes des Moï," in *Revue d'Ethnographie et de Sociologie,*   iv. (1913) pp. 27 *sqq.*
[2] C. E. Fox, *The Threshold of the Pacific*, p. 280.

who should sin in this way. They believe that the whole
island of Yap would perish if a certain grove at Tomil were
destroyed. Ordinary mortals are forbidden to set foot within
a sacred grove. They think that such a sacrilegious in-
truder would be killed by the spirit of the grove.[1]

The Cheremiss of Russia have many sacred groves, some
of which cover large areas of the forest. These groves are
inviolable, and are sometimes enclosed by walls, but the
anger of the gods and the zeal of the faithful afford them a
better protection than any material barrier. No one is bold
enough to cut even a branch in these sacred groves, and if a
tree is thrown down in a storm no one dares to touch it, and
the fallen tree is allowed to lie upon the ground. The
sacred groves look like portions of virgin forest. If some
impious hand should violate the sanctity of a grove, an expiatory sacrifice is deemed necessary to atone for the sin.
A living goose or hen is taken into the grove. They cut its
rump and torture it till it dies. Then when they have
plucked and cooked it, they throw it into the fire. At the same
time they call down the vengeance of the god on the guilty
person, saying, " May you find and punish with a similar
death the sacrilegious person who has cut the tree." Among
the Cheremiss the sacred grove is not the abode or temple of
a single god, but all the gods loved by the people take up
their residence there at a time when a sacrifice is offered in it.
But it is necessary that in the sacred grove each of the gods
should have his own special tree assigned to him. That is
why the faithful plant a tree for each god and attract him
to it by offerings. The ritual of the sacrifice offered in the
sacred grove follows a form consecrated by tradition. On a
table raised on trestles are placed a pitcher filled with mead,
dishes containing food and bread, and goblets. The sacrificer sprinkles the blood of the victim on the trunk of the
tree, saying, " Receive this offering, receive this red blood."
In some cantons the roots of the tree are also sprinkled with
the blood of the victim. Further, they hang to the branches of
the tree little tin figures and small squares of bast to remind
the god of the sacrifice and of the person who offered it, for

---

[1] P. S. Walleser, " Religiöse Anschauungen der Bewohner von Jap," in
Anthropos, viii. (1913) p. 625.

the Cheremiss distrust the memory and good faith of their gods, and therefore think it well to give them these substantial reminders of the sacrifice that has been offered. Private individuals are not free to offer sacrifices in the sacred grove. For that purpose they must employ the agency of a professional sacrificer, who himself, in offering the sacrifice, implores the pardon of the god for any fault he may have involuntarily committed.[1]

Among the beneficent powers attributed to the spirits of trees is that of causing the rain to fall in the due season. Thus the Boussanses, a tribe of the French Sudan, have, at the village of Longa, a sacred tree to which they offer an annual sacrifice at the beginning of the rainy season. Every inhabitant, including the slaves, assists at the sacrifice. The offerings, which include hens, are presented by the oldest man of the village, and the flesh of the victims is eaten by all persons present. The object of the sacrifice is to obtain an abundant rainfall. If rain should not fall during the winter they offer another sacrifice to the tree, and this second sacrifice, we are told, always proves effectual.[2] Again the tree-spirit is sometimes believed to promote the growth of the crops. Thus the Gallas of East Africa have certain sacred trees to which they repair at various times, but especially before harvest. They take with them a green bough, which they deposit at the foot of the tree, imploring the divine blessing on the family and on the crops.[3]

Again, tree-spirits are often believed to possess the power of bestowing fecundity on the human sexes and cattle. Several examples of this belief have already met us ; [4] but a few more may here be added. The Gouronmossi of the French Sudan offer sacrifices to trees and pray to them for offspring. When a childless man finds a large tamarind tree in the forest he invokes it, together with the Lord of the Earth and the Lord of the Sun, that the tree and these divinities may grant him a son. And he promises that if his prayer be granted he will give them a hen and some millet

[1] J. N. Smirnov and P. Boyer, *Les Populations finnoises des bassins de la Volga et de la Kama*, pp. 180 *sqq.*

[2] L. Tauxier, *Nouvelles Notes sur le Mossi et le Gourounsi* (Paris, 1924),

p. 174.

[3] R. Chambard, " Croyances des Gallas," in *Revue d'Ethnographie et de Sociologie* vii. (1926) pp. 122 *sq.*

[4] See above, pp. 129, 131.

meal. If he obtains his wish by the birth of a son he fulfils his vow.[1] The Southern Buduma of Lake Chad worship the *karraka* tree, a kind of acacia and the largest tree that grows in the Chad region. Nothing would persuade a native of these parts to cut or burn it. They believe that if the tree is approached with the proper rites it has power to grant prayers. One way of ensuring a favourable answer is for a medicine-man to grind corn and mix it with milk in a bowl. Then he digs a small hole at the foot of the tree, and sets the offering within. The petitioners approach and wait humbly while their request is made. Usually this is that more children shall be granted, or that the cattle shall multiply.[2] At Ikotobo, in Southern Nigeria, there is an ancient tree, a specimen of the *Dolichandrone*, which is called "The Mother of the Town." To it come wives, young and old, to pray for offspring. Hither, too, come ancient women to beg a like boon for their children and grandchildren. In most Okkobor towns stands a great tree, named "Ebiribong," to which offerings are made twice a year, at the planting of new farms and during the harvest. This is done with the special purpose of drawing down the blessing of fertility upon the women of the place, as also upon farm and byre.[3] On the plateau above James Town in Southern Nigeria Mr. P. A. Talbot found a great old tree, which had been in past times an object of special veneration to the people. Women from all parts of the district came on long pilgrimages. It was supposed to have the power of granting fertility to those who performed the necessary rites, as well as to protect them in childbirth and at all times of danger.[4] Among the Baras of Madagascar, in order to obtain offspring a man will address himself to a tree, called *sakoa*, a species of fig. He clears a space round about the tree and prostrates himself at the foot of the tree, repeating the following vow : "If my wife gives me a child, I will kill a hen or a sheep to honour you, and will render you sacred." After that he returns once a day or oftener to renew his prayer to the tree. If by chance his

---

[1] L. Tauxier, *op. cit.* p. 161.

[2] P. A. Talbot, "The Buduma of Lake Chad" (a typewritten paper sent me by the author, who collected the information)

[3] D. A. Talbot, *Woman's Mysteries of a Primitive People*, p. 81.

[4] P. A. Talbot, *Life in Southern Nigeria*, pp. 303 *sq.*

wife makes him a father during the year, he will sacrifice a hen or a sheep to the spirit of the tree, and he will declare publicly that the tree is sacred. Everyone will then come to ask something of the sacred tree which has given proof of its fertilizing power.[1]

[1] M. C. Le Barbier, " Contribution à l'Étude des Bara-Imamono de Madagascar," in *L'Anthropologie*, vol. 31 (Paris, 1921), pp. 321 *sq*.

CHAPTER VII

RELICS OF TREE-WORSHIP IN EUROPE

MANY relics of the worship of trees have survived in the popular customs of Europe, as these are observed particularly on May Day and Whitsuntide. These I have dealt with elsewhere.[1] Here I may supplement what I have there said on English May Day customs by some notices which I have not hitherto used of similar May Day customs, now, or formerly, observed on May Day in Wales.

" The old customs and superstitions in connection with May Day are unknown in Wales at the present day. Once, however, May Day dances and revelling were most popular, especially in Pembrokeshire, as the following interesting account, which appeared in the *Cambrian Journal*, proves. ' On May-eve, the inhabitants would turn out in troops, bearing in their hand boughs of thorn in full blossom, which were bedecked with other flowers, and then stuck outside the windows of the houses. Maypoles were reared up in different parts of the town (of Tenby), decorated with flowers, coloured papers, and bunches of variegated ribbon. On May Day the young men and women would, joining hand in hand, dance round the Maypole and *thread the needle*, as it was termed. A group of fifty to a hundred persons would wend their way from one pole to another, till they had thus traversed the town. Meeting on their way other groups who were coming from an opposite direction, both parties would form a *ladies' chain*, and so pass on their respective ways.' The Maypole was once most popular in Wales, but the old custom has entirely died out, though we still hear occasionally

[1] *The Golden Bough: The Magic Art and the Evolution of Kings*, ii. 59-96.

of a May Queen being selected in some places. The May-pole in Wales was called Bedwen, because it is always made of birch which is called in Welsh Bedwen, a tree associated with the gentler emotions ; and, to give a lover a birchen branch is for a maiden to accept his addresses. Games of various sorts were played around the bedwen. The fame of a village depended on its not being stolen away, and parties were con-stantly on the alert to steal the bedwen, a feat which, when accomplished, was celebrated with peculiar festivities. This rivalry for the possession of the Maypole was probably typical of the ancient idea that the first of May was the boundary day dividing the confines of winter and summer, when a fight took place between the powers of the air, on the one hand striving to continue the reign of winter, on the other to establish that of summer."[1]

Again we read, " On the morning of May Day—that is, at the first glimmer of dawn—the youths and maidens in nearly every parish in Wales set out to the nearest woodlands. The gay procession consisted of men with horns and other instruments, which were played, while vocalists sang the songs of May-time. When the merry party reached the woodlands each member broke a bough off a tree and decorated the branch with flowers unless they were already laden with May blossoms. A tall birch-tree was cut down, and borne on a farm-wagon drawn by oxen into the village. At sunrise the young people placed the branches of May beside the doors or in the windows of their houses. This was followed by the ceremony of setting up the Maypole on the village green. The pole was decorated with nosegays and garlands of flowers, interspersed with bright-coloured ribbon bows, rosettes, and streamers. Then the master of the ceremonies, or the leader of the May dancers, would advance to the pole, and tie a gay-coloured ribbon round it. He was followed by all the dancers, each one approaching the pole and tying a ribbon around it until a certain number had been tied. The dance then began, each dancer taking his or her place according to the order in which the ribbons had been arranged around the pole. The dance was continued without intermission

[1] J. C. Davies, *Folklore of West and Mid-Wales* (Aberystwyth, 1911), p. 76.

until the party was tired, and then other dancers took their place." [1]

In Tuscany and Romagna " once the young lovers were accustomed to plant, the first night of May, a branch before the door of their sweethearts with gifts hung up : at present they bring it about singing." [2]

A somewhat fuller description of the Hobby Horse on May Day at Padstow runs as follows : " The *Hobby Hoss*, a formidable-looking creature with tall cap, flowing plume and tail, savage looking snappers, and ferocious mask, sallied forth, accompanied by the Pairs, carrying each a musical instrument, of which the drum is the most prominent.   Before the *Hobby Hoss* danced a man in a terrible dwarf mask, carrying a club.   This dancer led the way everywhere, followed throughout the day by the *Hobby Hoss*, and a vast crowd of men and women gaily decorated with flowers and singing the May songs, while the men fired in all directions pistols loaded with powder." [3]

---

[1] M. Trevelyan, *Folk-lore and Folk Stories of Wales* (London, 1909), p. 24.

[2] Extract from a letter written to me by Mr. Ludovico Limentani and dated Ferrara, Via Columbara 36, 20th Sept. 1912.

[3] *The Padstow Hobby Hoss*, a pamphlet published by Williams and Son, Padstow, 1903.   Cf. *The Magic Art and the Evolution of Kings*, pp. 67 *sq.*

CHAPTER VIII

THE INFLUENCE OF THE SEXES ON VEGETATION

ELSEWHERE I have shown that in the opinions of many peoples the intercourse of the human sexes has a potent influence in stimulating the growth of vegetation, particularly of the food-bearing plants or trees on which man is in large measure dependent for his subsistence. Where such beliefs prevail the intercourse of the sexes is often regulated at the seasons of sowing and planting by rules which have for their object to promote the growth of the crops.[1] Thus, for example, among the Banyankole of Uganda, " during the time of the sowing, husband and wife had to be careful to have sexual relations only with each other, lest the seeds should fail to germinate and the weeds grow."[2] Again, among the Fan or Pangwe of West Africa, the night before a man sows earth-nuts he has intercourse with his wife for the purpose of promoting the growth of the earth-nuts, which he will plant next morning.[3]

The belief in the fertilizing influence of the human sexes on vegetation is brought out in the most unmistakable manner in the rites observed by the Kiwai of British New Guinea in the planting of the yam, sweet-potato, sugar-cane, banana, and so forth. Details of the rites will be found in the work of Professor Landtman on the Kiwai. Here I will only mention that for the purpose of fertilizing the sago-palm these people resort to promiscuous sexual intercourse, in order to obtain the life-giving fluid which is to be directly

---

[1] *The Magic Art and the Evolution of Kings*, ii. 97 *sqq.*
[2] J. Roscoe, *The Banyankole*, p. 97.
[3] G. Tessmann, *Die Pangwe*, pp. 90 *sq.*

M

applied to the trunks of the sago-palms.[1]

A power of fertilizing the food-plants has sometimes been ascribed to twins or to the parents of twins, who have given a living proof of their fecundity in the birth of the twins.[2] Thus among the Basoga of the Central district on the northern shore of Lake Victoria Nyanza, " when a woman has twins, the people to whose clan she belongs do not sow any seed until the twins have been brought to the field. A pot of cooked grain is set before the children with a cake of sesame and all the seed that is to be sown. The food is eaten by the people assembled and afterwards the seed is sown in the presence of the twins ; the plot is then said to be the field of the twins. The mother of the twins must sow her seed before any of the clan will sow theirs." [3] Some African peoples suppose that the parents of twins possess the further power of multiplying animal life. Thus with reference to the tribes inhabiting the great plateau of Northern Rhodesia, we are told that " pigeon cotes are erected in the majority of villages. The first stakes of such cotes are driven in by a woman who has borne twins, in order, they say, that the pigeons may multiply." [4] On this subject another writer, speaking of the Bantu tribes of Central Africa, observes " in laying the foundations of pigeon houses, chicken houses, or goat pens, or anything for breeding purposes, a similar favourable concession is made to either a father or a mother of twin children. It is supposed to have a beneficial or prolific effect. There is a native woman I know who has had twins three times, and she is in great demand for laying the foundations of pigeon and chicken houses, goat and sheep pens, and even a cattle kraal." [5]

The belief in the influence which the human sexes exercise on the growth of plants is further proved by the rule of continence which some people impose on persons at sowing or planting the food-crops. Thus among the Berbers of

[1] G. Landtman, *The Kiwai Papuans of British New Guinea*, pp. 70, 76, 78, 79 *sq.*, 81 *sq.*, 84, 90, 101, 357 *sq.*, 355 *sq.*

[2] *The Magic Art and the Evolution of Kings*, ii. 102 *sq.*

[3] J. Roscoe, *The Northern Bantu*, p. 235.

[4] C. Gouldsbury and H. Sheane, *The Great Plateau of Northern Rhodesia* (London, 1911), p. 307.

[5] D. Campbell, *The Heart of Bantuland*, p. 155.

Morocco, " sexual cleanness is required with those who have anything to do with the corn ; for such persons are otherwise supposed to pollute its holiness, and also, in many cases, to do injury to themselves.   In most parts of Morocco it is considered necessary for the ploughman to be sexually clean ; otherwise there will be no *baraka* (holiness) in the seed, or there will grow mostly grass and weeds on the field.   So also the reapers and anybody who comes to the threshing-floor when the corn is there must be clean ; and the same is the case with the women who clear the crops of weeds in the spring, lest their work should be without result and they should become ill themselves.   If an unclean person goes into a granary, it is believed that not only will the grain lose its *baraka*, but that he himself will fall ill. . . .   Nor must an unclean individual enter the vegetable garden, for such a visit would do harm both to the garden and to the person who went there."[1]   Again, among the Bakongo of the Lower Congo, " women must remain chaste while planting pumpkin and calabash seeds, and they must wash their hands before touching the seeds.   Neither may they eat pig-meat during the planting of these particular seeds.   If a woman does not observe these taboos, she must not plant the seeds, or the crop will be a failure ; she may make the holes, and her baby girl, or another who has obeyed the restrictions, can drop in the seed and cover them over."[2]   Again, among the Fan or Pangwe of West Africa, the women who have planted the yams are bound to remain chaste for three months after the planting, for if they were to break this rule it is believed the yams would fail to grow, or would be devastated by grubs.[3]

Among the Oraons of Chota Nagpur in India the night before a husbandman goes to sow the first seeds of the rice, he remains sexually continent and does not lie on the same bed with his wife.[4]   The Bare'e-speaking Toradyas of Central Celebes remain chaste during the harvest, for they believe that otherwise the rice would diminish in quantity.[5]

Again, many peoples believe that sexual offences, and

[1] E. Westermarck, *The Moorish Conception of Holiness* (Baraka), p. 125.
[2] J. H. Weeks, *Among the Primitive Bakongo*, p. 252.
[3] G. Tessman, *Die Pangwe*, p. 98.
[4] S. C. Roy, *The Oraons*, p. 142.
[5] N. Adriani and A. C. Kruijt, *op. cit.* ii. 274.

particularly incest, have the effect of blighting the crop. Hence among the Bare'e-speaking Toradyas of Central Celebes, before planting rice, generally before clearing the ground, there is a ceremony called "the driving away of sins." The sin here contemplated is incest, which is supposed to spoil the rice, either through severe drought or heavy rain. The more venial incest (between uncle and niece or aunt and nephew), is expiated by a sacrifice called "covering the sky," because it hides the sin on earth from the dwellers in heaven. Incest may escape detection. Even the report of incest committed is enough to draw down the calamitous consequences on the land. Hence, to make sure, the Toradyas offer this atoning sacrifice every year. It is sometimes called "asking for rain." Almost all the inhabitants of the village repair to the bank of a river. A great stone is then placed on the way leading to the river, to close it. A sacrificial table is set up and a pig tied to the foot of it. The leader, with one foot on the pig, spits betel in the air, and invokes the gods. He prays : "O gods above and gods below, perhaps we have sinned with mouth or hands or feet ; perhaps our ears have heard the sin of men of another village. We have put away our sinful ears and mouths. Here are a pig, a buffalo, and a goat. In return we ask you to give us rain. If you give no rain, what shall we eat this year ? Saroe and Sarengge (two spirits whose bodily hair is in the form of rice stalks), we give you this that you may give us rain." Then the pig is killed, and its blood is dabbed on the cheeks and foreheads of the people. Also the sacrificial victims are killed and cooked, and their livers offered. Meantime a small ship has been laden with rice, coins, betel, tobacco, cloth, and so forth, to which every person present must contribute. Then the people are beaten with prickly plants to drive out all guilt. Finally the little ship is allowed to drift down the stream. Afterwards the people splash water on each other as a rain-charm. The stone is then removed from the path, with the words, "Lightness in the stone, heaviness in the rice."[1]

---

[1] N. Adriani and A. C. Kruijt, *op. cit.* ii. 247 *sq.*

CHAPTER IX

THE SACRED MARRIAGE

The mimic marriage of the king and queen of May in Europe was probably in origin a magical rite intended to promote the growth of plant-life in spring by representing dramatically the bridal of a young man and a young woman who personated the male and female powers of vegetation. A similar ceremony is still observed in spring by some of the Berbers of Morocco, and it has been interpreted in a similar sense by the French writer who reports it. The ceremony takes place at the little village of Douzrou in the Anti-Atlas Mountains, and the time of it is the return of spring. In the morning, at daybreak, the young girls of the village go out into the forest to pluck grass and gather dead wood. Their return is signalled by the shot of a musket. Immediately the women remaining in the village advance to meet them, escorting a young girl called the Bride of the Good (*Fiancée du Bien*). The bride, apparelled as for a wedding, dressed entirely in white, is mounted upon a white she-ass, and holds in her hands a white hen. When the two processions meet the young girls put down their bundles of grass, and begin to dance, singing some such words as these :

We shall accompany the bride of the good to the mosque of the village,
That God may bring, for the Musulmans, health and abundance.

For their part, the boys go into the gardens to gather wood, which they take to the mosque. Then, like their sisters, they go into the forest to gather dry grass. They have chosen from among them a young man who is the Bridegroom of the Good (*Fiancé du Bien*). Dressed in white like the bride, he is also mounted upon a white male ass, and holds in his hands a cock of white plumage. He goes at the head of the small procession which makes its way into the fields ; but when they have got half-way his companions leave him, committing him to the care of one of their number who stays by him, armed with a musket to protect him against the evil spirits, or jinn. Then the boys, bringing armfuls of grass, return and take their places round the bridegroom. Then one of them hobbles the feet of the ass, and with the same rope ties the neck of the bridegroom, who is stooping over the shoulders of his mount. At this moment the guardian fires a shot with his musket. This signal, heard in the village, excites there a lively agitation. The men, seizing their arms, rush towards the bride, seated upon her ass in the centre of the group of women, and lead her, in wild career, towards the hobbled bridegroom. They call out, " Hold on. Do not fall, that the new year may be favourable to us. Do not fall." The procession stops near the bridegroom. Then, without losing a moment, the young girl cuts with a knife the rope that binds the bridegroom, after which she calls out : " We have cut the neck of Hunger : May God resuscitate the neck of the Good." Accompanied by the young man who guards the bridegroom, the bride then returns alone to the village, and when she has taken her place among the women, her guardian discharges his musket. This is another signal, for at once the men and boys lead, with the same precipitation, the now delivered bridegroom. They shout to him from all sides, " Hold on. Do not fall, that the new year may be favourable to us." Songs, dances, cries, and musket-shots announce the happy return of the bridegroom. That ends the first part of the ceremony. Doubtless the bridegroom, freed from his bonds and returning triumphant, personifies the renewal of Nature, and the bride the spirit of vegetation. Their union is expected to influence the renewal of the life of spring and render it fertile. The bride and bridegroom side by side now march at the head of the procession, in which the boys follow behind the bridegroom and the girls behind the bride, all singing, but without mingling with each other. The happy crowd repeats incessantly, " We are bringing back the Good."

In this curious and picturesque array the emblematic couple are conducted to the mosque. Bride and bridegroom alone enter the sanctuary, in accordance with prescribed custom. The two doors close upon them. Upon the threshold of one the crowd remains, keeping silence : on the other a severe guardian, his musket loaded, mounts guard, and keeps at a distance the curious and indiscreet who might wish to pierce the mystery that is taking place in the temple, become, for an hour, the scene of sacred prostitution. What takes place there is little known ; but it is said that the bride and bridegroom go to the place called " The Tomb of the Archangel Gabriel," and that there the bridegroom cuts the throat of the white cock which he has not abandoned in the course of the preceding ceremonies, and then does the same to the white hen of his bride. After having cooked and eaten the flesh of the two victims, he claims the rights which his bride does not contest, for on the consummation of their transitory union depends the prosperity of the clan. When night falls the bride and bridegroom separate to follow different paths.   Then follows the third and last act of the ceremony, a tragic act, in the course of which the bride is to die.   The bride and bridegroom separate and each go towards a door of the sanctuary. " Fire ! " cries the bridegroom to his guardian. At this signal the men rush towards the bridegroom's door, and kindle large heaps of dry grass which are placed there. And when the bridegroom comes forth he is confronted by high flames which he leaps over at a single bound, while the bride, languid and exhausted, lets herself fall into the small fire that her sisters have kindled for her at her door. It is further said that the young people of the village imitate the example set by the bride and bridegroom of the good, to facilitate, in the same manner, the return of the life of the spring. They meet in couples in a public place, and pass together, the girls and boys, that which they call " the night of happiness." [1]

This Berber ceremony furnishes an example of what we may call a sacred marriage, that is, a marriage of two divinities, one or both of whom are represented by living human beings. Antiquity furnishes examples of such sacred mar-

[1] E. Laoust, *Mots et choses berbères*, p. 191.

riages in which living women were wedded to the gods,[1] and in India similar ceremonies are still performed. Thus, among the Ra Deo of Malana, a village in the Punjab, " there is a peculiar custom in connection with the worship of Jamlu, namely, the dedication to him of a handmaiden (called Sita), taken from a family of the Nar caste resident at Manikaran. The handmaiden is presented as a wife to the god at a festival (*kaika*), which occurs at irregular intervals of several years, on the first of Bhadron. On dedication to the god the girl, who is four or five years old, receives a gift of a complete set of valuable ornaments from the shrine. She remains in her parents' house, getting clothes and ornaments at intervals. If she goes to Malana she is fed. She does nothing in the way of worship of Jamlu. When she is 15 or 16 years old a new handmaiden is appointed in her place. She is supposed to be really a virgin while she is Jamlu's wife." [2] Again, " in old days in the Panjab a Dhimar or water-carrier girl used to be married to Bhairon, an old Earth godling, at his shrine in Baodada in Rewari, but it is said that she always died soon after. The Bharbhunjar or grain-parchers in the Gurgaon District of the same Province worship Bhairon, to whom the Mallah boatmen of Agra used to marry their daughters. It is said that the godling once saved a sinking boat, and ever after the family which owned it used to marry one of their girls to him, leaving her at his shrine where she survived for less than a year ; but now only a doll made of dough is formally wedded. In the Central Provinces a Jain bride was, it is said, locked up in a temple and was considered to be the bride of the Tirthankara or saint to whom the temple was dedicated, but now she is locked up there only for a minute or two, and is then released." [3]

In the second half of the seventeenth century a case of a sacred marriage was reported by the French traveller Bernier at Juggernaut, a town of Bengal. He says, " The brahmins select a beautiful maiden for the bride of Juggernaut, who accompanies the god to the temple with all the pomp and

---

[1] See *The Magic Art and the Evolution of Kings*, ii. 129 *sqq.*

[2] H. A. Rose, *A Glossary of the Tribes and Castes of the Punjab and North-West Frontier Province* (La-hore, 1913), iii. 265.

[3] W. Crooke (and R. E. Enthoven), *Religion and Folklore of Northern India* (Oxford, 1926), p. 246.

ceremony which I have noticed, where she remains the whole
night, having been made to believe that Juggernaut will come
and lie with her. She is commanded to enquire of the god if
the year will be fruitful, and what will be the processions, the
festivals, the prayers, and the alms which he requires in return
for his bounty. In the night one of the brahmins enters the
temple through a small back door, enjoys the unsuspecting
damsel, makes her believe whatever may be deemed necessary, and the following morning when on her way to another
temple, whither she is carried with the usual forms and
magnificence, she is desired by the brahmins to state aloud to
the people all she has heard from the lustful priest, as if every
word had proceeded from the mouth of Juggernaut." [1] This
form of the sacred marriage was still continued at the town
of Juggernaut down at least to about the beginning of the
nineteenth century.[2]

The Oraons of Chota Nagpur in Bengal worship the Sun
as a God and the Earth as a Goddess, his wife. They celebrate
the marriage of the two deities every year at the time when
the *sal* tree is in blossom. In the marriage ceremony the
Sun-God is represented by the priest and the Earth-Goddess
by his wife. I have described the ceremony elsewhere.[3] It
has since been described in much greater detail by the eminent
Indian ethnographer, Sarat Chandra Roy ; [4] but his description is too long for quotation.

In Africa the gods of the Baganda had human mediums
who acted purely as the mouthpieces of the deities. "When
a woman was chosen to be a medium, she was separated from
men, and had to observe the laws of chastity for the rest of her
life ; she was looked upon as the wife of the god."[5] Nende,
one of the war-gods of the Baganda, had six human wives
who were princesses, and these never left the sacred enclosure
when once they had been dedicated to the deity. They had
seats in the temple, on either side of the dais on which the god

---

[1] F. Bernier, *Travels in the Mogul
Empire*, trans. T. Brock, (London,
1826), ii. 7.

[2] J. Forbes, *Oriental Memoirs*
(London, 1813), who after quoting
Bernier's account adds, " it is well
known that this infamous practice still
continues."

[3] *The Magic Art and the Evolution
of Kings*, ii. 148.

[4] S. C. Roy, *Oraon Religion and
Custom* (Ranchi, 1928), pp. 193
sqq.

[5] J. Roscoe, *The Baganda*, p. 275.

was supposed to sit.[1]   At Ngeri-gbaw-ama, amongst the
Ijaw of Southern Nigeria, there is worshipped a water-spirit
who is represented by a great python.   To his shrine women
who aspire to be diviners or prophetesses resort.   These
women used to hold a great position in the tribe, and nothing
of importance was done without their inspired counsel.   They
are hedged round with many taboos and in ancient times were
allowed no human husband, since they were regarded as
wedded to one of the sacred serpents.   The water-spirit is
supposed to rise out of the river every eighth day ; on that
day, therefore, she keeps herself untouched, sleeps alone, does
not leave the house after dark, and pours libations before the
symbols of the water-spirit.[2]

The Tumbuka of the Nyasa region in East Africa worshipped a god Chinkang'onme whose body is said to resemble
that of a great snake, with a mane like that of a lion.   Now
and then a girl was dedicated to the god to be his wife.   After
this dedication she lived apart, and was greatly honoured.
She dressed her hair with beads to resemble the mane of the
god, and remained throughout her life unmarried.   In her
the deity was believed to be incarnate.[3]

Elsewhere I have suggested that stories like that of Andro-
meda, in which the heroine is exposed to a sea-monster, may
reflect an ancient custom of sacrificing virgins to water-
spirits to be their wives.[4]

Here I may cite a few African instances of human victims,
especially girls or virgins sacrificed to water-spirits.   Almost
all over the Western or French Sudan towards the beginning
of May, after the first day of heavy rain, a procession took
place which was destined to call down from heaven a benedic-
tion on the fields.   At Bamaka this procession ended with a
sacrifice offered on the banks of the Niger to the spirit of the
river, a sacrifice which, before the French occupation, consisted in throwing into the river a virgin who was devoured by
the crocodile representing the spirit of the water.[5]

Again, at Mahilane on the seashore, in the territory of the

---

[1] J. Roscoe, *op. cit.* p. 308.

[2] P. A. Talbot, *The Peoples of
Southern Nigeria*, ii. 100 *sq.*

[3] D. Fraser, *Winning a Primitive
People*, p. 122.

[4] *The Magic Art and the Evolution
of Kings*, ii. 155 *sq.*

[5] M. Delafosse, *Haut-Sénégal-Niger
(Soudan Français)* (Paris, 1912),
pp. 111, 175.

Ronga or Thonga tribe, " there are two great rocks on the
beach.   When the great waves dash against them with a
fearful roar, people go and sacrifice : they pray thus : ' Oh
sea, let vessels be wrecked, and steamers also, and let their
riches come to us and help us.'   In former times a young girl
was sometimes exposed there as a prey, or an offering to the
power of Mahilane." [1]   The Bangala of the Upper Congo
think that the river is haunted by certain malevolent water-
spirits who do their best to hinder all fishing operations.
Hence it was no uncommon thing, when a village was unsuccessful in its fishing, for the inhabitants to join their brass
rods together to buy an old man or old woman—old by preference, because cheap—and throw him or her into the water
to appease these water-spirits.[2]   Among the Baganda of
Central Africa " certain wells have been famous for many
generations ; they are thought to have been protected by the
special intervention of water-spirits ; they were passed down
from family to family, or from chief to chief, and were venerated and kept sacred.   In some places a new chief, on his
appointment to the charge of the district, offered a human
sacrifice ; oftentimes he had to take for this purpose his own
child, whom he offered to the water-spirit at the well, as a
means of securing prosperity.   In other places an animal was
offered, and the people assembled to eat a sacred meal and to
drink beer by the well ; after the meal the chief placed a new
hoe in a shrine which had been built for the water-spirit by
the well." [3]

Again, the ancient Chinese used to worship the god of the
Hoang-ho or Yellow River, whom they called by a name
which we may translate by the Count of the River.   He is
described as a tall being with the face of a man and the body
of a fish ; sometimes he is said to ride in a chariot drawn by
two dragons.   The great seat of his worship was at the
confluence of the Yellow River and the River Lo, the very
heart of ancient China.   There the water-god was honoured
with splendid dramatic ceremonies, in which human beings

[1] H. A. Junod, *The Life of a South
African Tribe*, ii. 825.
   [2] J. H. Weeks, in *Journal of the
Royal Anthropological Institute*, xl.

(1910) p. 370.   Cf. *id.*, *Among Congo
Cannibals*, pp. 98 *sq.*

   [3] J. Roscoe, *The Baganda*, p. 458.

were drowned. White horses were also sacrificed to him by being plunged in his stream.[1] Tradition runs that formerly it was the custom to provide the Yellow River every year with a bride. The marriage was celebrated at Ye on the river. There a college of witches was entrusted with the duty of annually choosing a beautiful girl to be the bride of the water-god. The chosen maiden was bathed, dressed in red garments, and shut up in a red tent, where she was fed on beef and wine, but in other respects had to observe rigid abstinence. After ten days' seclusion in the tent she was dressed as a bride and placed on a nuptial couch which was set floating on the river ; and down the stream it drifted until it sank with the maiden into the depths. Thus the mortal bride was committed to the arms of her immortal bridegroom. All the nobles and the people in their thousands witnessed these nuptials of the river-god. In the year 417 B.C. the Emperor Tsin, the founder of a new dynasty, began the practice of thus marrying royal princesses to the god of the river ; as an upstart he desired to strengthen his claim to the imperial throne by making the river-god his kinsman by marriage. But not long afterwards the barbarous custom was abolished by the Marquis Wen de Wei (428–387 B.C.), a disciple of Confucius.[2]

Water-spirits are often thought to bestow offspring on childless women. To the examples of this belief which I have given elsewhere[3] may now be added the following : at Gujarat in India " waterfalls are not very familiar to the people. There is a belief, however, that barren couples obtain issue if they bathe in a waterfall, and offer a coconut."[4] In the Bombay Presidency, " About a month and a quarter after the delivery of a woman, a ceremony called *Zarmazaryan*, is performed, when the woman goes to a neighbouring stream or well to fetch water for the first time after her delivery. Near the stream or well five small heaps of sand are made and

[1] M. Granet, *Danses et légendes de l'ancienne Chine* (Paris, 1926), ii. 466-482.

[2] M. Granet, *op. cit.* ii. 473-478. For other sacrifices to water-spirits, see my commentary on Ovid, Book v. line 621, vol. iv. pp. 99-109, and *Folk-* *Lore in the Old Testament*, ii. 414 *sqq.*

[3] *The Magic Art and the Evolution of Kings*, ii. 159 *sqq.*

[4] A. M. T. Jackson, *Folklore of Gujarat*, p. 40 (appended to the *Indian Antiquary*, xli. 1912).

daubed with red lead.   Next, a lamp fed with *ghi* is lighted,
and seven small betel-nuts are offered to the stream or well.
A coconut is then broken, and a part of it thrown into the
water as an offering.   Next, the woman fills a jar with the
water of the stream or well and returns home, taking with her
six out of the seven betel-nuts offered to the stream or well.
On her way home she is approached by barren women, who
request to be favoured with one of the betel-nuts, as it is
believed that swallowing such a betel-nut causes conception.
Some believe that only the smallest of the seven betel-nuts
has the power of producing this result.   Others hold that
this betel-nut must be swallowed on the threshold of a
house." [1]   Again, in the country of the Ait Sadden, a
Berber tribe of Morocco, there is a river called Igi with a
waterfall, named Amazzer.   Barren women resort to the
waterfall to obtain offspring.   They hope to obtain the wish
of their hearts by pouring the water from the waterfall
down their backs.   When Professor Westermarck asked his
informant whether there was a saint at the waterfall, the man
smilingly answered that he did not know. [2]

[1] R. E. Enthoven, *Folklore of Bombay*, p. 288.
[2] E. Westermarck, *The Moorish Conception of Holiness (Baraka)*, pp. 54 *sq.*

CHAPTER X

THE KING'S FIRE

ELSEWHERE I have argued that in ancient Rome the Vestal Virgins were of old the King's daughters, charged with the duty of maintaining the fire on the royal hearth, and supposed to be the wives of the fire-god.[1] With these Roman Vestals we may compare the African Vestals, who in Uganda are charged with the duty of maintaining the perpetual fire in the temples of the gods. Of these latter Canon Roscoe has given us the following account : " In most of the temples there were a number of young girls dedicated to the god. Their special duties were to keep guard over the fire in the temple, which had to be kept burning by day and by night ; to see that nothing which was taboo was brought into the temple ; to provide an ample supply of firewood and water ; to keep the grass floor-covering replenished ; and especially to guard the sacred pipe and tobacco which were used by the medium before giving the oracle. The persons of these girls were sacred, and men had to be careful not to be unduly familiar with them, nor to attempt to take any liberties with them. These girls were brought to the temple when they were weaned ; they were offerings of parents who had prayed to the god for children, promising to devote them to his service if he granted their request. When such a girl was born, she was dedicated to the god ; and as soon as she was old enough to be separated from her mother she was brought into the temple enclosure to live. She remained in office until she reached the age of puberty, when the god decided whom she was to marry. She was then removed from the temple, because no woman might

[1] *The Golden Bough : The Magic Art and the Evolution of Kings*, ii. 195.

enter a temple or have anything to do for the gods during her periods of menstruation ; consequently the office of temple virgin was restricted to girls of immature years."[1]

Moreover, in Uganda the King and the chiefs had their consecrated virgins bound to chastity and charged with the duty of tending the fire on the royal or chiefly hearth.   Canon Roscoe's account of these domestic Vestals, as we may call them, runs thus : " The King and each important chief had a girl in personal attendance wherever there were restrictions and taboos to be observed.   This girl was called *kaja buwonga* ; she lived in her master's house, and was ready for any service.   Her birth had been predicted by a priest ; she was dedicated to some god from her birth ; and when old enough to perform the office called *kaja*, she was given to a chief to perform the duties of this office.   These duties were, to tend the fire in the evening, and by night, to bring the chief water with which to wash his face in the early morning, to bring him the butter or medicine with which he smeared his body, and to hand him the fetiches which he required, after obtaining them from his principal wife who had the charge of them.   When he went on a war expedition, she accompanied him for a short distance, carrying in front of him his fetiches which were to protect him from danger ; these she afterwards restored to the principal wife.   No boy was ever permitted to play with her, or even to touch her, for she was a consecrated person.   When she attained puberty the god to whom she was dedicated ordered her marriage, and another *kaja* girl from the clan was sent to take her place.   The king and the chiefs often took these girls to wife.   The clan from which she came profited by receiving presents and other favours from the King or the chiefs, as the case might be."[2] Among the Barundi, a tribe living to the west of Lake Victoria Nyanza, there is a class of virgins whom our authority calls " Vestals."   In the tribe there is a sacred drum which is worshipped with almost divine honours.   The Sultan or King brings offerings to it, and the charge of the drum is committed to three girls.   One of their duties is to see that the regular offerings are duly brought to the drum. Such a girl is known as " the wife of the sacred drum."

[1] J. Roscoe, *The Baganda*, p. 276.   [2] J. Roscoe, *op. cit.* p 9.

She is bound to observe strict chastity, and if she fails to do so, like a Vestal Virgin at Rome, she is put to death.[1] The Bergdama of South-west Africa attach great importance to their domestic fire. We are told that a man of the tribe would rather be without his hut than without his fire. The chief's fire is tended by his first wife. If it should go out it is rekindled, like the Vestal fire at Rome, by the primitive apparatus of the fire-drill.[2]

[1] H. Meyer, *Die Barundi*, p. 188.
[2] H. Vedder, *Die Bergdama* (Hamburg, 1923), pp. 20-38.

CHAPTER XI

THE FIRE-DRILL

As we have just seen, whenever the perpetual vestal fire at Rome happened to go out it was solemnly rekindled by the primitive apparatus known as the fire-drill, that is, by a pointed stick made to revolve so as to make a hole in a flat board and elicit a flame by the friction of the wood. This is perhaps the oldest of all modes of kindling fire known to man, and it seems to be the most widely diffused among savages before they came into contact with civilization. Elsewhere I have given references to some of the tribes who are known to practise or formerly to have practised this method of obtaining fire.[1] I will now subjoin a list of some other peoples who are known to practise or to have formerly practised this primitive mode of securing fire.[2] But it may be well to illus-

[1] *The Golden Bough : The Magic Art and the Evolution of Kings*, ii. 206 *sq.*

[2] G. St. J. Orde Browne, *The Vanishing Tribes of Kenya* (London, 1925), pp. 120 *sq.*; F. Fülleborn, *Das Deutsche Nyassa- und Ruwumba-Gebiet* (Berlin, 1906), p. 91 ; E. Kotz, *Im Banne der Furcht* (Hamburg), p. 137 ; C. K. Meek, *The Northern Tribes of Nigeria* (London, 1925), i. 172 ; S. S. Dornan, *Pygmies and Bushmen of the Kalahari* (London, 1923), pp. 116 *sq.*; *id.*, " The Tati Bushmen and their Language," in *Journal of the Royal Anthropological Institute*, xlvii. (1917) p. 46; D. Livingstone, *Last Journals*, i. 58 ; R. Schmitz, *Les Baholoholo* (Brussels, 1912), p. 51 ; J. Vanden Plas, *Les Kuku* (Brussels, 1910), p. 69 ; H. Rehse, *Kiziba Land und Leute* (Stuttgart, 1910), pp. 19 *sq.*; R. Neuhauss, *Deutsch Neu-Guinea*, iii. 24 ; A. F. R. Wollaston, *Pygmies and Papuans* (London, 1912), pp. 200 *sq.*; A. R. Wallace, *The Malay Archipelago*, ii. 34 ; H. Riedel, *De Sluik-en Kroesharige Rassen tusschen Selebes en Papua* (The Hague, 1886), p. 187 ; W. Marsden, *The History of Sumatra* (London, 1811), p. 60; A. L. Van Hasselt, *Volksbeschrijving van Midden-Sumatra* (Leyden, 1882), pp. 177 *sq.*; S. J. Hickson, *A Naturalist in North Celebes*, p. 172 ; P. J. Veth, *Java* (Harlem, 1875-1884), i. 564 ; E. Modigliani, *Un Viaggio a Nias* (Milan, 1890), p. 385 ; D. Bray, *Ethnographic Survey of Baluchistan*,

trate the practice by a few particular examples. Thus with regard to the primitive Embu tribes who inhabit the vast southern slopes of Mount Kenya in East Africa, their method of kindling fire has been described as follows by Major Orde Browne, who administered the tribes and knows them well. " All the Embu tribes are clever at producing fire by friction, though the art is naturally rapidly disappearing with the introduction of matches. The principle utilized is the friction set up between a drill of soft fibrous wood, working in a socket of hard dense wood. A stick some twelve or eighteen inches in length, and about the thickness of a pencil, is cut from some light fibrous wood and dried. Another piece of wood is cut, of some hard dense material, and shaped to about the size and thickness of the back of a small clothes brush ; the edges are rounded off and several ' nicks ' are cut in them. This piece of wood is held firmly on the ground under one toe, and the operator squats with the drill between his two hands, the point resting in one of the ' nicks.' It is rotated rapidly, the hands quickly rising to the top again as they reach the bottom of the stick. Friction soon rounds the nick until it becomes a small socket with a gap at one side from which the powder produced runs out in a pile on the ground ; continued friction increases the heat, until a glowing point is observed on the little pile of dust. This is half covered with a wisp of dry grass kept ready for the purpose, when a few puffs are enough to ignite the grass. The time taken is surprisingly short, when the two sticks are ready and thoroughly dry ; after a little practice I was myself able to produce a light within a minute, under favourable conditions. The secret lies in putting a few grains of sand in the socket before starting, to increase friction ; without this aid, blistered hands would probably be the only result."[1]

Again, with regard to the tribes of Northern Nigeria, we are told that " two methods of obtaining fire are used by all the tribes : (*a*) the percussion, and (*b*) the drill method. . . .

i. 33 ; L. Hearn, *Glimpses of Unfamiliar Japan*, i. 198 *sq.* ; W. B. Grubb, *An Unknown People in an Unknown Land* (London, 1911), p. 74 ; F. Boas, *The Quakiutl* (Jesup North Pacific Expedition, vol. v. Part ii.), p. 407. As to the fire-drill, see further my *Myths on the Origin of Fire* (London, 1930), pp. 217 *sq.*

[1] G. St. J. Orde Browne, *op. cit.* pp. 120 *sq.*

The drill method is a dry-season one, and is only resorted to in the absence of steel and flint. A stalk of guinea-corn, bul-rush-millet, or *Hibiscus* is split into two. One half is taken, and a groove is made in it by twirling into it a smaller stalk. Underneath the groove some dried cow's or horse's dung, or old dried rags, are placed. The rotatory movement is con-tinued until the stalk is pierced, when the heat generated ignites the dried dung or rags. Among some tribes, (*e.g.* the Mbarawa), where the percussion method is commonly followed, the more ancient drill method is ceremonially carried out each year by the religious chief. All fires are extinguished in the town, and the religious chief, with the elders, goes through the process of twisting one stick into another. The resultant fire is believed—by the women, at any rate—to have been obtained by magic means, and is for-mally distributed throughout the village." [1] The practice of these Nigerian tribes, who in daily life have discarded the ancient method of kindling fire by the fire-drill, but retain it at the solemn annual ceremony of kindling the new fire for the whole village, is an interesting example of that con-servatism in ritual which is characteristic of many religions. Practice is always more stable than theory ; men shed their opinions more easily than their habits.

Once more, with regard to the very primitive Bushman of the Kalahari Desert in South-West Africa, their mode of kindling fire is described as follows : " As soon as a Bush-man has killed a buck, he lights a fire, cooks a portion of it, and devours it. The method of making fire is as follows : a short length of hardwood, about twelve inches, of acacia or mopani, is chosen. This is as thick as a lead pencil, and is the drill. It must be quite dry. Another piece of about the same length, but twice as thick, of some soft wood, such as commiphora, is placed on the ground, and firmly held by the operator's feet, who sits down. The drill has a pointed end which fits into a notch in the lower piece. It is rapidly twirled between the hands, with a double motion right and left. In a short time the dust thrown out of the notch by the drilling begins to smoke. Rapid and more rapid becomes the motion till the dust begins to glow. It is then covered with

[1] C. K. Meek, *op. cit.* i. 171 *sq.*

a little moss, and gently blown upon by the mouth, when it bursts into a flame, and is immediately thrust into some dry grass, when there is a fire. It is astonishing how quickly a Bushman will produce a fire. Anything from five to seven minutes is enough. Long practice is required to get the requisite pressure on the lower piece of wood. If it is too heavy the drill becomes blunted, and if too light, nothing beyond a smoking is produced. Considerable deftness is required to keep the drill in motion when sliding the hands up and down. This is what produces the alternation of movement. I have tried several times, after watching Bushmen make fire, but could never get the thing beyond the smoking stage." [1]

Many savages see in the working of the fire-drill an analogy to the intercourse of the sexes, and accordingly they identify the upright pointed stick with the male, and the flat notched or socketed stick with the female. Among African tribes this holds true of the Bakitara and the Basabei, two tribes of Uganda, of the Bushongo, a tribe of the Upper Congo, of the Ba-Ila speaking tribes of Northern Rhodesia, the Wasu of Tanganyika, and the Antandroi of Madagascar.[2] The Thonga or Ronga of South-East Africa call the upright pointed stick the husband, and the flat notched stick the wife.[3] With regard to the Kikuyu, a tribe of Kenya, who treat the two fire-sticks as male and female respectively, we are told that " it is curious to note that a woman is not allowed to make fire by friction, the reason given for this being that a man has to squat to make fire, and that if a woman does the same it is unseemly, as she thereby exposes her nakedness. It is believed, however, that there is more in it than this, and that only a male is supposed to manipulate the masculine portion of the apparatus." [4] Very different from this was a practice of the people of Loango. Public fires were kept perpetually burning during a king's reign, and were ex-

[1] S. S. Dornan, *op. cit.* pp. 116 *sq.*

[2] J. Roscoe, *The Bakitara*, p. 47; id., *The Bagesu*, p. 58; E. Torday and T. A. Joyce, *Les Bushongo*, p. 135; E. W. Smith and A. M. Dale, *op. cit.* i. 143; J. J. Dannholz, *Im Banne des Geisterglaubens*, p. 43; R. Decary, " L'Industrie chez les Antandroy de Madagascar," in *Revue d'ethnographie et des traditions populaires*, vii. (1926) p. 38.

[3] H. A. Junod, *The Life of a South African Tribe*, ii. 33.

[4] C. W. Hobley, *Bantu Beliefs and Magic* (London, 1922), p. 68.

tinguished at his death.   When the new king came to the throne the new public fire was rekindled by the friction of two sticks, regarded as male and female respectively, which were appropriately manipulated by a youth and a maiden.   After performing this solemn function they were compelled to complete the analogy with the fire-sticks by cohabiting with each other in public, after which they were buried alive.[1]

In India the Birhors, a primitive tribe of Chota Nagpur, still produce fire by the old method of the fire-drill, the sticks of which they recognize as male and female respectively. Their mode of kindling the fire is as follows.   " The orthodox method of making fire is with two pieces of split bamboo, about two feet long.   These fire-sticks are called *gulgus*, one of which has a slight notch cut into it towards the middle of its length and is called the *enga* or the female stick.   The *enga* stick is placed on the ground with the notch looking upwards and one end pressed under the operator's left foot and the far end placed in a slightly inclined position over a stone to keep it steady.   The other stick which is called the *sanre* or male stick is inserted perpendicularly into the notch on the *enga* stick and rapidly twirled round and round between the hands until the charred dust produced by this process of drilling takes fire.   The Birhor does not keep fire continually burning, but produces it with the *gulgu* whenever required." [2]

[1] *Die Loango Expedition*, iii. 2, pp. 170 *sq*.

[2] S. C. Roy, *The Birhors*, pp. 516 *sq*.

CHAPTER XII

FATHER JOVE AND MOTHER VESTA

IN treating of the worship of Vesta, the Roman goddess of the domestic hearth and of the fire that burned in it, I have suggested that the widespread custom of leading a bride round the hearth may have been intended to fertilize her, by that generative virtue of the fire which from legends is known to have been an article of the ancient Latin creed, and further, that the practice of passing new-born infants over the fire may have been a mode of introducing them to the ancestral spirits supposed to haunt the old domestic hearth.[1] The conception of ancestral spirits haunting their old domestic hearths appears to be familiar to the Ba-Ila speaking tribes of Northern Rhodesia, for with regard to them we are told that " for a hut to have no fire in it is reckoned very bad, not only for the convenience of the living, but also for the family ghosts who live in the hut." [2]

Further I have suggested that the Vestals were regarded as embodiments of Vesta as the mother-goddess who bestowed offspring on cattle and on women.[3] With this their character as priestesses of the sacred fire was probably closely connected, for whenever the sacred fire went out they appear to have assisted the pontiff in rekindling it, by means of the fire-drill. We may conjecture that a Vestal held the flat board of the drill while the pontiff twirled the other fire-stick between his hands, so as to elicit the flame by friction. We may compare a custom observed by the Palês of South Hsenwi

[1] *The Golden Bough : The Magic Art and the Evolution of Kings*, ii. 227-252.
[2] E. W. Smith and A. M. Dale, *op.*
cit. i. 142.
[3] *The Golden Bough : The Magic Art and the Evolution of Kings*, ii. 229.

in Burma.   " Among the Palês of South Hsenwi there is a
village custom that once a year all the village fires must be
extinguished and new fires made.   A man and a woman are
chosen, who rub two pieces of wood together in order to get
fire by friction.   All other fires in the village are lit from this
source." [1]   In this custom we may assume, with a fair degree
of probability, that the fire is kindled by means of the fire-
drill, and that in the operation the drill, the male element, is
twirled by the man, while the flat board, the female element,
is held by the woman.   Maori legend has preserved the
memory of a fire thus solemnly procured by a father and
daughter acting together.   " Kai-awa resolved to remove
the *tapu* which Wheke-toro had put on the Whanga-o-keno
Island, and his purpose was approved by all the people.
He and his daughter Po-nui-a-hine went to the island.   His
daughter accompanied him that she might stand on and hold
steady the wood which her father would use to procure fire by
friction, and perform her part of the ceremony and represent
the female gods. . . . Kai-awa took some wood, and, whilst
his daughter pressed one end firmly on the ground, he by
friction produced fire from it.   When smoke was first seen,
he called it Pinoi-nuku (hot stone of the earth).   When he
made the fire blaze he called it Pinoi-a-rangi (hot stone of
heaven).   He put his daughter to sleep, and went to light
the sacred fires—one for the gods of men, the others for the
gods of females." [2]   In this legend it is to be observed that
the woman who assisted her father in kindling the new
fire claimed to represent the female gods, thus answering
exactly to the part which I have conjecturally assigned to
the Vestal Virgin who helped the pontiff to relight the sacred
fire at Rome, for on my theory the Vestal personated the
goddess Vesta.   We have seen that in Loango a new fire,
lit at the beginning of a king's reign, was always kindled by
a youth and maiden with the use of the fire-drill.[3]

But while the sexual interpretation of the fire-drill which
the Vestals used in relighting the sacred fire is obvious and
unmistakable, the Vestals themselves had to be chaste, or

[1] Mrs. L. Milne, *The Home of an Eastern Clan*, p. 207.

[2] J. White, *The Ancient History of*   the *Maori* (London, 1889), ii. 192.

[3] See above, p. 173.

otherwise it was believed that they could not elicit the fire. The same demand for chastity in persons who make cere-monial fires meets us among the Angami Nagas, a tribe of Assam.   A certain ceremony, called the *Derochü* " is per-formed in the case of any illness or by reason of being talked about, either for good or for ill.   A pig is killed, and two chaste unmarried boys, one a Pezoma and the other a Pep-fuma, are sent into the jungle to bring a bit of tree, to make a wooden hearth, some firewood, and some wormwood.   They make a new fireplace and make fire with a fire-stick, the Pezoma boy being the first to work the stick.   If he fails to get fire the owner of the house works it." [1]

It is a widespread belief in Germany that if a person can blow up into a flame the almost extinguished embers of a dying fire he or she is chaste.   The belief is said to be current in Silesia, Oldenburg, Bavaria, Switzerland, and the Tyrol,[2] to which we can add Mecklenburg.[3]   Elsewhere I have con-jecturally suggested a motive for this requirement of chastity in fire-making.[4]

---

[1] J. H. Hutton, *The Angami Nagas* (London, 1921), p. 234.

[2] A. Wuttke, *Der deutsche Volks-aberglaube der Gegenwart* (Berlin, 1869) p. 206, § 312.   For Bavaria, cf. F. Panzer, *Beitrag zur deutschen Mytho-logie* (München, 1848), i. 258.

[3] K. Bartsch, *Sagen, Märchen und Gebräuche aus Mecklenburg* (Vienna, 1880), ii. 58.

[4] *The Golden Bough : The Magic Art and the Evolution of Kings*, ii. 239.

CHAPTER XIII

THE ORIGIN OF PERPETUAL FIRES

ELSEWHERE I have suggested that the custom of maintaining a perpetual fire, like the fire of Vesta, originated in the difficulty of kindling a new fire by the laborious process of friction.[1] Hence many savages keep a fire perpetually burning or glowing in their hut, and if the fire goes out they borrow a light from a neighbouring house rather than take the trouble of kindling it in the usual way by friction ; and, for the same reason, on journeys savages will often carry a glowing ember with them rather than elicit fire by the friction of the firesticks. Thus, speaking of the black population of the Western or French Sudan on the Ivory Coast, the experienced French ethnographer, M. Delafosse, tells us that these people, having given up the practice of kindling fire by the friction of wood, and not yet having learned the method of making fire by flint and steel or matches, they carefully preserve the fire in each village or in each habitation and in shifting their habitations they carry with them a glowing ember to light the fire in their new abode. M. Delafosse witnessed for himself this custom in use among the Baoule, the Senoufo, the Ouobe, the Toura, the Dan, and other tribes of the Ivory Coast. He tells us that certain facts bear witness to the high importance, not only utilitarian but quasi sacred, which these peoples and others attach to the conservation of the family fire. They carefully guard the piece of charred wood from which the founder of the village or the house kindled the first fire on the soil which he transmitted to his descendants. In many parts of Western Sudan the remains of the ancestral ember are

[1] *The Golden Bough : The Magic Art and the Evolution of Kings*, ii. 253.

piously preserved by the patriarch and his descendants, as a sign of his territorial authority, and as a proof of the first occupation of the soil by the ancestor of the family. At Bondoukou on the Ivory Coast, when a discussion takes place between the two most ancient tribes of the country on their respective rights to the possession of the soil, it is the production, by the chief of one of the tribes, of the ancestral ember that decides the dispute in his favour.[1]

In Kiziba, a district to the west of Lake Victoria Nyanza, the natives are careful to keep fires perpetually burning, or at least glowing, by day and by night in their houses, because they shrink from undertaking the tedious process of kindling fire by friction. If the fire in the house should happen to go out the people will borrow fire from a neighbouring house rather than kindle it by friction, but they are acquainted with the method of kindling fire by the friction of a soft and a hard wood, and they resort to it on long journeys when there is no means of borrowing fire from somebody else.[2] Similarly among the Barundi, a tribe of the same region, to the west of Lake Victoria Nyanza, it is customary to maintain the domestic fire by day and night on a hearth in the centre of the hut, and if the fire should go out the people borrow a light from a neighbour, rather than be at the pains of rekindling it by friction. At the same time they are acquainted with the process of making fire by the friction of wood, and sometimes resort to it on long journeys, though at such times they sometimes carry with them a glowing ember to save themselves the trouble of eliciting fire by the fire-sticks.[3] Speaking of the natives of Loango, a good authority tells us that they rarely resort to the laborious process of kindling fire by friction. On journeys they always carry a fire with them smouldering in the pith of a plant or in rotten wood.[4]

Often the maintenance of a perpetual fire is an appanage of royal dignity. It is maintained throughout the life of the king, extinguished at his death, and rekindled at the accession of his successor. We have seen that this was the case with

[1] M. Delafosse, in *Revue d'ethnographie et des traditions populaires*, iv. (1923) p. 195.

[2] H. Rehse, *Kiziba, Land und Leute*, pp. 19 sq.

[3] H Meyer, *Die Barundi*, p. 24.

[4] *Die Loango Expedition*, iii. 2, pp. 171 sq.

the kings of Loango.[1] Among the Banyankole of Uganda all the king's fires were extinguished at his death, and all the goats and dogs in the neighbourhood of the royal kraals were killed, because they were supposed to retain the evil of death.[2] Among the Bakerewe, who inhabit an island on Lake Victoria Nyanza, at the accession of a new king a new fire was solemnly kindled by a man who must be a member of the Bahembe family. He did so by twirling a stick on a small log, and as soon as the flame appeared the people hastened to extinguish and throw out all the remains of the fires in the king's houses. After that the fire-maker distributed the new fire to all the people.[3]

Among the Thonga or Ronga of South-East Africa a perpetual fire was maintained in the hut of the chief's first or principal wife, the queen, who had the charge of it. If she allowed it to go out the fire had to be rekindled by the royal priest or magician, which he did by rubbing together two sticks of a certain wood called *ntjopfa*. The fire produced from this wood is deemed dangerous. It is taboo to cut the branches of the tree from which the wood is taken, or to use its wood for warming themselves. The queen or principal wife who had charge of the royal fire and royal medicine had on that account no sexual relations with the chief or king. " I do not know," says M. Junod, " if absolute continence is always enforced on the keeper of the sacred fire, as was the case for the Roman Vestal Virgins. But I have been told by Mboza that this woman prevented her co-wives from coming near her hut: it was taboo."[4] In any case the analogy between the Vestal fire at Rome and the royal fire of the Thonga is sufficiently close.

Some peoples attribute a special virtue to a fire kindled by lightning, and employ it to relight the fires in their huts. Thus among the Kagoro, a tribe of Nigeria, " if any tree or house is set on fire by lightning, all the people will at once quench their fires and hasten to the spot with bundles of grass to get new fire to rekindle them. To neglect this would be to show that the person so doing possessed black magic, and did

---

[1] See above, p. 173.
[2] J. Roscoe, *The Banyankole*, p. 51.
[3] P. E. Hurel, " Religion et Vie

domestique des Bakerewe," in *Anthropos*, vi. (1911) p. 71.
[4] H. A. Junod, *op. cit.* i. 391.

not want to change his fire." [1]   Similarly among the Oraons of Chota Nagpur in India, " although fire is not ordinarily considered sacred, ' lightning-fire ' is regarded as sent by Heaven.   Thus not so long ago, at village Haril (in *thana* Mundar), a tree on whose branches an Oraon cultivator had stacked his straw, was struck with lightning and the straw caught fire.   Thereupon all the Oraons of the village assembled at a meeting, and decided that as God had sent this ' lightning-fire,' all existing fire in the village should be extinguished, and a portion of this Heaven-sent fire should be taken and carefully preserved in every house, and should be used for all purposes.   And this was accordingly done." [2]   Again in some tribes of Northern Rhodesia " when a thunderbolt falls the chief kindles a new fire from it, and dispenses the embers, ordering his people to use this fresh flame sent from God." [3]

Some peoples appear to think that the virtue of fire is impaired or diluted by a death, and that consequently after such an occurrence it is necessary to extinguish the old fire and obtain a new one.   Thus among the tribes at the southern end of Lake Nyasa in Africa, " after the death of anyone in the village all fires are extinguished, fresh fire is made outside the dead man's house to cook for all, and from this fire is taken to every hut." [4]   The Wemba, a tribe of Northern Rhodesia, put out all fires in the village as soon as a death in it is notified.[5]   Among the Tumbuka, a tribe of Nyasaland, " if a man is killed by lightning, as happens every year, a ' doctor ' is called, and, after sacrifice, he washes all the villagers with some medicine of which he has the secret, and all the fires are taken from the houses, and thrown down at the cross-roads.   Then the doctor kindles new fire by friction and lights again the village hearths." [6]   Among the Thonga or Ronga of South-East Africa, as soon as a death has taken place,

[1] A. J. N. Tremearne, *The Tailed Head-Hunters of Nigeria* (London, 1912), p. 193.

[2] S. C. Roy, *The Oraons*, pp. 170 *sq.*

[3] C. Gouldsbury and H. Sheane, *The Great Plateau of Northern Rhodesia*, p. 286.

[4] H. S. Stannus, " Notes on Some Tribes of British Central Africa," in *Journal of the Royal Anthropological Institute*, xl. (1910) p. 326.

[5] G. Gouldsbury and H. Sheane, *op. cit.* p. 184.

[6] D. Fraser, *Winning a Primitive People*, p. 132.

"the fire which was burning in the funeral hut is removed and carried out into the square.   It must be carefully kept alight. This is a taboo.   Should there be rain, it must be protected. All the inhabitants must use this fire during the next five days. It will be put out by the doctor, with sand or water, on the day of the dispersion of the mourners.   He will then light a new one, and everyone will take from it embers to kindle his own fire in the different huts.   It is one of the conditions of the purification of the village." [1]   Among the Banyoro of Uganda, after the death of a king " no fires were allowed to burn during the period of mourning, they were all extinguished when the king's death was announced ; a fire might be lighted by friction with fire-sticks for cooking necessary food, but it was extinguished immediately the cooking was done and fresh fire obtained when it was wanted. . . . Upon the king's return from the funeral of his father, sacred fire was brought to him by the keeper of the sacred fire, who had the title of *Nsansa Namugoye* ; the king took the fire from the keeper and held it for a few moments ; he then returned it to the keeper and told him to light the fires in the royal enclosure. All the fires in the country were supposed to be lighted from this fire.   The original fire was supposed to have been brought to the fire by one of the first kings." [2]

Among the Birhors of Chota Nagpur in India " when the pall-bearers return home after burial or cremation, all old fires in the village (*tanda*) are extinguished and the cinders and ashes in hearths of all the houses in the village are thrown away, and every Birhor in the settlement takes a bath. Then a new fire is kindled in some hut by the friction of two pieces of wood, and all the other families in the village light their fires from it." [3]

[1] H. A. Junod, *op. cit.* i. 135 *sq.*   pp. 51 *sqq.*
[2] J. Roscoe, *The Northern Bantu,*   [3] S. C. Roy, *The Birhors*, p. 264.

CHAPTER XIV

THE SUCCESSION TO THE KINGDOM IN ANCIENT LATIUM

ELSEWHERE I have shown some grounds for thinking that in the old Latin kingship the crown descended, not to the king's son, but to the man who married one of the king's daughters, kinship being traced in the female instead of in the male line.[1] This seems to have been originally the rule of descent with the kingship in Burma, as we learn from the following account of it. When Mindon became king of Burma in 1853, " he had to follow the custom prescribed for the maintenance of a line of succession having the pure blood royal. For this purpose one of the king's daughters, known as the *Tabindaing* Princess, always remained unmarried in order to become the wife of the next monarch. In case of any accident befalling the *Tabindaing* with regard to producing heirs, the second available Princess nearest of blood to the royal blood was also wedded to the new king. The former became the ' chief ' queen (*Nanmadaw*), and the south palace was assigned to her use ; while the latter became the ' middle ' queen (*Alenandaw*), in contradistinction to any and all queenly wives raised to queenly rank. Thus Mindon received his stepsister and his cousin as royal consorts. This had now become nothing more than the survival of an ancient custom, since the throne did not descend by direct lineal succession, but was filled by any prince, usually a brother or a son, who had been nominated as heir apparent by the King. The only requisite qualification was that he should be a son of one of the four chief queens of a king." [2]

[1] *The Golden Bough : The Magic Art and the Evolution of Kings*, ii. 266 *sqq.*

[2] J. Nisbet, *Burma under British Rule* (London, 1901), i. 194 *sq.*

Among the Garos, a tribe of Assam, who have the system of female kinship, a man's sons receive nothing of his property at his death.   It all goes to the man who married his favourite daughter, on condition that, at the death of his father-in-law, he must marry the widow, his mother-in-law, through whom he succeeds to the whole of his father-in-law's estate.   The sons of the deceased, inheriting nothing from their father, have to look to the family into which they marry for their establishment in life.   Amongst the Garos, as amongst the Khasis, another tribe of Assam, the wife is the head of the family, and through her all the family property descends.[1] Elsewhere I have suggested that among the ancient Latins succession to the throne may have been regulated by a rule which combined the hereditary with the elective principle, and I have shown that such a combination is found in the rule of succession in not a few African kingdoms.[2]   To the examples there cited I may now add a few others.   Among the Wafipa, a tribe to the east of Lake Tanganyika, " royalty is at once hereditary and elective.   It is hereditary in the sense that the King must always be chosen from the same family, that of the *Watwaki*.   It is elective, since the candidate for the throne must be recognized and approved by the Great Council.   The heir presumptive to the throne bears the name of *Wakouchamdama*.   His title is conferred even in the lifetime of the king.   Usually he is one of the King's brothers, or one of his nephews, rarely one of his children." [3]

In the kingdom of the Shilluk, a tribe of the Upper Nile, the kingship is hereditary " in so far as the king must always be a member of the royal family, that is, of the descendants of Nyikang, and only a person whose father has been a king may be elected.   There are three houses of the royal family, and the king is elected from each of these royal branches in turn.   If there are several brothers in the branch whose turn it is to have the kingship, upon the death of the king one of these brothers will be elected.   But in case there is no vacancy

---

[1] W. W. Hunter, *A Statistical Account of Assam* (London, 1879), ii. 154. Cf. A. Playfair, *The Garos* (London, 1909), p. 68. As to the system of female kinship among the Khasis, see P. R. T. Gurdon, *The Khasis* (London, 1914), pp. 82 *sq.*

[2] *The Golden Bough : The Magic Art and the Evolution of Kings*, ii. 292 *sqq.*

[3] Mgr. Lechaptois, *Aux Rives du Tanganyika*, pp. 78 *sq.*

during the life of these three brothers, then the sons of the eldest will be in line for the throne." [1]

Among the Ila-speaking peoples of Northern Rhodesia the succession to a chief is partly hereditary and partly elective, the new chief being generally chosen from one of the late king's family or clan. The following is an instructive account of the discussions to which the selection of a chief's successor among these peoples commonly gives rise. " The chiefs and headmen select their fellow-chief in an assembly after the funeral of the deceased chief. In setting about the selection of the heir, they call over the names of his children and nephews, and then discuss among themselves whom they shall instal, saying, ' Who shall it be ? Let it be a proper man from among his children or his nephews.' And then comes the argument. Because some wish to put in a child whom they think a suitable heir, but others when his name is suggested are hesitant and doubtful, and do not haste to agree, or if they seem to agree it is not heartily, ' they will answer from the outside of their hearts.' Or they will speak out and say, ' He whom you wish to instal to-day, has he left off doing certain things which he is used to doing ? Is he really competent to rule the people ? ' The others, hearing this, reply : ' Well, name the one you consider the proper person.' So they put forward the name of their candidate for the chiefship, saying, ' We wish for So-and-So, one of the deceased's nephews, he is the proper person.' So they come to a decision. And the child of the chief, if he does not fall in with it, will leave the village : there is no room there for him who thought that the chiefship should be his : there cannot be two chiefs. . . . The clan relationship of the deceased chief is respected in so far that in selecting the heir an endeavour is made to find a suitable successor of the same clan ; thus when a *Munasolwe* dies they seek a *Munasolwe* in his place." Among these Ila-speaking peoples, when several candidates are proposed for the chieftainship the choice is sometimes determined by a trial of skill among the candidates. Several instances of such a choice were known to Messrs. Smith and Dale, our authorities on these tribes. They cite one of them, which was as follows : " One such case was at

[1] D. Westermann, *The Shilluk People* (Berlin, 1912), p. xlvi.

Itumbi. Shimaponda, the first chief, on his death-bed nominated Momba ; but others were proposed. To settle the matter several competitions were held, in one of which a large-eyed needle was thrown into a pool and the candidates were set to fish for it with their spears. The one who succeeded in spearing it through the eye was to be chief. Momba was the only one who succeeded, and he became chief." [1] Elsewhere we have seen that among the personal qualities which in Africa recommend a man for the position of chief, corpulence is one.[2] Among the Baya, a tribe in West Africa on the borders of the Cameroons, succession to the chieftainship is hereditary. When he is about to reign, a new chief is not submitted to any physical test of endurance, but he is shut up in a house for three months, where he is gorged with manioc, flesh, beer, and maize. And not until he has attained a high degree of corpulence is he brought forth to be enthroned.[3]

Elsewhere I have cited examples or races for a bride.[4] I will here add one from Formosa. In the Pepo tribes of that island " there was generally freedom of marriage for both sexes. Among some of them, however, there was a custom of holding, on a certain day specially announced, a running race in which all young bachelors competed. The prize was the privilege of marrying the most beautiful girl of the tribe." [5]

[1] E. W. Smith and A. M. Dale, The Ila-Speaking Peoples of Northern Rhodesia, i. 299 sqq.

[2] The Magic Art and the Evolution of Kings, ii. 297.

[3] A. Poupon, " Étude ethnographique des Baya," in L'Anthropologie, xxvi. (Paris, 1915), p. 118. In Africa, the wives of chiefs and princesses are similarly fattened artificially. See J. Speke, Journal of the Discovery of the Source of the Nile, p. 172; Emin Pasha in Central Africa (London, 1888), p. 64, and G. Casati, Ten Years in Equatoria, ii. 71.

[4] The Magic Art, etc., ii. 299 sqq.

[5] J. W. Davidson, The Island of Formosa (London and New York, 1903), p. 580.

CHAPTER XV

ST. GEORGE AND THE PARILIA

ELSEWHERE we have seen that in many parts of Eastern Europe herdsmen are wont to drive out the cattle to pasture from the winter quarters for the first time on St. George's Day, the twenty-third of April, a date that nearly coincides with that of the Parilia, the shepherds' festival held at Ancient Rome on the twenty-first of April.[1] The custom is observed on St. George's Day in various parts of Hungary ; but before driving out the cattle on that day the herdsmen are careful to lay a ploughshare on the threshold for the purpose of guarding the animals against the insidious arts of " the wicked ones," the witches. A powder made of the holy wafer burnt at Christmas, of onions and the bones of the dead, is a powerful specific against the witches, and on St. George's Day shepherds strew this powder on the fields as a protection against wild beasts. In some districts of Hungary women stark naked run round the herd before they drive it out and commit it to the care of the herdsmen. In the district of Baranya-Ozd they put an egg on the ground for every head of cattle that is driven out. The shepherd takes the eggs in his hand and says, " God save the master and his cattle, and may they come home as round as this egg." At Vep, in the county of Vas, Western Hungary, when the cattle are driven out they are beaten with the branches of the elder and green twigs, and a chain with eggs is put before the stalls. It is believed that their feet will then be as strong as the chain, and the poor, who get the eggs, will pray for the cattle. At Gömör, northern Hungary, there is another explanation for the same

[1] *The Golden Bough: The Magic Art and the Evolution of Kings,* ii. 324 *sqq.*

custom.   There is a lock on the chain, and this is said to ensure that the cattle will never be hungry ; the egg means that they should be as round as an egg.   Here again the cattle are whipped, this time that they may grow like young trees.   When they arrive at the end of the village there is another chain with an ants' nest in the middle ; and so the cattle will stop together like the ants in a nest.   At Besen-yotelke the cattle are never driven out to pasture before St. George's Day, because on the eve of that day the witches are prowling about to gather the profit or virtue of the cows. They manage to do this by pulling a blanket in the grass and collecting all the dew.   It is against these maleficent beings that all sorts of precautions are taken on the eve of St. George's Day.   Branches of the birch are then stuck on the fence, the cattle are beaten with wild-rose branches, and so on.   In Eastern Hungary people strew millet round the stalls on St. George's Eve.   The witch must collect all the grains before she can steal the milk.   In 1854 there was a witch's trial at Kolozsvar.   The charge against a certain woman was that she had been gathering dew in a three-cornered blanket on the eve of St. George's Day.   At Kecskemet it is the shepherds who do this, and when they do it they say " I gather, I gather the half of everything."   In Borsod they say " I gather, but I leave some," and the ceremony is performed either on St. George's Eve or on Good Friday.   They must be naked to do this.[1]

[1] G. Róheim, " Hungarian Calen-   *Royal Anthropological Institute*, lvi.
dar Customs," in *Journal of the*   (1926) 366 *sq.*

CHAPTER XVI

THE OAK

ELSEWHERE in speaking of the worship of the great European god of the oak and the thunder I had occasion to notice the widespread popular belief that prehistoric flint weapons are thunderbolts which have fallen from heaven to earth.[1] To the evidence I have there cited I may here add a few details. The subject has been discussed in a learned monograph by the Danish scholar, Dr. Blinkenberg, from whose work I may be allowed to quote a few passages. " Denmark has three portions of territory in touch with the neighbouring countries in the east and south, each with its special kind of thunderstone. In the greater part of the country, viz. in Sealand with the neighbouring islands, in Langeland, Funen, Bornholm, and in Vendsyssel, Mors, and the eastern parts of Jutland, the common flint axes of the stone age or occasionally other flint antiquities (dagger blades, even the crescent-shaped flint saws) were the objects supposed to fall down from the skies in thunderstorms. Partially in Sealand and on the islands to the south of it, Falster, Lolland, and Bornholm, belemnites (' fingerstones ') were regarded as thunder-stones ; whereas in western and southern Jutland fossilized sea-urchins passed as such. . . . The stone protects the house in which it is kept against strokes of lightning. . . . In Norway the thunder-stone belief does not seem to have such importance as in Denmark. In the greater part of the country certain round and smooth stones have been looked upon as thunder-stones ; whereas the axes of the stone age are so regarded only in the southern part of Norway, nearest Vendsyssel. . . . It is quite

[1] *The Golden Bough : The Magic Art and the Evolution of Kings*, ii. 373.

otherwise in Sweden, where the thunder-stone belief has been widely spread until the latest times. It is usually the implements of the stone age (not only the flint axe, as in Denmark, but quite as often the pierced axe) that are supposed to have come down with the thunder, though in certain parts (as in southern Skaane, close to the Danish Islands) it is the belemnite that is so regarded ; in other parts the same is said about rock crystals, stones worn by water, etc. . . . The power attributed to it in the affairs of daily life is partly the same as or at any rate akin to, that known in Denmark. . . . It is a protection not only against lightning, but also against other forms of fire. . . . In Germany we have many records of the popular belief in thunder-stones in various parts of the country. Here, in the main, the same ideas occur which are known in Scandinavia, but besides these we find individual features foreign to the Danish and Swedish traditions. Some of these occur in other countries as well, but others seem peculiar to German districts. Not only flint axes, belemnites, and echinites pass for thunder-stones, but also, in certain parts at any rate, pierced stone axes. The thunder-stone comes down with the lightning ; it penetrates a certain depth into the earth but comes to the surface again after the lapse of a certain time ; when a thunderstorm is brewing the stone perspires and moves. It is a protection against lightning, for which purpose it is carefully kept, put up under the roof, or hung up near the fireplace. In some parts of East Prussia, where the belief is associated with the pierced axe, when a thunderstorm is coming on, the peasant puts his finger through the hole, swings the axe round three times, and then hurls it vigorously against the door—thus the house is freed from strokes of lightning."[1]

In Auvergne polished stone axes are known to the farmer under the name of thunder-stones (*pierres de tonnerre*). The peasants consider them as lucky charms for the fields in which they are found. When they no longer protect the fields they are placed in the houses, which they guard against lightning and fires.[2]

---

[1] Chr. Blinkenberg, *The Thunder-weapon in Religion and Folklore* (Cambridge, 1911), especially pp. 1-6.

[2] G. Charvilhat, in *L'Anthropologie*, xxiii. (1912) p. 461.

Again, the natives of the western Sudan, whatever their race or degree of culture, are reported to consider polished stone axes, and in general all polished pebbles, as thunderstone, which are called in Bambara *samberini* and in Sarakole *sankalima*. These two words mean lightning as well as thunder. According to them, wherever the lightning strikes it leaves behind a polished stone axe. It is this axe which is the cause of the ravages, and it becomes indispensable to extract it, else the lightning will strike again in the same place. But it is very dangerous to extract the thunder-stone, or to touch any person or animal that has been struck by lightning. It is necessary to have recourse to the rain-maker. In the region of Yelimane, at the village of Kocke, there is only one rain-maker, but his authority is very great. Whenever he hears that a thunderbolt has fallen, he by means of a charm ascertains the exact spot where the lightning has struck. He repairs to the spot, digs up the thunder-stone, and carries it away after receiving a present from the owner of the house which has been struck by the lightning. But if the owner of the house wishes to retain the thunder-stone he may do so on paying the rain-maker for it with a bull, an enormous sum for the country. And if the owner places it in his granary it will secure for him a superb crop.[1]

With regard to thunder-stones in Africa, Dr. Blinkenberg observes, " On the Guinea Coast and its hinterland the belief in thunder-stones is very common. The ancient stone axes which are regarded as such are called ' thunderbolts,' ' lightning stones,' ' stone gods,' or ' thundergods,' and are supposed to fall from the sky in thunderstorms. When the lightning splits a tree, kills a man, or sets fire to a house, the thunder-stone is held to be the agent. As a protection against lightning it is placed under the rafters, and sacrifice is made to it of cowries, poultry, or kids, when it is smeared with the blood of the sacrificed animals, or with milk. The Danish missionary Monrad mentions this belief in his description of the Guinea Coast, and makes the interesting statement that no negro dares to take a false oath when near such a thunderbolt." [2]

[1] Fr. de Zeltner, " Notes sur le préhistorique Soudanais," in *L'An-* *thropologie*, xviii. (1907) pp. 543 *sq.*
[2] C. Blinkenberg, *op. cit.* pp. 7 *sq.*

In India the tribes inhabiting the Naga hills of Assam regard prehistoric stone axes or celts as thunderbolts and keep them as charms to promote the fertility of the rice crop or of the bean crop. " These celts are mostly more or less triangular with a plano-convex cutting edge, polished usually at that end only, though occasionally all over. As a rule they are roughly shouldered, probably to fit into a socket like the shouldered iron hoes still in use. Mr. Henry Balfour considers from the condition of their cutting edges that they were mostly axes, but the occurrence of specimens worn down at one corner, exactly like well-used iron hoes, suggests that some at any rate were used as such." [1]

In discussing the worship of the oak I had occasion to mention the old Prussian chronicler, Simon Grunau, who described the sacred oak at Romove in Prussia, and I said that I did not know whether Simon Grunau was the same person as the Symon Grynaeus, editor of the work, *Novus Orbis regionum ac insularum veteribus incognitarum* which was published in Paris in 1532. On this subject my late learned and lamented friend, Salomon Reinach, in *Revue Archaeologique*, 1919, p. 244, pointed out that the author of the *Novus Orbis* was quite distinct from the Prussian chronicler, the former being an eminent Greek scholar, a friend of Melanchthon and Luther, and editor of the Almagest of Ptolemy, Euclid, Plato, Pollux, Proclus, and John Chrysostom.

---

[1] J. H. Hutton, " The Use of Stone in the Naga Hills," in *Journal of the* *Royal Anthropological Society*, lvi. (1926) p. 71.

CHAPTER XVII

DIANUS AND DIANA

ELSEWHERE I have argued that the two pairs of deities, Jupiter and Juno and Janus and Diana were originally identical, both in name and in function. With regard to the etymological identity of their names I will quote the opinion of the eminent philologist, Max Müller. He says, " It may be useful to dwell a little longer on the curious conglomeration of words which have all been derived from the same root as Zeus. That root in its simplest form is DYU. . . . In Latin, initial *dy* is represented by *j* ; so the *Ju* in *Jupiter* corresponds exactly with Sanskrit *D y o*. *Jovis*, on the contrary, is a secondary form, and would in the nominative singular represent a Sanskrit form *Dyavih*. Traces of the former existence of an initial *dj* in Latin have been discovered in *Diovis*, according to Varro an old Italian name for Jupiter, that has been met with under the same form in Oscan inscriptions. *Vejovis*, too, an old Italian divinity, is sometimes found spelt *Vediovis*, dat. *Vediovi*, acc. *Vediovem*.

" That the Greek *Zen, Zenos*, belongs to the same family of words has never been doubted ; but there has been great diversity of opinion as to the etymological structure of the word. I explain *Zen*, as well as Latin *Jan*, the older form of *Janus*, as representing a Sanskrit *dyav-an*, formed like Pan from the root *pû*, raised to *pav-an*. Now as *yuvan*, juvenis, is contracted to *jun* in *junior*, so *dyavan* would in Latin become *Jan*, following the third declension, or, under a secondary form, *Janus*. *Janus-pater* in Latin was used as one word, like *Jupiter*. He was likewise called *Junonius* and *Quirinus*, and was, as far as we can judge, another personification of Dyu, the sky, with special reference, however, to morning, the beginning to the day (*Janus matutinus*), and later to the spring, the beginning of the year. The month of January owes its name to him. Now as Ju : Zeu = Jan : Zen, only that in Greek *Zen* remained in the third or consonantal declension, instead of migrating, as it might have done, under the form *Zenos, ou* into the second. The Latin *Jun-o, Jun-on-is* would correspond to a Greek *Zenon* as a feminine." [1]

[1] F. Max Müller, *Lectures on the Science of Language* (New Edit., London, 1880), ii. 493 *sqq.*

CHAPTER XVIII

ROYAL AND PRIESTLY TABOOS

IN discussing the burden of royalty I have elsewhere given some account of the many burdensome prohibitions or taboos which have been laid on royal or priestly personages in all parts of the world.[1]   The list of such taboos may be much extended.   Here I will add a few examples.   Among the Ibos of Southern Nigeria the king of Nri or Aguku is bound to observe the following taboos.   He may not see a corpse, not even of one of his own children.   If the king sees a dead body he must take an egg, pass it before his eyes, and throw it away.   He may not see an *alose* (certain pole or image) carried along the road.   After his consecration he may not see his mother ; his son will undertake her burial rites when she dies, or, if there is no son old enough, her family.   No one of the king's wives may enter the room in which his sceptre (*alo*) is kept.   No one may take corn into the house in which the sceptre is kept, for they would fall sick.   A woman who has not washed in the morning may not salute the king nor come to his place.   Until she has washed, a king's wife may not salute him, which she does by clapping her hands.   The king may not touch the water of the lake with his foot.   He may use it for washing and drinking, but it must be carried to his house by small boys and girls.   When water is being carried up for the king the children are not to speak on their way back ; if they speak the water is to be thrown away.   When the king is bathing no one is allowed to rub his back for him.   Only Adama people may enter the bath-house, but the bath water is thrown away by the king

[1] *The Golden Bough*, Part ii., *Taboo and the Perils of the Soul*, pp. 1-17.

himself. When the king gets up in the morning he may not go out without washing his feet, hands, and face. His wives are not allowed to wash with other women. No one is allowed to step over his wives' legs, nor may anyone commit adultery with them. The shaving of his head is attended with various ceremonies. Yams are roasted and fish and meat prepared for an old woman. She takes a rod and eats the food transfixed on it while she is shaving his head. The cut hair is put in the bush on a wooden shelf resting on four posts by the king himself : no one else may touch it. No one may enter the room in which he is being shaved, unless it be one of his servants. The king himself must remove his cap on this as on other occasions. It appears that his wives also may now shave his head. A widow, for whose husband the rite of second burial has not yet been performed, may not come to the king's house and the king may not speak to her. The rules with regard to touching the king or using his seat are very severe. No adult may touch him when he is sitting and no young man may touch his skin under any circumstances. The king will even refuse to take an object from the hands of a young man. He may not sit upon the ground, but a mud seat with a mat are not forbidden to him. Beside the king himself only young children may use it. He may not use the same stool as anyone else. If a friend of the king eats food in his house he must not wash his hands after it, only rub them ; if he washed his hands there would be a famine in the land. Nor may he lick his fingers : the result would be the same. The king does not eat food in the house of another, but he may eat kola and drink. If he is to eat kola, a child or a woman may break it for him or give him palm wine. If he breaks kola himself, no one else may eat it. He does not eat kola which has been offered as a sacrifice. Certain kinds of food are forbidden to the king. He does not eat cassava or banana. If he eats banana he must wash his mouth. He may, however, eat plantain. No one may see the king eat, and no boy above the age of puberty may cook for the king, nor may any woman ; small girls, however, may do so. He may eat palm nuts. He also forbids coco yams and a kind of yam known as *ona* ; he may however eat *igu*. When the

king is about to eat and after he has eaten, the double bell
is sounded, which is beaten by a small child.   He may eat
kola, or dried meat, or fish in public, but would have to
cover his mouth.   When a boy cooks for him he may not
taste anything.   The king throws four pieces of food as an
offering to the ancestral spirits (*Ndicie*).   The Adama boy
who serves him puts out four pieces of mashed yam, and the
king may not eat more.   If it is not sufficient, or if he
wishes to make some complaint, the king points with his left
hand.   If he speaks, his complaint is limited to the words,
" This Adama boy."   The remains of his food were formerly
thrown away or eaten by the Adama boys.   But he has now
offered a goat and a hen to the sacred shrine (*Ajana*) so
that his own children may be permitted to eat the remains
of the food.   If he attends a festival at which the food is
cooked by women, his food is not taken by him but given to
other people.   When the king begins to eat, his servant
says, " Let no one talk, let my father Nri become a leopard."
(If a leopard is killed its body is brought to the king.   It is
called his son.   There is an obvious connection between this
and the name of the town Aguku, which means " big leopard.")
After these words have been spoken no one may open his
mouth until the king has finished and the bell has been rung
again.   When the servant has washed the pots, the dirty
water and any remains of food are thrown away ; the ashes
of the fire are also thrown in the same place.   The king
is not allowed to eat in the house of any man, except in
Umudiana.   When the king's yams are being planted, he
must plant either yams or coco yams in a single row, that is
after having finished one row he may not turn back and
begin another row on the same day.   When he is working
on the farm the king may not use a hoe, because in bending
down he would look backwards.   Before the coming of the
white man he was not allowed to cross water, but he may
sleep away from home.   He may not climb a tree or carry
a load on his head.   He may not enter a woman's house nor
go to market.   If a dog enters his house it may be driven
out or killed ; its body is carried out and everything
which it touches.   The king may not cross the door-frame.
It must be taken out, or, failing that, he may climb over the

wall.   He may not lament for his children, but he mourns
for his wives like an ordinary man.   If they die a " bad
death," sacrifice is offered for them in his house by the
Adama people.[1] With regard to the king of Onitsha,
which is an important town of the Ibo on the Lower Niger,
we are told that " the announcement of the death of the
late king of Onitsha was not made until a full year had
elapsed after his decease.   The fact that no one saw him
during the interval signified nothing, as but few beyond his
own personal attendants ever did see him, he being forbidden
by royal custom from leaving his compound.   To venture
outside the gate would be to commit an act of grave
sacrilege, except occasionally by night, when he might
surreptitiously slip out to visit some of his near relatives." [2]

Similarly the king of Loango may never leave the neighbourhood of his dwelling, he may never see the sea, nor any
white person : he may not see nor handle any objects of
European manufacture.   Every subject who approaches him
must wear exclusively articles of native manufacture.   Strict
quiet must prevail about him.   He may not see any person
eating or drinking, or performing any natural function.   And
the remains of his food and drink, and of his person, must be
secretly disposed of.   His spittle is collected by a confidential
attendant, who wipes it up in a towel of bast.[3]

Among the Wafipa, a tribe inhabiting the eastern shore of
Lake Tanganyika, the royal family is forbidden by ancient
superstition to see the lake or to eat fish.[4]   With regard to the
curious taboo which in Africa forbids royal personages to
behold the sea or a lake, we may note that in Mindanao, one
of the Philippine Islands, there is reported to exist a whole
tribe living in a crater-like valley, every member of which
believes it would be death for him or her to behold the sea,
which they have only heard of, but never seen.[5]

Among the Kam, a semi-Bantu tribe of North Nigeria,

---

[1] N. W. Thomas, *Anthropological
Report on the Ibo-speaking Peoples of
Nigeria*, Part i. (London, 1913)
pp. 52 *sqq.* Cf. P. A. Talbot, *The
Peoples of Southern Nigeria*, iii.
597 *sqq.*

[2] G. T. Basden, *Among the Ibos
of Nigeria* (London, 1921), p. 115.

[3] *Die Loango Expedition*, iii. 2,
p. 162.

[4] Mgr. Lechaptois, *Aux Rives du
Tanganyika*, p. 57.

[5] Fay-Cooper Cole, *The Wild
Tribes of the Davao District, Mindanao*, p. 183.

" the chief regards himself as a semi-divine personage and is so regarded by his people. He leads a secluded life and is subject to numerous taboos. He must not be seen eating, must not eat food outside his own compound, must not eat food cooked by a menstruous woman, must not smoke, must not see people smoking or chewing tobacco, must not pick up anything from the ground, must not put his foot in running water, and must not point his finger at any person. He eats ceremonially in private, his food being cooked by a favourite wife, provided she is not in a menstruous condition ; it is brought to him by a male attendant who averts his eyes while he eats. A second attendant, a sister's son, performs duties such as fetching water for the chief's use (and he is required to fetch it on his shoulders), and sweeping the chief's enclosure every morning (the chief may not enter the enclosure if it has not been swept). Both these attendants were in former times put to death when the chief died, with the intention that they should attend to him in the next world. The chief acts the part of the character ascribed to him. He speaks in a low voice (always through an interpreter), in an expressionless, impersonal manner. He told me himself that he was a deity, and that I could be sure, therefore, that in giving me information about the other deities or cults of the Kam it would be impossible for him to mislead me, as deities do not lie. The chief of the Kam, like the king of the Jukun, is closely associated with corn, and carries out a daily ritual by which he feeds his royal ancestors, particularly the last deceased chief, who are regarded as the life and soul of the crops." [1]

Again among the Kilba, another tribe of Northern Nigeria, " the chief was regarded as a divine person, and was subject, in consequence, to numerous taboos. He might not visit the village where he had formerly resided, for if this rule were broken disaster would fall on the inhabitants. He might not engage in any agricultural work, nor was he permitted to visit any farm. He might not pick up anything from the ground lest the dynamism of his person should blast the crops. If he struck the ground in anger the people would be confounded with fear. If he shook his fist in a man's face that man would go mad. He might not receive any article from the hand of

[1] C. K. Meek, *Tribal Studies in Northern Nigeria*, ii. 539 *sq*.

any save the official known as the Biratada.   If he fell off his
horse all persons riding in his company had to fall off also.
The mat on which he sat was regarded as charged with divine
dynamism, and no one could touch it except for the purpose
of swearing an oath.   The chief was not supposed to require
the ordinary nourishment of mortals, and he therefore ate his
food in private, attended only by the Biratada.   While the
chief was eating or drinking the attendant official sat with
head averted, and the chief signified the conclusion of the
meal by uttering a cough.   The official then smoothed the
ground in front of the chief in order, it is said, to cover up any
of the sacred food that may have dropped on the ground
The chief's meals were cooked by an old woman past the age
of menstruation.   The morning meal consisted of beer taken
at sunrise.   The evening meal of porridge and stew was eaten
at sunset, and it is said that if the cook had failed to prepare
the meal before sunset the meal would not be eaten. . . . The
Kilba chief was not permitted to eat from a decorated calabash ; and the remnants of the food were either eaten up by
the attendant official (in his capacity of priest in attendance on
the god) or else were given to the chief's dogs.   If any other
were to eat the remnants of the chief's meal he would go mad
and die.   If the chief had to be absent from Hong he was
surrounded by grass matting when he wished to eat and drink.
No one might go near the chief's lavatory, and if a new lavatory were required it had to be prepared by a particular family
to whom this special duty was delegated.   Such were the
ancient rules of Kilba chieftainship, but few of them are
observed at the present time.   They are the rules still observed
by the kings of the Jukun." [1]

Among the Ibo of Southern Nigeria the king (Ezenri) is
not the only person who is subject to many taboos.   The
same is true of a certain priestly official, who bears the title of
Ezana, or priest of the ground.   (In the Ibo language *ana*
means ground or earth.)   When any law is abrogated or
violated the priest of the ground has to offer a sacrifice.   There
is usually a priest of the ground in each quarter as well as for
a whole town.   It is for him to decide where the farms are to
be made, and he chooses his own farm, which is worked for

[1] C. K. Meek, *op. cit.* i. 185 *sq.*

him by men of the different families.   When the new yams
come in, a sacrifice is offered to the Earth (*ana*), but the priest
of the ground eats the first yam prepared on the spot the day
before by his daughter or sister.   The priest of the ground is
subject to many taboos : he may not sit upon the bare ground
nor upon the same skin as another person ; earth may not be
thrown at him, nor may he be assaulted ; he may not sacrifice
at night, nor travel at night ; he may not see a corpse, much
less carry one.   When he meets a corpse on the road the priest
of the ground of Acala passes his wristlet over his eyes and
calls an Nri man to sacrifice a chicken.   He may not carry
things on his head, nor climb palm trees, nor eat cassava, nor
things that have fallen on the ground.   No one may drink
palm wine nor eat before him.   No one but his wife may cook
for him.   In Awka a dog that enters his house is thrown out.
He may not touch a child whose head has not been shaved.
Except on the first day after a birth he may not enter the room
where it has taken place for twelve days.   He may not put on
a mask, nor touch one, and a masked man may not enter his
house.   As a rule he is not allowed to sleep in another man's
house or to eat there.   His wives may not allow the ashes of
his fire to remain until morning, for the ancestors would
punish them for the neglect.   At certain times his wives are
not allowed to cook for him, and other menstruous women
may neither salute nor touch him.   His wives must wash
before returning into the house in the morning.   He is safe
from seizure, safe in war.   In addition to the ordinary forbidden animals the priest of the ground of Awka does not eat
eggs, all birds, dog and ewe sheep, bush-buck, civet cat, giant
bush rat, bush fowl and yams that it has touched, ground
squirrel, and a kind of fish.   In one quarter of Awka, however, the priest of the ground may sacrifice eggs and eat them,
and bush fowl is the only bird he may not eat.   In Agolo he
forbids snails and a tuber called *ona*, like a yam.   He may
not eat a cock before it can crow, nor a snake.   If his wives
do not wash after going out it means that they wish his death.
They may not cook for him.   If they commit adultery they
must come to the priest of the ground and bring cowries, a
ram and a fowl, and offer excuses.   All the quarter join in
levying a fine upon the lover.   At Nneni he may not eat any-

thing that has been sacrificed on account of the violation of a taboo, nor may he cross a river until a sacrifice has been performed by a Nri man. The corpse of a dead priest of the ground is not carried upon men's heads but upon their shoulders.[1]

Among the Sema Nagas, a tribe of Assam, there is a personage called the *Amthao* or *First Reaper* who is subject to many taboos. The office may be held either by a man or by a woman. It is his or her business to start the cutting of each crop, and in the case of paddy and Job's tears—not always, however, of the millet crop—the harvest is accompanied by strict prohibitions. And on the day when the First Reaper initiates the cutting of the paddy every house in the village gives him or her a measure of paddy (about a *seer*), except those who are so poor that they can only give beans. The office is unpopular, as the unfortunate First Reaper is liable to die if he makes any mistake in the conduct of a ceremony, in particular that of the village ritual (*genna*) known as *asukuchu*, which is only observed occasionally in a year when the harvest promises to be exceptionally good, each ward of the village (*asah* or *khel*) sacrificing a pig on the outskirts of the village. The office sometimes runs in families, the nearest suitable male relative being compelled to succeed in the place of a deceased First Reaper. A man or woman who is fastidious about food is selected, at any rate if possible, and the food restrictions are often very onerous. So long as the harvest lasts (the millet harvest excepted) the First Reaper may not eat the flesh of an animal killed or wounded by any wild beast, nor that of the kalij pheasant or *dorik*, nor of the Arakan Hill partridge or *duboy*, nor the grubs and honey of bees and wasps, nor smell beans, nor bamboo rat's nor dog's flesh. The last two of these are in point of fact taboo to the whole village during the harvest, but in some cases they all, or some of them, are taboo to the First Reaper at all times.[2]

---

[1] N. W. Thomas, *op. cit.* pp. 56 *sq.*
[2] J. H. Hutton, *The Sema Nagas* (London, 1921), pp. 216 *sq.*

CHAPTER XIX

THE PERILS OF THE SOUL [1]

LIKE many other peoples the natives of Yap, one of the Caroline Islands in the Pacific, conceive of the soul (*ya'al*) as an invisible body dwelling within the visible body and resembling it in form exactly. The soul is thus a faithful image of the body. This primitive conception of the soul is perhaps the principal reason which leads many persons to identify a person's soul with his likeness. Hence when any mischievous spirit of the sea catches a man's reflection in the water, the man must die, because the spirit has robbed him of his soul. For the same reason many old women on the island are afraid to be photographed, and one native expression for photographing is *fek ya'al*, " to take away the soul." The native entertains a similar opinion concerning animals and lifeless things ; they too, in his opinion, have souls. The dead can take away the things that have been deposited with him in the grave because he carries off with him their shadow-picture (*fon*). Hence the native expression for photographing lifeless things is *fek fon*, " to take away their shadow-picture." [2]

Similarly the Bare'e-speaking Toradyas of Central Celebes conceive the human soul as a miniature likeness of the man, but they think that on occasion the soul may assume other forms, particularly that of an animal, such as a butterfly, a worm, a snake, or a mouse. The soul can quit the body for a time in life, but if it does not soon return, the person dies.[3]

The ancient Egyptian doctrine of the soul was defined as

---

[1] Cf. *Taboo and the Perils of the Soul*, pp. 26 *sq.*

[2] S. Walleser, " Religiöse Anschauungen der Bewohner von Jap," in *Anthropos*, viii. (1913) 610 *sq.*

[3] N. Adriani and A. C. Kruijt, *De Bare'e-sprekende Toradjas van Midden-Celebes*, i. 250 *sq.*

follows by Professor Alexandre Moret : " In like manner the Egyptians believed that everything that lives—gods, men, animals, trees, stones, and all objects whatsoever— encloses its own diminutive image, which is its soul.   They called that image or projection of the individual Ka ; we translate it as Double or Genie ; the Ka is represented as a being somewhat smaller than the person in whom he is in- dwelling but in other respects exactly like him." [1]

Savages commonly believe that the soul can leave the body in life and return to it, but that if the absence is prolonged the owner of the soul dies.   Hence in order to save the life of the sick or dying they attempt to detain the soul in the body by plugging or tying up those parts of the patient's body by which they believe the soul to depart, hoping thus to detain the soul, and so to prolong the life of the sufferer. The soul is very often supposed to depart through the nostrils or mouth.   Hence the Boloki or Bangala of the Upper Congo tie up the mouth and nostrils of a dying person in order to prevent his soul from escaping.   Our informant, Mr. Weeks, observes : " I noticed that the mouths and nostrils of the recently dead were always plugged and tied, and to my questions on the subject I always received the same reply, ' The soul of a dying man escapes by his mouth and nose, so we always tie them in that fashion to keep the spirit, as long as possible, in the body.' " [2]

The Bare'e-speaking Toradyas of Central Celebes suppose that the soul lodges in the crown of the head, but that it passes out of the body at the wrists and other joints.   Hence when a person is very sick his friends tie up his joints to prevent the escape of his soul, or according to others the ingress of the demon who is causing the sickness.[3]   The Palaungs of Burma think that they can detain the soul of a dying person by tying a white thread round his or her wrists, while they say, " We shall not let thee fly away, we would tie thy spirit here." [4]

Among the Mailu of British New Guinea, when a man is

[1] A. Moret, In the Time of the Pharaohs, p. 188.

[2] J. H. Weeks, Among Congo Cannibals, p. 262.

[3] N. Adriani and A. C. Kruijt, op. cit. i. 248.

[4] Mrs. L. Milne, The Home of an Eastern Clan, p. 307.

dying a medicine-man (*vara*) is sent for, " probably when some relatives are away, to tie the patient. After uttering a spell and using gentle massage he fastens round the patient a cord or strip of cane, not in hope of recovery but to retard death until the absent relatives return. They call this attempt to retard death *nena badibadi* (breath-tying), and it is regarded as tying the soul of the man to his body. People have come to me and told me that so-and-so is sitting tied—really propped up in the arms of someone—that his soul may not leave his body yet. This is not to be confused with the tying of string or cane to relieve pain." [1]

But even when the soul of a sick or dying person is thought to have escaped from his body, savages often believe that they can recall the truant soul and restore it to the patient's body, so that he will recover. Elsewhere I have given examples of restoring lost souls to their owners.[2] Here I will illustrate it with some fresh instances. Thus for example in the Shortlands group of the Solomon Islands " if a man falls and hurts himself during the day his friends and relatives at evening make a tripod of sticks 5 or 6 feet high, and in a cocoa-nut shell placed on the top a small fire is made. This is about sundown, and the friends or relatives then retire to a distance of 25 or 30 yards away, and call on the hurt man by name, telling him to come back. This is repeated until an ember falls out of the fire. During this ceremony the old men will be seated with their hands to their ears listening so that they can hear the spirit answering, and questions will be asked, such as, ' Do you not hear me ? ' Then, ' Oh yes, we hear you,' and so on. The idea seems to be that the man's shade (*nununa*) has been taken away from the body by the fall, and it has to be called back, or other spirits may get between it and the body and prevent its return, and so cause the latter's sickness or even death. When the ember falls out of the cocoa-nut in which the fire is placed it is regarded as conclusive evidence that the shadow or spirit has safely returned to the body. When the man has recovered from the effects of the fall the stem of the wild plantain, which is about eight or nine feet high, is placed on the ground, and is sup-

---

[1] W. J. V. Saville, *In Unknown New Guinea*, p. 319.

[2] *Taboo and the Perils of the Soul*, pp. 43 *sqq.*

ported by several men.   The man who fell down climbs up
this plantain stem, and as soon as he reaches the top the men
holding it let go, and plantain and man fall together to the
ground.   This is repeated three times, with intervals consisting of days, or even weeks.   This ceremony is supposed to
prevent further falls." [1]   At Sa'a in Mala, one of the Solomon
Islands, when a child is sick its strayed soul is sought for by
a priest who holds a sprig of dracaena in his hand.   The
wandering soul then lights on the dracaena, from which it is
transferred to a pandanus umbrella, where it is heard scratching.   The umbrella is then held over the child, and the soul
returns to the child, who gives a convulsive shudder and
recovers. [2]

In San Cristoval, one of the Solomon Islands, the task of
recovering the lost soul of a sick person is entrusted to a
magician, who sends out his own soul in pursuit of the fugi-
tive, and brings it back to the patient.   For this purpose the
magician goes into a trance.   He retires to his own house,
darkens it, strips off all his clothing, and lying down goes to
sleep.   While he is in this state no one may disturb him, for
if he were so disturbed his own soul might not return to him
and he might die.   His business is to find the strayed soul of
the sick man.   Perhaps the sick man's soul has gone to a
place where there are ghosts or spirits (*adaro* or *hi'oni*), or
perhaps the soul has been captured by one of these ghosts or
spirits.   A sickness so caused is a dangerous matter.   A whole
crowd of ghosts or spirits may be seated gloating over the
captive soul and refusing to let it go home.   Still more
dangerous is it if the sick man's soul has been caught by a
spirit of the sea, for the soul of the magician cannot go to the
place of its imprisonment.   But most serious of all is it if the
strayed soul has gone to the Winged Serpent in the sky.   But
usually the soul has simply departed to Rodomana, the abode
of the dead, from which it is a comparatively easy matter for
the magician to rescue it.   One magician told how his own
soul pursued the soul of a patient to Rodomana, where he
found the soul of the patient dancing with the souls of the

[1] G. Brown, *Melanesians and Polynesians*, pp. 208 *sq.*
[2] W. G. Ivens, *Melanesians of the*
South-east Solomon Islands (London,
1927), p. 78.

dead, and refusing to return, but with the help of a friend
whom he had among the dead the magician contrived to seize
the patient's soul and to hurry back with it to earth.   If the
soul of the sick man is detained in one of the sacred places, the
soul of the magician goes in search of it.   He looks in at all
the likely places, such as burial places, sacred stones, and very
often in the hollows in the trunks of trees.   He adopts the
same means as before.   But if the soul of the patient has been
captured by a spirit of the sea the matter is, as we have seen,
more serious, because the soul of the magician cannot follow
it out to sea.   In this case he again resorts to the help of a
friend.   He goes down to the sea and gets a garfish.   This
he brings back and lays on the patient's navel and waves it
four times round his head.   He then puts the fish back in the
sea.   After that he waits till evening and then falls into a
trance.   In his trance his soul goes down to the shore to the
place where he let the garfish go back into the sea.   There he
waits for his friend, who by and by brings back the lost soul
of the sick person.   The garfish is the fish of the spirit of the
sea, with which he shoots men on the reef.   But if the magician looks in vain in Rodomana, the sacred places, and the sea,
he concludes that the Winged Serpent must have taken the
strayed soul.   This is the case in very serious sicknesses, and
probably in epidemics.   In this emergency the magician
takes the fat of a sacrificed pig (formerly of a dog) and burns
it, and goes into his trance in the evening, and his soul
ascends in the column of smoke to the sky.   There also he
finds a friend to speak for him, and this friend asks the
Winged Serpent to give up the sick man's soul.   He may ask
three times, but if he asks a fourth time and is refused, the
magician must return without the patient's soul, and the sick
man will die, for there is no snatching of the soul possible
in the abode of the Winged Serpent.[1]

The Kiwai of British New Guinea identify the soul with
the shadow, reflection, or picture.   A man can steal the soul
of somebody else by catching his shadow at night in a piece
of bamboo open at one end, which he afterwards plugs and
keeps over his fireplace until he chooses to release the soul.
The owner of the soul will gradually grow thin, and if the

[1] C. E. Fox, *The Threshold of the Pacific*, p. 243.

bamboo be burnt, the man will die. For this reason a man
who goes out at night carries his torch high in the air, so that
his body may cast as short a shadow as possible. A Kiwai
man once refused to take part in a dance with some visiting
bushmen, because in the midst of the many flickering fires
his shadow could easily have been caught. The souls of sick
persons are in danger of being abducted by malevolent spirits
or otherwise leaving the body, as for example in sleep.
Hence a sick person is not allowed to sleep too much, for the
natives are afraid lest he might not wake up any more, and
for that reason they wake him up at short intervals. In
cases of serious illness the patient's friends light a fire outside
his hut and watch the road which the spirits are supposed to
take, apparently in order to bar the departure of the patient's
soul. If the wandering soul of a sick person be seen in the
company of some spirit, it may be brought back by people
versed in such things. Such a sage, holding one end of a
plaited arm-guard or bracer in his hand, goes and catches the
soul in the bracer, which he closes with his other hand.
Carrying the bracer, he hastens into the sick man's house
through the west entrance, which is the direction in which the
spirits depart. He touches both door-posts with his shoulders
to block the way so that the soul cannot go out again, and at
the same time pretends to throw the soul into the house. The
patient is sitting with his back towards the door, and the
" doctor " or wizard runs up to him and pushes in the soul,
hitting him on the back, a gesture which is connected with
the idea that the soul is situated in the back. The patient at
once comes round as his soul returns. But if the doctor fails
to capture the strayed soul, the patient will die. In the same
way the soul of a sick child is snatched away in a basket from
spirits who have come to carry it off.[1]

For the purpose of catching wandering souls of sick persons
or others a Kiwai wizard or medium goes about carrying a
long wicker-work glove for covering the wrist, a gauntlet.
It is carried in the left hand, and with the right hand the
medium catches the spirit or soul and puts it into the gauntlet.
He then takes it and places it against the back of the sick
man ; the spirit enters his body, and the invalid makes a quick

---

[1] G. Landtman, *The Kiwai Papuans of British New Guinea*, pp. 269 *sq.*

recovery. The spirit of a woman who is about to give birth to a child may be seen sitting on the veranda of the house. A wizard is called. He may catch the spirit in his gauntlet or drive it away with his broom. If he brings the spirit back to the woman, she is at once delivered of her child.[1]

Among the Kai of Northern New Guinea when a native doctor or magician is called in to visit a patient, the only question with him is whether the sickness is caused by a sorcerer or by a ghost. To decide this nice point he takes a boiled taro over which he has pronounced a charm. This he bites, and if he finds a small stone in the fruit, he decides that ghosts are the cause of the malady; but if on the other hand he detects a minute roll of leaves he knows that the sufferer is bewitched. In the latter case the obvious remedy is to discover the sorcerer and to induce him, for an adequate consideration, to give up the tube in which he has bottled up a portion of the sick man's soul. If the magician refuses to give it up the resources of the physician are not yet exhausted. He now produces his whip or scourge for souls. This valuable instrument consists, like a common whip, of a handle with a lash attached to it, but what gives it the peculiar quality that distinguishes it from all other whips is the small packet tied to the end of the lash. The packet contains a certain herb, and the sick man and his friends must all touch it in order to impregnate it with the volatile essence of their souls. Armed with this potent implement the doctor goes by night into the depth of the forest; for the darkness of night and the solitude of the forest are necessary for the delicate operation which this good physician of souls has now to perform. Finding himself alone he whistles for the lost soul of the sufferer, and if only the sorcerer by his infernal craft has not yet brought it to death's door, the soul appears at the sound of the whistle; for it is strongly attracted by the soul-stuff of its friends in the packet. But the doctor has still to catch it, a feat that is not so easily accomplished as might be supposed. It is now that the whip of souls comes into play. Suddenly the doctor heaves up his arm and lashes out at the truant soul with all his might. If only he hits it, the business is done, the soul is captured, the doctor carries it back to the house in triumph, and restores it

[1] E. Baxter Riley, *Among Papuan Headhunters*, pp. 296 *sq.*

to the body of the poor sick man, who necessarily recovers.[1]

The Yabim of Northern New Guinea believe that there are water-spirits who steal the souls of children. To guard their offspring against them women do not bathe their children in a stream but in an artificial bath. If, however, a child sickens, and the water-spirits are thought to have stolen its soul, an experienced woman takes a coconut shell used as a vessel and attaches it by a string to a cross-bar, and goes with it to a stream. There she puts the coconut-shell in the water, and holding it like a fishing-line by the cross-bar or handle, she draws it to and fro, so that the coconut shell bobs up and down in the water. Attracted by the apparatus the water-spirits bring the child's soul to the coconut shell. The woman then carries the shell full of water to the house and bathes the sick child in the water of the shell. Thus the little sufferer recovers its lost soul.[2]

Among the Bare'e-speaking Toradyas of Central Celebes there are priestesses whose chief business it is to bring back the souls of sick people which have been carried away by demons or ghosts. Also they watch over people's souls when they move into a new house, for souls can then be easily damaged by angry tree-spirits. The priestesses also bring back the soul of the rice, and procure rain or dry weather. Every priestess has her familiar *woerake* spirit who descends to her and accompanies her up into the air. Yellow-coloured rice, an egg, and a fowl are provided, that she may take them with her in her flight as an offering to the great spirits. She sits under a hood hung from a rafter ; holding dracaena leaves in her hand, she chants, with closed eyes, her litany, in which she describes her soul's flight and adventures. The language of the litany is not the common language : it is supposed to be the language of the spirits. There are three parts of the litany. The stem (*watanja*) or principal part of the litany describes the journey of the priestess's soul in search of the patient's lost soul. The ship of the spirit, who comes to help the priestess, is the rainbow ; in it she and her familiar spirit fly aloft. She describes her arrival at the house

---

[1] Ch. Keysser, " Aus dem Leben der Kaileute " in R. Neuhauss, *Deutsch-Neu-Guinea*, iii. 134. Compare my *Belief in Immortality* (London, 1913), i. 270.

[2] R. Neuhauss, *op. cit.* iii. 294.

of Poeë di Songi, the chief god.   She finds the deity asleep,
and wakens him.   The fire has gone out.   Fresh fire having
been procured from the spirits, the drum in the temple is
sounded, and at the signal all the spirits assemble in the
temple.   In the assembly the chief god asks the priestess her
errand.   She tells him she has come for so-and-so's soul.
The god gives it back to her, and she carries it down to
earth in a calabash.   The priestess restores the lost soul to
the patient's head with a bunch of dracaena leaves.   After
restoring the soul she puts some cooked rice and a piece of a
boiled egg in the patient's hair on the crown of his head.
This is known as the feeding of the soul.   At the end of the
ceremony the priestess sends back her familiar spirit into the
air by throwing up a roll of dracaena leaves.   Of this
ceremony of the recall of the soul there are branches or variations, according to the nature of its object or of the spirit
which has caused the sickness.   The dead draw away the
souls of their relatives to the spirit-land ; hence after every
death a priestess comes to fetch back the abstracted souls to
earth.   The soul is in most cases supposed to be carried off
by a tree-spirit or cave-spirit, and often an attempt is made
to recover it without the help of a priestess.   A relation goes
to the tree, makes an offering to the spirit, and asks him to
give back the soul of the sick man.   Sneezing is a sign that
the man's soul has returned to him.   In serious cases when
the priestess has brought back the patient's soul, a wooden
puppet is made and dressed as a man if the patient is a
woman, but is dressed as a woman if the patient is a man.
A small sacrificial table is set up, and on it are laid rice,
wooden models of a knife, a sword, a spear, and so on.
Bamboo ladders are constructed to serve as ladders for the
tree-spirit or cave-spirit to descend to the offering.   The
puppet is offered to the spirit in exchange for the sick person's
soul.   While the patient holds one end of a string, of which
the other is attached to the sacrificial table, the priestess
recites a litany in which she tells the tree-spirit or cave-spirit
that he has come to the wrong place, and that he had better
go elsewhere.   A fowl is thrown into the air to carry the
offering to the spirit.   Omens of recovery or death are drawn
by hacking through the bamboo stalk that has served as a

ladder.   If one cut suffices to sever the bamboo the patient
will recover ; if more cuts are necessary, he will die.   When
all other remedies have failed, recourse is had to the *mowase*,
a more elaborate form of the preceding ceremony.   The
offering is generally brought for all the inhabitants of a house
or of a village.   Sometimes it is brought to get children.
A little house is made for the spirits, and a sacrificial table is
erected.   Two small ladders are brought of very hard wood
to bring back the spirit and fix it firmly in its place.   All who
take part in the ceremony hold a line which is fastened to the
sacrificial table.   An address is made to the spirits, who are
told that a buffalo, a pig, and a fowl, bearing the guilt of the
people, are offered to them.   As before, omens of recovery or
death are drawn from the hacking through of a bamboo.
The sacrificial animals are killed, and their blood is smeared
on the patient, and on all persons present.   The priestesses
receive portions of the victims ; the rest of the flesh furnishes
a banquet.   When the necessary victims are wanting, a vow
is made to offer them later.   Sometimes the soul of a sick
person is thought to have been carried off by the souls of the
dead who live in the temple.   In that case the priestess offers
seven pieces of ginger on a board to the spirits in the temple
in exchange for the patient's soul.   Or a warrior may vow
to bring back a human head in case the patient should recover.
If the sickness is thought to be caused by the spirits of the
smithy, a small model of a smithy is made and waved seven
times over the patient's head ; after which it is wafted aloft
by the litany of the priestess.   If the sickness is thought to be
caused by the spirits of the ricefield, the priestess makes a
chain of beads on a string and waves it over the patient, who
afterwards wears it round his neck.   If the spirits cause a
man pain in one of his limbs, he offers them a string of *kalide*
fruits, and then wears it on the ailing member till it drops off.
When a man returns from a journey or an expedition, he
sometimes leaves his soul behind him and brings back some
injurious substance in his body instead.   So the priestess must
come and recall the soul and eject the foreign substance from
the sufferer.   After invoking the spirits, the priestess strokes
the patient's body and limbs with a bunch of life-giving plants.
The patient is then covered with a blanket, and the priestess

strikes the blanket with a bunch of thorny plants in order to drive the evil out of the sufferer's body.   She then shakes the blanket out of the window, in order to rid it of the evil which has been transferred to it from the patient.   When a man has been frightened, as by the attack of a wild buffalo, a crocodile, or a python, it is thought that his soul has quitted his body and must be recalled.   The priestess makes the figure of a serpent out of leaves and strokes it over the man's body, chanting her litany, while she beats the figure with a bunch of leaves.   Then she hangs the figure through a hole in the floor.   The effigy is then put in a basket with rice, betel, and an egg, which last is given to the serpent to bite instead of the man.   Sometimes a rope is used instead of an image of a snake, especially in cases of chronic rheumatism.   The rope is passed over the aching joints, while the priestess beats it with a bunch of leaves and says that she is " unbinding " the malady.   Then the rope is let down through an opening in the floor.   Or the rope, representing the sickness is placed in the model of a boat and carried out of the village.   At the dedication of a new house the priestess comes to fix the souls of the inmates in their bodies.   Each person's soul is in a packet of life-giving herbs which is brought from the old house to the new.   When the rice does not grow well, its soul is supposed to be absent and the priestess goes and fetches it back from the spirits in the sky.   The soul of the rice is seen in the form of some grains of rice, which she lets fall from a bunch of dracaena leaves.[1]   When rain is wanted, the priestess professes to make it by collecting the buffaloes in the spirit land and driving them into a pool, so that the water of the pool overflows and falls in the form of rain.   But this rain-making ceremony belongs to another part of our subject.[2]

Among the Dyaks inhabiting the Dusun district of Southern Borneo, in case of a serious illness sacrifice is offered. If that produces no alleviation, a medicine-man (*balian*) is called in.   He is received in the principal room of the house, where the patient lies.   In the middle of the room a sort of altar is erected, on which stands a vessel containing *bras*, an egg, and dainties.   A light ladder, composed of reeds,

---

[1] N. Adriani and A. C. Kruijt, *op. cit.* i. 376-393.

[2] See above, pp. 68-93.

extends from the altar to the ridge of the roof; it is to facilitate the descent of the spirits, and the *bras* and dainties are
bait to allure them. The guests sit along the walls to watch
the proceedings. The medicine-man wears heavy metal
bracelets on his wrists. He throws up grains of rice, variously
coloured, and tries by all kinds of endearing names to draw
the spirits to himself, while he sways his arms about so that
the heavy bracelets rattle. In his hands he holds *rirong*
leaves, which he waves to and fro. He chants the words in
sing-song tones. In the intervals of his chant the drums beat
loudly. Thus attracted, the spirits are supposed to alight on
the ridge of the roof and descending the ladder to enter
into the medicine-man, who becomes possessed (*pasoa*). His
dance-movements grow more violent; he runs through the
room, shrieking and clinking bells, and at last rushes out
of the door into the darkness, for the time is night. However,
he returns, dances about mumbling to himself, and after a
good deal of hocus-pocus, in which he is assisted by a woman
helper, he kneels beside the patient, puts his mouth to the
body of the sufferer, then stands up, rushes to the door, and
spits out the sickness.

Thus with the help of the spirits he has got rid of the
illness. The next thing to be done is to recall the absent
soul (*amiroe*) of the sufferer. As the expulsion of the malady
has occupied the whole night, the recalling of the soul
has to be reserved for the following night. After the medicine-man has ascertained what spirit has carried off the
patient's soul, he prepares a puppet and offers it to the spirit
instead of the sick person, begging him to release the captive
soul. But the method of procedure varies according to the
nature of the spirit that has carried off the soul. If it is a
spirit of the air which has abstracted the soul, the medicine-
man may employ the small model of a boat (*sampan*) with a
little wooden bird attached to the top of the mast. The bird
typifies the flight through the air, and the soul of the medicine-man goes with it to seek and find the lost soul of the
patient. He brings the soul back in a little box, and drawing
it cautiously out, mixes it with oil, and rubs the oil on the
patient's head. The lost soul returns to the patient's body
through the fontanel.

If the soul of the patient has been carried off by a forest spirit a board is employed on which the body of a snake is painted, with a wooden snake's head attached to it. This board is hung by cords from the roof ; the medicine-man seats himself on it and swings to and fro. He is supposed to be thus searching all the nooks and corners of the wood for the lost soul, till he finds it and restores it to the sufferer in the manner already described. If the soul has been carried off by the spirit of a dead relation, the medicine-man brings it back from under the earth. A common way to recover a lost soul is to set a little lamp burning before the door. The first insect that flies into it is regarded as the lost soul. The medicine-man rubs it in pieces with oil, and smears the oil on the patient's head. If a water-spirit, for example the spirit of a fish, is thought to have caused the sickness, the medicine-man makes a similar fish out of dough, into which the guilty water-spirit creeps, taking with him the soul of the sick person. By a dexterous movement the medicine-man draws the soul out of the fish and restores it to the body of the sufferer. Then he stabs the dough image of the fish with a spear and threatens to kill the water-spirit if he will not leave the man's spirit alone. When cholera is raging, a rough gateway, consisting of uprights with a cross-piece, is erected at the entrance to the village, and rude effigies in human form, one for every person in the village and representing him or her as a substitute, are attached to it. This structure is intended to arrest the spirit of cholera, and to induce him to accept the puppets instead of the people.[1]

Among the Kayans of Sarawak in Borneo in cases of serious illness of mysterious origin that seem to threaten to end mortally, the theory generally adopted is that the patient's soul has left his body, and the treatment indicated is therefore an attempt to persuade the soul to return. For this purpose recourse is had to the services of a professional soul-catcher or medium (*Dayong*). Among the Kayans the professional soul-catcher is generally a woman who has served a considerable period of apprenticeship with some older member of the profession, after having been admonished to take up this

[1] P. te Wechel, " Erinnerungen aus den Ost- und West Dusun-Ländern (Borneo)," in *Internationales Archiv für Ethnologie*, xxii. (1915) pp. 44-53

calling by some being met with in dreams.   If on being called
in the medium decides that the soul (*Blua*) of the patient has
left his body, and has made some part of the journey towards
the abode of departed souls, his task is to fall into a trance
and to send his own soul to overtake that of his patient and
persuade it to return.   The ceremony is usually performed
by torch-light in the presence of a circle of interested relatives
and friends, the patient being laid in the long public gallery
of the house.   The medium struts to and fro chanting a
traditional form of words well known to the people, who join
in the chorus at the close of each phrase, responding with the
words, " Oh powerful medium."   The chant opens with a
prayer for help, addressed, if the medium is a man, to the
high god (*Laki Tenangan*), or, if the medium is a woman, to
the god's wife (*Doh Tenangan*).   The medium may or may
not fall and lie inert upon the ground in the course of his
trance ; but throughout the greater part of the ceremony he
continues to chant with closed eyes, describing with words
and mimic gestures the doings of his own soul as it follows
after and eventually overtakes that of the patient.   When
this point is reached his gestures generally express the difficulty and severity of the efforts required to induce the soul to
return ; and the anxious relatives then usually encourage
him by bringing out gongs or other articles of value, and
depositing them as additions to the medium's fee.   Thus
stimulated, he usually succeeds in leading back the soul
towards the patient's body.   One feature of the ceremony
is that the medium takes in his hand a sword, and, glancing
at the polished blade with a startled air, seems to catch in it
a glimpse of the wandering soul.   The next step is to restore
the soul to the body.   The medium comes out of his trance
with the air of one who is suddenly transported from distant
scenes, and usually exhibits in his palm some small living
creature, or it may be merely a grain of rice, a pebble, or bit
of wood, in which the captured soul is supposed to be contained.   This he places on the crown of the patient's head,
and by rubbing causes it to pass into the head.   The soul
having been thus restored to the body, it is needful to prevent
it from escaping again ; and this is done by tying a strip of
palm-leaf about the patient's wrist.   A fowl is then killed,

or, in very severe cases of sickness, a pig, and its blood
sprinkled or wiped by means of the sword or knife upon this
confining bracelet.   In mild cases the fowl may be waved
over the head of the patient without being killed.   The
medium then gives directions as to the taboos (*malan*) to
be observed by the patient, especially in regard to articles of
diet, and retires, leaving his fee to be sent after him.   The
catching of souls is practised in very similar fashion among
all the peoples of Borneo, even by the Punans, though the
details of the procedure differ from tribe to tribe.[1]

Among the Kachins of Burma when sickness is complicated by delirium or unconsciousness, friends attribute this
state to the absence of the patient's soul from his body, for
they believe that the soul may depart, above all in sleep, on
an outing of its own, or may be carried off by spirits.   If the
diviner declares that the soul has been captured and detained
by spirits (*nats*), they free it from their clutches by honouring
them with a festival.   When they suppose that the soul has
gone off of its own account, the medicine-man (*dumsa*), or
in his default the persons present, seek it and call it in a loud
voice, first of all in the neighbourhood of the house ;   then
some people set off with a small basket of provisions to scour
the paths and the woods, shouting, " O Soul of such a one,
do not remain in the forest where the mosquitoes bite and the
tigers devour ;   return to the house to rejoin your friends, to
drink this spirit, to eat these eggs, this flesh, and so forth."
When they believe they have discovered it they lead it back
to the house, where they offer it a small feast.   If the patient
continues unconscious, they have recourse to the domestic
spirits.   A priest gives or promises them eggs, dried fish,
fowls, and so forth, and sends them in pursuit of the wandering soul, to seek and find it in whatever quarter of earth or
heaven they may discover it.[2]

Among the Palaungs of Burma, " if the wise man sees
that his patient cannot live, he tells the mother or any near
relative to call back the spirit that he fears is departing from

---

[1] C. Hose and W. McDougall, *The
Pagan Tribes of Borneo* (London,
1912), ii. 30.

[2] R. P. Ch. Gilhodes, " Maladies

et remèdes chez les Katchins (Bir-
manie)," in *Anthropos*, x.-xi. (1915–
1916) p. 25.

the sick person.   If there is a woman who is able to call, men never do it.   This calling is done at night or in the early hours of the morning while it is still dark.   White paper flags, white flowers—if it is possible to find any—a few grains of cooked rice, a little curry, water in a tiny joint of bamboo, and a few strands of white thread are placed in a bag and carried outside, down the stairway of the front veranda, and set on the lowest step.   The mouth of the bag is opened wide, then, standing on the ground beside the steps the mother calls to the departing spirit.   Repeating the name of her child again and again, in accents of grief, she continues, ' O my darling child !   I have come out to call thee.   Do not wander, do not fly from us into the dark night.   The spirits may hurt thee, the fireflies may burn thee.   Come back to me, O my child !   Fall into this water, alight on this food. Here it is dark and cold, in our home the fire burns brightly on the hearth.   I do not set thee free, I will not let thee go. I take and keep thy shadow.   I take and hold thy spirit. Come back, come back, my darling child !   Come to me quickly.'   She repeats this invocation several times.   A sister, wife, or friend may call, but only one person calls at a time.   The invocation ends with a long, wailing cry.   When people in the neighbouring houses hear that cry they shut their doors, so that the wandering spirit may not mistake its own home and enter theirs.

"When the calling is finished, the bag is closed and carried as quickly as possible into the entrance-room, where relatives and friends are sitting round the fire.   The woman who has been calling says, ' It may be that the spirit of X has re-turned.'   The others, when they hear this, call words of encouragement to the sick person, announcing the return of his spirit, and the mother, hurrying into the inner room, says, ' We have called back thy spirit, it is here in thy food.   Try to eat this rice and curry, drink this water, smell these flowers, so that thy spirit may return into thy body.'   The patient tries to eat and drink, and the white threads are tied round the wrists." [1]

The Lakhers of Assam think that a sore throat or swell-ings on the throat are caused by a snake having been killed

---

[1] Mrs. L. Milne, *The Home of Eastern Clan*, pp. 287 *sq.*

in a rat-trap belonging to the sick man or by one of his family. If it is known that a snake has actually been caught in the sick man's rat-trap or killed by one of his family, a sacrifice must be offered at the place where the snake was killed. If it is only suspected that the killing of a snake has been the cause of the disease, the sacrifice is offered outside the village by the side of the path. Small earthen images of men, *mithun*, cows, lizards, tortoises, brass basins, gongs, and *pumtek* beads are prepared and placed in an old basket. An image of a snake is fashioned out of an image of bamboo by cutting the surface of the bamboo to represent the snake's markings. The sacrificer ties a string round the neck of the bamboo snake and goes out to the place of sacrifice, holding the basket of clay images in one hand and dragging the snake along behind him. The idea is that the soul of the dead snake will follow the bamboo snake as it is dragged along the ground, and when it reaches the place where the sacrifice is held will see all the clay figures and, thinking them real, will accept them instead of the sick man, who will then recover. A dog and a fowl are sacrificed and their blood sprinkled on the clay images. The bodies of the dog and the fowl are never eaten by the people, but left on the spot for the snake, who would think himself defrauded if portions of the victims had been devoured by the people. Among the Hawthais the ritual in such a case is still more elaborate. In addition to the ceremonies and sacrifice already described, a small rat-trap is placed on the veranda of the sick man's house. Near it are placed a chopping-knife (*dao*) and an old earthen pot. Having done this, the sacrificer goes outside the village and lights a fire, so that if the sick man's soul has been taken some distance away it may see the smoke and return to its home. He then lays down the clay models and other articles as before, kills a small fowl, which he leaves where he killed it, and returns to the village, taking with him two small pebbles. Before entering the sick man's house he stops on the ladder and calls out to the sick man " Has your spirit returned to you ? " The sick man replies, " It has returned." The sacrificer and his companions then enter the house and shut the door. The notion is that while they are inside the house with the door

shut a snake may come and be crushed in the rat-trap, cut
by the cutting-knife, and cooked in the earthen pot, the rat-
trap, chopping-knife and earthen pot having been made in
case the snake should refuse the sacrifices and try to re-enter
the house.   The two pebbles are placed on the floor of the
house, and another fowl is sacrificed on them to prevent the
sick man's soul from going outside the house again.   The
two pebbles represent the sick man's soul, which is brought
back into the house again, and to which a fowl is sacrificed
to induce it to remain.   The meat of this fowl is cooked and
eaten by the sacrificer, the sick man, and their families.
The use of pebbles to represent the soul of a sick man is
common among the Lakhers.[1]

Among the Garos, another tribe of Assam, in a case of
very serious illness, recourse is had to a certain ceremony,
called *denjaringa*, which is performed in the following manner.   Near the stream from which the invalid obtains his
supply of water a place is cleared in the jungle, and on this
spot a sort of altar (*sambasia*) is erected, together with various
bamboo receptacles for offerings of rice, cotton, and so forth.
The officiating priest (*kamal*) sacrifices a fowl, smears its
blood as usual over the altar, and plasters the bamboos with
the bird's feathers.   He then ties one end of the cotton thread
to the altar, leads it to the sick man's house, and fastens the
other end in the room in which the patient is lying.   On the
string a sprig of *kimbal* (*Callicarpa arborea*) leaves is hung.
The notion is that if the sick man's spirit leaves his body it
may be induced to return by the prayers of his friends, and
will be able to find its way back by means of the thread as a
guide.   Outside the house the priest takes up his stand, and
during the whole day calls upon Tatara-Rabuga (the God
of the Earth) to cure the sick person.   A horn is blown
continuously the while to frighten away the evil spirit which
is afflicting the sufferer.   When night falls, if there has been
no change in his condition the priest addresses his prayers
to the spirit Bidawe, who steals the souls of men, and continues his intercession as before.   This having been kept up
until a late hour, the cotton string is examined where the
leaves were hung, and if it shows any sign of having sagged

[1] N. E. Parry, *The Lakhers*, pp. 457 *sqq.*

it is believed that the sick man's soul has come back, and that he will recover.   The string is then broken, and a piece of it tied round the neck of the invalid, drums and musical instruments strike up in his room, and his relations greatly rejoice.[1]

Among the Lushais, another tribe of Assam, it sometimes happens that a man returning from a shooting expedition experiences a sudden feeling of fear near the water supply, and on reaching his house feels ill and out of sorts.   He then thinks that he has lost one of his souls (*thlarau*) in the jungle. So he calls in a wizard (*puithiam*), and requests him to call back the wanderer.   The wizard then hangs the head of a hoe on to the shaft of a spear and goes down to the water spring chanting a charm and calling on the soul to return. As he goes the iron hoe head jingles against the iron butt of the spear and the soul hears the noise and listens.   The wizard returns to the house still chanting and calling, and the soul follows him, but should the wizard laugh or look back the soul is afraid and flies back to the jungle.[2]

In Kan-sou, a province of China, when a man returns on a journey on which he has had an accident and been wounded, it is thought that he has left his soul behind him on the spot. An exorcist is then employed to recover the lost soul.   Taking a pair of the wounded man's trousers with him, he repairs to the spot where the accident took place, recalls the soul of the sufferer, folds it up in the trousers, and conveys it back to the wounded man, to whom he restores it by dressing him in the garment.[3]

In Africa, among the Mossi, a tribe of the French or Western Sudan, a sacrifice which is called " the hidden sacrifice " is offered for a person who is at the point of death. A native doctor or medicine-man, being called in, may declare that the patient's soul has passed out of his body, and that it may be found in the *tangande*, or sanctuary of the Guardian Spirit of the village, who in the shape of an animal has his sanctuary in the forest.   Without the knowledge of the patient, whence comes the name of " the hidden sacrifice," his father goes to the sanctuary in the forest,

[1] A. Playfair, *The Garos*, pp. 91 *sq.*
[2] J. Shakespear, *The Lushei-Kuki Clans* (London, 1912), p. 76.
[3] P. J. Dols, " La Vie chinoise dans la Province de Kan-sou," in *Anthropos*, x.-xi. (1915-1916) pp. 729 *sq.*

accompanied by another child who carries the victim and the water, and the mother of the patient, who carries a large calabash half filled with water, in which she places a smaller calabash floating.   At the sanctuary the fowl is sacrificed, and while the child is roasting the fowl the sacrificer throws upon the earth three cowries if it is a boy who is ill, four if it is a girl, and pours out a little water, then calls the patient by his name, " Bila, come, answer me."   He calls a boy three times, a girl four times.   Then he takes the cowries and a lump of earth mixed with water and the blood of the victim.   His wife takes up the small calabash which floats in the water, the sacrificer puts the bloody mud and the cowries in the large calabash, and his wife quickly puts the small calabash inverted over everything and holds it at the bottom of the water.   The same performance is repeated three or four times according to the sex of the patient, then the woman takes the road home, bearing the large calabash in one hand, and always holding the small calabash so that it does not come to the surface, while the sacrificer follows her, brandishing his sword or his spear behind her to drive off evil spirits.   The soul of the sick person is believed to be at the bottom of the water, among the bloody mud and the cowries, and it is necessary to prevent it at all costs from escaping anew.   When the procession reaches the patient's house they make him sit down, and the woman pours over his head the water from the large calabash, always without raising the small one.   If the patient, surprised by this unexpected splash of water, gives a sudden start, he is saved, his soul has returned into his body ; but if he does not, there is nothing to do but to abandon him to his unhappy fate ; the Guardian Spirit of the village will not give up his soul.   The sacrificer and his assistants eat of the flesh of the victim, but the sick man himself does not partake of it.[1]

The Eskimo of the Mackenzie River in North America thinks that sickness is often caused by the absence of the patient's soul, which has been stolen from him by a shaman. When that happens another shaman is called in to recover the missing soul, and restore it to the sufferer.   The shaman who has been invoked to act as physician has nothing to do

[1] P. E. Mangin, " Les Mossi," in *Anthropos*, x.-xi. (1915–1916) p. 203.

but to summon his familiar spirits and send them out over all the earth in search of the place where the soul has been forcibly confined. Eventually one of the spirits will find the soul, unless indeed it has been placed in some cavity or hole the mouth of which has been greased with seal or whale oil, for in that case neither will the soul be able to pass out of such a confinement nor will the spirit which is searching for the soul be able to enter in order to find it. When a shaman steals a man's soul and wants to be sure that no other shaman shall be able to recover it for him, the favourite hiding-place of the stolen soul is one of the foramina of the lower maxillary bone of the bow-head whale.[1]

We have seen that some primitive people believe a person's soul to be in his shadow or reflection, so that any injury done to the shadow or reflection is felt by him as an injury to himself.[2] Among the Baganda of Central Africa "no man liked another to tread upon his shadow, or to have his shadow speared; and children were warned not to allow the fire to cast their shadow upon the wall of the house, lest they should die from having seen themselves as a shadow. At meals no one sat so as to cast his shadow over the food, for this was considered dangerous to all who were at the meal."[3] Similarly among the Banyoro, another tribe of Uganda, "a man's shadow was supposed to be a part of himself. He therefore took care it should not be speared, trodden upon or in any wise injured, lest he too should suffer in like manner."[4]

It is a Hausa belief that a person's soul is in his shadow, and that it may be caught in the following manner. "If a wizard sees a person whom he wishes to injure coming along, he will wait near a stone or a wall, or close to any projection upon which the shadow of the enemy must fall as he passes. When this has happened, the wizard at once claps his hand upon the shadow, and picks out the soul, keeping it in his fist until he has reached his house, when he quickly places a vessel over his hand and transfers the soul to it—as one does a rare beetle."[5]

---

[1] V. Stefansson, *My Life with the Eskimos* (London, 1913), pp. 393 *sq.*

[2] See above, pp. 202 *sq.* Cf. *Taboo and the Perils of the Soul*, pp. 77 *sqq.*

[3] J. Roscoe, *The Baganda*, p. 23.

[4] J. Roscoe, *The Northern Bantu*, p. 97.

[5] A. J. N. Tremearne, *The Ban of the Bori*, p. 133.

Among many tribes of Southern Nigeria it is believed
that if the shadow is hurt the body also will be damaged.
The shadow is often believed to be a representation of one
of a man's souls.   Among the Yoruba a person can be injured
or killed by throwing a " medicine " made of " alligator "
peppers upon his shadow or by slashing at it with a knife.
If the shadow hand is touched, the medicine is thought to
enter into the man's own hand, make a big sore and cause
blood-poisoning, which will bring about his death unless
counteracting medicines are obtained.   The Ijaw are much
afraid of being injured through their shadow ; they are
greatly vexed if another sets his foot upon their shadow,
while if a dagger is thrown at it it is thought that the man
will suffer great harm.   All the Ibo, save those in the
Abakiliki and Obolo Divisions, believe that a man can be
hurt by " medicine " put upon his shadow.   Some in the
west think that it harms, and might even kill, a man if
another treads on his shadow.   Most Semi-Bantu have
similar beliefs.   Many Ibibio think that the soul is affected
by physical or magical action on the shadow.   Men sometimes tread on that of their enemies or throw a dagger at
it, while " doctors " place medicines on it.   The Bantu
think that " doctors " can make a medicine which will
destroy a man's shadow, as a consequence of which he will
die.[1]   Similarly the Kai of Northern New Guinea identify
the shadow with the soul, and a man is therefore much concerned if anyone treads on his shadow.[2]   Among the Boloki
or Bangala of the Upper Congo " the shadow of a person, his
reflection in water, or in a looking-glass, and more recently
a photograph, is called by a word (elilingi) that is often used
interchangeably with the word for soul (elimo).   They
repeatedly informed me that ' a dead person casts no shadow,'
and that therefore he has no soul, hence to say that So-and-
So has no shadow is, with them, the equivalent to saying
that he has no soul, i.e. that he is dead. . . . If for some
reason a man does not see his shadow reflected when he
looks into some water, he thinks someone has taken his
spirit away, and that he will soon die.   Even if at midday

[1] P. A. Talbot, The Peoples of   Life in Southern Nigeria, p. 119.
Southern Nigeria, ii. 183. Cf. id.   [2] R. Neuhauss, op. cit. iii. 111.

he does not see his shadow, because he is standing on it—
the sun being absolutely vertical at noon so near the Equator
—he will go to a witch-doctor, who will make medicine that
he may recover his shadow or soul."[1]

But in the opinion of some primitive peoples, not merely
the shadow or reflection is a source of danger to the person
who casts it. The likeness of another person to him may be
equally dangerous, because he thinks that the other must
have abstracted some portion of his own soul. This fear is
particularly entertained with regard to children who resemble
their parents. Thus according to the Toradyas of Central
Celebes the commonest death is due to the absence of the
soul. And they say that the reason why so many children
die is because they resemble their father or mother. They
say that such a child has taken part of the soul-stuff of one
of his parents. If the greatest part of the soul-stuff remains
with the parent, the child soon dies. But if the child has
the greatest part, then his father or his mother dies.[2] Similarly " the exact likeness of a male child to his father, that
is, the possession of two hosts by the same soul, causes alarm
to a Malay ; one of the boy's ears must be pierced, otherwise
either the father or the son is likely to die. Curiously, the
resemblance of a girl to her father or of a boy or girl to the
mother is of no moment."[3]

Elsewhere we have seen that primitive peoples have often
been in the habit of laying the foundations of buildings upon
the bodies of human victims in order that the souls of the
victims may guard or strengthen the foundations.[4] To the
examples there cited I may here add a few more. When
King Mindon laid the foundations of the new capital,
Mandalay, in 1857, " he acted on the advice of his chief
astrologer, and a pregnant woman was slain one night in
order that she might become the guardian spirit of his
palace. Throughout the whole of his reign offerings were
openly made by the king to the spirit of the murdered
woman, which was supposed to be incarnated in the body
of a snake. This is a strange and strong proof of animistic

[1] J. H. Weeks, *Among Congo Cannibals*, pp. 262 *sq.*

[2] N. Adriani and A. C. Kruijt, *op. cit.* ii. 56, 84.

[3] R. O. Winstedt, *Shaman, Saiva, and Sufi*, p. 14.

[4] *Taboo and the Perils of the Soul*, pp. 90 *sqq.*

worship on the part of one who was most unquestionably a most religious Buddhist, and the most enlightened of all the monarchs of the Alaung Paya dynasty. . . . At all the gates in the city walls, and at the four corners, male victims were also done to death—being buried alive, it is said, along with large jars of oil—according to the ceremony known as *Sadé*, for the purpose of providing guardian spirits to keep watch and ward over all the lines of approach to the city. Small white-washed pagoda-like tumuli outside the gates and the corners of the outer walls still form the abodes of these guardian spirits of the city (*Myozade*)." [1] " In old times it was the custom in the Shan States, as in Burma, to bury alive a man or woman under the palace or the gates of a new city, so that the spirits of the dead in guarding the place from human enemies should also keep evil spirits, that bring sickness, at a distance." [2]

The Toradyas of Central Celebes used to bury slaves alive under the foundations of the houses which they were building. We read of one case in which a man visiting a district found the people engaged in building a temple. They had just dug a deep hole to receive the central post, and they invited him to go down into the hole and dig it deeper. He consented and went down into the hole, but no sooner had he done so than they struck him down, and lowered the main post upon him, crushing him under its weight. [3]

About the middle of the nineteenth century an Englishman, John Jackson, saw men buried alive with the posts of a new house of the king of Fiji. [4] In Mala, one of the Solomon Islands, it is said that formerly when a chief's house was building, the first of the three central posts used to be lowered on a human victim buried alive beneath it. The practice is mentioned in many folklore stories current among the natives. [5] A similar practice seems to have been observed by the Maoris of New Zealand at building a chief's house, temple, or other important edifice. On this subject Mr.

[1] J. Nisbet, *Burma under British Rule* (London, 1901), pp. 195 *sq.*

[2] Mrs. L. Milne, *The Shans at Home* (London, 1910), pp. 178 *sq.*

[3] N. Adriani and A. C. Kruijt, *op. cit.* i. 203 *sq.*

[4] J. E. Erskine, *Journal of a Cruise among the Islands of the Western Pacific* (London, 1853), p. 464.

[5] W. G. Ivens, *Melanesians of the South-East Solomon Islands* (London, 1927), p. 32.

Tregear, a good authority on the people, writes as follows :
" A more terrible ceremony accompanied the opening of
very grand houses, such as a temple or council-hall. A
member of the tribe was killed and his heart was cut out,
cooked, and eaten by the officiating priest, with many
incantations uttered the while. Among the East Coast
tribes the body was buried inside the house at the base of the
end-slab (*poupou-tuarongo*) next the back of the building,
on the left side looking from the entrance. Among the
Arawa, Urewera, and many other tribes the body was
buried at the foot of the central pillar, the *pou-tokomanawa*.
The body of the victim was called a ' stone ' (*whatu*) for he
was the foundation-stone of the new edifice. In some cases,
after a lapse of time, exhumation took place and the bones
would be taken to a shrine or altar (*tuahu*) to be deposited
as a spiritual influence (*manea*) for the owner of the house.
Not only was a near relative needed as a sacrifice of this
kind, but even a favourite child of the ruling chief might be
selected. Taraia, to make sacred his new house at Herepu,
near Karamu, Hawke's Bay, slew his youngest boy and
offered him as a *whatu*. Thus goes the lullaby-song (*oriori*) :

> Then Taraia built his house,
> Placing his youngest child
> As a *whatu* for the rearmost pillar
> Of his house Te Raro-akiaki.

Instances have been known of the sacrifice of slaves as *whatu*,
but ordinary men were not of sufficient consequence for
such a purpose. If, however, a distinguished captive were
available the victim might suffice, as Te Whakororo, when
captured by the Ati-Hapai tribe, was used as a *whatu* for
their great temple, Te Uro o Manono. His bones, exhumed
and hung up within the building, guided by their rattling
his son Whakatau to the place to wreak vengeance for the
insult." [1]

In Africa, when a king of Agbor in Southern Nigeria
built a shrine for his ancestral spirits, he caused a man and a
woman to be killed and buried under the foundations of the
edifice. [2]

---

[1] E. Tregear, *The Maori Race*
(Wangammi, New Zealand, 1904), pp.
279 *sqq.*

[2] P. A. Talbot, *The Peoples of
Southern Nigeria*, iii. 863.

CHAPTER XX

TABOOED ACTS

SAVAGES are commonly very shy of entering a strange land, because they fear the spirits of the unknown country and the magic of the inhabitants. Accordingly before crossing the boundary they often observe ceremonies for the purpose of disenchanting the land, and assuring for themselves a safe passage through it. In such a case the Maoris of New Zealand used to perform a ceremony called *Uruuru-whenua*. " This is a ceremony performed by a person who, for the first time, ascends a mountain, crosses a lake, or enters a district never before traversed by him. The term implies ' to enter or become of the land.' It is an offering to the spirits of the strange land. It is generally performed at a tree or rock situated on the trail by which travellers pass into the district. Every person on passing such places for the first time would pluck a twig or piece of fern and cast it at the base of the tree or stone, at the same time repeating a short invocation to the spirits of the land. After passing on such a person would never look back towards the tree ; it would be an evil omen were he to do so." [1]

Savages commonly fear to be injured through the relics of their food, because if these fall into the hands of an enemy he might cast a spell upon them which would react with serious, or even fatal effect, on the original eater. For example in the Kakadu tribe of Northern Australia " another form of practising evil magic amongst the Kakadu consists in

---

[1] Elsdon Best, " Notes on Some Customs and Superstitions of the Maori," in the *Sixth Report of the* *Australasian Association for the Advancement of Science* (1895), pp. 765 *sq.*

a man who desires to injure an enemy securing some fragment of food that the latter has been eating.   First of all he ties it up in paper bark and takes it away, unknown to anyone else, to his own camp where he pounds it up and sings over it, thereby projecting evil magic into it.   Then he ties it up again and takes it to an ant-hill, at the base of which he makes a small hole, pushes the food inside, and closes the hole so that it cannot be seen.   This form of magic is supposed to be very effective and to act rapidly.   Within three days the man becomes very hot, continually cries out for water and soon dies." [1]

Among the natives near Cape King William in Northern New Guinea a sorcerer who desires to injure an enemy obtains some relics of the man's food, ties them up in a packet, and hangs it over a fire.   As the relics dry up, so the strength of his enemy wastes away, and he finally dies.   But sometimes the magical treatment lasts longer.   The sorcerer retires with the packet into the solitude of the forest.   He there under an overhanging rock kindles a fire, and puts the packet in a hole below the fire.   After one or two days he takes the packet out and strikes it with a stone.   This is thought to give the final blow to his enemy ; but the sorcerer remains in seclusion until the news of his victim's death is brought to him.   But if his intended victim obstinately persists in living it often ends by the sorcerer hanging himself. [2]

[1] Baldwin Spencer, *Native Tribes of the Northern Territory of Aus-* *tralia*, p. 260.

[2] R. Neuhauss, *op. cit.* iii. 248 *sq.*

CHAPTER XXI

TABOOED PERSONS

WE have seen that kings and chiefs in primitive society are subject to many taboos.[1] To the examples already given one or two more may here be added. The king of the Banyoro in Uganda might not touch his food with his hands, hence he had to be fed by another. The ceremony of feeding him is thus described by Canon Roscoe : " When the cook took the food to the king he smeared his head, face, arms, and chest with white clay after the manner of the milk-men who were going to milk the sacred cows. He had two iron prongs with sockets to fit on his finger and thumb, these prongs being used to lift the meat and put it in the king's mouth, as the king was not permitted to touch his food with his hands. The cook had to be careful not to touch the king's teeth with the iron prongs, as such an offence was punishable with death." [2]

Some interesting details as to the taboos observed with reference to chiefs in Samoa are furnished by a missionary, as follows : " Much order and, in case of chiefs, some ceremony was formally observed during meals, in their heathen state. Chiefs of rank, called *Alli pa'ia*, or sacred chiefs, always partook of their meals separately, since whatever they touched was supposed to partake of their sacredness, so that all food left by them at the close of a meal was taken to the bush and thrown away, as it was believed that if a person not of this sacred class ate of it, his stomach would immediately swell from disease, and death speedily ensue ! " [3] The sacredness

---

[1] See above, pp. 194 *sqq.*
[2] J. Roscoe, *The Northern Bantu,* p. 13.
[3] J. B. Stair, *Old Samoa* (London, 1897), p. 121.

attributed to many chiefs of high rank gave rise to observances which were irksome to their families and dependants, since whatever they came in contact with required to undergo the ceremony *lulu'u*, or sprinkling with a particular kind of coconut-water both to remove the sanctity supposed to be communicated to the article or place that had touched the chief, and also to counteract the danger of speedy death, which was believed to be imminent to any person who might touch the sacred chief, or anything that he had touched ; so great was the mantle of sanctity thrown round these chiefs, although unconnected with the priesthood. Thus the spot where such a chief had sat or slept was sprinkled with water immediately he had left it, as were also the persons who had sat on either side of him when he received company, as well as all the attendants who had waited upon him. This remarkable custom was also observed on other occasions. It was always used on the occasion of deposing a chief, and depriving him of his *Ao* or titles, in which case the ceremony was either performed by some of those who had either conferred the titles or had the power to do so. In the case of O le Tamafainga, the usurper who was killed in A'ana in 1829, his body was first sprinkled with coconut-water, and his title of *O le Tuia'ana* recalled from him, before he was hewn in pieces. The ceremony consisted of sprinkling the body with coconut-water, and the officiating chief or *Tulafale* saying, ' Give us back our *Ao*,' by which means the title was recalled, and the sacredness attaching to it was dispelled. It was also used over persons newly tattooed, and upon those who contaminated themselves by contact with a dead body. In each of these cases the ceremony was carefully observed, and reverently attended to, as very dire consequences were considered certain to follow its omission." [1]

Mourners, like chiefs, are subject to many taboos, in consequence of their contact with, or relation to, the dead. Thus in Annam mourners are not allowed to marry or to have any sexual relations whatever. The prohibition formerly extended to the whole period of mourning, but it is now re-

---

[1] J. B. Stair, *op. cit.* pp. 128 *sq.* As to the Samoan purifications by sprinkling with coconut-water, compare G. Brown, *Melanesians and Polynesians*, p. 231.

stricted to the three days after the death, during which it is absolute, and during these days they are further forbidden to chew betel, to drink alcohol, and to eat flesh.[1]

Women, again, are the subjects or objects of many taboos at menstruation and childbirth. For example, among the Ila-speaking people of Northern Rhodesia the doctor or medicine-man warns a hunter against allowing a menstruous woman to enter the hut in which he keeps his gun, for she would inevitably render it useless. And when traders are about to start on a journey he warns each of them to beware especially of menstruous women, bidding him not to allow one of them to touch his food on the journey. To do this would be to destroy his luck.[2]

In primitive society such women are commonly supposed to be in a dangerous condition which might infect anyone who came into contact with them. Hence at such times they are isolated and subject to many taboos. Among the Birhors of the Chota Nagpur in India a parturient woman, except in a few clans, has a new doorway made for the room in which she is to be confined, and for a certain number of days after delivery, during which her touch is taboo to others, she must use this new door only ; but the number of days varies in different clans. Thus in the Ludamba clan the woman is allowed to use the old door after seven days from the day of delivery, in most other cases after twenty-one days, and in the Maghaia Hembrom clan after five weeks if the new-born baby is a female and after six weeks if it is a male. In most clans, again, but not in all, long wooden fences are put up on both sides of the pathway leading to this new door, so that the woman's dangerous spirit may not fall on other people.[3] In the Kawan clan of the Birhors when a woman is about to be confined, " her husband makes for her a separate shed with leaves and branches in which she is left alone. As soon as a baby is born to her, a tiger, it is said, invariably enters the shed, cleanses the limbs of the baby by licking them, and opens a back-door to the shed for the woman to go out and come in during her days of ceremonial taboo." [4]

---

[1] P. Giran, *Magie et Religion Annamites*, p. 405.
[2] E. W. Smith and A. M. Dale, *The Ila-speaking Peoples of Northern Rhodesia*, i. 262 *sq.*
[3] S. C. Roy, *The Birhors*, pp. 114 *sq.*
[4] S. C. Roy, *op. cit.* p. 110.

A pregnant Hindoo woman " must not wear clothes over which a bird has flown. She must not wear a knot in her dress (*sari*) where it is fastened round her waist. In order to avoid the contact of evil spirits she must not walk or sit in the open courtyard of her house, and must wear a thin reed five inches long in her hair. . . . When the hour of birth draws near, as a mother is ceremonially unclean for three weeks if she has given birth to a son, and if to a daughter for a month, her touch is defiling, and she cannot remain in the house. A shed is therefore provided for her temporary home. In the houses of the poor a lumber-room is generally used ; whilst in the large mansions a separate building is kept for this purpose. These places are destitute of furniture, a little straw being spread for the woman to lie upon. Here she must remain until the day of her purification. . . . The skull of a cow smeared with red paint is reared against the wall to drive away evil spirits. An image of Sasthi, the goddess who presides over married women and children, made of cow-dung, is placed in a conspicuous place and specially honoured. During all this time neither husband nor father, sister nor mother, may touch her, lest they be defiled, the poor woman being left entirely to the tender mercies of a barber's wife, whose reign is supreme over her and her child. When European ladies try to induce the friends to show a little more consideration to the invalid, their entreaties are met by the assurance that any departure from the custom of ages would anger Sasthi." [1] In Annam it is believed that the effusion of blood at child-birth is productive of effluvia which are extremely powerful and almost always dangerous. That is why in Cochin-China, when the moment of birth approaches, the woman retires to a house specially prepared for the purpose. Under her bed a continual fire is kept smouldering. This house she inhabits for thirty days after the birth, after which they abandon the house or burn all the things which the woman had handled.[2]

Among the Kai of Northern New Guinea as soon as a pregnant woman feels the first premonitary pangs of child-birth she must leave the village and go into the forest, near

[1] W. J. Wilkins, *Modern Hinduism* (Calcutta, N.D.), pp. 5 *sqq.*

[2] P. Giran, *op. cit.* p. 109.

some water, there to be delivered.   She must observe the
same custom at her monthly periods.   They build for women
at such times a small hut outside the village.   The people
believe that if the pigs were to eat of the blood of women, or
their afterbirth or their menstrual flow, they would imitate
the women by going into the fields and grubbing up the fruits
of the earth, just as the women dig them up.   If the pigs con-
trive to break into the fields in numbers, they blame the
women for not observing the rule of seclusion during their
periods, or at childbirth.[1]   Again, among the Yabim, another
tribe of Northern New Guinea, the husband of a pregnant
woman may not go fishing for bonito, for if he did the fish
would avoid the boat and refuse to be caught, and the
morning after a woman has been delivered of a child the
people may not go out into the fields, for they think that if
they did so the crop of taro would fail.   Evidently they fear
to convey the infection of childbed to the fields by visiting
them too soon after the birth.[2]   Among the Bukaua, another
tribe of Northern New Guinea, a pregnant woman may not
walk on the sea-shore or near the mouth of a river because
it is believed that her blood would kill all the fish.   And her
husband may not go fishing with other men, though he is
not forbidden to try his luck by himself.[3]

   In Efate, one of the New Hebrides, after childbirth, " the
woman is isolated and regarded as unclean until the thirtieth
day, on which day, for the first time, the mother and child
go out of the house and are both purified with sea water.
According to the Efatese notions the *sea* is the great purifying
medium. . . . The name in Efatese for *uncleanness* is *nimam*,
and that of childbirth is called *nimam nafiselan*.   The men
are afraid of it and keep away from the house in which the
birth has taken place.   They say that men by going to or
near the house would contract the *nimam* or uncleanness,
and that in consequence ' their eyes would be darkened
(that is, they would be weak) in war,' and that if, having
contracted it, they went to their plantations, the yams would
rot.   This applies to the day of birth.   A sacred man
(*natamole tabu*) who inadvertently goes near such a house,

[1] R. Neuhauss, *op. cit.* iii. 91.   [3] R. Neuhauss, *op. cit.* iii. 425 *sq.*
[2] R. Neuhauss, *op. cit.* iii. 294.

R

immediately purifies himself by a religious ceremony, as the uncleanness would be fatal to his sacredness or holiness (natabuen)."[1]

Among the Maoris when a male child is born to a chief all his tribe rejoice. But the mother is separated from the inhabitants of the settlement, to prevent her coming in contact with persons engaged in cultivating the sweet potato (*kumara*), lest anything belonging to the mother should be accidentally touched by them, and lest the sweet potato should be affected by her state of *tapu* (taboo) ; for the sacredness of any nursing mother (*rehu-wahine*) is greatly feared.[2]

In Africa among the Bangala of the Upper Congo, " a woman is unclean for a month after confinement, and then she washes and is accounted clean, although she will have washed every day of the month. During this time no man will go near her, nor will a man eat anything she has cooked, but children who have not arrived at the age of puberty will visit the house freely."[3] Among the Kikuyu, a tribe of Kenya, when a woman has recently been confined and the discharges are still unfinished, it has sometimes happened that a cow has come along and licked the stool upon which she was sitting. In such a case she must immediately tell her husband : if not, he will become defiled (*thahu*) and die, and all the other people in the village will become defiled in a lesser degree and will fall ill. The cow must be killed without delay by the elders and is eaten by them ; no person of the village may eat of the meat unless he has been circumcised Masai fashion. Three elders in Kikuyu are said to have died from this defilement (*thahu*) within recent years.[4]

In primitive society again, many taboos are observed by warriors in time of war. Thus for example in Southern Nigeria " special taboos had to be observed before, during, and after fighting ; failure, and perhaps death, would, it was

[1] Rev. D. Macdonald, " Efate," in *Fourth Report of the Australasian Association for the Advancement of Science*, 1892, p. 721.
[2] E. Shortland, *Maori Religion and Mythology* (London, 1882), p. 40.
[3] J. H. Weeks, " Anthropological Notes on the Bangala of the Upper Congo River," in *Journal of the Royal Anthropological Institute*, xl. (1910) p. 417.
[4] C. W. Hobley, " Kikuyu Customs and Beliefs," in *Journal of the Royal Anthropological Institute*, xl. (1910) p. 434.

thought, follow any infraction of them. Almost always it was forbidden to have intercourse with a woman, to eat women's food—soft things such as yams, coco-yams, fish, etc., or for an adult female to cook for them. If a wife had committed adultery and had not informed her husband—or if she committed adultery while her husband was away fighting—it was commonly believed that he would die. No warrior would, if possible, touch another, or his ' medicines ' might be rendered useless." [1] Among the tribes of Southern Nigeria, the Mbo Abaw, who are Bantu, "˙gave the enemy notice of war and fixed a time and place for the fighting, otherwise they would have regarded themselves as ' no better than thieves.' From the day war was decided on, which was generally at least a month beforehand, all the warriors were kept in certain rooms in the king's compound, which were guarded by sentinels with orders to allow no one to go in or out. During the whole of this period they were not permitted to hold intercourse with women nor to eat anything which these had cooked ; they might only partake of foods sanctioned by the ' doctors.' " [2]

Among the Embu, a primitive tribe inhabiting the southern slopes of Mount Elgon in Kenya, before they engage in war "a small hut is constructed in the bush under the supervision of a doctor, who erects in the middle of it a bundle of various branches tied up with charms. The hut is a temporary structure, and only serves as a sort of central shrine. In the bush round this the warriors, sometimes as many as a hundred, go and camp for perhaps a month. There they live quite separate from the rest of the population. They strip off all clothes, but wear their ornaments and use a waist-band of wild sodom apples. Each day for some hours they perform a very monotonous dance in two lines on a sort of follow-the-leader principle. The step is quick and very short. The performers carry weapons and the leaders carry horns, which they blow at intervals. The performers are largely restricted in their behaviour, and are supposed to consume large quantities of meat, if available.

[1] P. A. Talbot, *The Peoples of Southern Nigeria*, iii. 823 *sq.*, 835, 848, 850, 852, 853 *sq.* ; *id.*, *Life in*   *Southern Nigeria*, p. 232.
[2] P. A. Talbot, *The Peoples of Southern Nigeria*, iii. 854 *sqq.*

They must drink no milk or beer and must abstain from sexual intercourse." [1] With regard to the Wa-Giriama, a Bantu tribe of Kenya, we are told that " during war time men do not cohabit with their wives, as they say it brings bad luck to them. They believe that if they do cohabit with their wives during war time they will be unable to kill any of their enemies, and that should they themselves receive a trifling wound it will prove fatal." [2]

Among the Ila-speaking tribes of Northern Rhodesia in time of war " before the actual fighting certain ceremonial observances took place, the principal being a solemn sacrifice to the *muzhimo* or spirit of the district, with prayers for victory and a safe return. All sexual intercourse was avoided, and the women were instructed to remain chaste while their husbands were away fighting, lest harm should befall them. They were also forbidden to throw anything at one another for fear lest their relations should be speared, or to imitate any kind of blow." [3] With regard to these same tribes we are told that " there are a number of particular occasions when sexual intercourse is prohibited to men and women. . . . Above all, men going to war must absolutely have nothing to do with women from the time that preparations are begun and the doctors have started to doctor the army. Breach of this would mean certain death in the fight ; and likely enough bring disaster to the army." [4]

Similarly with regard to the Kiwai Papuans of British New Guinea we read that " before going to war a man must not cohabit with his wife, which under the circumstances is a bad thing, and may cause his death. During the days preceding a fighting expedition the warriors eat in the men's house, and at least in the notions of certain people must avoid having their food cooked by women who are used to sexual intercourse. The young warriors abstain from playing with the girls and do not even speak to them." [5] So

[1] G. St. J. Orde Browne, *The Vanishing Tribes of Kenya*, p. 176.

[2] W. E. H. Barrett, " Notes on the Customs and Beliefs of the Wa-Giriama, British East Africa," in *Journal of the Royal Anthropological Institute*, xli. (1911) p. 22.

[3] E. W. Smith and A. M. Dale, *op. cit.* i. 176.

[4] *Ibid.* ii. 44.

[5] G. Landtman, " The Magic of the Kiwai Papuans in Warfare," in *Journal of the Royal Anthropological Institute*, xlvi. (1916) p. 323. Cf. W. N. Beaver, *Unexplored New Guinea*, p. 173.

again the Melanesians of New Britain " were very particular in preserving chastity during or before a fight, and they believed that if a man slept with his wife he would be killed or wounded." [1]

Warriors who have slain a foe in battle have commonly to submit to a number of special taboos, followed by purification, for the purpose of guarding them against the vengeful ghosts of the slain. To the examples of these customs which I have given elsewhere,[2] I may add the following. Thus among the Banyankole, a tribe of Uganda, " the warrior who had killed a man was treated like a murderer or a hunter who had killed a lion, leopard, antelope, or hyena (because these animals belonged to the gods) ; he was not allowed to sleep or eat with others until he had been purified, for the ghost of the man was upon him." [3] Among the Elgeyo, a tribe of Kenya, " the slayer of a foeman did not return immediately to his hut, but went to a cave or overhanging rock for ten days. During this period he daily from 4 A.M. till 7 P.M. chanted his prowess as a warrior. His food was brought to him by male friends. No females or young children were allowed to approach him. Old men who in their time had killed enemies cut on his right forearm eight parallel rings, called *caulli*. Each ring was formed by making a series of small parallel cuts in line round the arm. The *caulli* were cut on the left arm of a left-handed man. In cases where, say, four spears pierced a foeman before he died, the thrower of the first spear was entitled to have five rings, the second to four, the third to three, and the fourth to two. A few survivors of the ' Kimnyegeo ' and the ' Kablalach ' age-clans still proudly display their *caulli*. At the end of the ten days a white goat was slaughtered by the men who had operated on his arm. They took the undigested contents of its stomach and rubbed this on the warrior's face and body. Until this was done, the young man was not allowed to wash, as it was feared that if he did so the stream or spring at which he washed would dry up. After this ceremony he was permitted to mix again with his fellows." [4]

---

[1] G. Brown, *Melanesians and Polynesians*, p. 154.

[2] *Taboo and the Perils of the Soul*, pp. 165-190.

[3] J. Roscoe, *The Banyankole*, p. 161.

[4] J. A. Massam, *The Cliff Dwellers of Kenya*, pp. 39 *sq.*

The Lango, a Nilotic tribe of Uganda, stand in great fear of the ghost (*tipo*) of a man who has been slain in battle. They think that it afflicts the slayer with attacks of giddiness and frenzy, during which he may do himself or the by-standers mortal mischief. For this reason, and also lest in the heat of the conflict a leprous or cancerous man has been speared, the slayers sacrifice goats and sheep, which may be of any colour, unless the slayer feels the influence of the ghost already beginning to affect him, in which case he must kill a black goat. The undigested matter from the intestines of the slaughtered goats is smeared over the bodies of the warriors to guard them against the ghosts of the slain. The ghost has further to be appeased by the cicatrization of the killers, each slayer cutting rows of cicatrices on his shoulder and upper arm, the number varying according to his ability to stand the pain up to three and a half rows. And finally each slayer has to shave his head after the fashion known as *atira*." [1] Among the Wawanga, a tribe of Kenya, " a man returning from a raid, on which he has killed one of the enemy, may not enter his hut until he has taken cow-dung and rubbed it on the cheeks of the women and children of the village and purified himself by the sacrifice of a goat, a strip of skin from the forehead of which he wears round the right wrist during the following four days." [2]

Among the Kipsikis or Lumbwa, another tribe of Kenya, when a warrior returns from a raid on which he has killed a man he " washes his blood-stained spear, allows the water and blood to drip upon a handful of grass which he licks ; there is no stated intention of partaking of the virility of the slain. On returning home the warrior arrives screaming the name of the tribe of which he has killed his man ; the villagers come out to meet him and throw grass upon him ; he goes far down the stream to bathe ceremonially, and plasters red earth (*ngariet*) on the right of his face, white earth (*ewaret*) on the left of his face ; he draws red parallel lines criss-cross upon his right arm, right leg, and on the right of his body,

[1] J. H. Driberg, *The Lango* (London, 1923), pp. 110 *sq.*

[2] K. R. Dundas, " The Wawanga and other Tribes of the Elgon District, British East Africa," in *Journal of the Royal Anthropological Society*, xliii. (1913) p. 47.

and similarly in white upon the left.   The shield and spear
are both half-plastered with red and white earth.   He may
not wash or oil his body now for a month, and if this is his
first killing he must slaughter a white goat, on a second killing the colour is of no moment.   The skin of this animal is
given to a woman past child-birth to wear.   A ring made
from this skin is worn on the big finger of the right hand,
with a strip extending to the wrist, where it is wound round
as a bracelet.   This form of ornament is also worn after
other ceremonial slaughter of animals.   Women and children
may not eat of the leavings of his food, and women shun his
presence until the month of seclusion is over.   This month
being over, the killer seeks a strange woman, especially one
who is thought barren, and has connection with her, the
husband, should he know (and if there is a child he must
know) shows no resentment ;   the next child born to the
woman, if a male, is called Kipkoli (*kolit*—a white goat)—the
name is fairly common." [1]

Among the Boloki or Bangala of the Upper Congo " a
homicide is not afraid of the spirit of the man he has killed
when the slain man belongs to any of the neighbouring towns,
as disembodied spirits travel in a very limited area only ; but
when he kills a man belonging to his own town he is filled
with fear lest the spirit shall do him some harm.   There are
no special rites that he can observe to free himself from these
fears, but he mourns for the slain man as though he were a
member of his own family.   He neglects his personal appearance, shaves his head, fasts for a certain period, and laments
with much weeping." [2]

With regard to the practice of head-hunting among the
Ibibio of Southern Nigeria we are told that should a slayer
find that the ghost of the slain is very strong and is haunting
him to his hurt, he will sacrifice a dog to the ghost of his foe.
If this sacrifice proves unavailing he catches a male lizard,
and with this carefully caged goes to a place where cross-
roads meet.   There by the wayside he makes a tiny gallows,
and, taking out the lizard from its cage, passes it three times

[1] J. Barton, "Notes on the Kipsikis *logical Institute*, liii. (1923) p. 47.
or Lumbwa Tribe of Kenya Colony,"   [2] J. H. Weeks, *Among Congo Canni-*
in *Journal of the Royal Anthropo-* *bals*, p. 268.

round his head, crying, " Here I give you a man instead of me. Take him and leave me free." After this he places a thin noose round the neck of the lizard and hangs it upon the miniature gallows.[1]

Among the Tumbuka, a tribe of Nyasaland, when a victorious army returns from battle they sit down by a stream about a mile from the village and the men who have slain foes in battle smear their bodies and arms with white clay. They rest beside the water one night and next morning the army returns to the royal village. The warriors who have slain others sleep that night in the open kraal with the cattle, and do not venture near their own homes. In the early morning they run again to the stream, and wash off the white clay with which they have bedaubed themselves. The witch-doctor is there to give them some magic medicine to drink, and to smear their bodies with a fresh coating of clay. For six days the process is repeated, until their purification is completed. Their trappings and war dress are hung up on a tree, the head is shaved, and being pronounced clean, they are at length allowed to return to their own homes. [2]

Among the Ila-speaking peoples of Northern Rhodesia when an army returned from battle a medicine-man or doctor went round among the slayers and put a little medicine on each man's tongue in order that the ghost of the slain might not trouble him. " Another cleansing process is called *kupu-pulula*. The warrior was bathed in the fumes of certain medicines burnt in a sherd : the ashes were afterwards placed in a koodoo horn and planted at the threshold of his hut to drive off the ghost of the person he had killed." [3] Further, among these tribes, every person who has slain a man, whether in battle or otherwise, must be careful to cut a short stick, split it partly down the middle, stretch the two sides apart, and jump through the cleft three or four times in order to avert the evil consequences.[4] Doubtless this precaution is taken in order to give a slip to the ghost of the slain.

[1] P. A. Talbot, *Life in Southern Nigeria*, p. 245.
[2] D. Fraser, *Winning a Primitive People*, pp. 39 *sq.*
[3] E. W. Smith and A. M. Dale, *The Ila-speaking Peoples of Northern Rhodesia*, i. 179.
[4] *Ibid.* p. 415.

The Thonga or Ronga of South-Eastern Africa believe that the slayers of men in battle are exposed to the very dangerous influence of the ghosts (*nuru*) of the men they have slain. The ghost of the slain haunts the slayer and may drive him into insanity : his eyes swell, protrude, and become inflamed. He will go out of his mind, be attacked by giddiness, and the thirst for blood may lead him to fall upon members of his own family and stab them with his assegai. To prevent such misfortunes a special treatment is required to free the slayers from the ghosts of their victims. The slayers must remain for some days at the capital. They are taboo. They put on old clothes, eat with special spoons because their hands are " hot " and from special plates and broken pots. They are forbidden to drink water.· Their food must be cold. The chief kills oxen for them ; but if the meat were hot it would make them swell internally " because they are hot themselves, they are defiled." If they ate hot food, the defilement would enter into them. " They are black. This black must be removed." During all this time sexual relations are absolutly forbidden to them. They must not go home to their wives. In former times the Ba-Ronga used to tattoo them with special marks from one eyebrow to the other. Dreadful medicines were introduced into the incisions and there remained pimples which gave them the appearance of a buffalo when it frowns. After some days a medicine-man comes to purify them, " to remove their black." The treatment seems to vary. According to one account seeds of all kinds, together with drugs and the un-digested contents of the stomach of a goat, are put into a broken pot and roasted on a fire. The slayers inhale the smoke which emanates from the pot. They put their hands into the mixture and rub their limbs with it, especially the joints. After this ceremony the slayers say : " Phee ! phee ! " viz. " Go down, sink." This means : " May you go deep into the earth, you, my enemy, and not come back to torment me." The last part of the treatment consists in rubbing the biceps, the legs, and the whole body with milk which had been mixed with the embers in the pot. The medicinal embers are carefully collected and reduced to a powder ; this will be put into small bags of skin called *tintebe* which the slayer will wear round his neck.   They contain the medicine of the slayers of men.[1]

The taboos observed by man-slayers among the Zulus have been described as follows : " Every Zulu man who might, whether in war or otherwise, have killed another man, was, before being able to return and mix with his family, required to go through a certain elaborate ceremony of purification or fortification called *ukuqunga*.   This, in the case of an army, was regularly arranged for by the king.   After having killed his adversary, the victor (now called an *inxeleha*, his assegai also being called by the same name), would immediately do off his *ibetshu* and put on that of the man he had killed.   He would then go to the river and wash the whole body, after-wards doctoring himself with certain prescribed herbs. Affixing a sprig of *ipinganhlola* in his hair, he could now direct his course home, but must keep a look-out for any strange female he may come across, as, before he can take up his residence in the kraal, he must first have sexual intercourse with some female or other of a tribe not his own, otherwise even at home he must continue to live out on the veldt. Upon entering his kraal, he must *ncinda* a large number of medicines, or fighting charms, called *izembe elimnyama*— this before partaking of any kind of food.   He then *ncinda*'s milk mixed with other medicines or cleansing charms, called *izembe elimhlope*.   This done, he is clean, and may again freely enter society and partake of *amasi* ; but until he dies he must never again eat *amasi* made from the milk of a cow whose calf has not yet shown the horns ; and every year he must refrain from eating the *ihlobo* or first-fruits of the new season, *i.e.* the pumpkins, calabashes, and the like, nor par-take of any beer made from the first corn of the new year, unless, in all cases, he shall have first fortified himself by certain medicinal charms." [2]

Among the Lakhers, a tribe of head-hunters in Assam, as soon as the warriors have returned from a successful raid, all those who have been lucky enough to take an enemy's head must perform the *Ia* ceremony over it.   The object of this ceremony is two-fold : first to render the spirit of the slain,

---

[1] H. A. Junod, *The Life of a South African Tribe*, i. 479 *sq.*

[2] W. Wanger, in *Anthropos*, x.-xi. (1915–1916) p. 272.

which is called *saw*, harmless to his slayer, and secondly to ensure that the spirit of the slain shall be the slave of his slayer in the next world.   It is believed that unless the *Ia* ceremony is performed over the heads of men killed in war, their spirits will render their slayers blind, lame, or paralysed, and that if by any lucky chance a man who has omitted to perform the *Ia* ceremony escapes these evils, they will surely fall upon his children or his grandchildren.   Again, unless the *Ia* ceremony is performed, the spirits of those slain in war go to a special abode called *Sawvawkhi*, where dwell the spirits of all those who have suffered violent deaths, so it is only by performing the *Ia* ceremony that a man can ensure that the spirit of his dead enemy shall accompany him to *Athikhi*, the abode of the dead, as his slave.   The ceremonies performed at *Ia* vary somewhat.   Among the Sabeu and Hawthai heads are never taken into the village, and so each man who has taken a head erects a bamboo pole in front of his house, and on it places an imitation head made out of a gourd.   He then sacrifices a pig, the flesh being used for a feast for his family and friends, and dances round this imitation head.   In the other villages the head of the man slain is taken to the place where the *Ia* ceremony is being performed, and the man and his friends dance the *Sawlakia* round and round the head. When the real head is used at the ceremony, rice and meat are placed in its mouth, in order that the dead man's spirit may not wander about on the night of the ceremony, the idea being that it will eat its fill of the food and remain near the head.   Three dances are performed at the *Ia* ceremony —the *Sawlakia*, the *Chochhipa*, and the *Dawlakia*.   The meaning of *Sawlakia* is " the dance of the Spirits of the slain " and Lakhers believe that the Spirits of the slain willy nilly have to dance round with their slayers.   On the night of the *Ia* ceremony and all the next day dancing, feasting, and singing continue.   The day after this the whole village is on holiday (*aoh*), no work is done and no one leaves the village.   The next day each man who has taken a head kills a pig, washes his hands in its blood, and then goes and bathes and thoroughly cleanses himself of all blood-stains, so that the spirits of the dead shall not be able to recognize their slayers.   While the *Ia* ceremony is in progress the man performing it may not sleep with his wife.   It is not till he has cleansed himself that he can resume conjugal relations.   The belief is that during the *Ia* ceremony the spirit of the deceased is hovering round, and if it saw the man who had slain him sleeping with his wife, it would say, " Ah, you prefer women to me," and would inform all the spirits, and the man who had done what was forbidden would not be allowed to take any more heads.[1]

Among the primitive natives of the Andaman Islands if a man kills another in a fight between two villages, or in a private quarrel, he leaves his village and goes to live by himself in the jungle, where he must stay for some weeks, or even months.   His wife, and one or two of his friends may live with him or visit him and attend to his wants.   For some weeks the homicide must observe a rigorous taboo.   He may not handle a bow or arrow.   He may not feed himself or touch any food with his hands, but must be fed by his wife or a friend.   He must keep his neck and upper lip covered with red paint, and must wear plumes of shredded *Tetrathera* wood in his belt before and behind, and in his necklace at the back of his neck.   If he breaks any of these rules it is supposed that the spirit of the man he has killed will cause him to be ill.   At the end of a few weeks the homicide undergoes a sort of purification ceremony.   His hands are first rubbed with white clay and then with red paint.   After this he may wash his hands and may then feed himself with his hands and may handle bows and arrows.   He retains the plumes of shredded wood for a year or so.[2]

Among the Kiwai of British New Guinea " the warrior who has killed is, as only might be expected, in continual danger from the ghosts of those he has slain.   Consequently he must for a month refrain from intercourse with women and eat no crabs, crocodile, sago, or pig.   If he did, the ghost would enter into his blood and he would certainly die.   As a further precaution against the power of the ghosts, food and a bowl of gamada (a native drink) are set aside and flung away with a warning to the dead to return to their own place." [3] Among the Orokaiva, a tribe in the east of British New Guinea,

---

[1] N. E. Parry, *The Lakhers*, pp. 213 *sqq.*
[2] A. R. Brown, *The Andaman*   *Islanders*, p. 133.
[3] W. N. Beaver, *Unexplored New Guinea*, p. 174.

a man who has slain another in a raid must perform certain
rites and observe certain taboos.   He may not drink pure
water out of the river, but only that which has been stirred
up and made muddy by the feet of a non-slayer.   He may not
eat taro cooked in the pot, but only that which has been roasted
in the open fire.   He must abstain from sexual intercourse.
These restrictions lasted for a few days and then the slayer
ate the same purificatory stew (*suna*) which is given to initiates
at the end of their seclusion.   Mr. Williams witnessed a
mock demonstration which immediately preceded the eating
of the *suna*.   The slayer climbs into a small tree which contains
a nest of those large and aggressive insects commonly called
" green " ants.   The tree should properly be of the kind
called *Bobo*, which is always swarming with them.   While he
crouches in a fork of the tree, branches are broken and laid
over him so that he is almost completely covered and thoroughly
bitten.   Having endured this for some time he climbs down
and eats the *suna*, steaming himself over the dish and spon-
ging his joints with handfuls of the stewed leaves.   Another
rite (also performed at the end of the initiate's seclusion) was
to break a coconut above the head of the slayer and souse his
head with the milk.   " It seems likely that all these observances and tabus are in a sense not only purificatory but
defensive.   As a rule, informants have no explanation to
offer, but I have been informed directly that they are meant
to drive away the *asisi* or spirit of the slain man.   In support
of this view I may quote what W. N. Beaver has written :
' I am not disposed to the sole view that the killer is *unclean*.
It seems to me rather that rites are necessary to throw off the
power of the ghost or ghosts of the slain.' " [1]

Among the Kai of Northern New Guinea when a party of
warriors return to the village after a successful raid in which
they have killed their enemies they are carefully avoided for
several days by the villagers, who will not touch them
because they believe that some of the soul-stuff of the slain
men is adhering to the bodies of their slayers.   If during
these days of seclusion any one in the village suffers a bodily
pain, he thinks that it must be caused by his having sat down

[1] F. E. Williams, *Orokaiva Society*, pp. 174 *sq.*, quoting W. N. Beaver, in
Annual Report (1918–1919), p. 97.

on the place where one of the slayers had sat before him. If any one complains of the pangs of toothache, he thinks that he must have eaten a fruit that had been touched by one of the slayers. All the remains of the food of the slayers must be carefully disposed of, lest a pig should eat of it, for were it to do so it would die. The remains are therefore either burned or buried. The soul-stuff of the enemies cannot seriously hurt the slayers, because these men protect themselves against it by smearing their bodies with the sap of a liana, a tropical climbing plant.[1]

In Mangaia, one of the Hervey Islands, the inhabitants of which are Polynesians, when a warrior had slain an enemy he became taboo (*tapu*). He might, for a certain time, only kiss his wife and children. On no account might he cohabit with his wife until the taboo had been removed. During this period of taboo all the warriors who had taken part in the raid lived together, receiving immense presents of food. When a sufficient interval had elapsed, in preparation for the removal of the taboo, they would go unitedly to fish.[2]

Among the Eskimo of Langton Bay in North America, a man who has killed an Indian or a whale had to refrain from all work for five days and from certain foods for a whole year. Notably he might not eat the intestines of any animals or their heads.[3] Among the Eskimo of Chesterfield Inlet, " it is the custom that when an Eskimo kills a person, he must not handle rocks for a certain time, and he must eat only straight meat, and when he eats, he must be under some shelter from the sun. Ouang-Wak was made to observe these customs, and did so while I was there. This was proof that Ouang-Wak killed these two men." [4]

Elsewhere we have seen that in primitive society hunters and fishers have often to observe taboos and undergo rites of purification, which are probably dictated by a fear of the spirits of the animals or fish which they have killed or intended to kill.[5] To the examples of such taboos which I have

[1] R. Neuhauss, *op. cit.* iii. 132.
[2] W. W. Gill, " Mangaia, Hervey Islands," in *Second Report of the Australasian Association for the Advancement of Science* (1890), p. 333.
[3] V. Stefansson, *My Life with the* *Eskimo* (London, 1913), p. 367.
[4] *Report of the Royal Canadian Mounted Police* for 1921 (Ottawa, 1922), p. 36.
[5] *Taboo and the Perils of the Soul*, pp. 190 *sqq.*

there cited I may here add a few more. Thus among the Basoga of Uganda " during their expedition huntsmen are careful to abstain from washing and from any contact with women." [1] Among the Kwottos of Northern Nigeria the magical preparation of the bows and arrows for the hunt is a matter of great importance to the success of the enterprise. " But this is not all, for the hunter has to put himself into a fit state to handle his weapons after their being thus saturated with spiritual potency. To this end the conscientious hunter abstains from sexual intercourse for a considerable time before the hunt ; otherwise his touch would spoil the efficacy of his weapons. No woman is allowed to touch the latter for the same reason. Should she do so, it is believed that she herself would become afflicted with a skin disease which would cause her continually to scratch herself in much the same way as a person might be scratched with an arrow. After returning from a hunt, men commonly eschew sexual relations for the space of up to two months. A breaking of this taboo, it is believed, would result in illness." [2] Among the Wa-Sania of Kenya a man does not cohabit with his wife during the hunting season. Otherwise he believes he would have bad luck in the chase. [3]

Among the Wandamba, a tribe of Tanganyika, "in each locality there is usually a principal *fundi* (skilled man), who makes the medicine and directs operations in the hunt, in which he is assisted by several lesser *mafundi*, all of them being in the employ of the chief of their tribe. For seven days prior to the setting out of an expedition each member of the party abstains from sexual intercourse and retires morning and evening to a place of privacy, either in the bush or in the enclosed courtyard (*uanja*) of his house, where he bathes his whole person thoroughly from head to foot. During the last three days he fasts, and on the eighth day, *i.e.* the day before starting, all the hunters meet together at a lonely spot in the bush where the head *fundi* makes a fire and boils in a large pot a concoction of water and the bark and leaves of the

---

[1] J. Roscoe, *The Northern Bantu,* p. 239.

[2] J. R. Wilson-Haffenden, *The Red Men of Nigeria* (London, 1930), p. 176.

[3] W. E. H. Barrett, in *Journal of the Royal Anthropological Institute,* xli. (1911) p. 31.

following seven trees. . . . The resultant mixture is sticky and unpleasant ; nevertheless, each man bathes in it, after which they proceed to cut small gashes in each other with sharp knives. These gashes are from 1 cm. to 2 cm. in length, and vary considerably in number, but always consist of double sets of two or more, one set on each side of the radius or humerus, close to the bone. An average number is half a dozen double sets of two to four on each arm, but a fellow who fancies himself as a fire-eater will often continue the sets almost unbroken from thumb to shoulder, and even have a set at the back of each shoulder. The head *fundi* then pounds the mixture upon a stone and rubs it into the cuts with small twigs of *msoro*, after which they all lick the stone clean. The ceremony, which is said to serve the threefold purpose of diminishing their scent, helping them to shoot well, and preserving them from attack, must be performed before each trip, though after the first time it is not necessary to make fresh cuts, but only to reopen the old ones. On the rare occasions when a man goes out alone, he observes the same procedure, enlisting the services of another old hunter. Later, in the evening, the party dance before the people in the *uanja* (open space in the village), thrusting their spears at insects and other marks even though they hunt with guns, singing hunting songs and invoking the spirits of dead hunters not to haunt them. Then, after another night of abstinence, they set out on their adventure." [1] Among the Wahehe, another tribe of Tanganyika, it is strictly forbidden for a hunter to cohabit with a woman the night before he goes out to hunt. Were he to do so, it is thought that he would only have himself to blame if he lost his life in the hunt.[2] Among the Boloki or Bangala of the Upper Congo the hunters who set traps for special game, such as elephants, had, from that moment, to abstain from all intercourse with women until an animal had been caught in the trap and killed. Otherwise their luck would be bad and their trap unsuccessful. The same prohibition was enforced on hunters who made traps

[1] A. G. O. Hodgson, " Some Notes on the Hunting Customs of the Wandamba," in *Journal of the Royal Anthropological Institute*, lvi. (1926)
p. 60.

[2] E. Nigmann, *Die Wahehe* (Berlin, 1908), p. 120.

for bush-pigs and burrowing animals.[1]   In the same tribe a
similar taboo is observed by fishermen, who while they are
making their traps must abstain from all intercourse with
women, and this prohibition continues until the trap has
caught some fish and the said fish has been eaten, otherwise
they will have no luck in fishing.   This abstinence may last
some few weeks, or only a few days.[2]   Among the Bakongo
of the Lower Congo, before hunters go out to hunt they pay
a visit to the grave of a famous hunter, where they worship
his spirit.   From that time until they kill an animal they must
abstain from all intercourse with women, for otherwise their
hunting magic would not work.[3]

Among the Badjo, a tribe of the Belgian Congo, on the
eve of departure for a hunt and during the whole time of the
hunt a hunter must abstain from cohabiting with his wife.
During his absence a fire must be kept up continually in his
hut.   To maintain it is the duty of his first or principal wife,
and the hunter may eat only the food which she has cooked
upon it for him.   If the hunter is a bachelor, he heaps up the
fire in his hut before his departure, and if on his return the fire
has gone out he lights it, with a particular kind of bark, which
gives out a sweet odour.   In the same tribe fishermen observe
a similar rule of chastity the night before they go out fishing.
Menstruous women, and women who have been pregnant
for at least three months, and their husbands, may not participate in the fishing.[4]

Among the Tumbuka, a tribe of Nyasaland, the taboos
observed at the hunting of elephants were particularly strict.
" When all the preparations for the expedition were made,
and sacrifice had been offered to the spirits of the dead, the
chief hunter charged the villagers that remained that there
must be no quarrelling or immorality indulged in within
the village.   None were to leave their homes to visit other
places, but all were to remain quiet and law-abiding lest the
game disappear, or turn in anger and rend the hunters.   As
he left the village he blew a loud blast on a little horn he

---

[1] J. H. Weeks, *Among Congo*
Cannibals, p. 233.
[2] *Ibid.* p. 244.
[3] J. H. Weeks, *Among the Primi-*

tive Bakongo, p. 183.

[4] M. G. Bernard, *Notes Sur les*
Badjo (Brussels, 1914), pp. 36 *sq.*

carried, and shouted back to the people, ' Let those who have gone before go in peace ; let him that utters my name die.' The curse was to prevent any talk about the projected hunt lest the game hear about it and hide away. . . . Throughout these days of travel and sport the chief hunter lived alone, slept and ate by himself, and was held in great reverence. Those who accompanied him had to guard most carefully their moral conduct, and husbands had no intercourse with their wives."[1] Among the Ila-speaking tribes of Northern Rhodesia " men going to fish, or to set traps, or to dig game-pits must not visit their wives or other women the night before. Some men will not do it before going to hunt, lest, as they say, they should be hurt on the way or be mauled by a wild beast. Others, on the contrary, regard intercourse as giving them good luck during the hunt. The *bashilwando* must abstain all the time they are fishing."[2] Speaking of the tribes of Northern Rhodesia in general, other writers tell us that " in the important enterprises of life such as hunting and fishing, natives will submit to certain taboos. While a weir is being built and fish baskets are set, the Bisa fisherman who cuts the weir stakes must live apart from his wife, and the majority of the Hunters, members of the society of *Uwanga wa nzovu*, are bound to abstain from certain foods, and live in the bachelors' quarters some days before starting in pursuit of a dangerous animal."[3]

With regard to hunters among the Thonga or Ronga of South-East Africa we are told that " these professional hunters are subject to many taboos. . . . They must undergo a purification before starting, and also be inoculated in the wrists with special drugs, the most important being those of the *tintebe*, the same which is used by the slayers of enemies in battle. . . . In some cases they have to prepare themselves for their expeditions by daily ablutions and by absolute continence for a certain number of days. The sacrifice of a fowl is also sometimes made before starting. It is taboo for adults to eat the meat of this fowl ; it might

[1] D. Fraser, *Winning a Primitive People*, p. 136.
[2] E. W. Smith and A. M. Dale, *op. cit.* ii. 44.

[3] C. Gouldsbury and H. Sheane, *The Great Plateau of Northern Rhodesia*, pp. 97 *sq.*

endanger the success of the expedition.   Little children may
eat it : ' they are quiet ' (*i.e.* they have no sexual relations),
and so the hunting will not be spoilt."[1]   At some of the
rivers in the country of the Thonga there are men who make
it their profession to hunt the hippopotamus.   They are
called *batimba*.   " This is the manner in which these batimba
hunt.   During the day the hunter fishes, watching the movements of the hippopotami all the time.   When he sees that
the propitious moment has come and is ready to undertake
hunting operations lasting a month, he first calls his own
daughter to his hut and has sexual relations with her.   This
incestuous act, which is strongly taboo in ordinary life, has
made him into a ' murderer ' : he has killed something at
home ; he has acquired the courage necessary for doing
great deeds on the river !   Henceforth he will have no sexual
relations with his wives during the whole campaign."[2]

In India the Birhors of Chota Nagpur observe an annual
hunt.   All the able-bodied men of a number of villages
assemble for the hunt.   In each village on the night preceding the hunt the chief hunter and his wife must observe
strict sexual continence.   And during the absence of the
hunters all the women of the village are bound to observe
the same rule, for otherwise it is believed that the hunters
would certainly be unsuccessful.[3]   The Oraons, another
tribe of Chota Nagpur, similarly hold a communal hunt
every summer.   " The huntsmen leave home on a Thursday
evening and return to their villages generally on the Tuesday
following.   During all these days not only do the men of the
party, but all the members of their families left behind in
their villages must observe strict sexual continence.   It is
believed that if this tabu is disregarded by any Oraon, male
or female, his or her fellow-villagers, or at any rate the
members of his or her family who may have joined in the
hunt, are sure to have ill success at the hunt.   Another tabu
which the stay-at-home Oraons of such villages have to observe
is that they must not kill, beat, or even purchase any eatable
fowl or animal so long as the hunters are away from home."[4]

[1] H. A. Junod, *The Life of a South African Tribe*, ii. 60.
[2] H. A. Junod, *op. cit.* ii. p. 68.
[3] S. C. Roy, *The Birhors*, pp. 77 *sq.*
[4] S C. Roy, *The Oraons*, pp. 231 *sq.*

Among the Lakhers, a tribe of Assam, "when a hunter has killed any of the larger animals, on his return home he performs a sacrifice called Salupakia, the object of which is to give him power in the next world over the spirit of the animal he has killed, to please the dead animal's soul, and so also to help him to kill many more animals in future. Either a pig or a fowl may be sacrificed. If a fowl is used, the sacrifice is performed immediately the hunter returns home; if a pig, the sacrifice is postponed till next morning. When a fowl is killed, the women may not eat any part of it, but if the sacrifice is a pig, women may eat any part of it except the head, which may be eaten only by men. . . . For the day and night of the sacrifice the sacrificer and his family are *pana* (taboo), and the women of the house may not weave. That night it is *ana* (forbidden) for the sacrificer to sleep with his wife or any other woman; he must sleep on the place where the sacrifice was made. The Lakhers believe that on the night of this sacrifice the spirit of the animal shot comes and watches the man who has killed it, and if it saw him sleeping with his wife, would say, ' Ah, this man prefers women to me,' and would go and inform all the other animals that the man who had shot him was unworthy to be allowed to shoot any more animals, as he was fonder of women than of the chase. A man who broke the prohibition on sexual intercourse on *Salupakia* night would therefore be unable to kill any more animals."[1]

Among the Kiwai of British New Guinea, "a man must not go out hunting or fishing while his wife is in childbed or in her menses, or he will be killed by a pig or a shark, or meet with some other calamity. The blood flowing from his wounds in such a case is associated with that of his wife. . . . Previous to a hunting or fishing tour a man must not have connection with his wife, as this would cause the same misfortune. If a woman is ' humbugged ' by another man while her husband is away hunting or fishing, the latter will meet with nothing but ill-luck. A man who is going out hunting will not speak of it beforehand to anybody, for in that case he is sure to fail; nor is it considered good form for any one to ask a hunter where he is going. Everybody must

[1] N. E. Parry, *The Lakhers*, p. 140.

judge for himself ; sometimes even the people living in the same house feign sleep and pretend not to notice when the hunter gets up in the early morning and quietly goes out. Supposing two men are arranging to go out together the next day, they will speak to each other with marked caution, and in the morning before starting no mention whatever must be made of the enterprise, each must get ready independently by the right moment. The only sign which may be given is a low whistle, by which the one man lets his friend know that he is going and expects him to follow. Not even the hunter's wife may speak to him about his undertaking. If he is obliged to refer to it, he will do so in a whisper, only hinting vaguely at his object. The reason for all these precautions is plainly stated by the natives : if a hunting trip were openly discussed beforehand, some invisible spirit might hear what was being said and carry the news to the animals in the bush." [1]

Among the Bukaua, a tribe of Northern New Guinea, there is a magician whose special business is to secure a good catch of the bonito fish. He takes a bowl, at each side of which there is a small representation of the bonito rod, fills the bowl with sea-water, and throws into it certain leaves and portions of plants. Then he takes the bowl and hides it in a secret place in the forest till the contents of the bowl are foul and stinking, and worms appear in the water. These worms represent the bonito fish which are to be caught. All the time that this bowl remains in the forest the fish-maker has to observe certain taboos. He may not come into contact with running water, he may have no sexual intercourse, and he may chew no betel. But he should eat much taro, which is brought to him by a small girl or a young boy. The more taro he eats, the larger will be the fish, and the more numerous the catch. From time to time he goes to the sea and makes movements with his hands, as though he would draw the fish from all directions, and he imitates their leaps. When the bowl in the forest is full of worms and maggots, which represent the bonito and other fish to be caught, the fish-maker takes the bowl to the beach and empties the bowl into the sea. On that day no one in the village may work, and they offer a

[1] G. Landtman, *The Kiwai Papuans of British New Guinea*, pp. 114 *sq.*

sacrifice to Balum, that he may not eat the bonito fish. The sacrifice consists of nuts, banana, and taro, from which a great feast is prepared. The fish-maker himself may not eat of the bonito fish, or his body would break out in dreadful sores, and his whole magic would be rendered useless.[1]

In the Caroline Islands every man who is preparing to go fishing may, according to established conventions, have no commerce with his wife for the preceding eight or nine days, and is obliged to pass the same number of nights in the communal house assigned to the unmarried men. This custom is maintained with the utmost rigour, and whoever has received the slightest favour from any woman is forced to submit to it, or to renounce his part in the fishing, if he does not wish, according to the general belief, to contract the most dangerous maladies, particularly inflammation of the legs. Moreover, he may not touch the fishing apparatus for twenty-four hours after he has had commerce with his wife. These customs are reported by a French voyager in the early part of the nineteenth century.[2] They may to some extent now be obsolete. A writer of the twentieth century, in speaking of Yap, one of the Caroline Islands, merely says that before going to fish a man may not cohabit with his wife, and that after his return he may for a time eat only the flesh of ripe coconuts.[3]

But in primitive society warriors and manslayers, hunters and fishers were by no means the only persons who were bound to practise strict continence for a longer or shorter period. The same rule was observed by many other persons on many other occasions of life. To the examples of this custom which I have given elsewhere I may briefly add a few more, as illustrative of the high importance which, under many circumstances, primitive or savage man attributes to sexual purity.[4] Thus for example the custom is often observed in time of mourning, probably out of respect for the spirit of the deceased, who might be offended by any breach of the rule. The practice is enjoined, for instance, in the Banyoro and Basoga tribes of Uganda, in Annam, and in the Marshall Islands of

---

[1] R. Neuhauss, *op. cit.* iii. 454 *sq.*

[2] F. Lutké, *Voyage autour du Monde* (Paris, 1835–1836), iii. 151 *sq.*

[3] P. S. Walleser, in *Anthropos*, viii.

(1913) p. 1062.

[4] Compare *Taboo and the Perils of the Soul*, p. 200.

the Pacific.[1]   In Loango and Urundi, a district to the west
of Lake Victoria Nyanza, it is observed after the death of a
king, and in the latter country, during the mourning for a
king, the rule of continence is extended to animals.   Cattle,
sheep, goats, and fowls are all prevented from breeding.   The
people believe that if a child were begotten during the mourning for a king his successor would die.[2]   Among the Banyankole of Uganda, during the mourning for a king or queen,
the scrotums of bulls were tied to prevent their breeding, and
after the mourning they were killed.[3]   Among the Banyoro
of Uganda " during the time that the smelters are engaged in
making charcoal, digging the iron-stone and smelting, they
live apart from other men and their wives and observe strict
rules of chastity." [4]   So among the Ila-speaking tribes of
Northern Rhodesia, " during the time the smelters (*bashin-
ganzo*) are sojourning in their shelters they are in a state of
strict taboo (*balatonda chinini*).   If one wishes to visit the
village, he must on no account have connection with his wife.
. . . Should a man transgress by having intercourse with his
wife or any other woman, they say the smelting would be a
failure." [5]   In the Gogodara tribe of British New Guinea
while a canoe is building the builder and his assistants are
bound to observe strict continence, and the women are forbidden even to look at the canoe while it is building and at
the men who are doing the work.   They think that if any of
these customs were neglected, some evil would befall the
canoe.[6]   Among the Kiwai of British New Guinea while a
man is making a drum he refrains from cohabiting with his
wife.   It is believed that if he broke the rule the drum would
break.[7]   In the same tribe " during the whole time that the
harpoon-maker is engaged in his work, he must refrain from
sexual connection with his wife, and she is not even allowed

[1] J. Roscoe, *The Northern Bantu*,
pp. 59, 201, 226 ; P. Giran, *Magie et
Religion Annamites*, p. 405 ; P. A.
Erdland, *Die Marshall-Insulaner*,
p. 326.
[2] H. Meyer, *Die Barundi*, p. 187 ;
Die Loango Expedition, iii. 2, p. 155.
[3] J. Roscoe, *The Banyankole*, p. 60.
[4] J. Roscoe, *The Northern Bantu*,
p. 75.

[5] E. W. Smith and A. M. Dale, *op.
cit.* i. 206.   As to a similar taboo
among the Fan, see below, p. 259.
[6] A. P. Lyon, " Notes on the Gogodara Tribe of Western Papua," in
*Journal of the Royal Anthropological
Institute*, lvi. (1926) p. 349.
[7] G. Landtman, *The Kiwai Papuans of British New Guinea*, p. 45.

to come near the place in the bush. The presence of a menstruous woman is particularly disastrous, as it would infallibly cause the cleaving of the tree to go wrong. Even the married sister of the harpoon-maker can injure his work from a distance, through the magic tie which exists between her and her brother, if she does not take care as to her conduct at that time. On the critical day when the cleaving of the tree is to take place, the harpoon-maker will ask his sister to leave her home and stay at his house, where she and his wife will spend the day together. The reason for this precaution is that otherwise the sister and her husband might happen to have intercourse on that very day, which would ruin the cleaving of the tree. The sister and her husband willingly submit to this arrangement, well knowing that the making of the harpoon will in time benefit them as well as the whole village." [1] In the same tribe again a man may not cohabit with his wife the night before he goes to work in his garden, nor on his way to the garden nor during an interval in the work there. It is thought that a breach of the rule would cause the pigs to break into the garden.[2] In the Kai tribe of Northern New Guinea when a sorcerer is preparing his enchantments for the destruction of an enemy he may not even touch a woman, nor receive food at the hands of men who have had intercourse with women. It is believed that a breach of these rules would endanger the success of his enchantment.[3]

---

[1] G. Landtman, *op. cit.* p. 122.
[2] G. Landtman, *op. cit.* p. 68.

[3] R. Neuhauss, *op. cit.* iii. 137.

CHAPTER XXII

TABOOED THINGS

IN the opinion of the savage certain things as well as certain persons are subject to the mysterious influence of taboo, and according to circumstances their use may be forbidden or enjoined. Among such objects of ambiguous potency in the thinking of primitive man is iron. To the examples which I have elsewhere given of the superstitions that cluster round iron in the mind of primitive man I may here add a few more.[1] Thus the Wajagga of Mount Kilimanjaro in East Africa think that the magical power which resides in iron is inimical to life and to peace. Hence when two men are forming a covenant of blood brotherhood, if both intend to be faithful to the compact they are very careful to have no scrap of iron about their persons, for the smallest morsel of the metal would render the covenant invalid. But if one of the parties is treacherous, and seeks for a loop-hole by which to escape from his obligation, he will secrete a small piece of iron about his person, if it be only a needle in his hair, to give him an excuse for renouncing the covenant. Some neighbours of the Wajagga suspect that tribe of often practising this treachery, and are therefore very distrustful of them in any dealings they may have with the tribe.[2] In Kitui, a district of Kenya, the natives will not use iron in the fields, for they think that this would drive away the rain. Mr. Dundas, who reports this custom and belief, adds, " probably the same reason underlies the objection to the railway. I talked to an old man on the

[1] See *Taboo and the Perils of the Soul*, pp. 224 *sqq.*

[2] B. Gutmann, " Der Schmied," in *Zeitschrift fur Ethnologie*, xliv. (1912) p. 93.

subject, but got very little out of him but a look which plainly said that if I did not know that to lay an iron band all across the country was enough to drive all rain away, what did I know." [1] The Wakikuyu, another tribe of Kenya, have certain periods when sacrifices for rain are offered, and during these periods no man may touch the earth with iron. It is a very common belief among the natives of this part of Africa that iron is antagonistic to rain. In Ukamba the women for long refused to use iron hoes for this reason. [2]

The Toradyas of Central Celebes are careful not to place any piece of iron in a coffin, because they think that the dead person might throw it out, and that falling on the fields it might blast the rice-crops. [3]

But primitive man thinks that the magical potency of iron may be turned to good as well as to evil account ; in particular it may serve to guard him against dangerous spirits. " The Oraon and Munda practice of wearing rings and armlets (*bera*) made of iron previously exposed to an eclipse of the sun, so that the wearer may offer to the ' evil eye ' of witches, and the evil attentions of ghosts and spirits, a resistance as strong as that of iron so hardened, is an instance in point. The person wearing the armlet is believed to acquire the strength of the iron ; and the iron itself is believed to have acquired greater virtue through the sympathetic influence of the eclipse. Such rings and armlets are believed to be most effective in averting a thunderstroke." [4] To frustrate the assaults of evil spirits a pregnant Malay woman must always carry a knife or iron of some sort as a talisman whenever she goes abroad. [5] Similarly the protective virtue of iron against spirits is recognized by the Mountain Jews of the Caucasus. They believe that there is a water-spirit called Ser-Ovi, who has the appearance of a tender snow-white maiden. On moonlight nights she sits by the wells and watches over the water to prevent people from defiling it. Often she lures

[1] C. Dundas, " History of Kitui," in *Journal of the Royal Anthropological Society*, xliii. (1913) p. 525.

[2] C. Dundas, " Native Laws of Some Bantu Tribes," in *Journal of the Royal Anthropological Institute*, li. (1921) p. 238.

[3] N. Adriani and A. C. Kruijt, *op.* *cit.* ii. 95.

[4] S. C. Roy, " Magic and Witch-craft on the Chota Nagpur Plateau," in *Journal of the Royal Anthropological Institute*, xliv. (1914) p. 332.

[5] R. O. Winstedt, *Shaman, Saiva, and Sufi*, p. 117.

older people and drowns them, but she leaves young people
in peace.   But she is afraid of steel and iron, and flees from
them.   Hence when people go to fetch water by night, they
take with them some implement of steel, and wave it about in
the air and over the well.   For the same reason almost all
men and women wear steel rings on their fingers.[1]

In Africa the craft of the smith is looked on with awe
by the natives, who attribute magical or semi-magical powers
to him.   For example among the Ndia Kikuyu of Kenya
the Ithaga clan, who are mostly smiths, are supposed to be
the masters of specially potent curses, and to be able to ward
off or summon rain.   Several cases are known in which
general indignation was caused by the alleged action of a
smith in preventing rain for a considerable period.[2]   Among
the Fan or Pangwe, a tribe of West Africa, the workers in
iron have to observe many taboos, especially of the sexual
kind.   The taboos have to be observed for two months
before the working of the iron begins, and last throughout
the work.   The restrictions are so burdensome that they
render the work of iron-smelting very unpopular.[3]

The use of sharp-edged weapons is sometimes tabooed
lest they should wound spirits.   Among the Banyankole of
Uganda when a king died all work ceased in the land and
the blades of all weapons had to be wrapped up in grass or
fibre.   Even an axe might not be used for cutting fire wood,
which had to be broken by hand.[4]   We may suppose that
the rule was dictated by a fear of wounding the king's ghost,
which might be hovering in the air.   Among the Ten'a
Indians of Alaska after the birth of a child both parents
abstain from using any sharp instrument, such as an axe,
a knife, scissors, and so forth.   Neighbours have to saw and
split wood, and do the sewing for them.   It is supposed that
the parents, by using those cutting instruments, might per-
chance clip and sever an imaginary thread of life of the child.[5]

Again among primitive peoples blood is the subject of
many taboos.   The divine king of the Bushongo was pro-

[1] C. Hahn, *Aus dem Kaukasus*
(Leipzig, 1892), pp. 189 *sq.*
[2] G. St. J. Orde Browne, *The
Vanishing Tribes of Kenya*, p. 201.
[3] G. Tessmann, *Die Pangwe*, i. 225.

[4] J. Roscoe, *The Banyankole*, p. 52.

[5] F. J. Jetté, " On the Superstitions
of the Ten'a Indians," in *Anthropos*,
vi. (1911) pp. 705 *sq.*

hibited by ancestral custom from spilling any blood, even in war.[1] Among the Wa-Giriama of Kenya blood of a human being accidentally shed is covered up with earth, as it is considered to bring bad luck to others to look at it.[2] The taboo on blood is probably based on the conception of blood as the vehicle of life. Hence in Morocco " From the time the pilgrim has assumed the *ihram* or pilgrim's garb until he takes it off he is not allowed to kill any living creature, not even the vermin troubling him ; a louse which he finds on his body or his dress may be removed by him to another part of it, but must not be thrown away. Nay, even his relatives at home are obliged to refrain from killing lice during the three days preceding the Great Feast and until the sacrifice has been performed, as otherwise some misfortune would befall the pilgrim. Many holy men avoid killing lice altogether ; and persons who are in the habit of praying only kill them after they have removed them from their clothes, or at any rate remove those they have killed before they begin their prayer. Contact with carcasses is polluting. Even meat may have to be kept away from *baraka* (holiness). A scribe from the Hiaina told me that if meat were brought to the field at ploughing or reaping time, the crops would suffer by it ; that the shepherd must take no meat with him when he goes out with the animals ; and that neither raw meat nor grease must be carried on a horse which has on it a riding-saddle." [3]

" Flies and mosquitoes were not killed in Tonga, but were driven away with a whisk of coconut fibre. The mosquito might have bitten the sacred king (the Tui Tonga) and so his sacred blood would be spilled by the man who crushed the mosquito." [4] The Noofoor Papuans of Dutch New Guinea are very much afraid of spilling the blood of their own kinsfolk. They also carefully avoid places where the blood of members of their family has flowed, and to the third and fourth generation they will not eat the products

---

[1] E. Torday and E. J. Joyce, *Les Bushongo*, p. 61.

[2] W. E. H. Barrett, " Notes on the Customs and Beliefs of the Wa-Giriama," in *Journal of the Royal Anthropological Institute*, xli. (1911) p. 35.

[3] E. Westermarck, *The Moorish Conception of Holiness (Baraka)*, pp. 131 *sq.*

[4] Rev. G. Brown, D.D., in a letter to me dated 7th May 1912.

of a spot where the blood of one of their relatives has been shed. Dr Adriani says that people are especially afraid to shed the blood of those who have been guilty of incest.[1] In Bombay the blood of a king is not allowed to touch the ground.[2]

In the human body the head is particularly tabooed or sacred. In Cambodia the head of every person must be respected, and most especially the head of the king. No one may touch the head of a nursling at the breast ; formerly, if any one were so malicious as to do so he was put to death, for only thus could the sacrilege be atoned for.[3] Again the Wa-Singi of Kenya perform a great ceremony at the circumcision of youths. During the whole of this ceremony they have to take particular care not to touch each others' heads or their hair falls off, so they cover their heads with a cloth or skin.[4]

Again the human hair as part of the head is also very sacred and subject to many taboos. We hear of a chief of the Baganda who while a temple was building might neither shave his head nor cut his nails, and consequently at the end of the period presented the appearance of a mourner.[5]

In primitive society people are generally very anxious about the disposal of their cut hair and nails, because they fear that if these fall into the hands of a sorcerer or witch he might perform ceremonies over them which by the force of contagious magic would injuriously affect the original owner of these personal relics. Thus among the Tumbuka, a tribe of Nyasaland, " the commonest method of bewitching was by getting possession of some discarded part of the body. Hence precautions were taken to conceal whatever might give an enemy opportunity to hurt the owner. When a man or woman had the hair clipped or shaved, all the hair was gathered and laid in deep ant-holes, lest a sorcerer should find it out and knowing the owner do him harm.

---

[1] T. J. F. van Hasselt, " Nufoorsche Fabeln," in *Bijdragen tot de Taal-, Land- en Volkenkunde van Nederlandsche Indie,* lxi. (1908) p. 572.

[2] R. E. Enthoven, *The Folklore of Bombay,* p. 87.

[3] R. Verneau and Pennatier, " Con-tribution á l'Étude des Cambodgiens," in *L'Anthropologie,* xxxi. (1921) p. 317.

[4] C. W. Hobley, *Ethnology of the A-kamba* (Cambridge, 1910), p. 73.

[5] J. Roscoe, *The Baganda,* p. 303.

The sorcerer might mix the hair with medicine and cause people to drink it in their sleep by some occult power, or he might curse the mixture saying, ' If this hair is So-and-So's let him die, but if not let him recover.' And such a curse was most potent. Chiefs used to get their hair cut by a slave who was sent to throw it away in some secret place ; but sometimes the slave had a cause of enmity in his heart, and before he hid it he would curse the hair, and the chief would immediately fall sick, and perhaps die. When finger-nails were cut, the clippings were hidden away or buried in the earth lest an enemy should find them and slice them up, causing the owner's death. When a man's tooth is pulled, he is careful not to leave it lying about, also to cover with earth the blood he spits out, lest someone use these parts of himself for evil magical purposes." [1] For a similar reason the Ila-speaking peoples of Northern Rhodesia are usually careful to bury their cut hair lest it should fall into the hands of warlocks, who might injure them thereby through their magic.[2] To prevent their hair and nails from falling into the hands of a hostile magician, the Kpelle of Liberia are careful to burn these personal relics.[3] So again among the Malays, " clippings from hair or nails are hidden or de-stroyed for fear possession of them may give an enemy possession over their owner's soul and so over his life. . . . So strong is the soul-substance in the hair shorn at a girl's first tonsure that it is buried at the foot of a barren tree to bring fruit as luxuriant as the girl's tresses." [4] So again the natives of San Cristoval, one of the Solomon Islands, are careful to bury the cuttings of their hair and nails lest these personal relics should fall into the hands of a wizard, who by means of them might do them a mischief.[5]

The ceremonies which the malignant sorcerer or witch performs over these personal relics for the injury or destruc-tion of his enemy vary considerably. Thus in Yatenga, a district of the Western Sudan, the enchanter puts the cut hair and nails in a receptacle of some sort (*zoullotoga*),

[1] D. Fraser, *Winning a Primitive People*, pp. 142 *sq.*

[2] E. W. Smith and A. M. Dale, *op. cit.* i. 66.

[3] D. Westermann, *Die Kpelle*, p. 206.

[4] R. O. Winstedt, *Shaman, Saiva, and Sufi*, p. 65.

[5] C. E. Fox, *The Threshold of the Pacific*, p. 257.

which he compresses and binds tightly. The soul of his victim suffers in this confinement, and the man himself soon dies. But against these charms by ligature and compression there are magical remedies which may be used to counteract their baneful effect.[1] Among the Gouro of the north, in the same region, the wizard puts the cut hair and nails of his enemy in an ant-hill, whereupon the victim pines away and dies, unless his friends by using counter-magic can annul the effects of the hostile charms.[2] Among the Sinsoro Koulangos, another tribe of the western Sudan, the enchanter simply buries the hair and nails of his foe along with a certain charm, and the victim is supposed to die.[3]

Among the Kiwai of British New Guinea " one means of causing a sick person to die is to take a little of his hair and excrement, together with some earth bearing traces of his urine and saliva, and burn it all in the middle of the night in a small ant-hill. The person will die while the fire is burning." [4] Hence the Kiwai are very careful about the disposal of their cut hair and nails, lest they should fall into the hands of a hostile magician.[5]

As cut hair and nails are supposed by primitive man to remain in a sympathetic relation with their original owner, they may obviously be employed as hostages for his good behaviour. Thus among the Ekoi, a tribe of Southern Nigeria, when a man received a new slave in his house, in order to prevent him from attempting to escape, the master used to cut off a lock of the slave's hair and some parings of his nails, and then took a piece of an old cloth which the slave had worn. These personal relics he carried to the fetish or Juju, and there prayed that death or recapture might overtake the slave should he attempt to escape. After the ceremony the pieces were carefully kept in a secret place, and the slave believed that, should he run away, the Juju would infallibly catch him.[6] Similarly, among the Wajagga of Mount Kilimanjaro in East Africa, when a child or boy

---

[1] L. Tauxier, *Le Noir du Yatenga*, p. 397.

[2] L. Tauxier, *Nègres Gouro et Gagou*, p. 258.

[3] L. Tauxier, *Le Noir de Bondoukou*, p. 181.

[4] G. Landtman, *The Kiwai Papuans of British New Guinea*, p. 321.

[5] W. N. Beaver, *Unexplored New Guinea*, p. 134.

[6] P. A. Talbot, *In the Shadow of the Bush*, p. 327.

is restless and prone to wander away from home, they seek to attach him to his home by means of his soul. In the night, while he sleeps, his anxious mother cuts his finger-nails and some locks of his hair. Next day a magician is called in. He binds these personal relics magically by spitting on them and hiding them with certain formulas in a beam of the house. By these means the boy will be at-tached to the house and freed from his tendency to wander. And when a young slave has been captured in war and brought to the house a similar ceremony is performed to pre-vent him from attempting to escape.[1]

People who believe that they can be magically injured through their shorn hair or the parings of their nails com-monly take great care to hide these relics of their person, so as to put them beyond the reach of animals and the maleficent arts of sorcerers. Thus for example among the Tigre people of Abyssinia, " Everybody gathers his hair when it has been shaved off and buries it under a green tree or hides it in a secret place. For a small boy the parents take it until he grows up. But when he arrives at the age of dis-cretion, they say to him : ' Gather thy hair ! ' And he him-self like the grown-up people puts his hair in a secret place. If the wind carries the hair away, or if a man treads upon it, or, again, if an animal eats it, they say it is not good, and they are afraid. And some say that if a man has not hid his hair, God will account with him in the other world, say-ing : ' Why hast thou not gathered thy hair ? ' Others say that if a man does not hide his hair it will be scanty, or that he will lose his reason. Others again say that if the wind scatters the hair of a man, his family will be scattered all around ; or that if an animal eats it and is choked by it, the responsibility for the animal will be upon the owner of the hair. And because they are afraid of all this, everybody hides his hair. Men take great care that the nails of their fingers and the nails of their toes are not lost. And every-body, at the time when he cuts his nails or when the nail is broken off by itself, takes great care that they do not slip away from him ; and he wraps his nails in a rag and buries this in the ground. Or even if he buries them without a

[1] B. Gutmann, *Dichten und Denken der Dschagganeger*, p. 65.

rag it does not matter. And all of them bury their nails thus. But if anybody does not pay attention to gathering his nails, he is asked about them at the day of resurrection, and it is said to him : ' Where hast thou put thy nails ? ' And he is told to seek them, but he does not find them. And they say that in this way his account grows heavier, or else that his body becomes deficient. And because they fear this, they all keep their nails." [1]

Among the Baganda one of the king's wives had to act as his hairdresser ; she also cut the king's nails, and took care of the hair and nail clippings, and stored them in a house built for the purpose.[2] Among the Nilotic Kavirondo after the birth of a child " when the new moon appears, the parents shave, and bathe their heads, taking care to keep separate the hair which is cut off. This hair is hidden away in some place near, by preference in a rat-hole or in some hole where it is not likely to be found again." [3] Among the Hausa of West and North Africa " a man will not have his hair shaved in the presence of any one who owes him a grudge. After his hair has been cut, he will look around, and if there is no enemy about he will mix his cuttings with those of other men and leave them, but if he fears some one there he will collect the cuttings, and take them secretly to some place and bury them. With a baby this is said to be unnecessary, as he has no enemies—a surprising statement. Nails are always cut with scissors, and they are always buried in secret." [4] The Boloki of the Upper Congo always hide the parings of their nails and the clippings of their hair, because these might be used for their hurt by enchanters.[5] For a similar reason the Bakongo of the Lower Congo always bury the clippings of the hair and the parings of their nails, because they believe that if an enemy got hold of them he could quickly do them to death by mixing some of these relics with their food.[6]

Among the Malagese or natives of Madagascar the first

---

[1] E. Littmann, *Publications of the Princeton Expedition to Abyssinia*, vol. ii. (Leyden, 1910), pp. 312 and 315.

[2] J. Roscoe, *The Baganda*, p. 85.

[3] J. Roscoe, *The Northern Bantu*, pp. 282 *sq.*

[4] A. J. N. Tremearne, *The Ban of the Bori*, p. 57.

[5] J. H. Weeks, *Among Congo Cannibals*, p. 272.

[6] J. H. Weeks, *Among the Primitive Bakongo*, p. 238.

cutting of a child's hair is a solemn ceremony, which may be performed at any time from soon after birth up till the age of five or six years, according to the usage of the different peoples. It is always accompanied by prayers to God and to the ancestral spirits, and by feasts in which all the members of the family take part. Among all the peoples, except those who defer the ceremony for five or six years, the hair cut from the left side of the child are regarded as *faditra*, that is, as connected to the child by sympathetic magic, so that they can influence him for good or evil. The hairs are carefully buried or thrown into running water, or are deposited at a distance in some desert place, that no sorcerer may procure them and use them to compose a philtre for the purpose of injuring the child. On the other hand, the hairs cut from the right side of the child are sacrificed to God and to the ancestors, for the purpose of obtaining the divine favour for the child.[1] When the Lamas in Tibet shave their heads they carefully preserve the shorn hair and hide it in a hole in the wall; for if they were to lose it they believe that some great evil would overtake them.[2]

Another bodily relic through which a person can be magically injured is his spittle. Hence precautions have to be taken to guard the spittle against the arts of the sorcerer. For this reason the Baganda were careful to cover up their spittle with earth so as to leave no trace of it behind.[3] Speaking of the natives of the Mekeo district in British New Guinea, a missionary tells us : " Accusations of such magic were extremely common in the Mekeo district on the south coast some fifteen years ago. As examples of the kind of material used I may mention that a fragment or two of a woman's grass petticoat, or the fibrous part of a piece of sugar-cane after it had been chewed and spat out, are very commonly used. I remember once chewing some sugar-cane in an unfriendly village and a very loyal village police-man from Waiuan village, on the north-east coast, simply insisted on the collection and hiding of the fibrous material I spat out. He feared that the unfriendly village people,

[1] A. and G. Grandidier, *Ethnographie de Madagascar*, iv. 292.
[2] Prince Henri d'Orleans, *From Tonkin to India* (London, 1898), p. 234.
[3] J. Roscoe, *The Baganda*, p. 344.

who had deserted their village on our approach, would be able to do me harm if they found such material."[1]   In New Britain and New Ireland "the natives always blow the spittle from the mouth in a fine spray lest it should be gathered up by anyone and used for the purposes of sorcery."[2] For the same reason no Maori would spit in the presence of any person whom he suspected of a wish to injure him, because he feared that his enemy might use the spittle to bring down upon him the anger of an ancestral spirit, especially of a child spirit, for the spirits of dead children were believed to be particularly mischievous.[3]

"The saliva of the king of Hawaii was carefully preserved in a spittoon, in the edges of which were set the teeth of his ancestors.   Should his enemies get possession of any of it, they were supposed to have the power to occasion his death, by sorcery and prayer."[4]   Speaking of Tamaahmaah, king of Hawaii, a voyager in the early part of the nineteenth century tells us that "the bearer of his spitting-tray does not quit him a moment, as he always holds the tray ready, which is made of wood, in the form of a snuff-box, and provided with a lid, which is opened when the king intends to make use of it, and then immediately closed.   This careful preservation of the royal saliva, is in consequence of a superstition that so long as they are in possession of this treasure their enemies are not able to send him any sickness by conjuration."[5]

Among the things which many primitive people regard with fear as magically potent, and therefore dangerous, are knots.   Accordingly it is sometimes prescribed that a sacred person shall have no knots in his garments, and the same taboo is observed by women at certain times.   Thus knots fall under the class of things which are often tabooed.   The underlying idea seems to be that the physical constriction of the knot exerts a magical constriction on the person of the wearer.[6]   Thus, for example, among the Baganda, when a

[1] W. M. Strong, "Some Personal Experiences in British New Guinea," in *Journal of the Royal Anthropological Institute*, xlix. (1919) p. 293.

[2] Rev. George Brown in a letter to me dated 7th May 1912.

[3] E. Shortland, *Maori Religion and Mythology*, p. 31.

[4] J. J. Jarves, *History of the Hawaiian or Sandwich Islands* (Boston, 1843), p. 197.

[5] Otto von Kotzebue, *A Voyage of Discovery* (London, 1821), i. 313.

[6] See *Taboo and the Perils of the Soul*, pp. 293 *sqq*

certain medium was accused of having spoken against the king by command of the gods, he was bound and brought before the offended king. When the king asked him to repeat the oracle which he professed to have received from the gods, the man refused to do so while he was bound, saying that it was contrary to custom to bind a medium or medicine-man.[1] Among the Bakongo of the Lower Congo River when a fetish or charm has been made for the protection of a town or village " there is one prohibition that must be scrupulously observed—nothing tied in a bundle may enter the town, or the charm will become non-effective. Women returning with firewood must untie the bundle before reaching the ' town charm ' ; men with bundles of grass for thatching must unfasten them ; carriers with loads must loosen the cords, or make a wide detour ; and people must remove their girdles or belts." [2]

It is a common belief that a knot on the garment of a woman in childbed would retard or prevent her delivery and that the presence of a lock in the room would have the same effect. Hence among the Ibibio Efik people of Southern Nigeria it is customary to untie all knots and open all locks in a house where a woman is in childbed. " A case was related of a jealous wife, who, on the advice of a witch doctor versed in the mysteries of her sex, hid a selection of pad-locks beneath her garments, then went and sat down near the sick woman's door and surreptitiously turned the key in each. She had previously stolen an old waist-cloth from her rival, which she knotted so tightly over and over that it formed a ball, and, as an added precaution, she locked her fingers closely together and sat with crossed legs, exactly as did Juno Lucina of old when determined to prevent the birth of the infant Hercules." [3] Among the Malagese when a woman is in hard labour all the women about her are enjoined to untie or unbutton their garments as a means of facilitating the delivery.[4] A pregnant Hindoo woman may not wear a knot in her dress at the point where it is fastened round her waist.[5]

[1] J. Roscoe, *The Baganda*, p. 227.
[2] J. H. Weeks, *Among the Primitive Bakongo*, pp. 220 *sq.*
[3] D. A. Talbot, *Woman's Mysteries of a Primitive People*, p. 22.
[4] A. and G. Grandidier, *op. cit.* p. 261.
[5] W. J. Wilkins, *Modern Hinduism*, p. 5.

Among the Malays at a childbirth " all locks on door or box are opened, the sufferer's hair is unbound, and any knot in her clothes is untied." [1] Among the Looboos, a primitive tribe of Sumatra, while a birth is taking place all chests and boxes must be open, and the clothes and hair of the woman must hang loose.[2] So among the Kooboos, a primitive aboriginal race in the south-east of Sumatra, when a woman remains in the house to bring forth, and the birth is difficult, all doors and chests in the house are opened, and the same custom is observed by the ordinary natives of Sumatra.[3] Among the Toradyas of Bada in Central Celebes, when a birth is taking place, everything that can be opened or loosened, including the band of the betel-bag, the trouser-band, chests, windows, and so forth, is opened or loosened, in the belief that this will facilitate the delivery.[4] Ideas and customs of the same sort are not unknown in Scotland. In the county of Fife, at a birth, when the labour was long and tedious, an old woman would often open the door of the chamber of the woman by way of helping the delivery.[5]

But in magic the obstructive power of knots may be turned to good account by opposing the inroad of disease or otherwise hindering an undesirable consequence. In short, knots may have their beneficent use. Thus among the Brahuis of Baluchistan " as for the fever that comes on every other day, we treat it at first like any other fever. But if it clings to the man, we go to one that was born a twin, and give him a blue thread, and bid him knot it in five or seven places. And the knotted thread is hung round the sick man's neck, and keeps the fever at a distance." [6] In the north-eastern part of British New Guinea, near the river Magavara, the natives have some fear of attending a festival where there is a great gathering of people, because they think that among

---

[1] R. O. Winstedt, *Shaman, Saiva, and Sufi*, p. 121.

[2] J. Kreemer, " De Looboes in Mandailing," in *Bijdragen tot de Taal-, Land- en Volkenkunde van Nederlandsch-Indie*, lxvi. (1912) p. 314.

[3] G. J. van Dongen, " De Koeboes," in *Bijdragen tot de Taal-, Land- en Volkenkunde van Nederlandsch-Indie*,

vol. lxiii., (1910) p. 231.

[4] A. C. Kruijt, " Het landschap Bada in Midden-Celebes," in *Tijdschrift van het Koninklijk Nederlandsch Aardrijkskundig Genootschap*, Deel xxvi. (Leiden, 1909) pp. 375 *sq.*

[5] *County Folk-Lore*, vii., Fife, p. 395.

[6] Denys Bray, *The Life History of a Brahui*, p. 106,

them there may be sorcerers who will do them a mischief. Still, they say " if you do go it is well to be forearmed, and so get some friend who knows how to do it to tie knots in your hair as a preventive against charms, and some thongs round your ankles and knees and wrists, so that the spirits are blocked and cannot get into your body and do mischief." [1] The Toradyas of Central Celebes attribute an obstructive power to knots, which they sometimes employ for a helpful purpose. At a feast when buffaloes are slaughtered and eaten they sometimes tie knots in palm leaves to prevent the flesh of the victims from diminishing too rapidly.[2] In Monferrato, a district of Piedmont, to cure a sprained ankle " the foot is tied with a thread which has never been used before, whilst the healer says in an undertone, ' Diau porta via vi mal ' (Devil take away the ill). The best result will be obtained if silk is used, and sometimes three knots are tied." [3]

[1] H. Newton, *In Far New Guinea*, p. 158.
[2] N. Adriani and A. C. Kruijt, *op. cit.* ii. 176.
[3] E. Canziani and E. Rohde, *Piedmont* (London, 1913), p. 143.

CHAPTER XXIII

TABOOED WORDS

UNABLE to distinguish clearly between words and things, a savage commonly regards his name as a vital part of himself, and thinks consequently that he can be injured magically through it, as well as through his hair, his nails, or other parts of his body. Hence he is often very cautious about uttering his own name, or allowing others to do so. Thus among the Barundi, to the west of Lake Victoria Nyanza, people are very unwilling to tell their own names or those of their children to strangers, lest the strangers through knowing the names might exert magical power over the bearers of the names, and bring harm down upon them.[1] The Bangala of the Upper Congo think that the eyesight of ghosts is defective, but that their hearing is very keen. Hence a man's name was never mentioned while he was fishing, for fear the ghosts might hear and deflect the fish from his nets and traps.[2] Among the Ila-speaking peoples of Northern Rhodesia, " a person is not allowed to speak his own name. This is particularly the case in the presence of older people. For any one sacrilegiously to pronounce his name in their presence would be a serious fault. They might sell him up, make him a slave, or drive him out of the community, unless his clansmen redeemed him. . . . If you ask a person his name he will turn to another and ask him to tell you. Nowadays they are getting accustomed to being asked their names by Europeans, who insist upon a man speaking for himself, but they get out of the

---

[1] H. Meyer, *Die Barundi*, p. 112.
[2] J. H. Weeks, " Anthropological Notes on the Bangala of the Upper Congo River," in *Journal of the Royal Anthropological Institute*, xl. (1910) p. 372.

difficulty by making up impromptu names for the occasion, or they take advantage of the grotesque names given them by European employers. . . . A man may not pronounce his wife's name, at any rate unless and until she has borne him children ; nor his father's nor his mother's, nor the names of his parents-in-law, nor those of his *bakwe*, *i.e.* the brothers and sisters of his parents-in-law, nor those of the brothers and sisters of his wife, nor the name of his uncle. . . . A woman must observe similar rules ; and she calls her husband by his *champi* names, or addresses him as *Munaisha*. The reason for these taboos is that by pronouncing a name you may bring misfortune upon the person or upon yourself. It is the same motive which forbids people staying in the village to speak by name of people away on business. An absent hunter may only be referred to as *Shimwisokwe* (' he who is in the veld ') ; a warrior as *Shilumamba* (' the warrior ') or *Shimpi* (' the fighter ') ; a fisherman as *Shimulonga*, ' the river man,' a merchant as *Mwendo* (' the trader '). Were you to mention the name of any of these, accidents would befall them. . . . Not only must one refrain from speaking the names we have mentioned, but one must avoid speaking of things by their names when those names bear a close resemblance to the persons' names."[1] The Bushmen of the Kalahari desert in South-West Africa " have an extensive range of terms of relationship among themselves. Some, but not all, of these are connected with taboos, as, for example, a mother-in-law must not see her son-in-law or mention his name unless it is absolutely unavoidable. He on his side must not see her or mention hers. A man's wife must avoid mentioning the name of her husband or any of his blood relations. To do so would be unlucky. It thus happened that a man had a name given to him at the time of his initiation which was used by his wife and relations, while his real name was known only to himself and his parents, who never used it when speaking to him. This secret name was only revealed to him after his initiation."[2] In certain provinces, or rather in certain families, of Madagascar, a person is forbidden to pronounce his or her own name, on pain of incurring some great

---

[1] E. W. Smith and A. M. Dale, *op. cit.* i. 367 *sq.*

[2] S. S. Dornan, *Pygmies and Bushmen of the Kalahari*, pp. 161 *sq.*

evil.[1]   The Toradyas of Central Celebes are very unwilling
to mention their own names, the names of their parents and
chiefs, and above all the names of their parents-in-law.[2]
Among the natives of British New Guinea " there is a marked
reluctance to mention the individual name of any person related by marriage, and in their intercourse the natives never
do so.   At every marriage they make at least a tacit agreement
to discontinue using the personal names in such cases, and at
times this is confirmed by means of the *karea*-rite.   There is a
similar reluctance to tell a person's own name.   In both cases
it often happened, when I asked some man for a name he
ought not to pronounce, that he would turn to somebody else
present, requesting him to say it.   It was impossible for
me to get the native explanation of this avoidance ;   the
only answer I obtained was that the people were ' shame ' to
utter the names of persons with whose daughter or sister they
were holding sexual intercourse." [3]   In British New Guinea,
" Fifteen years ago the Port Moresby native was very unwilling to tell you his name.   He always got a friend to tell
you his name.   Possibly there was some magical idea at the
back of this.   The name and the individual are closely identified in native thought.   At the present time names are
given without much reluctance." [4]

·Among the Kai of Northern New Guinea etiquette forbids
a man to ask another to mention his own name.   Such a
question would greatly embarrass the person addressed.
Parents-in-law and children-in-law may not mention each
others' names, and men who have gone through the ceremony
of initiation together may not mention each other's names.
A person who has uttered one of these forbidden names is
believed to run the risk of dying by consumption.   And he
must atone for his offence by paying the person whom he has
named a fine, consisting of a spear, or a pot, or something of
the kind.[5]   In Mala, one of the South-East Solomon Islands,
" when a man is asked his name he seldom gives a direct
answer.   If someone else is present he will turn towards him

[1] A. and G. Grandidier, *op. cit.*
p. 303.

[2] N. Adriani and A. C. Kruijt, *op.
cit.* ii. 67.

[3] G. Landtman, *op. cit.* p. 176.

[4] W. M. Strong, " Some Personal
Experiences in British New Guinea,"
in *Journal of the Royal Anthropological Society*, xlix. (1919) p. 297.

[5] R. Neuhauss, *op. cit.* iii. 46.

and either say, 'You,' or else a mere look will suffice and the
other person says the name. . . . To say one's name is to
put one's self in another person's power. My name is myself.
The question, ' What is your name ? ' is rendered not ' What '
but ' Who ' (after the idiomatic use), where personality is the
dominant thought." [1] In Siberia " every Yakut bears two
names, and is never called by the right, except in cases of
necessity ; thus they think they evade the search of the evil
spirits bent on tormenting them." [2]

In not a few savage tribes parents are named after their
children, not children after their parents, the husband being
called " the father of So-and-So " and his wife " the mother
of So-and-So." Thus, for example, among the Toradyas
of Central Celebes, the father is named " the father of
So-and-So ", and the mother is called " the mother of So-
and-So." Lads, less often girls, are named after nephews
or nieces, or after slave children or imaginary persons.
When a child has grown up, the father is no longer named
after it, but after a younger child. When all the children are
grown up, the parents are named after their grand-children.
This change of name is called " making one's self young."
A man who had lost four children named himself grandfather of the fifth in order to deceive the spirits into thinking
that he had no child. [3]

Among the Klemantan of Borneo " after the naming of
a couple's first child the parents are always named as father
and mother of the child ; *e.g.*, if the child's name is *Obong*,
her father becomes known as *Tama Obong*, her mother as
Inai Obong, and their original names are disused and almost
forgotten, unless needed to distinguish the parents from other
persons of the same name, when the old names are appended
to the new." [4] So among the Kayans, another tribe of Borneo,
the name which a child receives is borne by him until he
becomes a father, when he resigns it in favour of the name
given to his child, with the title of Taman (or father) prefixed,
while the mother takes the name of her child with the title

[1] W. G. Ivens, *Melanesians of the
South-East Solomon Islands*, p. 11.
[2] M. Sauer, *An Account of a Geographical and Astronomical Expedition to Northern Russia* (London,
1802), p. 125.
[3] N. Adriani and A. C. Kruijt, *op.
cit.* ii. 67 *sq.*
[4] C. Hose and Wm. McDougall, *The
Pagan Tribes of North Borneo*, i. 80.

Tinan or mother prefixed.[1] Similarly among the Kuki Lushai, a tribe of Assam, " on the birth of a child the name to be given is settled upon, not by the parents, but by the elders of the community. Subsequent to the birth the father and mother drop their own names, and are addressed by that borne by their offspring, the terms for father and mother being affixed : thus, ' so-and-so's father,' ' so-and-so's mother.' "[2] Similarly, among the Kachcha Nagas, another tribe of the same region, when parents have a child they drop their own names and take that of their offspring, with the title of father or mother prefixed.[3] The Barotse of South Africa " have family names. Each individual has a name of his own, and they add a kind of inverted surname, derived from their children. A man is called Ra (father of) and a woman Ma (mother of), with the name of the child added."[4] But we are not told that among the Barotse parents drop their own names after the birth of a child.

Elsewhere I have suggested that the custom of naming parents after their children is based on the common reluctance of a person to utter his or her name, lest a sorcerer or evil spirit should hear it, and by means of it work evil on the owner of the name. In favour of this view I would point out, first, that among the Kuki Lushais, who practise the custom of naming parents after their children, there is a strong and general dislike of all persons to mention their own names,[5] and second, that among the Yakuts, as we have seen, every man keeps his real name secret, lest an evil spirit should learn it, and so be able to harm the owner of the name. The custom of naming parents after their children can hardly have originated, as has sometimes been thought, in a transition from female to male kinship, since it takes account of the mother equally with the father.

We have seen that in primitive society people are often unwilling to mention not only their own names, but also those of their relations by marriage, including their own

---

[1] *Ibid.* ii. 161.

[2] C. A. Soppitt, *Short Account of the Kuki-Lushai Tribes* (Shillong, 1887), p. 16.

[3] C. A. Soppitt, *A Short Account of the Kachcha Naga* (Shillong, 1885), p. 9.

[4] L. Decle, *Three Years in Savage Africa* (London, 1898), p. 76.

[5] J. Shakespear, *The Lushei Kuki Clans*. p 19.

wives.[1] Some further examples of these curious taboos may
here be added. Among the Kwottos of Northern Nigeria
" another form of avoidance, practised by married couples
throughout life, is the refraining from uttering each other's
personal names, whether in their presence or absence. It is
explained that a husband would be regarded as slighting his
wife's kindred if he were to show her so little respect as to
address her familiarly by the birth-name given her by her
own kindred. He therefore gives her a new 'marriage-
name.' "[2]

Among the Wajagga of Mount Kilimanjaro relations by
marriage may not mention each others' proper names, but
must refer to them only indirectly, or by using the terms of
their relationship. A young wife is particularly careful to
avoid mentioning the names of her husband's blood relations.
In conversation a brother-in-law and sister-in-law use a
special designation in referring to each other. They call
each other the " greased lead-ring." If a sister-in-law either
addresses her brother-in-law or speaks of him in conversation
with another, she refers to him as " greased lead-ring," at
the same time licking the thick lead ring which, like all
women of the tribe, she wears on her wrist. Similarly, when
a brother-in-law is speaking to or of his sister-in-law he calls
her " greased lead-ring," and at the same time licks the part
of his arm where women wear the ring.[3] Among the Wa-
kamba or Akamba of Kenya, a man was until lately forbidden to mention the proper names of his father-in-law and
mother-in-law. If he was asked to name them he would
either give false names, or would give the polite reply, " I
may not pronounce that name ; that is taboo among the
Akamba."[4] Among the Konde in the north of Nyasaland
a daughter-in-law may neither see nor name her father-in-
law and the avoidance of naming him has given rise to a
special form of women's speech among the people. She may
not pronounce her husband's family name, not even a part
of the name which occurs in other words. Thus, for example,

[1] See above, pp. 272, 273.
[2] J. R. Wilson-Haffenden, *The Red
Men of Nigeria*, p. 271.
[3] G. Gutmann, *Dichten und Denken*

der Dschagganeger, p. 81.
[4] Karasek-Eichhorn, " Beiträge zur
Kenntnis der Waschambaa," in *Baessler-Archiv*, i. (1911), pp. 186 *sq.*

the wife of Muankenja may not say *mkenja*, which means
bachelor. If she wishes to say " bachelor " she uses instead
the word *kepiki*. So also she may not pronounce any syllable
that reminds one of Muanonda, because that is also a family
name. If a child remains small and weak it is said that the
child's mother must certainly have pronounced the name of her
father-in-law.[1]

Among the domiciled Hindoos in Baluchistan " a husband
will not call his wife by name, nor will the wife take the name
of her husband. He addresses her as ' Sethani ' or ' Wan-
riani,' and the wife in turn addresses him as ' Seth ' or
' Wanria.' If they have a son, she calls the husband ' father
of so-and-so ' (naming the boy). This is a matter in which
the women are more particular than the men." [2]

Among the Birhors of Chota Nagpur in India, " as
amongst most other tribes and castes of Chota Nagpur, the
names of a man's younger brother's wife and of his wife's
elder sister are taboo to the Birhor, and the names of the
husband's elder brother and of a younger sister's husband and
a younger brother's wife are taboo to a Birhor woman.
Even words resembling in sound names of such relatives
may not be uttered. Thus, if the name of a woman's husband's elder brother is Budhu, she will not call a Wednesday
by its proper name of *Budh*, but in referring to a Wednesday
she will use some such expression as ' the day after Tuesday.'
It is believed that the uttering of such a tabooed name is
sure to cause sickness or other misfortune to the person
uttering the name or to some one of his or her family. When
a Birhor wants to say something to a younger brother's wife
or his wife's elder sister he may not ordinarily communicate
directly with such relative, but should communicate through
somebody else such as his own wife ; and similarly, when a
woman wants to say something to her husband's elder brother
or sister or her younger sister's husband, she should, if
possible, communicate through some third person. If any
direct communication becomes absolutely necessary between
such relatives they may talk without going close to each other

[1] Dr. F. Fulleborn, *Das Deutsche
Njassa- und Ruwumba-Gebiet, Land
und Leute* (Berlin, 1906), p. 351.

[2] Denys Bray, *Ethnographic Survey of Baluchistan*, ii. 22 *sq.*

and without looking straight at each other's face.   They may not sit on the same mat nor even tread on each other's shadow."[1]

Among the Sakai, a dwarf people of the Malay Peninsula, " the prohibition with regard to mentioning the names of near relatives, either by blood or marriage, so common in the Malayan region, is also found among some of the Negrito-Sakai and Sakai-Jakun tribes, and also among the Sakai proper.   A man of a Sakai-Jakun tribe, which was living close to Kuala Tembeling in Pahang, told me that they were forbidden to mention the names of fathers-in-law, mothers-in-law, brothers-in-law, or sisters-in-law ; while a man from near Pertang in Jelebu, Negri Sembilan, said that his people did not dare to mention the names of their fathers, because they were afraid of being struck by the indwelling power (*daulat*) of that relation.   Among the Hill Sakai of Perak I was informed that the avoidance of the mother-in-law was strictly observed, and that it was not allowable to speak to her directly, to pass in front of her, or even to hand her anything. Among these people there seems also to be a certain prejudice against a person mentioning his own name."[2]   Among the Toradyas of Central Celebes a man may not utter the names of his wife's parents, uncles, and aunts, and if their names are also common words in the language, he may not use these common words, but must substitute others for them.[3]

Among the Alfoors of Halmahera, a large island to the west of New Guinea, the use of substituted words occurs in various circumstances, and the practice receives different names according to the circumstances.   Thus the name *saali* is applied to the principal use of substituted words, namely, the use of a different word in order to avoid uttering the names of elder members of the wife's or the husband's family, or words which resemble such names in their terminations.   This custom is very common.   If, for example, such a member of a family bears a name meaning " land," then in speaking of land you would use another word, such as country, or if his name is the same with the word for hand, you would call it

[1] S. C. Roy, *The Birhors*, pp. 136 *sqq.*
[2] I. H. N. Evans, " Some Sakai Beliefs and Customs," in *Journal of*

the *Royal Anthropological Institute,* xlviii. (1918) pp. 194 *sq.*
[3] N. Adriani and A. C. Kruijt, *op. cit.* ii. 28.

upper arm ; if his name means sand, you would say desert ; if his name means tooth, you would say biter ; if his name signifies " wind " you would say " what moves to and fro," and so on.[1] In the East Indian island of Ceram, south of Halmahera, a man may not mention the real name of his wife's parents, brothers, and sisters ; and similarly a woman may not mention the names of her husband's relations.[2]

Among the Kiwai of British New Guinea " a man may not mention the name of his wife's father, mother, elder sister, or elder brother, or of any male or female relative of her father and mother. The prohibition is reciprocal as between husband and wife, and holds good when both are members of the same tribe." [3] Among the Mailu people of British New Guinea " there is absolute, strictly observed name-avoidance between the following kin : (1) mother-in-law ; (2) father-in-law ; (3) son-in-law ; (4) daughter-in-law ; (5) husband's elder brother ; (6) man's younger brother's wife ; (7) girl's younger sister's husband ; (8) man's wife's elder sister. But the younger brother may mention the name of the elder brother's wife, or a younger sister may mention the name of the elder sister's husband. They explain it thus : ' in the first instance, she is his eldest sister, and in the second case he is her elder brother.' " [4] Among the Yabim, another tribe of Northern New Guinea, persons related by marriage may not touch each other nor mention each others' names. If the son-in-law mentions his father-in-law, he does not utter his name, but speaks of him as his father-in-law. And conversely the parents-in-law describe their son-in-law as their daughter's husband.[5] Among the natives of New Britain " there are many prohibitions against eating with, touching, speaking to, or calling by name certain relatives, such as mother-in-law, son-in-law, and others. A native will never speak of these by their names : they are his *nimuan*, that is, people whose names he is forbidden to mention, and with whom certain prohibi-

[1] M. J. van Baarda, " Nog iets angaande ' Heer Pokken ' auf Halmahera," in *Bijdragen tot de Taal-, Land- en Volkenkunde van Nederlandsch-Indie*, lxvii. (1913) p. 58.
[2] M. C. Schadee, in *Internationales Archiv für Ethnographie*, xxii. (1915)

p. 134.
[3] W. N. Beaver, *Unexplored New Guinea*, p. 67.
[4] W. J. V. Saville, *In Unknown New Guinea*, p. 31.
[5] R. Neuhauss, *Deutsch Neu-Guinea*, iii. 426.

tions are connected." [1]   In the Booandik tribe of South
Australia a woman is not allowed to mention the name of her
son-in-law as long as he lives. [2]

In primitive society, again, it is very often forbidden to
mention the names of the dead, probably in most cases from a
fear of attracting the dangerous attention of the ghosts who
may be supposed to be attracted by the familiar sound of their
own names.   The taboo is particularly common among the
aborigines of Australia.   Speaking of the aborigines of New
South Wales, an early voyager tells us that after a death they
consigned the name of the deceased to oblivion, and never
mentioned it again.   He adds that " the namesake (*Tomelai*)
of the deceased assumes, for a time, the name of *Bourang*,
which appears to be the general appellation for those in such
circumstances, and signifies that they are at present destitute
of a name, their name-father being dead.   This title they
retain until they become the namesake of another person." [3]
In the Andrawilla tribe of East Central Australia the names
of the dead are never mentioned ;   it is thought that the
deceased would never rest peacefully should his name be
spoken. [4]   And indeed " everywhere in Australia it is the
custom among the indigenous people never to mention the
name of the person whose death is being lamented.   This
rule is so far-reaching that should there be more than one
tribesman holding the same name, the one surviving his
namesake immediately changes his appellation.   If, too, the
name of the dead one happened to be that of an animal or
place, a new word is immediately introduced in the vocabulary
of the tribe in place of the former.   Thus allusion to the dead
man's name is entirely avoided.   The reason for this strange
custom is that the tribespeople want the spirit of the departed
not to be molested ;   by calling aloud the name of one who has
gone beyond, the spirit might be persuaded to come back and
haunt the camp ;   the natives are in constant dread of this." [5]

Similarly, concerning the very primitive but now extinct

[1] G. Brown, *Melanesians and Polynesians*, p. 275.
[2] Mrs. J. Smith, *The Booandik
Tribe of South Australian Aborigines*,
(Adelaide, 1880), p. 3.
[3] J. Turnbull, *A Voyage Round the*
World (London, 1813), p. 87.
[4] F. H. Wells, in *Fifth Report of the
Australasian Association for the Advancement of Science* (1893), p. 519.
[5] H. Basedow, *The Australian
Aboriginal*, pp. 212 sq.

aborigines of Tasmania, we are told that they had " a fear of
pronouncing the name by which a deceased friend was known,
as if his shade might thus be offended.   To introduce, for any
purpose whatever, the name of any one of their deceased
relatives, called up at once a frown of horror and indignation
from a fear that it would be followed by some dire calamity."[1]
In Buin, one of the Solomon Islands, the old names of the
dead are not pronounced.   The deceased are known by new
names, " names of the other world," which were usually
chosen by the persons in their lifetime.[2]   The Kiwai of
British New Guinea avoid mentioning the dead by their old
name, particularly the names of those who have died recently
and are feared after death.   They say that this is like calling
on the ghost, who might appear at the call and cause sickness
among the living.[3]   Among the natives of Dobu, an island off
the South-East coast of British New Guinea, one cause of war
was " naming the dead.   The dead may be named only when
a mighty oath is taken, or by a sorcerer when all other
remedies to save a sick man from death have failed."[4]   The
Yakuts of Siberia never mention the names of the dead, and
any hut in which a death has taken place is left by them to fall
into ruins as an abode of demons.[5]

   In Africa the Barundi, a tribe to the west of Lake Victoria
Nyanza, never mention the names of the dead, lest they should
call back their mischievous ghosts, and all persons and things
bearing the same name as the deceased have to change them
for others.[6]   So among the neighbouring Banyankole when
a king died his name was never spoken again, and if his name
happened to be that of a common object the name of the thing
was changed for that of a new one.[7]   Among the Bakongo of
the Lower Congo " the name of the dead is tabooed, and is
therefore never mentioned, but if it is necessary to refer to
the deceased one, they call him ' old what's-his-name ' (*nkulu*

[1] J. Barnard, " Aborigines of Tasmania," in *Second Report of the Australasian Association for the Advancement of Science* (1890), p. 605.
[2] R. Thurnwald, " Im Bismarck-
archipel," in *Zeitschrift für Ethnologie*, xlii. (1901) p. 129.
[3] G. Landtman, *op. cit.* p. 293.
[4] W. E. Bromilow, " Some Manners and Customs of the Dobuans of
South-East Papua," in *Eleventh Report of the Australasian Association
for the Advancement of Science* (1907),
p. 470.
[5] M. Sauer, *op. cit.* p. 125.
[6] H. Meyer, *Die Barundi*, p. 114.
[7] J. Roscoe, *The Banyankole*, p. 35.

U

nengandi), or ' old Peter ' (*nkulu Mpetelo*), or ' of the name of Peter ' (*ejina dia Mpetelo*). Any photographs of the deceased are torn up, all signs of him removed from the house, and every effort is made to forget him." [1] After a death the Bushmen of the Kalahari desert in South Africa leave the spot and never mention the name of the deceased again.[2] Similarly the Bechuanas of the same region usually abstained from ever mentioning the name of a dead person lest his spirit should be offended.[3] In most tribes of Madagascar it is sacrilege to pronounce the name of a dead relative, and still more the name of a dead chief or king. They fear that on hearing the familiar name the spirit of the deceased will return among them, and above all things they dread any contact with the spirits of the dead. Only a sorcerer would dare to commit such a sacrilege, an offence punishable with death. There are even peoples, such as the Sakalavas, among whom it is forbidden under the severest penalties to make use of words in the current language which enter into the names of dead kings or which have a similar sound, such words being replaced by synonyms created for the purpose.[4]

Under the heading of tabooed words may be included a common prohibition to tell fairy stories or myths at certain times and seasons, and particularly during the day. The Berbers of North Africa, for example, will not tell their fairy stories during the day, believing that if they did so before night has fallen some great misfortune would befall the narrator or one of his family. The taboo is said to be not confined to the Berbers, but to be observed all over the world from Alaska to South Africa.[5] For example among the Baluba of the French Congo stories may not be told in the day-time : it is a thing never done, but they may be told in the evening.[6] In the Solomon Islands stories may not be told by day, but only by night : if they were told by day it is believed that the hair of the story-teller would fall out.[7] Again, in Dobu,

---

[1] J. H. Weeks, *Among the Primitive Bakongo*, pp. 248 *sq.*

[2] S. S. Dornan, *Pygmies and Bushmen of the Kalahari*, p. 145.

[3] S. S. Dornan, *op. cit.* p. 279.

[4] G. Grandidier, " La Mort . . . à Madagascar," in *L'Anthropologie*,

xxiii. (1912) p. 348.

[5] H. Basset, *Essai sur la littérature des Berbères* (Alger, 1920), p. 104.

[6] E. Torday, *On the Trail of the Bushongo*, p. 41.

[7] R. Thurnwald, *Forschungen auf den Salomo-Inseln*, i. 430.

to the south-east of New Guinea, " the telling of legends was restricted to the night-time, under the penalty of the narrators and hearers becoming fixtures to each other and to the place where they were sitting." [1]

Sometimes the names of sacred chiefs and gods are tabooed, and may not be spoken. Thus for example in Samoa there was a sacred chief named *Pe'a*, which in the Samoan language means flying-fox. Hence the name Pe'a might not be pronounced in the district in which the chief lived, still less in his presence, and the name for a flying fox in that district was changed for another, which means bird of heaven. Again at Matautu in Samoa, neither the words *titi* nor *vave* could be used, because these were the names of two gods in that village. The former, which was the name of the girdle or apron of *ti* leaves worn by all the people, was changed to *noa*. *Vave*, which meant swiftly, had the synonym *taalise* substituted for it.[2] Again in Annam the people avoid mentioning the names of the gods, because they think that to name them is to evoke them, and to render their presence real, which is always dreaded by the profane. Thus it is prohibited to pronounce the exact name of certain villages, since the name designates at the same time the tutelary deity of the village.[3]

But in primitive society not merely the personal names of gods and men are often tabooed. The same interdiction is very frequently laid on the names of common objects of daily life in certain circumstances, and for a certain time.[4] Hence when men are engaged in certain special occupations they are often debarred from the use of many common words, lest the spirits should hear them and frustrate their efforts. Thus for example when a Maori is digging for a certain tuber called *perei* he may not mention the name of the tuber, he will call it *maukuuku*, for should he mention the name *perei* no roots would be found by his party. " In the bird-snaring season should a man mention that he is going to visit his snares to take the birds which have been caught, he

[1] W. E. Bromilow, " Dobuan Beliefs and Folk-lore," in *Thirteenth Report of the Australasian Association for the Advancement of Science* (Sydney, 1912), p. 413.

[2] G. Brown, *Melanesians and Polynesians*, p. 280.

[3] P. Giran, *Magie et Religion Annamites*, pp. 94 *sq.*

[4] Compare *Taboo and the Perils of the Soul*, pp. 392 *sqq.*

will not make use of the word *wetewete* (a plural form of *wewete*, to untie), for that would be a *puhore*, and would bring ill-luck. He will use, in place thereof, the term *wherawhera* (a plural form of *whera*, to open). Or should the snarer be going to look at his *waka* or water troughs, over which pigeon snares are set, he will not use the word *titiro*, ' to look at,' but substitute that of *matai*, that no *puhore* may be incurred."[1] Again in sailing northwards the natives of the Marshall Islands avoid the use of certain common words, and substitute others in place of them. Thus instead of *wut*, which means rain, they say *wajum*; instead of *wa*, which means canoe, they say *jidon*; and instead of *mane*, which means food, they say *kakuronron*.[2]

Among the Kiwai of British New Guinea when a man is waiting on the platform to harpoon dugong, he will not call the dugong by its proper name, for he thinks that to do so would spoil his luck, so he calls the dugong a pig.[3] The Alfoors of Halmahera, an island to the west of New Guinea, have a class of substituted words called *sirangi*, which they use in various circumstances instead of the ordinary words. Such words are employed in cases where to use the ordinary words would be deemed dangerous, for instance in making a long sea voyage, as from Obi to Ceram. Evil powers might drive the mariner out of his course ; hence he tries to deceive them as to the goal of his voyage. Thus, for example, instead of " straight ahead " or " forecastle " he would say " bird's beak ; instead of " right " or " starboard " he would say " sword " ; and instead of " larboard " he would say " shield." In this way a sort of " sea language " arises. So in other districts there is a sort of " forest language " employed in the search for products of the forest such as dammar and camphor : in such cases the searcher is careful to avoid all the usual words referring to the business he has in hand, in order that he may not be hampered by evil influences in the pursuit of his calling. Hence in the substituted words made use of during an attack of smallpox, as Mr. van Ossenbruggen correctly remarks, we have to do

[1] E. Best, in *Seventh Report of the Australasian Association for the Advancement of Science* (1898), p. 769.

[2] P. A. Erdland, *Die Marshall-Insulaner*, p. 341.

[3] G. Landtman, *op. cit.* p. 132.

with the belief in sympathetic magic, that is, the belief that
the dreaded event is brought about by simply naming it.
This belief, or rather superstition, is very strong among these
Alfoors. " So when I good-naturedly warned heathens to
abstain from such and such an evil course, lest a judgment
or visitation should overtake them, I saw that it made a very
disagreeable impression on them, because they considered
that the simple naming of the evil that might overtake them
was as dangerous and as effective as an attempt on my part
to bring down the calamity upon them." The reason why
the use of substituted words occurs almost only in cases of
smallpox is probably that in these regions smallpox is the
most dreaded malady ; cholera and pestilence have been
nearly or altogether unknown. Hence smallpox is spoken
of as a king—a pretty word to hide an ugly thing, and yet
an appropriate image, since the disease visits district after
district, village after village, like a prince making a royal
progress. He who can hide himself from the sickness is
supposed not to be attacked by it; hence the people try
to conceal themselves in all sorts of ways. In the villages
everything must be as quiet as possible. Fowls, especially
cocks, are killed ; and dogs would also be killed, if they
were not so necessary for the chase. Children must be
kept quiet ; if they squall, they are beaten. The festal drum
is never heard in the district. If anybody dies, no lamentation
is heard, no shot is fired to drive away the evil spirits from
the house of death. In everything an appearance must be
kept up as if the population of the village were extinct, so
that when " King Smallpox " comes he may imagine that
there is no one at home, and that he can therefore pass by.[1]
The Sakai in the centre of the Malay Peninsula believe that
animals have souls, and consequently intelligence. Hence
" the aborigines of the Ulu Kinta think that it is unlucky to
use the proper name of an animal when they are eating its
flesh, and substitute instead another appellation which is
often a periphrasis descriptive of some characteristic of it.
Thus the bamboo-rat, which is ordinarily called *takator*, when

---

[1] M. J. van Baarda, " Nog iets
aangaande ' Heer Pokken ' auf Halmahera," in *Bijdragen tot de Taal-*
Land- en Volkenkunde van Neder-
landsch-Indië, lxvii. (1913) pp. 58 *sqq.*

being eaten is described as *nyam awin*, or ' bamboo meat ' ; the bear (*ta'pus*) becomes *mes mat* (little eyes); the porcupine (*chekos*), *berjalak* (the thorny one); the ' brok ' (or coconut) monkey (*dok*), *hoi wet* or *hoi ket*, which is said to mean ' no tail ' ; and the fowl (*manuk*) *chep*, which simply means ' bird.' " [1]

The Malays have a whole system of tabooed and substituted words, based as usual on the conception of all Nature as animate and sensitive, and therefore as liable to resent human intrusion on its domain. I will borrow the excellent account of it given by Mr. Winstedt : " The Malay is afraid to attract the spirits of beasts. In the jungle the dreaded tiger is ' grandfather.' On a mine the elephant, whose heavy feet and roving trunk can undo the work of puny men, must be called ' the tall one,' the blundering water-buffalo ' the unlucky one,' the poisonous snake ' the live creeper.' In Patani Bay fishermen call a crocodile the ' gap-toothed thingummy-bob,' a goat or sheep the ' baa-baa,' a buffalo ' moo,' a sea-snake ' the weaver's sword,' a tiger ' stripes,' a monkey ' Mr. Long-Tail,' a vulture ' bald-head,' a Buddhist monk ' the yellow one,' and sea-spirits ' thingummies.' Smallpox is termed in many places ' the complaint of the good folk.' The mention of the real name may attract the capricious attention of the lords of the sea, the spirit of a disease, a human ghost, a king, a mammal or a mother-in-law : it may also frighten away such elusive things as ore in a mine or camphor in a tree. So on a tin-mine the ore must be called ' grass-seed ' and the metal ' white stone.' Collectors of camphor use an elaborate tabu vocabulary of aboriginal, rare and artificial words : the bamboo is called ' the drooper,' bananas ' the fruit in rows,' bees ' seeds on branches,' blood ' sap,' a cat ' the kitchen tiger,' a fire-fly ' a torch for the eyes,' the nose ' the smeller,' the jaws ' the chewers,' a bed ' the cuddling-place,' and so on. Not only is the name of camphor itself avoided, but no words are uttered which might lead the tree to suspect that Malays are in search of its treasures. So human in anger and fear are trees and minerals and beasts." [2]

---

[1] I. H. N. Evans, " Some Sakai Beliefs and Customs," in *Journal of the Royal Anthropological Institute,* xlviii. (1918) p. 181.

[2] R. O. Winstedt, *Shaman, Saiva, and Sufi,* pp. 69 *sq.*

The Lakhers of Assam have a similar system of tabooed and substituted words, based on a similar belief in the universal animation of Nature. " As Lakhers believe that the universe is peopled by spirits ready to harm man or to seize his possessions, they are afraid when travelling or in the jungle to mention the names of any animals they own, lest the evil spirits should hear what they say, and, wishing to get possession of the animals, should make the owners ill, in order that the animals may be sacrificed to them. Therefore, when referring to animals anywhere, except inside their own houses, Lakhers refer to them only indirectly. *Mithun* and cows are referred to as grass-eaters or *rabapa*, goats are referred to as medicine or *thanghnapa*, because they are frequently used for sacrifices. Pigs are referred to as *sahrang* (the animal) or *angchahritapa* (the dwellers below the house), dogs are referred to as *lomangbeupa* or the eaters of scraps that fall from men's meals, chickens are referred to as *pavaw* or birds. To save themselves from falling into the clutches of a wood- or mountain-spirit when travelling in the jungle, Lakhers, instead of calling each other by name, say ' *Eu heinaw*,' which means ' Ho, brother.' By such simple devices does the Lakher think to deceive the supernatural powers." [1] Among the Oraons of Chota Nagpur in India " there are tabus on names of certain persons, animals, places, or other things : it is believed that some names pronounced at certain times bring ill-luck to the person who pronounces them. Thus the names of certain villages are not pronounced by the men of certain other villages at night-time, for it is believed that some misfortune will befall the man who does so. Similarly some people's names are considered of bad omen if pronounced within an hour or so after sunrise. In the cases of certain beasts and reptiles, substitutes for their names are used at night. Thus a serpent is called a ' rope,' a tiger is called ' the long-tailed thing ' (*digha khola*), a sheep is called the ' wool-covered thing' (*khani chutti*). These prohibitions are not attended with any social consequences or social disapproval." [2]

[1] N. E. Parry, *The Lakhers*, pp. 477 *sq.*

[2] S. C. Roy, *The Oraons of Chota Nagpur*, p. 361.

In Africa the Wajagga of Mount Kilimanjaro believe
that the dangerous animals of their country are sent by the
spirits of the dead to attack them, and in order to avoid the
danger in certain circumstances they abstain from calling
the creatures by their proper names and adopt substituted
names instead.   When they fear that an elephant is near them
in the forest they speak of the animal only as the chieftain,
they speak of the lion as " the Lord from below," and they
refer to the leopard as " rope " apparently on account of
the lithe and supple body of the beast.   But they attempt to
work on the feelings of the beasts in other and less compli-
mentary ways.   Thus they call the elephant " woman's
bag," because his hide is as cracked and wrinkled as a
woman's market bag.   They think that, humbled by this
mode of referring to him, the elephant will sneak shame-
facedly away.   But the lion and the giant snake are sometimes referred to by the high-sounding title of " Lord of the
Underworld." [1]   The Ibibio of Southern Nigeria extract
a magical medicine from a crocodile, and for this purpose
they hunt and seek to capture the animal ; but in hunting it
they must abstain from mentioning the name of the crocodile,
and if only they observe this taboo they can approach the
brute in perfect safety.[2]   Among the Ila-speaking tribes
of Northern Rhodesia it is a maxim that in travelling through
the wilderness you should not speak of the lion by his proper
name, but must refer to him only as *Shikunze*, the outsider,
or *Kabwenga mukando*, the great hyena, for otherwise you
might bring the beast upon you.   Further, in smelting iron
you should not speak of fire as fire, but only as " the fierce
one," and when women are threshing corn they may neither
drink water nor speak of it by name ; they must, if it is
necessary at all, speak of it as *mawa Leza*, " that which falls
from the sky." [3]

In primitive society a common taboo forbids people to
step over things or persons lying on the ground, because they
believe that to do so would exercise an injurious effect of some
sort on the things or persons stepped over.   Elsewhere I

---

[1] B. Gutmann, *Dichten und Denken
der Dschagganeger*, p. 44.
[2] P. A. Talbot, *Life in Southern*

Nigeria, p. 99.
[3] E. W. Smith and A. M. Dale, *op.
cit.* i. 368.

have illustrated this rule by examples : [1] here I may add a few more instances to conclude the subject of taboo.   Thus among the Banyoro of Uganda " a potter is careful to place his pots when drying where they shall not be stepped over and where no pregnant woman shall come near them. Should either of the above precautions be disregarded, it is thought the pots will break when being baked." [2]   Among the Bakene, a small tribe of lake dwellers and fishers in Uganda, "when a man is making a new line or net, his father's wives must keep away from him lest they should accidentally step over the materials of his work ; such an action would have a disastrous effect, as the line or net would not catch thereafter unless he learned what had happened and was able to propitiate the spirit of the net by an offering of food which he fastened to the material where the woman had stepped over it.   If this is not done, they say that no net over which a woman has stepped will retain fish, they will merely pass through its meshes, unless the spirit is propitiated." [3]   In Loango it is believed that if a person steps over a sleeper he thereby transfers to the sleeper all the sorrows and sufferings with which he himself is afflicted, and that to step over a child is to stunt its growth.[4]   Similarly the Merinas of Madagascar believe that to step over children renders them weak and puny.[5]

The Wajagga of Mount Kilimanjaro think that if a person has stepped over the body of another he should at once turn back and leap over the body in the reverse direction, thus undoing his first action, but that if he fails to do so the man he stepped over will soon die.   Among these people if a she-goat has leaped over a man lying on the ground it is killed, and a he-goat which has leaped over the body of a woman lying on the ground is also killed.   But if the owner of the animals wishes to keep them he may do so on condition of leading them back and causing them to leap over again the body of the man or woman.[6]

[1] Compare *The Golden Bough : Taboo and the Perils of the Soul,* pp. 423 *sqq.*

[2] J. Roscoe, *The Northern Bantu,* p. 79.

[3] J. Roscoe, *op. cit.* p. 155.

[4] *Die Loango Expedition,* iii. 2. p. 330.

[5] A. and G. Grandidier, *op. cit.* p. 289.

[6] B. Gutmann, *Dichten und Denken der Dschagganeger,* p. 155.

CHAPTER XXIV

THE KILLING OF THE DIVINE KING

THE custom of killing a divine king upon any serious failure of his bodily or mental powers, because such failure is believed to entail the failure of the rain and the crops which are thought to be inseparably bound up with the divine life of the king, is very common in Africa. Elsewhere I have adduced some examples ; [1] but the evidence has since been considerably extended, notably by the researches of Mr. P. Amaury Talbot in Southern Nigeria, and of Mr. C. K. Meek in Northern Nigeria, and the whole subject has been admirably discussed by Professor C. G. Seligman [2] in a learned and instructive monograph. I shall take advantage of their labours to lay some of the new evidence before my readers.[3] The custom is of especial interest to us in this work because, if I am right, it furnishes a clue to the mysterious rule of the priesthood of Diana at Nemi, which obliged every priest, the King of the Wood as he was called, to be slain in single combat by his successor in office. At the outset I will only mention that the evidence for the closest parallel—that of the Shilluk kings on the Upper Nile—which I cited on information kindly furnished me by its discoverer, my friend Dr. C. G. Seligman, has since been published in full by Dr. Seligman himself,[4] and confirmed by the account of a Catholic

---

[1] See *The Golden Bough*, Part III., *The Dying God*, pp. 9 *sqq.*

[2] C. G. Seligman, *Egypt and Negro Africa* (London, 1934).

[3] Some of the new evidence has already been cited by me in my commentary on the *Fasti* of Ovid (London, 1929), vol. iii. pp. 72-87.

[4] C. G. Seligman, *The Cult of Nyakang and the Divine Kings of the Shilluk, General Science of the Fourth Report of the Wellcome Tropical Research Laboratories* (Khartoum, 1911). Cf. *id.*, in J. Hastings' *Encyclopaedia of Religion and Ethics*, xi. 459 *sqq.*, *s.v.* " Shilluk." Cf. his

missionary, Father W. Hofmayr, who laboured among the Shilluk for about ten years and is familiar with their language and institutions.[1] I need therefore say no more on that subject.

The Jukun are a tribe in Northern Nigeria whose country is situated in the basin of the Benue River, an important tributary of the Niger. Among them all Jukun chiefs, however minor, are regarded as being in some measure incarnations of deity, while the Aku or king of Wukari is regarded as the supreme incarnation. It is a common saying among the Jukun that the power of the Aku exceeds that of Chidô (the Jukun sky-god), for a man may incur the wrath of Chidô and still continue to live, but one who incurs the wrath of the Aku dies that very day.[2] The divine king is regarded as having a personal influence over the works of Nature and his primary function is to secure for the people a successful harvest. " This is certainly his main duty. He is not, and apparently never was, expected to be a leader of victorious armies, but he is expected to secure in his time a regular succession of rich harvests, and by his ability to do so is adjudged to be a true son of god. He is identified with the crops, and is addressed as *Azaiwo* (our Guinea-corn), *Afyewo* (our Ground-nuts) or *Asoiwo* (our Beans). . . . But to secure a good harvest there must be a bountiful, but not an undue, supply of rain at the proper times, and the ripening crops must be protected from the excessive winds. The king of the Jukun is, therefore, in virtue of his deity, able to control the rains and the winds. A succession of droughts or bad harvests is ascribed to his negligence or to the waning of his strength, and he is accordingly secretly strangled.

" According to Jukun tradition the Jukun king was only allowed to rule for a period of seven years, being put to death at any convenient time after he had reached this allotted span. . . . No reason is given to the limitation of the period of years to seven. The number seven is apparently a sacred number in all Jukun communities, based perhaps on an ancient Moon cult. But possibly the choice of seven is due

volume, *Pagan Tribes of the Nilotic Sudan* (London, 1932), pp. 90-92, 197-198, 423-428.
[1] W. Hofmayr, *Die Shilluk*, pp.

178-180.

[2] C. K. Meek, *A Sudanese Kingdom*, pp. 121 sq.

to the observation that famines seem to occur roughly at intervals of seven years in the Northern Provinces of Nigeria. Some Jukun state, however, that in former times the allotted span was no more than two years ; and with this we may compare the three years or four years traditionally allowed to the Yoruba chiefs of Abeokuta and Ijebu. The Jukun period of two years was subsequently extended to seven, it being said (after the extension) that if the king were killed before that time his ghost would pursue his slayers, but that if he were killed at any later time his slayers had nothing to fear. We have seen that there were rites performed some six or seven years after the king had been crowned, the object of which was to advance the king to a higher degree of sovereignty, or in other words to secure a prolongation of his period of office.   Kings might, therefore, reign for more than seven years, and if any credit can be attached to the chronology of the list of kings in the various Jukun communities, it would not appear that the septennial rule was enforced during the last two hundred years.   Further, if we are to believe the concurrent tradition that a king who fell sick was put to death it must have been permissible to kill the king before the completion of seven years.   It may be assumed generally that a popular king was allowed to remain in office so long as he was able to carry out the daily liturgy and as long as the harvests were satisfactory, but that at the end of seven years he was subjected to an ordeal which obtained for him a further probationary period.   It is possible that an unsatisfactory king met his death during the ordeal, *i.e.* during the *Ando ku* rites.

" It is not possible to give full and accurate details of the ritual of the killing and burial of the king, as these are known to only a few officials ; or it might be more correct to say that parts of the ritual are known to particular officials, and parts to other particular officials, it being taboo and dangerous for one official to breathe to another a single syllable of the secret duty pertaining to his office.   Even the king himself is ignorant of some parts at least of the procedure.   The following account is based partly on hearsay and partly on such details as were revealed by persons who had official or accidental knowledge of the ritual.

" When the king became sick, or infirm, or broke any of the royal taboos, or proved himself unfortunate, he was secretly put to death.   Whether any king was, in the olden days, permitted to die a natural death cannot now be known, but it is noteworthy that many Jukun kings are said to have reached a hoary old age, so that mere old age was not in itself considered a sufficient cause for the ritual murder of the king.   The mode of killing was by strangulation with a string or piece of cloth. . . . Those appointed to commit the murder entered the palace at night, having previously suborned the Akû Nako, Katô, and Iche [1] to assist, if not to take the principal part in the murder.   The two executioners tied a noose of cloth round the neck of the sleeping king, and going off in different directions pulled the cloth until the king was strangled.   It is said that if the king woke up and attempted to summon assistance the executioners reminded him that they were but performing the ancestral custom and that it behoved the king to behave quietly, as his royal ancestors had done before him.   Another method was for the conspirators to bore a hole in the wall of the king's sleeping apartment and pass a noose through to the king's wife, who fastened it round his neck, the conspirators then pulling on the noose from outside.   The king could only be killed by strangulation for two reasons :   (a) that the executioners might not look into the king's eyes as he died, for if they did his departing spirit would slay them ; and (b) that the king's blood might not be spilt.   It is also said that no one who had a claim to the throne might be present at the king's execution.

" The king's demise was and is kept a close secret, and is not, in fact, revealed until many months afterwards, when the body is formally buried.   Various reasons are assigned for this secrecy, such as that the counsellors may have time to choose a successor, that bloody contests between aspirants for the throne may be avoided, or that the royal slaves and wives may not run away.   But the real reason would seem to depend on the belief that the king is the crops.   If he dies between March and December an announcement of his death would be tantamount to a repudiation of the central feature of Jukun religion, viz. the identification of the king with the

[1] The Akû Nako, Katô, and Iche are three royal officials.

annual corn ; or to say that he had 'returned to the skies' would be the same thing as saying that there would be no harvest that year.   It would in fact be an invitation to the crops to wither up.   His body is therefore kept preserved until after the harvest.   Even at the present time, when it is no longer possible to preserve for long the secret of the king's death, it is believed that the crops harvested after his death are the late king's 'seed.'   If he dies in the dry season it might be supposed that his death could be announced with safety, his functions being handed over to his successor ; but even in this case the normal rule is observed, though the ensuing crop is regarded as being that of his successor." [1] After the king's death an incision is made in his body and the heart extracted.   It is placed on a pointed stick beside a fire.   When it is thoroughly dried it is ground into a powder which is handed over to a court official that it may be secretly and periodically inserted into the food of the king's successor. The body itself is desiccated by fumigation over a slow fire. " The period of fumigation varies from four to ten months, according to the time of the year at which the king had died. Being the personification of the life of the crops he cannot be buried during the dry season.   Otherwise the crops would die for ever.   He is usually buried at the beginning of the wet season when the bulrush-millet crop has attained the height of about one foot." [2]   When the time for burial has come the king's corpse is mounted on a horse behind a rider.   The horseman first faces south, then proceeds some paces north, then goes west, and returns eastward.   At this stage all the people burst into loud lamentation, throwing themselves upon the ground, and crying out, " Our lord, whither are you going ?   Return, oh return !   In whose hands have ye left us ?   Our Corn, our Beans, our Ground-nuts."   The horseman wheels the horse and the drummer plays a chant and sings, calling on the names of former kings, and saying that the king whom they know is leaving them ; may those who have gone before receive him well, and may he salute his ancestors on behalf of the people.   The horseman again wheels his horse as though to go, and again the people break into lamentation.   A certain official (the Angwo Tsi) falls

¹ C. K. Meek, *op. cit.* pp. 165 *sqq.*   ² C. K. Meek, *op. cit.* p. 169.

on the ground saying, " And are you going off thus and leaving us destitute of rain and corn ? "   At this the horseman discharges some millet from the dead king's hand, and some water from a flask.   Accompanied by the senior officials and the royal family the horseman then rides off, with the king's body behind him.   They proceed as far as a small hamlet where the Kû Za or priest of the corn bars their progress with a demand for the return of the seed which had been conferred on the king at his coronation.   A few seeds are handed to the priest who declares that they are worthless as they have been fully used.   The Kinda protests that this is not their fault but is the doing of the Sky-God (*Chidô*). They pray the priest to have patience and to allow them to spend the night there.   On the following morning they proceed to the hamlet of the Kû Vi, who had conferred the kingship on the king, and there the progress of the party is again barred by a demand for the return of the royal coat, cap, and whip.   The priestly official known as Katô also demands the return of the rain-making cloth.   The king is thus divested of his kingship and now becomes merely a corpse.   He is given a new personal name and under this name the body is finally handed to the Ba-Nando, the kindred which is responsible for carrying out the burial rites.

They deposit the corpse in a burial hut, which is then sealed up and surrounded by a stockade.   Close to the burial hut a horse is tossed on the ground and killed with clubs.   In former times two slaves, male and female, were killed by having their necks twisted, their bodies being left near the doorway of the royal tomb.   The male slave thus killed was known as the attendant of " the Corn," that is, of the king.   After death he became one of the slave ghosts whose cult is in the hands of the Ba-Nando.   These ghosts are propitiated ; and in times of drought, or when the harmattan wind is delayed, sacrifice may be offered to them, should the divining apparatus declare that the failure of the rain or wind was due to them, the king providing the sacrificial gifts.   The hut over the king's grave is not, nowadays, kept in repair, but in former times it was re-thatched when rites were occasionally offered on behalf of the living king.   The occasions for such rites would be when a drought threatened and the divining apparatus had indicated that the rains were being withheld by the former king. Two slaves, provided by the king, were sacrificed, their necks being broken and the blood which exuded from their mouth and nostrils being caught in a calabash and poured on the top of the grave of that king who had been declared to be inhibiting the rains. The formula used was, " Your grandchild has given you this offering. If it is you who are withholding the rains then accept the offering and send us rain that we may harvest our crops and make libations to you." In the burial hut beside the royal corpse is always deposited a bag containing the parings of the nails and the clippings of the hair of the late king, which are accumulated during his reign.[1]

A fuller account of the custom of killing the Jukun kings of Kororofa is given by Mr. H. R. Palmer, a high authority on the history of Northern Nigeria. According to him, the Jukun or (as he spells the name) Jukoñ kings were only allowed to reign two years and were then killed, until a king named Agudu enlisted a Hausa bodyguard, and so contrived to prolong his reign to eleven years. The procedure at the killing of the king and the enthronement of his slayer is reported to have been as follows :

" There was a king made every two years. When a king had reigned two years it was considered that he had enjoyed power long enough, and he was compelled to fight with the senior member of the royal family, who came forward and challenged him to fight until one of them was killed. The descent of the kingship did not go from the reigning king to his sons, but to any children of any deceased king. The would-be successor, at about the season of the great feast, used to come into the king's mess suddenly and walk round and then go out. Of course under ordinary circumstances this would have been a great affront, but the king understood that from that time forward the king must guard himself. At the first opportunity after this the successor attacked the king. If he killed him, the fight was over for the time ; if he did not kill him, another of his relations came forward and challenged the king in the same way. This went on until someone did kill the king.

[1] C. K. Meek, *op. cit.* pp. 170-175.

" After the king was killed his body was taken to the place of sacrifice, the internal organs were removed, and four men were put to guard the corpse, which was placed on a bed and smeared over with salt and butter. A slow fire was lighted underneath and the body thus kept often for two or three months. At the end of this period all the chief men of the country were summoned and the death of the king was officially announced. All the chiefs of the country assembled at the place of sacrifice, which was called *puji*, and all the male members of the royal family attended, among them the king-slayer. Then the chief priest stepped forward and said, ' We wish to make a king.' A chair, a bed, and five or six *turmi*'s ¹ were arranged in a circle. The chief priest and other important officers sat on the *turmi*'s, the king-slayer taking the chair. Then the chief priest advanced and asked if all were assembled. He then said : ' So-and-so our king is dead ; we wish to decide on someone who can maintain us. Here are the whip and the cap.' Then the senior chief present took the whip and the cap and gave them to the chief priest, saying : ' Give us a king.' The chief priest placed the cap on the head of the king-slayer and the whip on his neck, saying, at the same time : ' You have killed our elder brother, but to-day you are in his place. Do not let us lack food or drink. If you can give us these, let us see if this cap will remain on your head.' The cap was then put on the king-slayer's head, and he twisted his head round sharply with the cap on. If the cap did not fall off he was then made king.

" After that a black dog, a black ox, a black goat, and black fowls were sacrificed at the gate through which the new king would pass on going out. As he went through, the chief priest said : ' To-day the world is yours, but see the corpse of him whom you killed ; you must bury what belongs to you. See the blood on the ground ; cross it and pass.' Then the new king stepped over the body of the old king, and when he had crossed the chief priest said : ' What you have done to the dead to-day, to-morrow will be done to you. Do you agree ? ' And he replied : ' Who

¹ " *Turmi*—a wooden mortar for pounding corn, which is turned upside down and used as a seat."

has tried to escape the custom of our country, and how can I ? I agree ! '

" Then followed the burial, which took place the same night. The chief priest clothed the corpse of the dead king, and he, the senior chief, and the new king alone took the body to the place of burial. The new king mounted a horse, and the corpse was put astride the horse in front of him. They then went in solemn procession to the place of burial, which is called *puji*. This procession to *puji* took place at midnight, and no women, boys, or strangers were allowed to see it.

" The place of burial was a funeral chamber excavated beneath the floor of a large, domed, circular hut. A hole was made in the centre of the hut with a narrow opening about two feet across, widening out below to about the same size as the hut itself. Its general shape was therefore like an inverted funnel. The roof of this funeral chamber was supported by beams and rafters. The earth was all removed to a distance. The floor was beaten. A kind of ladder was made by which to descend into the tomb.

" The king, the chief priest, and the senior chief carried the old king's body down into the tomb. Prepared for its reception were a red cloak, twelve mats, *tulus* (water-jars), a washing basin, a calabash for drinking, pipe and tobacco, apparatus for making fire, a finger-bowl, some palm wine. The mouth of the hole is then covered over. The roof of the hut is covered by all the people of the village with old clothes, and it is left until it falls in. . . .

" The king might not sneeze. If he sneezed, coughed, had smallpox, or was sick in any way he was killed." [1]

Among the Fung, a tribe inhabiting the country south of the Gezira between the White and Blue Niles, but who seem to have migrated thither from Sennar, the custom of killing the king on magical or religious grounds seems formerly to have been regularly observed. It is recorded by the traveller Bruce,[2] who tells us that the king-killer was

[1] H. R. Palmer, " Notes on the Korórofawa and Jukoñ," in *Journal of the African Society*, No. 44, vol. xi., July 1912, pp. 407-409.

[2] J. Bruce, *Travels to Discover the Source of the Nile* (Edinburgh, 1790), iv. 459-461, cited by C. G. and B. Z. Seligman, *Pagan Tribes of the Nilotic Sudan*, p. 423.

a regular official who might in his time despatch several kings.

" Professor Evans-Pritchard's informants stated that the ruler would be killed by a relative (and by no other) who was ambitious to occupy his high office, but that this could not happen until the deed had been sanctioned by a family council, since the killing was no individual murder but rather a joint execution ; consequently only those kings who proved unsatisfactory to the Fung relatives were killed. The actual spearing appears to have been carried out by a brother of the king by the same father but having a different mother, though the mother's brother's son and the father's brother's son were also mentioned as fulfilling this function. When several brothers united to kill the king it was regarded proper that the eldest of them should succeed him. The slayer might try and spear the king at night, or might lie in wait for him with a party in the bush, but he would seldom find him alone, as the king always went about with an armed bodyguard of slaves. He would regularly change his sleeping hut, not only nightly, but several times during the night, sleeping only a little while in each hut and always surrounded by armed guards. It was the present head of the Fung line who told Professor Evans-Pritchard how little his ancestors dared to sleep at night ; ' he slept and woke, slept and woke, slept and woke,' he said, while another man added how restless the king was at night, ' always on the move, coming and going.'

" When it had been decided that the king should die, he was wakened in the night by his guard and told that there was a party of armed men outside. He and his bodyguard fought to the death, and all with him were slain by his relatives and their retainers. His wives were not slain but were inherited by a brother, though not by his slayer. Age and sickness were not regarded as reasons for killing the ruler as amongst the Shilluk and Dinka, nor was he specially protected from the dangers of war but took part in the fighting." [1]

Among the Mbum, a tribe inhabiting the district of Ngaundere in the French Cameroons, the chief is known as

[1] C. G. and B. Z. Seligman, *op. cit.* p. 427.

Belaka. " The Belaka is ' the father of the cults ' ; he is
likened to a lion or a leopard among animals ; he is a demigod—in fact, he is almost God himself. For he is the reposi-
tory of the life and prosperity of the community. Childbirth,
rain, crops, health are so intimately connected with him that
any deficiency in these is ascribed to his deliberate ill-will or
culpable neglect. When he goes abroad he is preceded and
followed by four men carrying torches of grass, for it is said
that though the chief may share with others the heat of the
sun, he alone may feel the heat of fire—for fire belongs to him.
The chief is the keeper of the seed corn. All the corn harvested on the royal farm is deposited in a huge granary close
to the rain and corn shrine. At sowing time the royal drum,
mounted on a platform, is sounded, and all farmers come to
receive the seed, which, being the king's, is regarded as
charged with magical power. Each farmer is given a little
of the seed and hurries home to plant it the same day (if he
waited until the following day the seed would lose its magical
efficacy). This custom is precisely that of the Wukari and
Kona Jukun. The chief is held responsible for drought
conditions ; for a drought may be occasioned either by the
failure of the chief to see that all due religious rites have been
performed, or merely because the general character of the
chief was displeasing to the gods. As an example of the
former a drought might occur as a result of the anger of the
gods because, during an epidemic, the chief had taken no
steps to stay the witchcraft which had caused the epidemic.
For in times of excessive sickness it is the business of the chief
to subject the entire town to an ordeal by sasswood in order
that witches may be detected and automatically removed. . . .

" The Mbum chief was not always put to death ; if things
went well and he was popular he was left alone. Otherwise
the members of his family would ask for the performance of
some religious rites, followed as usual by an orgy of beer-
drinking. While the beer bout was in progress the conspirators busied themselves boring a hole in the wall on the
other side of which was the royal couch. When the intoxi-
cated chief lay down and went to sleep the conspirators completed the last stage of boring, and thrust through a noose.
The chief's wife, having been suborned, fixed the noose round

his neck, and the conspirators on the other side of the wall pulled on the rope and strangled the chief." [1]

With regard to kings in Southern Nigeria, we are informed by Mr. P. Amaury Talbot, whose official position and long residence in the country have afforded him unique opportunities of observation, that "throughout the land, as a general rule, the king combines magico-religious with civil duties, acts as the representative and priest of the town or clan in all dealings with gods, jujus,[2] and ancestors, and regulates all religious ceremonies. He is often regarded as semi-divine, endowed with the spirit of his ancestors or the ancestral god, is confined to his house except on special occasions—chiefly, no doubt, so that the sanctity in which he lives should not be violated—and the prosperity of the countryside and the fertility of crops, animals and men are thought to be linked with his well-being and his performance of the proper magical and other rites. The power of bringing rain is often attributed to these chiefs." [3]

One of these priestly kings or kingly priests resides at Elele, an important market-town of the Ibo people, to the north of Degema Division. This priestly king, who is named Eleche, is the head of the worship of the yams, which furnish the people with one of their staple foods. The fetish associated with the worship is called Aya-Eke. It is kept in a compound called Omo Kpurukpu, " and there, from election until death—at most seven years later, even should the full term of office be completed—the priest dwells, carefully guarded by all his people and never crossing the threshold unless called forth by some grave emergency. The reason for this restriction is that up to a few years ago any man who succeeded in killing the holder of this office would reign in his stead.

" The whole prosperity of the town, especially the fruitfulness of farm, byre, and marriage-bed, was linked with his life. Should he fall sick, it entailed famine and grave disaster upon the inhabitants, and there is reason to believe that, in such a case, facilities were offered to a successor. Under no circumstances did the term of office last for more than seven

---

[1] C. K. Meek, *Tribal Studies in Northern Nigeria*, ii. 491 *sqq.*

[2] That is, fetishes.—J. G. F.

[3] P. A. Talbot, *The Peoples of Southern Nigeria*, iii. 563 *sq.*

full years.   This prohibition still holds ; but since the coming
of Government it is said that another of the same family, who
must always be a strong man, may be chosen to take up the
position in his stead.   No sooner is a successor appointed,
however, than the former priest is reported to 'die for himself.'
It was frankly owned that, before Government came—*i.e.*
some dozen years ago—things were arranged differently in
that, at any time during his seven years' term, the priest might
be put to death by one strong and resourceful enough to
overcome him.

" In answer to the question as to whether, in view of the
fate known to follow after so short a period, it was not difficult to find men willing to succeed to the office on such terms,
Mr. Braid answered in a somewhat surprised tone : ' Oh, no !
Many wish for the post, because so much wealth is brought
them at the annual festival that they become very rich—past
all others in the town.'

" Our informant also stated that, during his own term of
office, Chief Eleche has only once been known to pass beyond
the compound walls.   The occasion was as follows : A fellow
townsman accused him of making a Juju to kill the com-
plainant.   The case came into court and, all unconscious of
the excitement which such a proceeding must cause, the
chief was bidden to attend and answer the charge.   He
arrived, accompanied by nearly all the townsfolk, who not
only filled the courtyard, which is a very large enclosed space,
but thronged the market-place outside.   They came, in a
state of great anxiety, to watch over the sacred priest and
guard him, so far as in them lay, from any misfortune the
effects of which, it was believed, would react on all the
countryside.

" Doubtless Mr. Braid would have been less ready to
impart information of this nature, had it not been that he was
about to leave the place, in all probability never to return." [1]

Mr. Talbot visited Elele and questioned the priest himself
in his house, which is formed of elaborately carved wooden
panels, being apparently the only house of the kind in the
whole Division.   The priest told him : " No priest of Aya-
Eke may eat of the new season's yams.   All the harvest must

[1] P. A. Talbot, *Some Nigerian Fertility Cults* (Oxford, 1927), pp. 103 *sqq.*

be garnered and the festival held.   Then, though others may
eat, I may not until all the new farms have been cut and
planted.   Only when the last of the seed yams has been laid
in the ground do the people bring me those which yet remain
over in the yam racks.   These I eat, calling the first of them
' my new season's yam,' though in reality it was garnered at
the last harvest about seven moons before. . . . It is a very
strong law of the Juju that no yams, save such as are old
enough to plant, may be eaten by a priest of Aya-Eke.   None
has ever broken this rule ; for, should it be disobeyed, the
seed yams would die in the ground, bearing no increase.   All
the great men of our family have kept the law faithfully." [1]

One of Mr. Talbot's party inquired of Eleche, the priest,
whether he himself had power to appoint a successor, or in
what way one was chosen.   " No sooner was the word ' successor ' uttered than Eleche raised his arms over his head
twice as though to ward off threatened danger, while his head
wife, who kept close to him throughout, shrugged her
shoulders violently over and over again, repeating in an
agitated voice :   ' Mba !   Mba !   Che !   Che ! '   (Let it
not be !   Let it not be !).   Meanwhile the crowd of retainers
took up the cry, low but angry, like the rumble of distant
thunder, waving hands outward as if to drive off the ill effects
of such ominous speech.   Eleche answered excitedly, the
words tumbling over one another in his agitation :   ' No
successor is needed ; for I shall never die !   It is forbidden
even to mention such a word !   In the beginning of things,
when I came out of the world, it was arranged that I should
not be as other men but should live very long—looking after
my people and bringing them prosperity.   The fate of common men is not for me !   Thereupon, like a Greek chorus,
came the response of the crowd :   ' Oda !   Oda ! '   (Forbid
it !   Forbid it !)." [2]

The Bambara, a large tribe in the French territory of
Upper Senegal and Niger, have an ancient tradition that
formerly their kings were only allowed to reign so long as they
retained their strength and vigour.   When they noticed that
the king's strength was failing, they said " The grass is
withering !   The grass is beginning to wither," which had

[1] P. A. Talbot, *op. cit.* pp. 108 *sq.*   [2] P. A. Talbot, *op. cit.* p. 109.

a sinister significance for the ageing king whose hair was beginning to grow grey.[1]

According to a tradition of the tribe, when a new king of the Bambara was elected he had to submit to a test for the purpose of determining the length of his reign and of his life. One of the cloths which are used for baking the native bread was passed round the neck of the king-elect, and two assistants pulled the ends of the cloth in opposite directions, while the king-elect feverishly plunged his hands into a bowl containing a number of pebbles and of baobab leaves ; the number of pebbles he could succeed in clutching at one grasp was the number of the years of his reign.   When the number of the years was passed, the king was put to death by strangulation, the instrument of death being the cotton cloth which had determined the length of his reign.[2]

Among the Banyankole, a pastoral people of the Uganda Protectorate, the king is known by the title of Mugabe.   " No Mugabe ever allowed himself to grow old : he had to put an end to his life before his powers, either mental or physical, began to deteriorate.   It was even thought undesirable that the Mugabe should look old, and treatment was applied to prevent his hair from growing grey.   A bird, *kinyankwanzi*, was caught and killed, the body being dried and burnt to ashes, which were mixed with butter.   This mixture was prepared by the medicine-man, who pronounced some magic incantations over it, and, when the night was darkest before the new moon appeared, the Mugabe smeared his head with it.   The bird, *Kinyankwanzi*, was sacred, and if any unauthorized person killed one he was deprived of all his possessions.   No Mugabe ever went on living when he felt that his powers were failing him through either serious illness or old age.   As soon as he felt his strength diminishing he knew it was time to end his life, and he called his chiefs, and also his sons, who never came to see him except on this occasion. . . . When all was ready, he summoned the royal medicine-man and asked for the king's poison.   This was always kept in readiness in the shell of a crocodile's egg.   The white of the

[1] L. Tauxier, *La Religion Bambara* (Paris, 1927), p. 219 n.
[2] C. Monteil, *Les Bambara du Ségon et du Kaarta* (Paris, 1924), p. 305.

egg was dried and powdered and mixed with the dried nerve from the pointed end of an elephant's tusk and some other ingredients, the exact mixture being kept strictly secret. This had only to be mixed with a little water or beer to be ready for use, and when the Mugabe drank it he fell dead in a few moments."[1]

Another African king who is never allowed to die a natural death is the Sultan of Uha in Tanganyika Territory. When he is at the point of death he is strangled or his neck is twisted by anybody who happens to be present. The custom may be a relic of an older practice of killing him on the first symptoms of weakness or senility. No sooner is he dead than pandemonium reigns in the village. Everybody flees, driving away all beasts and snatching up any article they can lay hands on. The Bilu, who are said to be the children of certain slave women, alone remain and take charge of the body, and they seize all the cattle and other property left behind by the fugitives in their haste. The corpse may not be buried in the bare earth. A white cow is killed and the hide removed entire, the horns being detached from it. The body is placed in the hide, the head resting on the skin of the cow's head and the arms and legs resting on the skin of the cow's legs. The hide is then sewn up, and dried over fires which are fed (*sic*) with milk. When it is dry the body is deposited in a canoe-shaped wooden trough and carried to the burial-place of the sultans, where it is set on trestles, and a hut is built over it.[2]

Another African people who are, or were till lately, governed by a priestly king of the type we are here considering are the Konde, a Bantu tribe inhabiting the country round the northern end of Lake Nyasa. The title of the king is Chungu. " The Chungu of to-day is but a poor shadow of his great ancestors. European power has deprived him of many of his prerogatives, and stripped his person and his office of much that was picturesque, and might well have been preserved. But even in the heyday of their glory, the Chungus were but priest-kings, hampered in their divinity,

[1] J. Roscoe, *The Banyankole*, pp. 50 *sq.*

[2] Captain C. H. B. Grant, " Uha in Tanganyika Territory," *Geographical Journal*, lxvi. (1925) p. 419.

hedged in their kingship by advisers, limitations, customs, which could not be set aside. . . . Chungu himself, however, was and still is 'the man who speaks with God'; and as such he is hedged with a real divinity, which the limitations to which he has to submit, and the independence of the once subordinate chiefs, have not yet destroyed.   He remains pre-eminently the man of prayer, who carries to the ancestral spirits the petitions of the community, and speaks to them with an authority which no other possesses. . . .   The principal duties of the councillors were to put the Chungu to death when he became seriously ill, a duty which has necessarily lapsed under British rule. . . .

"The health of the priest-king and the welfare of the whole community were inseparably bound up together. A Chungu in health and vigour meant a land yielding its fruits, rain coming in its season, evil averted.   But a weak and ailing Chungu meant disasters of many kinds.   Smaller illnesses Chungu, very excusably, concealed from his councillors, hoping that his ancestors would hear the prayers which he offered secretly by night.   But when serious illness overtook him, the councillors were called to a full meeting by those who were about the person of the chief.   For Chungu must not die a natural death; the land would turn into water should such a calamity be allowed to happen. Having decided that the illness is really grave, the councillors one by one give their voice in the formula, ' *Siku na mwaka*,' literally, day and year; but actually meaning, ' Does God die ? '   In solemn procession these terrible persons enter the house and, having turned out the chief's wives, lay him down on the floor.   Two keep him in that posture, while a third stops his breath by holding his mouth and nostrils, a fourth meanwhile gently slapping him all over the body until the life has gone out of him.

"No announcement of the death was made.   One of the councillors lived in the royal dwelling, so that if any came to consult Chungu a response might be given, and as he was rarely seen by common men it was easy to keep up the deception.   The councillors with their own hands digged the grave, and on their shoulders, at midnight, carried the body, anointed with lion fat and enswathed in cloth, to the place of burial. Six or eight slaves, who did not return, went with them. Four went down into the grave to receive the body of their dead master, two at the head and two at the feet, and, in sitting position, held him in their arms. The remaining slaves being placed on top, the soil was filled in on living and dead." After the lapse of about a month the news of the king's death was conveyed to the people by the beat of a big iron drum.[1]

The successor of the dead Chungu is chosen by the councillors, with the help of divination, from certain families. But there are no candidates for the office; "for not only must Chungu himself be helped out of the world, but all his sons, born after his accession, are put to death at birth." [2]

Among the Mashona, a Bantu tribe of Southern Rhodesia, a chief would seem to have been regularly put to death whenever his bodily or mental powers were seriously impaired by sickness or old age. On this subject Mr. Bullock, who has given us a full description of the tribe, writes as follows : " As far as can be ascertained from comparatively credible native informants, a Chief ran the risk of being murdered when he became enfeebled by old age or sickness. The males of his entourage would expel all women from the kraal, then cut his throat. The blood from the chief's throat was mixed with grain, and this seed was accounted to gain immense fertility, because ' he must have eaten much strong medicine, being so old.' The motive of these murders was not said to be the acquisition of this fertility; but that WuMambo—the Kingdom (that is the attributes or state of the Chief) might not die. Asked as to whether the people would not eagerly seek the exceptional crops to be gained by this *madiwisi* (fertility medicine), and so demand frequent deaths of their Chiefs, informants stated 'No. For they were afraid of the Chief while his strength remained ; also they could use other potions as *madiwisi* (as they do to-day.)' " [3]

A more precise account of king-killing among the Mashona is given by the Rev. S. S. Dornan, as follows : " Among the Varozwe (Varozwi, a Shona tribe) the custom of killing the

[1] D. R. Mackenzie, *The Spirit-ridden Konde* (London, 1925), pp. 68-70.

[2] *Ibid.* p. 71.

[3] C. Bullock, *The Mashona* (Cape Town, N.D.), pp. 315 *sq.*

king prevailed.   Absence of bodily blemishes was considered absolutely necessary in the occupant of the throne. . . . Even when in full possession of his powers he was sometimes not allowed to reign very long.   If he showed any signs of physical decay, such as loss of teeth, grey hairs, failure of sight, or impotency—in fact, any of the indications of advancing age—he was put to death and a man was deputed to carry the resolution into effect.   He was waylaid on a path and strangled with a thong of cowhide.   I have heard it asserted that any man who saw the king declining in strength had the right to kill him, but I am not sure if this is true. . . ." [1]

Among the Balobedu of the northern Transvaal " the divine ruler is a queen, Modjagde, and it appears that this is not accidental, in the sense that the holder of the office happens to be a woman, but that each succeeding sovereign is a woman.

" ' Among the Balobedu the chief is even more closely bound up with the agricultural life of the country, for here we find the Sacred Kingship—with the queen's life is connected the welfare of the tribe and she may not grow old lest vegetation and the fertility of the crops be correspondingly weakened.   Therefore after every fourth initiation school the queen must drink poison called *ketaba* (used only by chiefs). Before she dies, however, she must impart her knowledge of the rain charms every day for six days to her successor.'

" The connection, it would probably be fair to say identity, between the Divine Ruler and the rain is shown by the nature of the chief ingredient of the rain medicine :—

" ' On the death of the queen, which is kept secret for a whole year, the body is washed every day and the dirt is made to fall into an earthenware basin.   This is done until all the skin comes off and only then is the chief buried.   This skin is put into the rain pots.'

" There are, as in many other instances, regalia.   The chief of these is a drum, *Rangoedi*.

" ' The *Rangoedi* appears to be important as giving power to the chief, for when the heir is being instructed and initiated

---

[1] S. S. Dornan, " The Killing of the Divine King in South Africa," in *South African Journal of Science*, vol. xv. (1918).   Cited by C. G. Seligman in *Egypt and Negro Africa*, p. 31.

into the secrets of rain-making prior to the queen's death she sits on this drum. And finally on the day of her coronation this drum is her chair.' " [1]

Once more, among the Sakalava of North-western Madagascar, when a king of the Volamena dynasty is on the point of death, it is customary to cut his throat with a knife reserved specially for this operation, thus hastening his death by at least some minutes.[2] The custom apparently originates in the common unwillingness to allow the king to die of weakness or old age, and that reluctance in its turn rests on the belief that the enfeeblement of the king's physical powers necessarily entails a corresponding decline in the state of his people and of the whole country. Thus the practice of cutting the throat of a Sakalava king when he is at the point of death, like the custom of strangling the Sultan of Uha under the like circumstances, is probably a relic of an older custom of killing him at the first symptom of bodily or mental decay.

From these and similar cases cited in my earlier work we may infer that the institution of a priestly kingship with a tenure not unlike that of Nemi was widespread in Africa down to recent years ; and in every instance, where the reason of the custom is reported, the motive for killing the king was apparently a belief that the welfare of the people, and particularly the fertility of the land, of cattle, and of women, were so intimately bound up with his health and strength that any impairment or failure of his bodily vigour through sickness or age would infallibly draw down calamity or even ruin on the country and its inhabitants, while his death from either of these causes would be fraught with incalculable evils for the community. In these circumstances his subjects had seemingly no choice but either to put him to death before the dreaded decay had sapped his energies, or to allow him to be attacked by a candidate for the kingship, who, by slaying him, demonstrated at once the incapacity of the deceased and his own fitness to discharge the onerous duties of the office. On this analogy we may suppose that the priest of Diana at

[1] C. G. Seligman, *Egypt and Negro Africa*, pp. 31 *sq.*, quoting Eileen Krige, " Agricultural Ceremonies and Practices of the Balobedu," *Bantu Studies*, v. (Johannesburg, 1931) 207 *sq.*

[2] G. Grandidier, " La Mort et les funérailles à Madagascar," *L'Anthropologie*, xxiii. (1912), 325.

Nemi, who bore the title of King of the Grove, was credited of old with possessing the same quickening powers over the fecundity of wild beasts, cattle, and women which seem to have been ascribed to the goddess herself, and that consequently any failure of his bodily strength was supposed to entail barrenness alike on man and beast, probably also on the fields, the orchards, and the vineyards. To avert these disastrous consequences it may have been at first customary to put him to death at the end of a period short enough to ensure that the fatal decline had not yet set in ; and in course of time this rigid limitation of his reign and life may so far have been relaxed that he was suffered to retain office so long as he could make good his title by defending himself against attack. It was under a tenure of this last sort that the priest of Diana at Nemi was held in historical times ; and though the custom in this mitigated form afforded the priest a chance of prolonging his life indefinitely, we need not wonder that candidates for the priesthood were few, and that they had, at least in later times, to be recruited exclusively from the ranks of runaway slaves. This explanation of the rule of the priesthood of Nemi is necessarily no more than an hypothesis, but in the light of the parallels which I have adduced the hypothesis appears legitimate, if not probable.[1]

In the powerful mediaeval kingdom of the Khazars or Khozars of South-eastern Russia the kings were not allowed to reign and live beyond a certain period, which is variously stated by the Arab travellers and geographers, who are our principal authorities on the kingdom. Elsewhere I have collected the evidence on the subject.[2]

Elsewhere we have seen that every Spartan king was liable to have his royal functions suspended every eighth year if on a clear moonless night the ephors observed a falling star, and that he could only be reinstated in his office by an oracle from Delphi or Olympia. The custom may point to a former limitation of the king's reign to eight years, and in illustration

---

[1] In this summary of the foregoing evidence, as in some of the preceding pages, I have allowed myself to quote from my commentary on Ovid's *Fasti*, vol. iii. 86 *sq.*

[2] J. G. Frazer, " The Killing of the Khazar Kings," *Folk-lore*, xxviii. (1917) 382-407. Reprinted in my *Garnered Sheaves* (London, 1931), pp. 212-234. Compare G. Roheim, " Killing the Divine King," *Man*, xv. (1915) 26-28.

of this omen drawn from a shooting-star I have cited some examples of similar superstitions about meteors among primitive peoples.[1] To these examples I may here add a few more instances.

Thus in Kiziba, a district of Central Africa to the west of Lake Victoria Nyanza, when the natives see a large, clear shooting-star, they think that it portends some evil to the earth brought by the star-spirit *Hangi*. And they seek to avert the danger by beating drums and offering sacrifices to the spirit.[2] Among the Wabende, a tribe inhabiting the country to the east of Lake Tanganyika, when a man sees a shooting-star he crouches down to the ground and says : " I have seen you, do not harm me." They think that the sight of a meteor presages some misfortune. It is the announcement of a curse which some sorcerer, paid by an enemy, has cast upon a whole family.[3] Among the Ila-speaking peoples of Northern Rhodesia when a falling star is seen it is greeted with curses. A man spits violently on the ground in the direction it is falling. *"Thu,"* he says, "may the people in that direction come to an end."[4] In Marsa Matruh, the classical Paraetonium, a district in North Africa to the west of Alexandria, the natives, who are Bedouin Arabs with a strong infusion of Berber blood, believe that the number of unfixed stars corresponds to the tally of all living creatures on the face of the earth, and that the falling of one of these stars signifies the death of some animal.[5]

When the Birhors of Chota Nagpur in India see a shooting-star or meteor, which they call *chandi*, they spit at it and say, " Thoo, thoo ! There goes *Chandi*." This is believed to ward off any calamity that might otherwise follow in the wake of the meteor.[6] In Konkan, a district of the Bombay Presidency, "whenever a great person or a very holy man is about to be born, it is believed that he alights on the earth in the shape of a shooting-star. Sometimes a big star falls on the

---

[1] *The Dying God*, pp. 58 *sqq.*

[2] H. Rehse, *Kiziba Land und Leute*, p. 146.

[3] Mgr. Lechaptois, *Aux Rives du Tanganyika*, p. 214.

[4] E. W. Smith and A. M. Dale, *The Ila-speaking Peoples of Northern Rhodesia*, ii. 219.

[5] Oric Bates, " Ethnographic Notes from Marsa Matruh," in *Journal of the Royal Asiatic Society* for 1915 (London, 1915), p. 736.

[6] S. C. Roy, *The Birhors*, p. 386.

earth, and thereby a noise like that of thunder is produced. When this happens, people believe that a great king or a holy saint whose merit has been exhausted is going to be born on earth. The sight of a shooting-star should be kept secret. In the Deccan it is held to indicate the death of a chaste woman or a good man. It is also said that the stars descend to the earth in human form when sins accumulate in the celestial world. The influence of meteors on human affairs is treated at length in the *Varahasanhita*. The phenomenon is popularly regarded as an evil omen : it is supposed to portend devastation by fire, an earthquake, a famine, an epidemic, danger from thieves, and storms at sea. The appearance of a bright shooting-star is supposed to foretell the death of some great man ; and on beholding one, it is customary to repeat the words ' Ram, Ram ' several times. A shower of meteors is believed to presage some civil commotion or a change in the ruling dynasties." [1] This last belief presents some analogy to the omen which, at certain times, the Spartans drew from the appearance of falling stars.

Among the Kai of Northern New Guinea, some people think that meteors are the souls of men who have been done to death by a magician, and are now seeking out the village where the wicked magician lives in order to reveal his identity to their friends and kinsfolk. Others are of the opinion that meteors are the souls of living persons who are now going with torches to the villages where the enchanters live. Others say that stars simply fall from the sky like fruit from a tree. Hence when they see a star falling, to prevent its fall from producing, by sympathetic magic, the falling out of their teeth, they spit, saying " O Star ! " [2] The Bukaua, another tribe of Northern New Guinea, think that the falling of a star is an omen of bad luck, and the taro plants that are touched by a falling star will put forth no tubers. Hence at the sight of a meteor they spit and cry out : " O falling star, go and spoil the taro of a bad man."[3]

" A shooting-star is to the savage of New Britain a thing of fear. On Duke of York group it is called *a wirua*. Now

[1] R. E. Enthoven, *The Folklore of Bombay*, pp. 70 *sqq.*, who gives more evidence on the subject.

[2] R. Neuhauss, *Deutsch Neu-Guinea*, iii. 159 *sq.*

[3] R. Neuhauss, *op. cit.* iii. 432.

wirua means to die by violence principally, and *a wirua* is the corpse for a cannibal feast.   Hence when a shooting-star flashes across the sky, people cry out 'A wirua, a wirua,' and the belief is that when the star flashes on its way a person has just been killed for cannibal purposes.   In New Britain the name given to a meteor is *tulugiai ra virua, i.e.* the soul of a body killed for cannibalistic purposes." [1]   Among the aborigines of Australia, whenever a shooting-star is seen travelling towards the earth, they are said to take it for the soul of a dead man returning temporarily to his old haunts on earth.[2]

Elsewhere we have seen that in Africa the souls of dead kings and chiefs are often supposed to be incarnate in lions. On this subject I will here adduce some fresh evidence.   Thus among the Manganja, a tribe inhabiting a hilly district on the Shire River in South Africa, " it is believed also that the souls of departed Chiefs enter into lions and render them sacred. On one occasion, when we had shot a buffalo in the path beyond the Kafue, a hungry lion, attracted probably by the smell of the meat, came close to our camp, and roused up all hands by his roaring.   Tuba Mokoro, imbued with the popular belief that the beast was a chief in disguise, scolded him roundly during his brief intervals of silence.   ' You are a chief, eh ?   You call yourself a chief, do you ?   What kind of chief are you to come sneaking about in the dark, trying to steal our buffalo meat ?   Are you not ashamed of yourself ? A pretty chief truly ; you are like the scavenger beetle, and think of yourself only.   You have not the heart of a chief ; why don't you kill your own beef ?   You must have a stone in your chest, and no heart at all, indeed ! '   Tuba Mokoro producing no impression on the transformed chief, one of the men, the most sedate of the party, who seldom spoke, took up the matter and tried the lion in another strain.   In his slow, quiet way he expostulated with him on the impropriety of such conduct to strangers who had never injured him. ' We were travelling peaceably through the country back to our own chief.   We never killed people, nor stole anything. The buffalo meat was ours, not his, and it did not become a

[1] B. Danks, " Some Notes on Savage Life in New Britain," in *Twelfth Report of the Australasian Association for the Advancement of* *Science* (1910), p. 453.

[2] H. Basedow, *The Australian Aboriginal*, p. 296.

great chief like him to be prowling round in the dark, trying, like a hyaena, to steal the meat of strangers. He might go and hunt for himself, as there was plenty of game in the forest.' The Pondoro, being deaf to reason, and only roaring the louder, the men became angry and threatened to send a ball through him if he did not go away." [1] When Speke was staying in Karague, a district on the shore of Lake Victoria Nyanza, he was told that when a certain old king had died his body, " after the fashion of his predecessors, was sewn up in a cow-skin and placed in a boat floating on the lake, where it remained for three days, until decomposition set in and maggots were engendered, of which three were taken into the palace and given in charge of the heir-elect ; but instead of remaining as they were, one worm was transformed into a lion, another into a leopard, and the third into a stick." [2] Again we have seen that in Africa the souls of dead kings and chiefs are often thought to be incarnate in serpents. [3]

In treating of the great games of ancient Greece I had occasion to notice the tradition that in all cases they were funeral games celebrated in honour of the dead, and in illustration of this tradition I cited some examples of other funeral games. [4] To these I can now add a few more. Thus in Samoa " the funeral obsequies of a chief of rank lasted from ten to fifteen days, during which time the house in which he died was watched night and day by men appointed for the purpose. After burial, and until the days of mourning were ended, the days were usually spent in boxing and wrestling matches, with sham fights; the nights being occupied with dancing and practising a kind of buffoonery, common to these seasons of mourning for the dead." [5] " Sometimes a chief died at a distance from his own settlement, when after a time his body was brought to the family burial-place with much ceremony and a kind of military show, called *O le langi*. It was followed by, or rather in part consisted of, sham fights, boxing matches, and dances, which took place after the skull of the deceased chieftain

[1] D. and C. Livingstone, *Narrative of an Expedition to the Zambesi and its Tributaries* (London, 1865), pp. 160 *sq.*

[2] J. H. Speke, *Journal of the Dis-*

covery of the Source of the Nile, p. 181.

[3] *The Dying God*, p. 84.

[4] *The Dying God*, pp. 92 *sqq.*

[5] J. B. Stair, *Old Samoa*, pp. 183 *sq.*

had been placed in the tomb."¹   Among the Ten'a Indians
of the Yukon Territory in Alaska " every year, or at least
every other year, the feast of the dead is held with great
solemnity. The proper time for this celebration is mid-
winter, *i.e.* the time of the winter solstice, which also coincides with the beginning of the Ten'a year. Sometimes
a celebration of secondary importance is held at midsummer,
but the neighbouring villages do not generally take part in
it, and it remains exclusively local, whereas for the winter
feast two or three villages join together, and even from the
remoter ones representatives are sent to participate in the
solemnities, and in the distribution of presents.

" These feasts are termed mourning celebrations, not in
the sense that they are attended with sadness or sorrow, but
because they are held in remembrance of those who died
during the year or, more exactly, since the last celebration.
Though mingled occasionally with the lamentations of the
dead ones' relatives, their dominant character is one of
rejoicing. The virtues of the deceased are commemorated,
and they receive a sort of apotheosis. . . . Among the
lower tribe, races, wrestling matches, and other sports
regularly take place during the feast, and contribute to
enliven the celebration. The upper tribe folk admit that
such was once their custom also, and their folklore bears
witness to it, but these manly amusements have been completely superseded by card-games, and reckless gambling
is now their only and prosaic recreation."²   In ancient Greece,
Teutamides, king of Larissa in Thessaly, is said to have
celebrated funeral games in honour of his dead father, at
which Perseus competed, and in throwing the quoit accidentally killed Acrisius, king of Argos.³

We have seen that in ancient Babylon there is some
evidence pointing to the conclusion that formerly the king's
tenure of office was limited to a single year, at the end of
which he was put to death.⁴ The Banyoro or Bakitara of
Uganda used to practise a remarkable custom which seems
to indicate that down to recent times they practised a similar

¹ J. B. Stair, *op. cit.* p. 179.   vi. (1911) pp. 709-711.
² F. J. Jetté, " On the Superstitions   ³ Apollodorus, ii. iv. 4.
of the Ten'a Indians," in *Anthropos*,   ⁴ *The Dying God*, pp. 113 *sq*

custom of limiting to a single year the tenure of the king's office and life. The custom is thus described by Canon Roscoe. "At or about the time of year when the king had been buried, the reigning king told *Bamuroga* [1] to prepare a feast for the departed king. *Bamuroga* chose a poor man of the Babito clan to impersonate the dead king, and the man so chosen lived in regal state in the king's tomb and was called by the name of the monarch he represented, for he was said to be the old king revived. He lived in the tomb, was feasted and honoured, and had full use of the women of the tomb, the widows of the old king. The king sent him presents and he sent his blessing to the king, the country, and the cattle. He distributed gifts of cows belonging to the king as he pleased, and for eight days lived like a king. When the ninth day came he was taken away to the back of the tomb and strangled, and no one heard anything more about him. This was an annual ceremony." [2] It seems probable that this mock king who held office for eight days every year was a substitute for the king himself, who thus died every year in the person of his deputy. In earlier times the king may have had no choice but to die every year in his own person, at the end of a brief reign of a single year.

Again, in Southern Nigeria, "among the Eket a faint tradition yet lingers of 'a priest who slew the slayer and must himself be slain.' This came to our knowledge through the following story, told, with slight variations, by two well-known Ibibio :

" ' In the olden time, far away from here, there dwelt a people called Ikot Ako Anyan. The last name was given them because they worshipped the great Juju 'Anyan.'

" ' Every year, at the time when the yam vines first clothe their poles with green, the people of Ikot Ako used to come down into the Ibibio country, and ask that an old chief might be delivered over to them, to become priest of their Juju until the same season came round again. When

---

[1] *Bamuroga*, one of the two chiefs appointed to take charge of the royal tomb.

[2] J. Roscoe, *The Bakitara*, pp.

126 *sq.* Compare J. Roscoe, *The Soul of Central Africa* (London, 1922), p. 202.

this request had been granted, they went away, leaving a blessing upon the farms. . . .

" ' Of all the Ibibio chiefs led away to be priests, none ever came back, for each died within the year, and another was chosen in his stead. Some say the Juju killed them ; but others state that each year the new priest slew his predecessor, knowing full well that in twelve more moons he must himself be slain.'

" It was, unfortunately, impossible to get more definite information. We were told, vaguely, that the Ikot Akos never came to this country any more, nor did the Ibibio go to theirs. Moreover, these were stories of long ago, forgotten by all save a few old men. Therefore it was no longer possible to learn anything further.

" A year later, while engaged on a study of the Ibo people, good fortune brought us to a town of some five thousand inhabitants, the spiritual ruler of which owns that each of his predecessors was ' a priest who slew the slayer and must himself be slain.' The present holder of the dignity naturally showed some reticence concerning the steps by which he himself succeeded to office." [1]

[1] P. A. Talbot, *Life in Southern Nigeria*, pp. 336-338.

CHAPTER XXV

THE FAIRY WIFE

ELSEWHERE I have had occasion to notice a widely diffused popular story of a fairy wife or husband which conforms to the type known as the Swan Maiden, or Beauty and the Beast, or Cupid and Psyche,[1] and I have cited examples of the tale. Here I will add a few more instances. A common story told all over Indonesia, if not over the whole Malay-Polynesian region, is that seven or nine heavenly women descended to earth every night to bathe in the form of birds, throwing off their wings and plunging into the water as girls. Once upon a time they were observed by a man, who took away the wings of the youngest. When the others were finished bathing, they donned their wings again and flew back to heaven. But the youngest, deprived of her wings, remained helplessly behind as a girl. She was taken by the man who had stolen her wings, and became his wife. Generally it is also told that the pair had a child, and that the wife, offended by her husband, returned to heaven, whereupon the disconsolate husband sought her everywhere for the sake of the child, but could find her nowhere.[2]

Thus in Efate, one of the New Hebrides, the story runs that " the people of the sky, perceiving that the tide was out and the reef bare, came down and took off their white wings and proceeded to fish with torches along the shore. At dawn they put on their wings, sang a song, and flew back to heaven. This they often repeated. One night, when they had come down, laid aside their wings, and were fishing, a man of the

---

[1] *The Dying God*, pp. 130 *sqq.*
[2] N. Adriani and A. C. Kruijt, *op. cit.* iii. 401.

country, who had been watching them, saw where they had laid their wings, and when they were out of sight he took the wings of one of them and hid them in a banana stem.   In the morning, at the peep of dawn, they came together, laid down the fish they had caught, and began to put on their wings for flight.   All did so but one, whose wings could not be found, and she was a woman.   The man who had stolen and hidden the wings came and took her for his wife.   They lived peaceably together, and had two sons ; the name of the one was Naka Tafaki, and the name of the other was Karisi Bum.

"By and by trouble arose in the household.   The man ill-treated his wife and said to her, ' You are a wicked woman, cause of trouble and sorrow ; go back to your own country.' This made her heart sore, and she sighed for the lost wings that she might fly away from all this turmoil and be at rest. One day she and her sons were out together, and the youths discovered a white thing in a banana stem.   It was their mother's lost wings.   Overjoyed, she resolved to put them on and fly away from earth to heaven.   But before she did so she told her sons of their kindred in heaven, in the hope that one day they would all meet there.   Then she put on her wings, sang the appropriate song, and, after swinging backwards and forwards a few times, flew swiftly away to heaven. The brothers went home and told their father. . . .

"Now the brothers were continually being taunted with being strangers and pilgrims, and they longed to depart to their mother's country.   One day it fell out that they were shooting birds with arrows, and one of the arrows lodged in the sky and stuck fast in the roots of a banyan tree.   Another arrow shot after it stuck fast in the end of the shaft of the first arrow, and so with arrow after arrow, until there was a chain of them extending from heaven to earth, and up it the two brothers climbed into the sky.   There they found an old woman cooking yams, and she knew her grandsons.   So all their troubles were over." [1]

A Maori version of the story runs as follows : " In days of yore, when gods and heroes deigned to dwell upon earth, one Tairi-a-kohu, a supernatural being, descended from the

[1] Dr. Macdonald," The Mythology of the Efatesi," in the *Seventh Report of the*   *Australasian Association for the Advancement of Science*, 1878, pp. 764 *sq.*

heavens, in order that she might bathe in the waters of this world. She was seen to descend, surrounded by mist, by one Venuku, who, captivated by the rare charms of the Mist Maiden, sought to capture her. But she only stayed with him during the night, and at break of day she departed every morning and ascended to the heavens, from which she again descended when the shades of night fell. And she told Venuku that he must not on any account mention anything about her or show her to his people. Were he to do so she would leave him, never to return. But when their child was born and well grown, then Venuku might inform his people as to who his wife was. So time passed by and at last the child was born, and was named Heheu-rangi. Then Venuku's heart became dry with desire to exhibit his wife to his own people. So he carefully closed all apertures through which light might enter his dwelling, and the next morning he managed to detain his celestial wife until broad daylight. Then, when Tairi rose to return to the heavens, she found that daylight was upon the world, and that many people had collected outside the house in order to view her. Then was the Maid of the Mist dismayed, so stood she beneath the window of the house, clothed with nought save her own long hair, which covered her as a shawl. And so she sang a song of farewell and upbraiding to her husband Venuku. Then she ascended to the heavens and left Venuku disconsolate." [1]

Among the Kiwai of British New Guinea the story runs thus : A handsome Puruma boy while steering a canoe was seen by an *oboubi* girl, that is, a water-maiden, who came to him the next night when he was sleeping in the canoe. He was very much attracted by her, and married her, keeping her hidden from the people. She bore him a child, and when she had recovered she was shown to the people. Some men asked the husband to let them have her, and the conversation was overheard by the girl, who, being a " devil-woman," could hear anything a long way off. She wept bitterly, and felt so mortified that when everybody was asleep in the night she took her child and went into the water, returning to her own place. [2]

[1] E. Best, " Maori Mythology," in the *Tenth Report of the Australasian Association for the Advancement of* *Science* (1904), pp. 450 *sqq.*
[2] G. Landtman, *The Kiwai Papuans of British New Guinea*, p. 305.

Among the Tami of Northern New Guinea the story runs somewhat differently. They say that in the Ngeng River a crocodile bore a girl. The girl lived in the body of her mother. When the girl was big she said to her mother, " All the people are away in the fields. Let me go on land that I may dance a little." But there was a woman in child-bed remaining in the village, who saw the girl as she danced. The woman said to herself, " O what a fine girl. My brother must marry her." The next morning, when the people went forth to the fields, her brother remained behind with her, and saw the girl dancing. When she wished to return to her crocodile mother, he seized her, and took her to his mother, and made her his wife. They lived happily, and after some time she bore him a son. One day the boy, her son, was taunted by a companion with having a crocodile grandmother. He returned in great grief to the house, and told his mother what had happened, and she called upon her crocodile mother, who received them both.[1]

Among the Kachari, a tribe of Assam, the story goes that " there was a certain lad whose father died before he was born. And one day, when he had grown a big boy, he asked his mother, ' What did my father do for his living ? ' And his mother, drawing a long breath, said ' Your father used to travel about selling things. Ah, if he were alive we should have no trouble to endure ! ' But the lad replied, ' Do not you think that I too could earn money in that way ? Bring out what money there is and let me see what I can do.' But his mother said, ' Ah, my son, you must not talk like that. If you go away into foreign lands and die there, what will become of me ? ' But her son would not listen to her, and by impor-tunity induced her to give him money, with which he bought goods and procured a boat, and hiring two or three men, took leave of his mother, and went into a far country to trade. Finally he came to a certain place where he moored his boat, at the place where men draw water, and sent his men to hawk his wares from village to village while he himself stayed in the boat. It happened that there lived hard by an old couple who possessed a white swan, which they fed and tended as though it were their own child. One day the lad saw this

---

[1] R. Neuhauss, *Deutsch Neu-Guinea*, iii. 564 *sq.*

swan strip itself of its swan plumage and become a beautiful
maiden, and bathe. From that time forth he paid great
attention to the owners of the swan, and gave them presents
of the oil and other things he had in his boat. And when the
merchandise had been sold and the time was come to go home,
he went to the old people's house and offering much money
begged them to sell him their swan. But they were for giving
him their swan for nothing. He, however, feared to commit
a sin if he took it as a gift, and, because it was the old man's
property, compelled him to take much money in exchange for
it, and went away.

" But when he came home with his boat, behold, the swan
remained a swan, and for disappointment the lad pined and
wasted away. Seeing which, his old mother consulted
various people, but got no help. Finally she went to a certain
wise woman, who said, ' Sister, do not you understand ?
Something has happened to him while he was away trading.
You must use a device to find out what it is.' To which the
mother replied, ' Tell me plainly what it is, and you will do a
good deed.' So the wise woman gave this advice. ' Some
day do you direct a maiden to search for lice in his hair. And
while she is doing this, let her pretend to be mightily grieved,
and let her ask him what is the matter. And he will feel
flattered, and will open out his heart to her.' And the mother
did as the wise woman directed her. The girl she sent wept
and snuffled as she tended the lad and said, ' Tell me why you
pine and grow thin, else I too will give up food and drink.'
And so he, heaving a sigh, explained thus : ' While I was
away trading, I saw the white swan which is in my boat turn
into a maiden. But now she remains a swan, and for her love
I am pining.'

" When her task was done, she told the lad's mother, who
sent word to the wise woman. The wise woman said, ' Let
the girl tell him that the swan maiden worships her own gods
in the dead of night. Let him pretend to lie asleep, and
when she divests herself of her swan plumage, let him seize it
and thurst it into the hearth, and then she will always remain
a girl.' The old mother directed the girl accordingly, and
the girl told the lad. One day he mixed ashes and oil in a
vessel, and procured a yak's tail, and when night was come he

lay down and pretended to be fast asleep. Presently the
swan crept out, and feeling his hands, feet, and body with her
beak, was satisfied that he slept. Then, slowly taking off her
swan skin, she became absorbed in the worship of her
country's gods. And the lad, seeing his opportunity, grasped
the swan plumage and thrust it into the hearth, so that it was
singed, and the smell of the feathers filled the place. And the
maiden, smelling the burning feathers, cried, ' What have
you done to me ?   What have you done to me ? '   So saying,
she fell down in a faint, and seemed as one dead. But the
lad, taking his vessel of oil, anointed her with it, and fanned
her gently with the yak's tail, till she came to. And so they
married, and begat many sons and daughters, and lived
happily ever after. And that's all ! " [1]

Among the Garos, another tribe of Assam, the story runs
that two brothers, Aual and Gunal, heard two doves talking.
They caught the birds, and Aual killed his bird, but Gunal
put his in a cage and took great care of it. One day, when
all the people had gone to their fields, the dove turned into
a woman, and coming out of the cage, boiled rice, drew water,
swept the floor and sprinkled it with water, and then, turning
into a dove again, entered the cage and waited. On their
return from the fields the brothers were much astonished,
for they did not know who had done this. The same thing
happened day after day, and the brothers thought that it
must be the work of ghosts or spirits. At last one day, to
solve the mystery, Gunal stayed behind in the morning and
feigned to be fast asleep. Seeing him, as she thought,
slumbering, the dove came out of the cage in woman's form,
and after cooking the rice and vegetables she swept the floor.
When she came by him sweeping, Gunal seized her by the
wrist. In order to free herself, she said, " Let me go, then
it will be well with you ; if not, it will not be well." But
Gunal would not let her go, so she said, " As you wish it, I
will marry you, but if from doing so any harm comes to you,
you must not reproach me." Gunal promised that he would
never reproach her, and she did not again turn into a dove,
but married him. [2]

[1] S. Endle, *The Kacharis* (London,   [2] A. Playfair, *The Garos* (London,
1911), pp. 119 *sq*.   1909), pp. 123 *sq*.

CHAPTER XXVI

TEMPORARY KINGS

ELSEWHERE I have described a custom of appointing a temporary or a mock king to represent the real king for a brief time, either annually or once for all at the beginning of the new king's reign.[1] To the examples which I have there cited I may here add a few more. To begin with temporary kings appointed for a brief time at the beginning of a reign, among the Banyoro or Bakitara of Uganda, after the death of a king, a solemn ceremony of purification was performed by a princess for the whole land and the people. Part of the ceremony was this. The prime minister, *Bamuroga*, went to one of the young princes and persuaded him that the people had chosen him to be their king. The boy was set upon the throne, and the real king, with all the chiefs, came to do obeisance as though they acquiesced in the choice and wished to take the oath of allegiance to him. They brought with them presents of cows and offered him gifts and congratulations. When all, including the real king, had presented their offerings, the prime minister asked the real king, " Where is your gift to me ? " The king gave a haughty answer, saying that he had already given his gift to the right person, whereupon the prime minister pushed him on the shoulder, saying, " Go and bring my present." The king thereupon called his followers and left the enclosure in feigned anger. The prime minister then turned to the mock king, saying, " Let us flee ; your brother has gone to bring an army," and, taking the boy to the back of the throne-room, he strangled him. This completed the death cere-

---

[1] *The Dying God*, pp. 148-159.

monies and the subsequent purifications, and the new king could take his seat upon the throne and begin his reign.[1] The meaning of this strange rite is thus explained by Canon Roscoe, who has reported the custom from his personal inquiries among the Banyoro, in which he was assisted by the king himself : " This boy-king was always chosen and killed during the ceremonies in order that death might be deceived and the real king secured from any evil that might attach itself to him during the rites or that might not be completely removed by the purification." [2]   In short, the young prince was killed in order that by his death he might save the life of his elder brother the king.

Again, among the Mossi, a tribe of the Western Sudan, after the death of a king (*Moro-naba*) the deceased monarch is replaced by his eldest daughter, who wears the royal insignia and exercises the royal power for seven days.   She puts on the huge crown, bracelets, and ornaments of her royal father.   Thus apparelled, she commands for seven days.   This institution does not exist exclusively for the king.   It is observed for all the chiefs of the country, great or small, chiefs of cantons, chiefs of villages, and even Chiefs of the Earth.   When they die their eldest daughter becomes their successor for a space of time which may last as long as a year, but which is generally very short.   The institution is thus general.   In the interval between the death of a king and the appointment of his successor, that is to say about seven days, robbery, pillage, violence, and murders were permitted indiscriminately throughout the country.   Another very notable custom observed by the Mossi is this : when the new king has assumed the regal power, they choose one of the sons or one of the nephews of the late king to perpetuate for some time the memory of the deceased monarch.   They give to him who plays the part the red cap, the bracelets, and a horse of the dead man, and two of his young wives.   The representative (*kourita*) of the deceased king has rights which are excessive but temporary : he may pillage at his ease ; when he lays his baton on an object or an animal the thing or the animal is his, and so on ; but he only exercises

[1] J. Roscoe, *The Soul of Central Africa*, pp. 201 *sqq.*
[2] J. Roscoe, *The Bakitara*, p. 130.

these rights until the new king has completed the ceremony of installation. The representative of the deceased king is allowed to retain all the objects which are given to him for his temporary royalty, except the horse of the dead king, which he must give up to the new king in order that the latter may sacrifice it before returning to the village.[1]

To come now to mock or temporary kings appointed annually to reign for a short period, among the Kwottos of Northern Nigeria the King of Panda used to be regarded as an incarnate divinity, who had power over the elements. Nevertheless, at an annual festival one of the king's slaves, a strong, handsome man, was allowed for a single day to wear a leopard's skin (the badge of royalty) and to adorn his head with a pair of buffalo horns ; thus arrayed, and attended by a bodyguard of fifty men, armed with stout sticks, he used to strut proudly about the town, exclaiming, " I am king at this festival. Let no one dispute my will." At sight of him in the distance the people scattered, believing that he had the power to cause anyone who might offend him to be struck down with a mortal sickness. Should he be minded to kill anyone he might do so, and no questions might be asked about it. He made a round of the town, visiting any house he pleased, and custom compelled the inmates to present him with money or gowns according to their means. Meantime the real king provided him with as much beer to drink and as many slave women for concubines as he cared to ask for. Even before he assumed the leopard's skin and the buffalo horns, the slave enjoyed for three days a privileged position in the King of Panda's palace, a special hut for eating in and a special hut for sleeping in being assigned to him inside the palace close to that of the King. When he had made his round of the town, he returned to the palace, and the real King thereupon invested him with a new white gown and turban. After receiving them the slave renounced his pseudo-royal privileges until the following year. At Toto to this day, under English rule, there lives a strong man of slave parentage, who acts the part of the principal slave in this ceremony every year, though on these festive occasions he naturally does not enjoy the licentious privileges which

---

[1] L. Tauxier, *Le Noir du Yatenga*, p. 352.

were accorded to his predecessors in the days when Panda
was an independent kingdom.[1]

In Bastar, a native State in the Central Provinces of
India, a temporary or mock king is still annually appointed
to replace the real king or Rajah for nine days. The occasion is the great autumnal festival of the Dasahra, which,
we are told, " is doubtless the autumn Saturnalia and celebrates the return of fertility." [2] According to another account, " the Dasahra festival probably marks the autumnal
equinox and also the time when the sowing of wheat and other
spring crops begins. Many Hindus still postpone sowing the
wheat until after Dasahra, even though it might be convenient
to begin before, especially as the festival goes by the lunar
month and its date varies in different years by more than a
fortnight. The name signifies the tenth day, and prior to
the festival a fast of nine days is observed, when the pots of
wheat corresponding to the gardens of Adonis are sown and
quickly sprout up. This is an imitation of the growth and
sowing of the real crop and is meant to ensure its success.
During these nine days it is said that the goddess Devi was
engaged in mortal combat with the buffalo demon Mahisasur
or Bhainsasur, and on the tenth day of the Dasahra she slew
him. The fast is explained as being observed in order to
help her to victory, but it is really perhaps a fast in connection with the growing of the crops. A similar nine days'
fast for the crops was observed by the Greeks. Devi signifies ' *the* goddess ' *par excellence*. She is often the tutelary
goddess of the village and of the family, and is held to have
been originally Mother Earth, which may be supposed to be
correct. In tracts where people of Northern and Southern
India meet she is identified with Anna Purna, the corn-
goddess of the Telugu country ; and in her form of Gauri
or ' the Yellow One ' she is perhaps herself the yellow corn." [3]

" In the Bastar State this festival is elaborately observed
and the Hindu rites are grafted in an ingenious manner on

[1] J. R. Wilson-Haffenden, "Ethnographic Notes on the Kwottos of
Toto (Panda) District, Northern Nigeria," in *Journal of the African
Society*, vol. xxvii., No cviii. (July
1928) pp. 385 *sq.*

[2] J. T. Marten, in *Census of India*,
1911, vol. x. Part i. (Calcutta, 1912)
p. 83.

[3] R. V. Russell, *Tribes and Castes
of the Central Provinces of India*
(London, 1916), iv. 13.

the indigenous ceremonies connected with the primitive autumn Saturnalia, which celebrates, in the worship of the mother goddess, the revival of the generative principles of the earth. . . . In the ceremonies themselves we have the incarnation in a girl of the spirit of the Devi, the annual abdication of the Chief, his period of taboo, the substitution for him of a chosen victim who is given his title of privileges, formally enthroned and no doubt till comparatively lately finally sacrificed, and the restoration of the king in pomp after his vicarious sacrifice." [1]

In Bastar the ceremonies which comprise the abdication of the Rajah and the enthronement of a mock Rajah in his room are called the Nawaratri and last nine days. They begin on the afternoon of the fifteenth day of the dark part of the month Kunwar (October). The Rajah first goes in procession to the temple of Kachin Devi, where a girl, seated on a thorny swing and rocking to and fro on it, is supposed to be inspired by the goddess and in that state prophesies how the ensuing year will end. The girl appointed to be the mouthpiece of the goddess is chosen from the sub-caste to which the priest belongs, and she is first ceremonially married to the priest. She is usually about seven or eight years old, but she is allowed to play her part in the ceremony every year until she arrives at puberty, and even after that, if she is chaste and continues to live peaceably with the priest. Armed with a stick and a shield, she, in the character of the goddess, fights and vanquishes a man similarly equipped, who represents an evil spirit come to prevent the Dasahra from taking place and to bring evil on the people. On his return from the temple to his palace the Rajah formally resigns the government to his prime minister (*Dewan*) in order to devote himself wholly to religious duties during the rest of the Nawaratri days. All that time he may wear no clothes except a *dhoti* and a *pichhori* : his body is smeared with sandalwood paste ; and instead of a turban he wears a wreath of flowers on his head. He may not ride in any vehicle nor put on shoes, and he must sleep on the ground. He may neither salute nor receive salutations. In short, he remains in a state of taboo from the first day of the festival to the ninth,

[1] J. T. Marten, *op. cit.* pp. 83 *sq.*

that is, throughout the whole duration of the Nawaratri ceremonies.

Meanwhile, by order of the Rajah, a responsible member
of his family and a State official go to the Durbar Hall to
consecrate and enthrone in his stead a devotee. The devotee
chosen for this distinction used to be taken from a special
class apparently connected with the Halba caste. Nowadays
a man from some Halba family is taken for the ceremony and
performs it yearly till he dies. Formerly, to compensate him
for the hardships he had to submit to during the rites, a
village was granted to him rent free, but he is now remunerated
in ornaments and cash. Once he is consecrated he must
remain on the same spot for the nine days of the Nawaratri
festival ; when hunger overpowers him he is given a small
quantity of milk and plantains, but otherwise he is not regularly fed during the nine days. Originally, when he was
released from his confinement on the ninth day, he was
allowed to plunder the bazaar, and the State reimbursed the
merchants for the loss of their goods. But at the present
time this old custom is forbidden, and the mock Rajah is
reduced to going about the bazaar and the villages soliciting
alms. The ceremony of the consecration and enthronement
of the devotee is as follows. In the middle of the Durbar
Hall a pit is dug six feet long from east to west, three feet
broad, and about a foot deep. In this pit, on the western
side, a raised platform of ashes is made, and on the middle
of the platform the devotee, now the mock Rajah, sits
covered with a new blanket or cloth. In front of him, on the
eastern side of the pit, are set holy water and a sword, and
wheat is sown on an altar. The devotee is placed in a sitting
posture, and a wooden plank is put across his thighs and
pegged to the ground. Another plank is placed behind him,
so that his head and back rest on it. Thus he is fastened
down to the throne. He receives sufficient clothing to keep
him warm during his irksome confinement. But neither
when he is first confined, nor when he is released on the
ninth day, nor in the interval may he and the real Rajah see
each other, and he is carefully screened from the Rajah's
sight. After the devotee has been enthroned in this strange
fashion, various ceremonies are performed in the temple, and

z

the real Rajah worships his arms. On the seventh day he
worships the Bel tree, and a fruit is picked from its branches.
On the ninth day nine unmarried girls are worshipped and
fed ; clothes are given to them, and Brahmans are feasted.
Between five and six in the evening the Rajah goes to the
shrine of Mawali, where he performs the closing ceremony.
The devotee is then released and brought screened to the
shrine, where he adores the goddess (Devi) and is set at large.
Next day the real Rajah formally resumes his duties as chief
of the State and is enthroned by the Brahmans, amid the
chanting of incantations, in the Durbar Hall, where the
devotee had reigned in durance for the nine preceding days.[1]

This is a typical case of an annual interregnum, including
the abdication of the real king and the brief reign of a mock
king, whose monarchy is of an extremely limited nature,
since during the whole of his tenure of office he is fastened
down to the throne and only receives sufficient nourishment to
keep him in life.[2] In all such cases it seems probable that the
temporary or mock king is a sort of dummy set up to divert the
powers of evil and especially of death, from the real monarch.

Elsewhere I have described the temporary Siamese king
who annually performs the ceremony of ploughing in the
spring.[3] He is still annually appointed for this purpose by
the king ; but he is now shorn of the remarkable privileges
which he formerly enjoyed. The ceremony as it is now performed is described by Mr. M. G. Quaritch Wales in his work
on the State festivals of Siam, who furnishes some further
details of the ceremony as it was celebrated in former times.[4]

[1] J. T. Marten, *op. cit.* pp. 83-86.
[2] In the foregoing account of the
temporary or mock Rajah of Bastar I
have allowed myself to quote from my
commentary on the *Fasti* of Ovid,
vol. ii. 57 *sqq.*
[3] *The Dying God*, p. 149.
[4] H. G. Quaritch Wales, *Siamese
State Ceremonies* (London, 1931),
pp. 256 *sqq.*

CHAPTER XXVII

SACRIFICE OF THE KING'S SON

WITH the case of the Swedish king Aun or On, who sacrificed nine of his own sons in order to prolong his own life, we may compare the case of some Chagga chiefs on Mount Kilimanjaro in East Africa. About them we are told that " it is said that formerly when a chief was seriously ill he would first sacrifice animals in great numbers to his own ancestors, then to the ancestors of those chiefs who had been vanquished and killed, and finally to the ancestors of all those whom he had killed in war. The great Chief Rongoma even sacrificed his own first-born son to Ruwa, and the same is told of other Chiefs in olden days." [1]

Elsewhere I have alluded to the vicarious sacrifice of animals instead of men. I may here illustrate the practice by a few examples. The Ekoi, a tribe of Southern Nigeria, appear to have formerly sacrificed human beings at their festival of first-fruits. But since they have been forbidden to do so by the British Government they have substituted Drill Apes or ant-hills, which they call " bushmen ", for the human victims. [2] At Urua Eye, as at Kwa Ibo, in Southern Nigeria, human sacrifices were offered by the fisher-folk to the God of the River in order to bribe him into sending rich hauls. Abassi Esuk, the God of the Beach, received similar offerings should the rainy season be unduly delayed, or if there was unusual dearth of water during the dry season.

[1] C. Dundas, *Kilimanjaro and its People*, p. 190. Ruwa is the chief god. His name is identical with that of the Sun, but whether he is identified with the great luminary seems to be doubtful. As to the Swedish king Aun or On, see *The Dying God*, pp. 160 *sq.*

[2] P. A. Talbot, *In the Shadow of the Bush*, pp. 77 *sq.*

331

Now under British rule goats have replaced human victims in these sacrifices. The blood of the goat is allowed to flow over the beach, and its head is thrown far into the current as an offering to the deity.[1] Again at Atabong, as at Ibeno and Eket, in Southern Nigeria, " in olden days, at the beginning of each fishing season, a man was chosen from among the poorer sort, and bound to a post at low tide, to be drowned by the rising water. Now a cow or bull is sacrificed in like manner, that the crawfish Juju may be pleased with the offering and, in return, bestow heavy catches upon its worshippers."[2] At Ondo, in Southern Nigeria, many human sacrifices used to be offered after the death of a king ; but under British rule horses are now substituted for human victims.[3] Among the Lesa, a tribe of the Belgian Congo, the graves of great chiefs are commonly surrounded by many paths, to allow the ghosts of the dead chiefs to walk about in them at their ease. From time to time these paths are ceremonially cleaned, and in old days the cleaning of the paths was regularly accompanied by the sacrifice of a slave. Now under Belgian rule a goat is sacrificed instead of a slave. The flesh of the goat is eaten by the sweepers of the paths.[4]

Elsewhere I have discussed the custom of killing or sacrificing the first-born children. I may here give a few more instances of the practice. Thus with regard to the Booandik tribe of South Australia we are told that " it is customary for the women to kill their first child, as they do not wish the trouble of rearing them. Others take revenge for the sufferings they undergo on the child, by allowing it to bleed to death."[5] In San Cristoval, one of the Solomon Islands, " the first-born baby is called *gare utaora* or *ahubweu*, ' the unlucky or stupid one.' This baby is immediately buried alive ; the father digs a little grave, puts his baby into it, places a large stone on top and firmly stamps down the stone upon the baby. The first-born baby they say will never be strong or clever, and is probably not the son of this man, but of someone else ; it is best to kill it at once. But if the baby

[1] P. A. Talbot, *Life in Southern Nigeria*, pp. 309 *sq.*

[2] P. A. Talbot, *op. cit.* p. 317.

[3] P. A. Talbot, *The Peoples of Southern Nigeria*, iii. 479.

[4] M. Baeyens. *Les Lesa, Peuplade du Congo Belge* (Brussels, 1914), p. 42.

[5] Mrs. J. Smith, *The Booandik Tribe*, pp. 7 *sq.*

is an *araha* (chief), or if his father is rich and means to raise his baby to that standing, ' to make him great,' as they say, then he is spared." [1]

In some groups of the Moï, a primitive people of Indo-China, the mother generally kills her first-born child because it is illegitimate, the fruit of ante-nuptial intercourse, and no man comes forward to claim it.[2]   In India, until the beginning of the nineteenth century, " the custom of offering a first-born child to the Ganges was very prevalent.   Especially was it the case with women who had long been barren and who made a vow to devote their first child to the sacred river if made fruitful." [3]   In regard to the Ibo of Southern Nigeria, speaking of the practice of killing twins at birth, Mr. N. W. Thomas observes : " In addition to this legal infanticide, as it may be termed, I have more than once heard that the first-born of every woman is killed ; my informants were Roman Catholic missionaries, who certainly know the native and his ways, and my own statistics seem to bear out the statement, for I had already observed that the number of children borne by women under twenty was much smaller than it should be, having regard to the age of marriage, which coincides with the age of puberty if it does not precede it." [4] On this subject of the sacrifice of the first-born, M. Delafosse observes the value of the first-born is indeed universal.   In Africa the sacrifice of a first-born is necessary to the founder of a tribe to conciliate the local divinities.   The passage of a river obtained miraculously by the sacrifice of a child is the legend attached to the name of Baoulé.   Bammako was founded thanks to the sacrifice of a first-born daughter to the crocodile divinity of the river.[5]

[1] C. E. Fox, *The Threshold of the Pacific*, p. 177.

[2] H. Baudesson, *Indo-China and its Primitive People*, p. 55.

[3] E. O. Martin, *The Gods of India* (London, 1914), p. 215.

[4] N. W. Thomas, *Anthropological Report on the Ibo-speaking People of Nigeria*, i. 12.

[5] M. Delafosse, in *Revue d'ethnographie et des traditions populaires,* v. (1924) 301.

CHAPTER XXVIII

KILLING THE TREE SPIRIT

ELSEWHERE I have illustrated the custom of substituting a mock human sacrifice. In India this substitution appears to be very common. On this subject Mr. Enthoven observes : " In ancient times human sacrifices were offered on certain occasions. Nowadays, in place of a human being, a coconut or a pumpkin (*Cucurbita maxima*) is offered. At the time of making the offering the coconut is plastered with red lead and other holy applications and covered with a silk cloth. The pumpkin is offered by cutting it into two pieces with a stroke of a knife or sword. Sometimes an image made of the flour of black gram is sacrificed in place of a human being. This sacrifice is generally made on the eighth or tenth day of the bright half of *Ashvin* (September–October). In place of human blood, milk mixed with red powder and molasses is offered. In ancient times, when a well was dug or a fort built, a human sacrifice was made to it in the belief that this would ensure a supply of water in the well, and render the fort impregnable. To-day, when a well is commenced, blood from the fourth finger of a man is sprinkled over the spot. It is also related that in ancient times, when a king was crowned, a human sacrifice was offered. Nowadays, instead of this sacrifice, the king's forehead is marked with blood from the fourth finger of a low-caste Hindu at the time of the coronation ceremony." [1]

Elsewhere we have seen that in Europe the transition from winter to summer is often celebrated by a popular festival which includes a dramatic contest between representatives of

[1] R. E. Enthoven, *The Folklore of Bombay*, pp. 340 *sq.*

334

the two seasons.[1]   Similarly among the Yakuts of Siberia :
" There are two tribal festivals of the Yakut, a spring festival
and an autumn festival.   As the name shows, the first is
intended for the good spirits in general, and for Urun-Aiy-
Toyon in particular.   After the sacrifice, which is followed
by certain sports or games, a dramatic representation of the
struggle between spring and winter is given.   One man,
called the *aiy-uola*, is dressed in white and mounted on a
white horse to represent the spring, while another, *abassy-
uola*, represents winter by being dressed in black or reddish
garments and mounted on a horse of corresponding colour." [2]

Speaking of the attitude of the savage towards Nature
and his want of confidence in the regularity of its order, I have
elsewhere suggested the possibility that he might conceive of
a time when the sun should not rise and there should be moons
no more.[3]   In point of fact we hear of an African tribe who
are in this state of uncertainty with regard to the moon.
The Gagou, a tribe of the Western or French Sudan, " do
not offer sacrifices to the sun, but among them some people
sacrifice a hen to the new moon, because they think that the
moon, if she were so minded, might not return every month.
They are therefore grateful to her for reappearing, and give
her a feast when she does appear.   They dance and sing to
celebrate the good divinity.   Among them the moon is a
beneficent deity." [4]

[1] *The Dying God*, pp. 254 *sq.*
[2] M. A. Czaplicka, *Aboriginal
Siberia* (Oxford, 1914), p. 298.

[3] *The Dying God*, p. 268.
[4] L. Tauxier, *Nègres Gouro et
Gagou*, p. 140.

CHAPTER XXIX

SWINGING AS A MAGICAL RITE

To the examples which I have given elsewhere I now add the following : [1] Among the Milanos of Sarawak in Borneo, swinging is adopted as a cure for sickness in very grave cases. The ceremony is conducted by one or more *Bayohs*, medicine men or women, who profess to have special power in the world of spirits. The apparatus which they employ for the purpose is as follows : firstly, a swing, which is hung from a nail at each end in the wall and has attached to it some tiny bells, which, hidden in tassels of plaited palm leaves, tinkle with the vibration of the swing ; secondly, a long ladder of plaited palm leaves, leading down into a square wooden lidless box containing four wooden images of anthropomorphic shape ; thirdly, a boat some eight or nine feet long, gaily painted, and hung from the ceiling by ropes attached at each end ; outside the room in the verandah of the house there is another boat containing a crew of images, but much more poorly made, often constructed of the pith of the sago palm.

The main part of the ceremony, which as a general rule is undertaken as a last resort for severe illness, consists in swinging in the swing, which is to some extent sacred. After chanting an incantation the medicine-man or woman mounts the swing, and sitting in it swings backward and forward many times, rhythmically swaying his head from side to side and gabbling an incantation in the obsolete Milano language. When he has done, the patient takes his place in the swing, and is swung to and fro under the direction of the medicine-man, who pushes him from behind. While the patient is

[1] *The Dying God*, pp. 277 *sq.*

swinging, the medicine-man continues to utter his incantations, and from time to time waves over the sick person his magic wand, " which passing from the head downward is supposed to sweep out the spirit of the sickness." When the sufferer retires from the swing or is removed from it in a swoon, the other sick persons present avail themselves of the opportunity to swing in the swing for the improvement of their health. The movements of the medicine-man when swinging are at first slow, but soon the motion accelerates, and the incantation becomes louder and louder until at last he is in a perfect frenzy and appears to be quite demented. The excitement amongst the onlookers increases when the bells of the swing begin to tinkle, for this is taken to indicate the presence of the spirit in the rattan. When the patient is too ill to support himself on the swing he enters the boat, which is set swinging by the medicine-man. If the patient is a young child, it is usual for the medicine-man to swing with the child on his knee. The instrumental music which accompanies the ceremony includes drums as well as gongs. The ceremonies are repeated night after night, till finally the temporary boat, with the images in it, is escorted by the musicians away from the house to its proper resting-place outside the village at the river-side, where it is fenced round with stakes to prevent it from floating away at high tide.

The patient, on the occasion of such ceremonies, warned in a dream, changes his name " so that the bad spirit may recognize him no longer : so during the ceremony and ever afterwards he is known only by his new name. Some Milanos indeed having experienced a number of such ceremonies have a corresponding number of names to their credit." [1]

---

[1] F. B. Mulder and J. Hewitt, " Two religious Ceremonies among the Milanos of Sarawak " in the *Journal of the Straits Branch of the Royal Asiatic Society*, No. 57 (January 1911), pp. 172-177.

CHAPTER XXX

THE MYTH OF ADONIS

IN discussing this subject I had occasion to point out that the Oriental, and we may add the primitive, mind, is untrammelled by logic, and insensible of the law of contradiction.[1] As to this I will quote two fresh testimonies. Thus, speaking of the mind of the native African, Captain Stigand observes : " A native can hold at the same time two absolutely opposite beliefs. He can believe in both of two conflicting statements. He does not compare or analyse them ; he just believes in that uppermost in his mind at the time. A little later he will believe in the second, but his faith in the first remains unshaken. For instance, he may give you at different times two different versions of the origin of his people ; perhaps one is that they all came out of a certain tree, and another that a single man and a cow were put by God in a country, and from them descended all the people and cattle now in the tribe. He has heard both stories from old men, and as he readily accepts anything he hears they must both be true. He has never compared them." [2] Again, speaking of the Chinese mind, an experienced missionary tells us that " it is always difficult to make a Chinese perceive that two forms of belief are mutually exclusive. He knows nothing about logical contradictories, and cares even less. He has learned by instinct the art of reconciling propositions which are inherently irreconcilable, by violently affirming each of them, paying no heed whatever to their mutual relations. He is thus prepared by all his intellectual training to allow the most incongruous

---

[1] *The Golden Bough*, Part iv., *Adonis, Attis, Osiris*, i. 4 n.   [2] C. H. Stigand, *The Land of Zinj*, p. 300,

forms of belief to unite, as fluids mingle by endosmosis and exosmosis. He has carried ' intellectual hospitality ' to the point of logical suicide, but he does not know it, and cannot be made to understand it when he is told." [1]

[1] A. H. Smith, *Chinese Characteristics* (London, 1900), p. 295.

CHAPTER XXXI

CONSECRATION BY ANOINTING

ELSEWHERE I have spoken of the practice of consecrating a person by anointing his head with holy oil.[1]   The custom was observed in various parts of Polynesia.   Thus in Samoa " Kings in ancient times were publicly proclaimed and recognized by anointing in the presence of a large assembly of chiefs and people.   A sacred stone was consecrated as a throne, or, rather, stool (*scabellum*), on which the king stood, and a priest—who must also be a chief—called upon the gods to behold and bless the king, and pronounced denunciations against the people who failed to obey him.   He then poured scented oil from a native bottle over the head, shoulders, and body of the king, and proclaimed his several titles and honours."[2]

Again in Tahiti there was an order of nobility called the Areoi, and when a member of it was raised to a higher grade he was consecrated by having his head anointed solemnly with oil.   The advancement of an Areoi from the lower classes took place at some public festival, when all the members of the fraternity in the island were expected to be present. Each individual appointed to receive this high honour attended in the full costume of the order.   The ceremonies were commenced by the principal Areoi, who arose, and uttered an invocation to *Te busa ra* (which seems to mean the sacred pig), to the sacred company of *Tabutabuatea* (the name of a principal national temple in Raiatea), belonging to Taramanini, the

---

[1] *Adonis, Attis, Osiris*, i. 21.
[2] S. Ella, " Samoa," in *Fourth Report of the Australasian Association* for the Advancement of Science, 1892, p. 631.

340

chief Areoi of that island.   He then paused, and another exclaimed, Give us such an individual, or individuals, mentioning the names of the persons nominated for the intended elevation.   When the gods had been thus required to sanction their advancement they were taken to the temple.   Here, in the presence of the gods they were solemnly anointed, the forehead of each being sprinkled with fragrant oil.   The sacred pig, clothed or wrapped in the cloth of the order, was next put into his hand and offered to the god.   Each individual was then declared, by the person officiating on the occasion, to be an Areoi of the order to which he had been thus raised.[1]   After death every member of the noble order was ceremonially divested of the rank to which he had been raised by the solemn consecration.   His body was brought to the temple, and there the priest of Oro, standing beside it, uttered a long prayer to his god.   " This prayer, and the ceremonies connected therewith, were designed to divest the body of all the sacred and mysterious influence the individual was supposed to have received from the god, when, in the presence of the idol, the perfumed oil had been sprinkled upon him, and he had been raised to the order or rank in which he died." [2]

Again, in the Konkan districts of the Bombay Presidency "there is a class of women known as Bhavins who are married to a dagger belonging to the god.   They are also called *deva yoshita*, *i.e.* prostitutes offered to the gods. . . . The following is the usual procedure for a woman who wishes to become a Bhavin :   She must repair to the temple of a village deity at night, and in presence of the people assembled in that temple she takes oil from the lamp burning in the temple and pours it upon her head.   This process is called *Deval righane*, *i.e.* to enter the service of the temple.   After she has poured sweet oil from the lamp upon her head, if she be a married woman, she has no further connection with her husband.   She becomes the handmaid of the temple, and is free to behave as she likes." [3]

[1] W. Ellis, *Polynesian Researches* (London, 1832), i. 242.

[2] W. Ellis, *op. cit.* i. 245. Cf. J. A. Moerenhout, *Voyages aux Iles du Grand Ocean* (Paris, 1837), i. 494.

[3] R. E. Enthoven, *The Folklore of Bombay*, p. 299.

CHAPTER XXXII

REINCARNATION OF THE DEAD

ELSEWHERE I have spoken of the sacred women among the Ewe-speaking people of the Slave Coast in West Africa, who act at once as wives of the python-god, as priestesses, and as temple prostitutes.[1] A similar institution exists among the Ijaw of Southern Nigeria. In that tribe these women used to hold a great position, and nothing was done without their inspired counsel. Each of the chief families possessed one, while several are attached to the service of the dominant Kalabari juju Awome-ka-so. They are hedged round with many taboos and in ancient times were allowed no human husband, since they were regarded as wedded to one of the sacred serpents. The water-spirit is supposed to rise out of the river and visit the priestess every eighth day ; on that day therefore she keeps herself untouched, sleeps alone, does not leave the house after dark and pours libations before the Owu (water-spirit) symbols, the chief one of which appears to be a cone-shaped piece of pottery surmounted by a head. It is the spirit of the sacred serpent which is said to enter the head of the priestess and causes her to gyrate in the mystic dance which always precedes the utterance of oracles. When she is inspired she dances for a period of three to seven days, during which time she may not touch a drop of water nor relieve nature.[2]

On the Afghan frontiers of India the Mohammedan ascetics or holy men, known as fakirs, are much addicted to the use of intoxicants, and when they are drunk they are

---

[1] *Adonis, Attis, Osiris*, i. 66.
[2] P. A. Talbot, *The Peoples of Southern Nigeria*, ii. 101.

known as *mast*, and are believed by the populace to be possessed by divinity, and to have miraculous powers of gaining favours from heaven from those who propitiate them. " Women who are childless will visit various faqirs, whose prayers have a reputation for being efficacious for the removal of sterility.   They write charms, and dictate elaborate instructions for the behaviour of the woman till her wish be fulfilled, and they take the gifts which the suppliant has brought with her.   Were this nothing more than a fraud dictated by avarice it would be reprehensible, but worse things happen ; and when a child is born after due time, the husband of the woman cannot always claim paternity." [1]

Elsewhere I have dealt with the common belief that the human dead come to life in the form of serpents, and revisit their old home in that form.[2]   The belief appears to be particularly common in Africa.   Thus for example the Tumbuka of Nyasaland believe that the spirits of the dead " live in many creatures, especially in snakes.   There are two little harmless ones which they particularly frequent : the blind worm and a snake with a saw-like backbone.   Should natives meet one of these on the path, they turn home, and the journey is not resumed, but a ' doctor ' is called to tell what ancestral spirit this was that had warned the traveller of danger ahead and oblations are made.   If a native meets a puff-adder in the scrub, he does not kill it, but returns to worship some spirit that inhabited the adder.   And when one of the little snakes enters a hut it is not driven forth, for it is a spirit come to live with the friends, and its intentions are good." [3]   The Barundi think that the souls of the dead migrate into snakes, lions, and leopards, which live in the sacred groves about the graves.   From there the snakes wander to visit the huts of their families, where they are regarded by the mothers as the souls of their dead children, and are fed with milk.[4]

The Banyankole believe that the spirits of dead kings pass into lions, but " the idea of transmigration is not confined to

[1] T. L. Pennell, *Among the Wild Tribes of the Afghan Frontier* (London, 1909), 238 *sq.*

[2] *Adonis, Attis, Osiris*, i. 82 *sq.*

[3] D. Fraser, *Winning a Primitive People*, p. 127.

[4] H. Meyer, *Die Barundi*, p. 118.

the king only ; the royal family at death pass into animals or reptiles, and the spirits of the king's wives enter into leopards. Princes and princesses go into large snakes ; the leopards, that is, the king's wives, have a part of the sacred forest in which the kings are buried ; and the snakes, that is the princes and princesses, have another part of the same forest. Each class has its own temple and priest who acts as mediums to consult the spirits when necessary. The burial rites are the same for each of these groups of spirits as for the king ; the leopards are fed with meat, and the snakes with milk from cows which are offered to them in sacrifice." [1]

Among the Wanyamwezi, a large tribe to the south of Lake Victoria Nyanza, a large serpent (boa) which enters a hut is regarded as a spirit or ghost and is not molested, else some disaster would befall the village or the inhabitants.[2]

In some parts of Transylvania and Lower Austria there exists, or existed down till lately, something like a cult of the snakes or adders which are allowed to live in the houses, though we are not told that these reptiles are supposed to contain the souls of dead members of the family. In many places people care for the domestic snakes by putting out a saucer of milk for them every evening, in order to ward off fire and misfortune from the house. On every farmstead there is an adder. If it were to be killed they believe that the whole family would die out. The domestic snake is here the protective and beneficent spirit of the house. And when you hear a cry of the house-adder you should put out a saucer of milk, half covering it with a white cloth, and the adder will come and drink.[3]

Elsewhere I have illustrated the belief that the souls of dead infants may enter once more into the wombs of their mothers and be born again.[4] The belief seems to be particularly common in Africa, where it is sometimes the practice to bury infants at places where their mothers often go in order to afford the spirits facilities for reincarnation. Thus, for example, among the Kassounas-Bouras of the Western Sudan,

---

[1] J. Roscoe, *The Northern Bantu,* p. 129.

[2] V. L. Cameron, *Across Africa* (London, 1877), i. 189.

[3] J. Haltrich, *Zur Volkeskunde der Siebenbürger Sachsen* (Wien, 1885), 310.

[4] *Adonis, Attis, Osiris,* i. 91.

infants who are still at the breast are buried beside the paths
leading to the villages from which their mothers came.   They
think that when the mother goes to her natal village, passing
the grave of her dead infant, its spirit will enter into her and
be born again.[1]   Among the Gouros of the Ivory Coast dead
infants are buried at the rubbish-heap outside the village,
because their mothers go thither every day to empty out the
sweepings of the house.   Hence it is believed that the dead
infants will have many opportunities of entering again into
their mothers' wombs.[2]   The Kanga-Bonou, another tribe
of the same region, practise the same custom of infant burial
for the same reason.[3]

Elsewhere I have treated of the common belief of the
Australian aborigines that conception in a woman is caused
by the entrance into her of an ancestral spirit, and is quite
independent of sexual intercourse.[4]   This belief, so far as I
know, was first discovered in Australia by the late Sir Baldwin
Spencer, among certain tribes in the centre and north of the
Continent.   The evidence for the belief has since been considerably extended, and its area summarised by Sir Baldwin
Spencer in a later work.   His summary runs as follows :
" One of the most striking features of the native tribes in
Central and Northern Australia, whose customs were in-
vestigated by the late Mr. Gillen and myself, is their universal
belief that children enter women in the form of minute spirits,
the representatives of formerly existing men and women, who
are thus reincarnated.   This belief in reincarnation, and in
procreation not being actually the result of sexual intercourse,
has now been shown to be prevalent over the whole of the
Central and Northern part of the continent—that is, over an
area four and a half times the size of Great Britain—amongst
many Queensland tribes and in a large part of West Australia.
It is now too late to secure reliable information, in regard to
matters such as this, from any part of Australia where the
natives have been at all closely in contact with whites, but,
though the belief was first described in connection with the
Arunta tribe, it has now been shown to be widely prevalent

[1] L. Tauxier, *Le Noir du Soudan*,   *Gagou*, p. 207.
p. 319.   [3] L. Tauxier, *op. cit.* p. 224.
[2] L. Tauxier, *Nègres Gouro et*   [4] *Adonis, Attis, Osiris*, i. 99 *sqq.*

over the continent, and I have little doubt but that at one time it was universally held among Australian tribes. From my own personal experience I know that it is, or was, held by the Urabunna tribe inhabiting the country on the West and North-West of Lake Eyre ; by the Arunta that extends to the north of the Urabunna up to and beyond the Macdonnell Ranges ; by the Kaitish and Unmatjera tribes whose territory extends beyond Barrow Creek ; by the Warramunga tribe inhabiting the country northwards to and beyond Tennant's Creek ; by the large Worgai tribe out to the east of the latter, towards the Queensland border ; by the Tjingilli tribe, whose country centres in Powell Creek ; by the Umbaia, Nganji, Binbinga, Mara, Anula, Mungarai, Nullakun, and other tribes, extending eastwards from the telegraph line to the Gulf of Carpentaria and occupying the vast area drained by the Roper, Macarthur, Limmen, Wickham, and other rivers ; by the Djauan and Yungman tribes ; north of the Tjingilli ; by the Waduman, Mudburra, and other tribes along the Victoria and Daly rivers running westwards ; by the Kakadu, Iwaidja, and allied tribes inhabiting the northern littoral, and by the natives on Bathurst and Melville Islands." [1]

A precisely similar belief as to conception in a woman being caused, not by the intercourse of the sexes, but by the entrance of a spirit (*Baloma*) of a dead person into her womb, was discovered by Professor Malinowski to prevail universally among the natives of the Trobriand Islands, to the east of New Guinea. [2]

So again among the Merinas, a tribe of Madagascar, when a woman is not pregnant for some time after her marriage, she consults the *mpisikidy* or diviner, then the wise woman. The diviner, after drawing the omens, tells her which of the ancestors of her family are displeased with her, and what offering or what sacrifice she must make to appease their anger, for they believe generally that the commerce of the sexes is not indispensable, and that conception is the work of God and the ancestors. [3]

---

[1] Baldwin Spencer, *Native Tribes of the Northern Territory of Australia*, pp. 263 *sq.*

[2] B. Malinowski, " Baloma," in *Journal of the Royal Anthropological Institute*, xlvi. (1916), 406 *sqq.*

[3] A. and G. Grandidier, *Ethnographie de Madagascar*, iv. 245.

CHAPTER XXXIII

VOLCANIC RELIGION

ELSEWHERE I have given some account of the worship which is paid to inflammable gases issuing from the ground at Juala-mukhi in the Lower Himalayas. I can now supplement the description of it by an earlier and somewhat fuller account of the worship. " Jwala-mukhi is about five kos to the north-west of Nadaun, and is situated upon an elevated nook immediately under the mountain of Caanga. It is a place of great sanctity in the estimation of the Hindus, and pilgrims come hither from all parts of India. Its holiness is owing to the inflammable gas which issues in various apertures in a temple dedicated to Devi, the wife of Mahadeo, who, as identical with the mysterious fire, is also called Jwala-mukhi, the goddess from whose mouth flame is exhaled. The vents through which the ignited gas, that is always burning in the temple of Devi, issues, are several in a shallow trough excavated on the floor, one in the north-western angle, and two others on the outside of the wall : there are also some in a well in a small detached building. Observing the water in this well apparently free from vapour, I applied a lighted wick to it, and the surface was immediately ignited, though but for a short period. The same test showed the exhalation of gas from several of the apertures which were seemingly quiescent. There was no smoke and but little smell. The interior of the temple was, indeed, blackened by smoke, but this had been generated by the offerings of Devi's worshippers, who place butter, sugar, and incense near the flame from the apertures as burnt-offerings to the goddess. The attendant Brahmans were very civil and allowed me to make what experiments I pleased. When a flame proceeded from any aperture longer and brighter than usual, an exclamation of *Ai Jwala* arose from the adoring multitude. The temple was about twenty feet square, not in any way remarkable for its architecture, except that the columns were without capitals, and were more massive than any I remember to have seen in Hindustan." [1]

At a place called " Fire-Cape " (*Tandjoeng Api*) on the coast of Celebes flames issue from the ground, and the natives, who are Toradyas, stand in great awe of these flames, and allow living fowls to fly as offerings to the divinities of the fire.[2]

Among the Basoga, a tribe inhabiting the northern shore of Lake Victoria Nyanza, in the Central district of the country " Kitaba is the god of earthquakes ; he is regarded as present in the form of a great stone or rock. A shrine is built beside this rock to receive offerings and is the place to which people go to pray to the god. Sometimes men disappear from the district and are said to have been spirited away by the god. Fowls and goats are offered at the rock, the blood is poured on the ground by the shrine, and the head of the goat or fowl sacrificed is buried by it. The meat is cooked and eaten in the vicinity of the rock.

" Sometimes the god is said to journey through the land and to cause the earth to quake, as he passes on his way. He is always followed by another god, Kibaho, who is greatly feared, because plague or sickness of some kind will almost be sure to happen, unless it can be averted. When, therefore, Kitaba passes, medicine-men set to work to avert the evil which his follower will cause. He passes, they say, from Mount Elgon to Lake Kyoga, and they call upon the people to cut a path for the god Kibaho that he may pass as rapidly as possible. In each sub-district the people cut down the grass and shrubs and smooth a road some ten feet wide, while others bring food and place it at the border of their territory to be carried on by those in the next sub-district. This road is said to expedite the god and to carry him through to Lake Kyoga without doing any harm. The people of the next region take up the work and pass on the food to their boundary; and in this manner the path is made and the food is carried

---

[1] W. Moorcroft and G. Trebeck, *Travels in the Himalayan Provinces of Hindustan and the Panjab* (London, 1841), i. 69 *sqq.*

[2] N. Adriani and A. C. Kruijt, *op. cit.* i. 71.

on with the additions from each sub-district, until Lake Kyoga is reached. There a canoe is ready, and the food is put into it and rowed to an island where a priest takes the food and offers it to the god by scattering it upon the water. This offering averts plague and death." [1]

The Kukis of Assam think that an earthquake is caused by the underground folk shaking the earth in order to ascertain whether there are still people alive on the surface of the ground. So when they feel the tremor of an earthquake they shout " Alive ! Alive ! " to reassure the underground folk.[2]

All the Friendly Islands of the Pacific " are subject to earthquakes, which are both frequent and violent. . . . One of the gods (some say Maui, and others say Lofia) is said to be reposing in the heart of the volcano at Tofua, and that the earthquake is either caused by the excessive nodding of the deity, or by the act of turning from the one side to the other, when too much irritated by the effects of his fiery bed. Whichever it may be, the natives invariably raise a great shout, during the continuance of the tremulous motion, for the purpose of thoroughly awakening the Plutonic deity, lest his nodding and uneasiness should, unhappily, overturn the world altogether. The custom still prevails ; although the belief of the native mind as to the supposed cause of the earthquake has long since been abandoned." [3]

In the Persian province of Rey, to the south of the Caspian, there is a lofty mountain, called Donbawend or Demavend, from the top of which a sulphurous vapour, accompanied sometimes by smoke and flames, is seen to issue from a number of holes in the ground. The popular opinion is that these are caused by the breathing of a certain Biourasf who was imprisoned in a cave on the mountain long ago, and whose groans can still be heard at the mouth of the cavern. Others will have it that the fiery breath comes from the mouths of the fallen angels whom King Solomon imprisoned there in the cave ; but we are not told that the people pay any homage, either to Biourasf or to the bad angels.[4]

[1] J. Roscoe, *The Northern Bantu,* pp. 250 *sq.*

[2] J. Shakespear, *The Lushei Kuki Clans,* p. 184.

[3] T. West, *Ten Years in South-* *Central Polynesia* (London, 1865), pp. 114 *sq.*

[4] Barbier de Meynard, *Dictionnaire de la Perse,* pp. 235 *sqq.*

CHAPTER XXXIV

THE GARDENS OF ADONIS

ELSEWHERE we have seen that the ancient gardens of Adonis have their analogy in modern India.[1] I may here quote some fresh evidence on the subject. Speaking of the Kurmis in the Central Provinces, who are the predominant cultivating caste of Hindustan, Mr. Russell says : " The sowing of the *Jawaras*, corresponding to the Gardens of Adonis, takes place during the first nine days of the months of Kunwar and Chait (September and March). The former is a nine days' fast preceding the Dasahra festival, and it is supposed that the goddess Devi was during this time employed in fighting the buffalo-demon (Bhainsasur), whom she slew on the tenth day. The latter is a nine days' fast at the new year, preceding the triumphal entry of Rama into Ajodhia on the tenth day on his return from Ceylon. The first period comes before the sowing of the spring crop of wheat and other grains, and the second is at the commencement of the harvest of the same crop. In some localities the *Jawaras* are also grown a third time in the rains, probably as a preparation for the *juari*[2] sowings, as *juari* is planted in the baskets or ' gardens ' at this time. On the first day a small room is cleared and white-washed, and is known as the *diwala* or temple. Some earth is brought from the fields and mixed with manure in a basket, and a male member of the family sows wheat in it, bathing before he does so. The basket is kept in the *diwala* and the same man attends on it throughout the nine days, fasting all day and eating only milk and fruit at night. . . . During the period of nine days, called the Naoratra, the plants are

---

[1] *Adonis, Attis, Osiris*, i. 241.   [2] *Sorghum vulgare*, a large millet.

watered, and long stalks spring up.   On the eighth day the *hom* or fire offering is performed, and the Gunias or devotees are possessed by Devi.   On the evening of the ninth day the women, putting on their best clothes, walk out of the houses with the pots of grains on their heads, singing songs in praise of Devi.   The men accompany them beating drums and cymbals.   The devotees pierce their cheeks with long iron needles and walk in the procession.   High-caste women, who cannot go themselves, hire the barber's or waterman's wife to go for them.   The pots are taken to a tank and thrown in, the stalks of grain being kept and distributed as a mark of amity.   The wheat which is sown in Kunwar gives a forecast of the spring crops.   A plant is pulled out, and the return of the crop will be the same number of times the seed as it has roots.   The woman who gets to the tank first counts the number of plants in her pot, and this gives the price of wheat in rupees per *mani*.[1]   Sometimes marks of red rust appear on the plants, and this shows that the crop will suffer from rust.   The ceremony performed in Chait is said to be a sort of harvest thanksgiving."[2]

Among the Bhils of Malwa, a district of north-western India, it is customary on the day when they begin their autumnal sowing to perform the mock marriage of two wooden dolls.   All the ceremonies of marriage are performed.   As soon as the rains commence the dolls are thrown into a stream to float away.   These dolls represent the deities who control the rain.   During the *Naoratras* (the nine days' fast which precedes the festival of Dasahra), a certain grain called *jowar* is planted in seven small baskets, which are then arranged thus, two to the north in the names of Chamunda-mata and Kachumar, two to the east in the names of Dharm-raj and Sharda, one to the south in the name of Rani Kajla, and two to the west in the names of Manora and Devi-mata.   They are sprinkled with water until they germinate.   Music and dancing are performed round them.   The *Badwas* or witch-finders present on these occasions become possessed and prophesy.   On the Dasahra the baskets are carried with music and singing to the nearest stream and floated down it.

---

[1] " A measure of 400 lbs."

[2] R. V. Russell, *Tribes and Castes of the Central Provinces*, iv. 84 *sqq.*

The person at whose house these baskets were prepared is obliged to remain bare-headed from the commencement of the ceremony.   After the baskets have been floated down the stream his relatives present him with a turban and he puts it on as a sign that all is completed.[1]

Again, among the Oraons of Chota Nagpur in India, " In the month of Bhado (August) seven days before the Karam festival,[2] the Oraon maidens of the village carry two basketfuls of sand to their own dormitory, deposit this sand on the floor of their dormitory, scatter over this sand a few handfuls of barley-seeds, and cover them over with a thin layer of sand. Every night up till the Karam festival on the eleventh night of the moon, the maidens sprinkle water over the sand and sit up late at night singing songs and watching the seeds germinating.   On the morning following the Karam festival, the maidens take up the seeds with shoots sprouting out of them, and distribute these germinated barley-seeds to the young Oraons of the village who all assemble at the village akhra [3] at the time and also to such other Oraons of the village who may happen to be present at the akhra at the time.   When the youth have received these mystic presents, the youth of both sexes dance together at the akhra.   Although the meaning of this rite is no longer remembered by the people, it looks like a magical ceremony designed to improve the fecundity of the young people, and also perhaps to stimulate the growth of the standing crops of the fields." [4]

---

[1] C. E. Luard, *Ethnographic Survey of the Central India Agency : The Jungle Tribes of Malwa* (Lucknow, 1909), p. 38.

[2] At the Karam festival three branches of the Karam tree are cut by young bachelors and brought into the village without touching the ground. See S. C. Roy, *Oraon Religion and Customs* (Ranchi, 1928), p. 240.

[3] The open space or dancing place of the village.

[4] S. C. Roy, *The Oraons*, p. 243.

CHAPTER XXXV

THE RITUAL OF ATTIS

ELSEWHERE I have mentioned that at the vernal festival of Cybele and Attis, the male worshippers mutilated themselves and flung the severed portions of their bodies at the image of the goddess, and I suggested that this may have been done to hasten the resurrection of Attis and the revival of the general life of Nature in the spring.[1] Some confirmation of this view seems to be furnished by certain evidence recorded by Mr. Talbot in Southern Nigeria. He tells us that some months previously at Idua Oronn, during the time of planting the new yams, a man, in a fit of religious frenzy, had mutilated himself, and thrown the severed portions of his body upon the newly hoed earth. And Mr. Talbot adds that small portions of the male organs removed at circumcision are brought down by Yoruba traders and sold in the markets, and that these are used as fertilizing agents in farm and byre as well as by the hearth.[2]

And in another passage, speaking of the Ibibio of Southern Nigeria, Mr. Talbot tells us that " very special and secret ceremonies used to be observed when a warrior in the prime of life was killed. Only married women relatives were allowed to touch the body, which was borne by them into the Owok Afai, the part of the thick forest reserved for those who have met with sudden death. There wedded women carried out rites, during which chants were sung that the virility of the dead man might not be lost but go forth to increase the fertility of the hearths, farms, and byres of his townsfolk.

---

[1] *Adonis, Attis, Osiris*, i. 217.
[2] J. Talbot, *Life in Southern Nigeria*, p. 275.

353

Sacred boughs were drawn over the pudenda, parts of which were cut off and secretly buried in the farm or under the marriage bed, that so new life might be won, like Isis from the body of the slaughtered Osiris." [1]

Among the Mossi, a tribe of the Western Sudan, we hear of a eunuch priest who, before the French occupation, had charge of a tomb of a dead king, and used to sacrifice an ass to him every year in the dry season. The priest took the name of the dead king, and was his living representative. He enjoyed special privileges. Escaped slaves and persons condemned to death who succeeded in reaching the tomb found sanctuary there, and became the property of the priest. [2]

---

[1] P. A. Talbot, *The Peoples of Southern Nigeria*, iii. 517.

[2] L. Tauxier, *Le Noir du Soudan*, p. 596.

CHAPTER XXXVI

ATTIS AS THE FATHER GOD

ELSEWHERE I have suggested that the story of the loves of Attis and Cybele might be in one of its aspects a version of the widespread myth which represents Mother Earth fertilized by father sky.[1] To take here a single example of that myth, the Manggerai, a people of West Flores, in the Indian Archipelago, personify Sky and Earth as husband and wife ; the consummation of their marriage is manifested in the rain, which fertilizes Mother Earth, so that she gives birth to her children, the produce of the fields and the fruits of the trees. The sky is called *langit* ; it is the male power ; the earth is called *alang* ; it is the female power. Together they form a divine couple, called *Moeri Kraeng*. Men and animals have also sprung from this divine marriage ; indeed they live and grow by eating plants, which are the offspring of Earth (*alang*) ; hence their bodies consist of the produce of Earth and are therefore also her children. The prayer which at the opening of tillage is uttered by the oldest man of the village amid the assembled villagers runs thus : " O Moeri Kraeng, give us a little rain, that the rice and the maize may thrive a little." Further, animals of various sorts are killed and their blood used to fertilize Mother Earth. Boiled rice is also offered. Afterwards all kinds of games are played.[2]

---

[1] *Adonis, Attis, Osiris*, i. 282.

[2] H. B. Stapel, " Het Mangger-aische Volk," in *Tijdschrift voor Indische Taal-, Land- en Volken-kunde*, lvi. (Batavia and the Hague, 1914) pp. 163 *sq.*

CHAPTER XXXVII

ON HEAD-HUNTING

ELSEWHERE I have mentioned that among the motives alleged by head-hunters for the practice of taking human heads is a belief that thereby they promote the fertility of the earth and the abundance of the crops.[1] On this subject I may here adduce some more evidence. Among the peoples addicted to the practice of head-hunting are the Naga tribes of Assam, and of them Mr. Hutton, who knows them well, says that : "All Naga tribes, like the Wa of Burma, regard head-hunting as contributive, if not essential, to successful cultivation."[2] And Mr. Mills, another good authority on these tribes, tells us that "a Naga who takes a head certainly wishes to bring home tangible proof of his valour, but he also wishes to add to the soul-force of his village by bringing home the soul of his enemy. This he can best do by securing the head in which it resides. This soul-force will add to the general fertility and prosperity of his village."[3]

Among tribes addicted to the practice of head-hunting must be numbered savages who occupy the mountains in the eastern part of the island of Formosa. Of them Mr. Davidson says : "Of all the savages in the island the Atayals are the most active and aggressive in head-hunting. This ferocious practice has entered into their life and plays so prominent a part in their whole social system as to have become almost

---

[1] *Attis, Adonis, Osiris*, i. 293 *sqq.*

[2] J. H. Hutton, "The Use of Stone in the Naga Hills," in the *Journal of the Royal Anthropological Institute*, lvi. (1926), 78. As to the Wa of Burma, see *Spirits of the Corn and of*

the *Wild*, i. 241 *sqq.*

[3] J. P. Mills, "Certain Aspects of Naga Culture," in *Journal of the Royal Anthropological Institute*, lvi. (1926), 34.

ineradicable so long as a remnant of their old life remains. The Atayals consider head-hunting justifiable, in fact obligatory," in certain cases, which Mr. Davidson enumerates. The first case which he mentions is : " to be assured of a year of abundance, the heads of freshly killed human beings must be offered up to their ancestors." [1]

The semi-Bantu tribes of Southern Nigeria practise, or rather used to practise, the same custom of head-hunting, and among some of the tribes offerings were specially made to the spirits of the slain that they might not injure the fertility of the farms. It is a common notion in this region that the ghosts have much to do with the granting of fertility to crops and human beings.[2] Among the Boki, a tribe of Southern Nigeria, the skull of a slain foe used to be placed on the roof of the house, and beer was offered to it for a period of fourteen days. Before the new farms were planted, ground guinea-corn was always offered up to the skull, otherwise they believed that the produce of the farms would be spoiled.[3]

The Jibaros, an Indian tribe of the Upper Amazon, are passionate head-hunters. They mummify the skulls of their slain foes and hang them up in their houses. On returning from a raid the successful head-hunters have to observe strict continence and a rigorous fast for a period lasting from several months to two years. At the end of this period the tribe celebrates a festival, by way apparently of reparation to the spirits of the slain, for they believe that the mummified skulls secure for them abundance of goods, fertility of the fields, the prosperity of the family and of the tribe, victory over their enemies, and immortality. When the crop is not abundant, or when the domestic animals do not breed, the women hold a festival of supplication, in which they dance alone holding each other, while an old man carries the mummified skull. If the ceremony remains without result, they shave the locks of the mummy, and throw them into the forest.[4]

---

[1] J. W. Davidson, *The Island of Formosa, Past and Present* (London and New York, 1903), 565.

[2] P. A. Talbot, *The Peoples of Southern Nigeria*, iii. 829.

[3] P. A. Talbot, *op. cit.* iii. 849.

[4] Dr. Rivet, " Les Indiens Jibaros " in *L'Anthropologie*, xix. (Paris, 1908), 244 *sqq.*

CHAPTER XXXVIII

THE TEARS OF ISIS

ELSEWHERE I have alluded to the ancient Egyptian belief
that the annual rise of the Nile about midsummer was caused
by the tears of Isis mourning for the dead Osiris.[1]   In modern
Egypt a night about midsummer is called the Night of the
Drop, because a certain marvellous drop is believed to fall
at that time into the Nile, and to initiate the swelling of the
river.   The drop is now spoken of as a drop of dew, but of
old it was probably thought to be the first tear dropped by
Isis in her annual mourning for Osiris.   The observances
customary on the Night of the Drop are thus described by a
modern writer : " Near Midsummer, it is said, a drop of dew
of marvellous power is elaborated in the remotest regions of
the heavens, and falls down always on the same night—
thence called the Night of the Drop—into the Nile, which is
at once, as it were, impregnated, and brings forth the annual
inundation.   Many believing people go out to watch for the
falling of this drop, and are often persuaded that they see it
shooting down like a star towards the river, now shrunk
within its narrowest limits.   On the same night superstitious
families number themselves, and make a little representation
of each of their members in clay or dough.   Generally it is
a mere square lump ; but sometimes the head and arms
are roughly indicated.   Of course this is entirely opposed to
the ordinances of El-Islam, and must be the remains of
some inveterate popular prejudice—as old, perhaps, as the
Pharaohs.   The object of the ceremony is to ascertain who
will live and who will die.   If the lump remain smooth and

---

[1] *Adonis, Attis, Osiris,* ii. 30 *sqq.*

entire, the omen is fatal; but if it crack, as it always does, a good old age is promised.   Christian maidens, who are very assiduous in the performance of this ceremony, do so with a very different object, and wish to know whether their husbands will be old or young, rich or poor.   This is not the only instance in which very similar superstitions may be found among the Levantines and the Muslims.   Both believe that there is some extraordinary influence in the air on the Night of the Drop." [1]

[1] B. St. John, *Village Life in Egypt* (London, 1852), i. 233 *sqq.*

CHAPTER XXXIX

THE STAR OF ISIS

ELSEWHERE I have shown the great importance which the ancient Egyptians paid to the rising of the bright star Sirius at sunrise about Midsummer. They identified the star with their great goddess Isis, and the observation of its rising served to correct the error of their civil year of three hundred and sixty-five days, though only after the lapse of fourteen hundred and sixty solar years.[1]

In modern times the same observation of the rising of Sirius at Midsummer was employed by the Bafioti of Loango to correct their calendar of twelve lunar months, which they did by inserting an intercalary month about every third year. As usual, they regarded the intercalary month as an unlucky or evil time when the hovering souls were playing their mischievous pranks at their maddest. But at the close of the month, when the rising of the new moon once more coincided with the rising of Sirius at Midsummer, the appearance of the bright star was greeted with shouts of joy as a sign of redemption for the world. This custom was observed in the old days, when Loango was an independent country under its own king. The king marked every intercalary month by inserting in the ground a post or carved elephant's tusk, and the post or tusk afterwards served to ornament his tomb, and so to record roughly the length of his reign. In modern times the ancient custom seems to have fallen into desuetude.[2]

---

[1] *Adonis, Attis, Osiris*, ii. 33 *sqq.*   [2] *Die Loango Expedition*, iii. 2. pp. 138 *sqq.*

CHAPTER XL

FEASTS OF ALL SOULS

IT is a common belief that the souls of the dead revisit their old homes once a year, when their friends and relatives welcome and feast the invisible guests. Elsewhere I have illustrated the belief and the custom by examples,[1] to which I may now add the following. Thus in the Trobriand Islands to the east of New Guinea, the spirits of the dead (*baloma*) are believed to return to their native village for a period varying from two to four weeks between the time of the ingathering of the yams and the resumption of field labour. To prepare for their reception stages or platforms are erected in front of the houses, laden with fruit and valuables for the purpose of gratifying the spirits by the sight. In every house food is offered to them, by being laid upon the bed, and suffered to remain there for about an hour, after which it is given away to a friend by the householder, who may not partake of it himself. At the end of the period the spirits are sent, or rather driven away. Their departure regularly takes place on the second day after the full moon. Then, about one hour before sunrise, when the leatherhead (*saka'u*) sings out, and the morning star appears in the heavens, the dancing, which has been going on the whole night, ceases, and the drums intone a peculiar beat, that of the *ioba*, the farewell roll. The spirits know the beat and prepare for their return journey. Such is the power of this beat that if somebody struck it a couple of nights earlier, all the spirits of the dead would leave the village, and go to their home in the nether world (Tuma). The *ioba* beat is therefore

[1] *Adonis, Attis, Osiris,* ii. 51 *sqq.*

2 B

strictly tabooed whilst spirits are in the village. While the drums are beating the farewell roll the spirits are addressed, entreated to go, and bidden farewell. The words of the address are brief: " O spirits, go away; we shall not go. We will remain." This solemn farewell is intended to drive away the strong spirits, the spirits that can walk. But next day, in the forenoon, there is a second farewell ceremony when the drums are again beaten. It is called the *pem ioba*, or chasing away the lame, and is intended to rid the village of women and children, the weak and the crippled. It is performed in the same manner, by the same beat, and with the same words. To the beating of the drums the procession moves through the whole of the village till it comes to the point where the road leading to Tuma (the underworld of the dead) is believed to start. There the drums cease, and the ghosts depart in silence to their own place in the underworld. This concludes the Trobriand Feast of All Souls.[1]

In East Shantung, a province of China, the people believe that the souls of their dead return to their old home on the eve of New Year's Day, and they make preparations for the ghostly visitors. The ghosts are supposed to return riding ghostly horses, so before each door a block of wood is laid, to which the ghost may tie up his horse before he enters the dwelling, and straws are spread out in the yard to serve as fodder for the steed. On the evening of the second day the spirits of the dead are reconducted to their graves by the family, who let off fireworks by the way, doubtless to light the ghosts on their journey to their long home.[2] Again, in Kan-sou, another province of China, the spirits of the dead are thought to return to their old homes for three days at New Year. At the end of the three days they receive a formal notice in writing to depart. In this the family explains to them that they are too poor to maintain them in comfort any longer, and that the spirits will find more comfortable quarters in heaven or in the temple. To console them for their enforced departure the spirits are informed that they will be welcomed home again on the thirteenth of the month, to

---

[1] B. Malinowski, " Baloma " in *Journal of the Royal Anthropological Institute*, xlvi. (1916), 370 *sqq.*

[2] P. A. Volpert, in *Anthropos*, xii.-xiii. (1917–1918), 1118.

share in the Festival of Lanterns.   But rich people, who can afford it, extend their hospitality to the spirits unbroken from the first to the twentieth day of the month.[1]

In Tibet there is a solemn annual festival of the dead, accompanied by the recitation of prayers, the tolling of bells, and a general illumination which, on the analogy of similar festivals elsewhere, we may fairly suppose to have been intended to welcome and light the spirits of the dead returning in the darkness to their old homes.   The festival was witnessed by an English envoy to the court of the Teshoo Lama, and he thus describes what he saw and heard.   " In Tibet, as well as in Bengal, an annual festival is kept in honour of the dead.   On the 29th of October, as soon as the evening drew on, and it became dark, a general illumination was displayed on the summits of all the buildings in the monastery ; the tops also of the houses upon the plain, as well as in the most distant villages, scattered among the clusters of willows, were in the same manner lighted up with lamps, exhibiting all together a brilliant and splendid spectacle.   The night was dark, the weather calm, and the lights burnt with a clear and steady flame.   The Tibetans reckon these circumstances of the first importance, as, on the contrary, they deem it a most evil omen if the weather be stormy, and their lights extinguished by the wind or rain. . . . The darkness of the night, the profound tranquillity and silence, interrupted only by the deep and slowly-repeated tones of the *nowbut*,[2] trumpet, gong, and cymbal at different intervals ; the tolling of bells, and the loud monotonous repetition of sentences of prayer, sometimes heard when the instruments were silent ; were all so calculated, by their solemnity, to produce serious reflection, that I really believe no human ceremony could have been contrived more effectually to impress the mind with sentiments of awe.   In addition to this external token of solemn retrospect, acts of beneficence performed during this festival are supposed to have peculiar merit, and all persons are called upon, according to their ability, to distribute alms and to feed the poor.   This is a festival of equal celebrity in Bengal and Hindustan, with both Mohammedans

---

[1] P. J. Dols, " La Vie Chinoise dans la Province de Kan-Sou " in *Anthro-* *pos*, xii.-xiii. (1917–1918), 986 *sq.*

[2] *Nowbut* : a sort of kettledrum.

and Hindoos ; by the former it is called Shubi-bauraut, by the latter Cherang-pooja." [1]

In Piedmont " on All Hallows E'en the dead leave their graves and return to their own firesides. They are personified by the chains hanging over the fire, and when they are raised a soul is raised from purgatory, and when dropped the souls suffer more. On this day rooms must not be swept, as the movements of the broom might wound the soul or send them away. A table is set with clean cloth and plates, for otherwise the dead persons would be offended." [2]

---

[1] S. Turner, *An Account of an Embassy to the Court of the Teshoo Lama in Tibet* (London, 1800), pp. 318 *sqq.*

[2] E. Canziani and E. Rohde, *Piedmont* (London, 1913), p. 141.

CHAPTER XLI

MOTHER-KIN AND MOTHER GODDESSES

ELSEWHERE I have discussed the system of mother-kin in its relation to the worship of the great Oriental goddesses, and have expressed a doubt whether the system of mother-kin, that is, the system which traces relationship through the mother instead of through the father, is ever found in conjunction with a system of gynocracy, that is a system in which the men are ruled by the women.[1] However, a system of pure gynocracy is reported to exist among the Valovale of South Africa, a tribe of the Marotse or Barotse nation. I will transcribe the report without attempting to estimate its value. " The system by which the local rulers of the tribe (the Valovale) is supplied is interesting. It is a pure gynocracy, and as such is probably unique. In most parts of Africa woman is practically a slave, a mere drudge. She tills the soil and ministers to the wants of her lord and master man, who, in many tribes, will not demean himself by taking his meals with her. Here, however, we find her in a position of power and honour surpassing even the most sanguine aspirations of the advocates of women's ' rights ' at home. All ' princesses of the blood ' are chieftainesses in their own right ; their female progeny inherit their rights in perpetuity so long as they owe their origin to the women of the line. The son of a chieftainess is a chief, but here the connection with the aristocracy ceases, for neither his sons nor his daughters inherit his rights ; they become mere subjects. Doubtless the very depraved moral condition of these people has given birth to the system, for it is a very wise Kalovale who can point with certainty to his own father, whereas he no doubt has less difficulty in arriving at a reliable conclusion where his maternal origin is concerned." [2]

[1] *Adonis, Attis, Osiris*, ii. 207 *sq.*

[2] A. St. H. Gibbons, *Africa from* *South to North* (London and New York, 1904), pp. 7 *sqq.*

CHAPTER XLII

MARRIAGE OF BROTHERS WITH SISTERS

ELSEWHERE I have referred to the ancient Egyptian custom of marrying full brothers with full sisters, which was practised, not only by the common people, but by the Pharaohs, and was inherited by their successors, the Ptolemies.[1] The same system of marriage between a brother and a sister was practised to a certain extent in the royal family of the Banyoro, a large and powerful tribe in the west of Uganda. The custom has been recorded by Canon Roscoe as follows : " Though the Banyoro clans are exogamous, this rule does not apply to royalty ; for in the royal family brothers frequently marry their sisters, and as there is no rule to prohibit them from having offspring, they sometimes have children by them, though princesses usually kill their children at birth. This seems to have been done rather to save trouble in nursing them than from any fear or sense of guilt. The custom of marriage with a sister is probably due to the fact that the royal family belong to some other race than the pastoral people, a race who followed the rule of succession through the female line, and the king married his sister to ensure his son succeeding him. The king had usually several princesses among his wives and often had children by them, and such children took their places with other princes as legitimate heirs to the throne, no difference being made between them and the king's sons born of women from pastoral clans. The practice of marrying a near relative was usually confined to couples of the same generation, though there was no rule which forbad a prince from marry-

[1] *Adonis, Attis, Osiris*, ii. 214.

ing a princess who was either his aunt or his niece; a father, however, refrained from marrying his daughter. When a princess became a wife of the king, she did not leave him to go with some other prince, but regarded herself as his sole property. The case was different with princes who married their sisters : with them there was no binding marriage contract, and a princess was free to leave her brother to go to some other prince, if she elected to do so. Such marriages being more of the nature of love-matches, the couple came together for a time and their union was rather of a secret than of a public nature." [1]

[1] J. Roscoe, *The Northern Bantu*, pp. 36 *sq.*

CHAPTER XLIII

CHILDREN OF LIVING PARENTS IN RITUAL

ELSEWHERE I have discussed the custom of employing in ritual children whose parents were both alive, and I have suggested that the custom may have been based on a notion that such children had a larger share of vitality than usual, and that therefore their presence was regarded as auspicious at any rite in which they took part. I have cited examples of this custom,[1] to which I will now add the following instances. Ancient Greek ritual appears to have prescribed that on the night before her marriage a bride should sleep with a boy whose parents were both alive.[2] In Africa to this day a precisely similar custom at marriage is followed by the Banyankole of Uganda, and they explain with perfect clearness the motive for observing the custom. I will transcribe Canon Roscoe's account of the usage. After performing with the bride a ceremony which sealed the marriage compact, " the bridegroom then returned to his companions near the fire, and they continued to drink until about four o'clock, when he was conducted to a small hut outside the kraal near the gate. The bride was also brought there and sat in front of the bridegroom. A cow that had one or two calves alive and well was milked, and the bridegroom took a mouthful of the milk and puffed it over the bride, who then took a mouthful and puffed it over him. A relative of the bridegroom, a boy whose parents were alive and well, was chosen to drink any milk that was left over. He was called *Mwana wa chora*, and in some cases he afterwards slept with the bride and bridegroom for a few nights to ensure that the bride would bear healthy children." [3] Again, at a birth

---

[1] *Adonis, Attis, Osiris*, ii. 236 *sqq.*
[2] Callimachus, *Aitia*, iii. i. 1-3.
[3] J. Roscoe, *The Banyankole*, p. 126.

among the cow-people of the Banyankole " the woman retired to bed as soon as the afterbirth came away and four small boys and girls whose parents were alive and well were sent to look for and bring to the house leaves of the trees *nyawera*, *kirikiti*, and *mulokola muhiri*. A hole was dug in the doorway and these were put in and the placenta laid on them ; it was covered with more leaves, and the hole was filled up with earth which was beaten hard. This was said to ensure that the child would grow up strong like the children who performed the ceremony, and that its parents would live, like theirs, to look after it." [1] Again, among the pastoral people of the Banyankole, " when the umbilical cord fell from the child, the mother kept it until the husband was present. He took a calf and bled it, using only a little blood. This his wife mixed with milk and added to it the cord chopped very small. The mixture was boiled slowly until it formed a cake. A number of small children, who were in good health and had both parents alive and well, came with a bunch of the purifying herb *enyamwerha*. A pot of fresh water was placed before each child and each dipped the bunch of herbs in the water and sprinkled the baby, saying, ' Grow up strong and good.' The children then ate the cake containing the cord and went away." [2] Once more, among the Banyankole, after the death of a king a ceremony of purification was performed in which a boy whose parents were both alive and who himself was in good health was chosen to fetch water for the ceremony from the royal well. He brought it in a trough, and a princess used it to sprinkle her royal brother the new king and the people by way of purification.[3] Similarly among the Bakitara or Banyoro, another tribe of Uganda, after the death of a king water was brought from the royal well by a boy whose parents were both alive and who himself was in good health. This boy went at dawn to draw the water and bring it to the gate of the royal enclosure. On his way from the well he had to be careful not to look behind him but keep his eyes fixed on the goal of his journey, where he found medicine-men and chiefs awaiting him. The water which he had brought was then

---

[1] J. Roscoe, *op. cit.* p. 111.
[2] J. Roscoe, *op. cit.* pp. 112 *sq.*
[3] J. Roscoe, *op. cit.* pp. 55 *sq.*

used by a princess to sprinkle the princes, the assembled people, and the royal cattle by way of purification.[1]

Among the Merinas of Madagascar there is a solemn ceremony of purification by bathing or sprinkling with water on the eve of New Year's Day. The ceremony takes place in the king's palace, and is intended to cleanse the king and the people from the pollution of any offences which they may unwittingly have committed during the past year. The water for the ceremony must be brought from a certain little lake by a man of the Alasora clan, whose parents are both still alive. After having served to purify the sovereign, it is used to sprinkle and purify all his subjects.[2] Among these Merinas again, when a child has been born, a propitious day is fixed by the diviner for carrying the infant out of the house for the first time. When the day has come, if the child is a boy, a man whose parents are both alive carries it on his back clad in a garment of red silk. He makes the circuit of the house several times, and as he passes the door he says, " May this child have a long life ! " But if the child is a girl the same ceremony is performed by a woman both of whose parents are alive.[3] Once more among the Merinas, on a propitious day fixed by the diviner a man whose parents are both alive cuts the first locks of a child's hair. They think that if the hair were cut by a man whose parents were dead the child would be an orphan.[4]

At a marriage among the Toradyas of Central Celebes when a bridegroom is brought to the bride's house for the ceremony his sword and betel-pouch are carried into the house by a woman or a girl, both of whose parents are alive, and who, if married, has never lost a child by death.[5]

Among the Bulgarians, shortly after a birth, the relatives are assembled in the house for a feast. They partake of cakes which have been baked by a girl of another family whose parents are both alive, and who has been invited to come to the house for the purpose. The first of the cakes which she bakes is given to the mother of the child to eat.[6]

[1] J. Roscoe, *The Bakitara*, p. 128.

[2] A. and G. Grandidier, " Céré-monies Malgaches " in *L'Anthropologie*, xxvi. (1915), 348-352.

[3] A. and G. Grandidier, *Ethno-graphie de Madagascar*, iv. 284 *sqq.*

[4] *Ibid.* pp. 289 *sqq.*

[5] Adriani and Kruijt, *op. cit.* ii. 19.

[6] A. Strauss, *Die Bulgaren* (Leipzig, 1898), p. 294.

CHAPTER XLIV

BLIND VICTIMS IN SACRIFICE

ELSEWHERE I have illustrated the custom of employing blind victims in sacrifice for the purpose of blinding, by sympathetic magic, the eyes of enemies.[1] Some further examples of the custom may here be cited. Thus among the Banyoro of Uganda, " should a report arise that an enemy was about to invade the country, or when some portion of the country had been raided and some people killed and others carried away into slavery, the medicine-man procured a blind cow, a puppy with its eyes still closed, and a basket of food which was carefully wrapped up so that no one could tell the kind of food it contained. The animals were killed and cut up into small portions and the food was also divided into a corresponding number of portions. These were taken and buried by every road by which it was possible for the foe to enter the country. This was supposed to be sufficient to ruin the powers of perception of any expeditionary force, when the members of it stepped over the hidden portions of food, minced cow, and minced puppy in the road." [2] Among the Bechuanas of South Africa an " important part of the witch-doctor's operations is the doctoring of armies and hunting-parties. An army before it goes to battle has to be prepared so as to be invisible. Before going out on an expedition the army assembled at a certain spot, where it was met by a doctor, and by a woman bearing a winnowing-fan. Keeping her eyes shut the latter rushed up to the army shouting out, ' The army is not seen,' while the doctor followed her and sprinkled medicine upon the spears

[1] *Adonis, Attis, Osiris,* ii. 249 *sqq.*　[2] J. Roscoe, *The Northern Bantu,* p. 96.

of the soldiers, repeating also the same formula. After this they seized a black bull and sewed up its eyelids with a hair from its tail, and drove it before them some distance on their journey. It was then killed, roasted whole, and every part of it eaten, with the exception of the stomach, which was preserved entire with its contents to lead the army to victory." [1]

Among the Marotse of the Central Zambesi there are public charms to preserve the tribe. Sometimes an ox is dedicated for this purpose. An ox which has never been used as a beast of burden or draught has its eyelids sewn up with the sinews of animals, and is then driven among the rest of the herd. It is carefully watched and after a time killed, and its blood, mixed with other ingredients, is kept in calabashes. In war the chief and the leaders besmear themselves with this mixture and wear on their persons little vessels containing it. [2]

On the same principle, in performing a magical rite a person will sometimes close his eyes in order, by sympathetic magic, to blind the animals or the vermin against which his incantations are directed. Thus among the Ila-speaking tribes of Northern Rhodesia a root called *Muto* is employed by a digger of game-pits to ensure capturing game. When he has dug the pit he sits by the side of it, closes his eyes, and prays : " I am humble ! Thou shouldst give me meat, thou who hast created this medicine, and hast created animals, and created me also, I pray for meat ! " He throws this medicine into the pit. The idea is that as he does this with his eyes closed, so animals will not be able to see the pit, but will fall into it. [3]

Among the Toradyas of Central Celebes at the sowing of rice in many families a woman, with her eyes shut, drops a few seeds in four holes beside a fig-tree. Her eyes are shut in order that mice, pigs, and other creatures that harm the crop may not see the rice. [4]

[1] S. S. Dornan, *Pygmies and Bushmen of the Kalahari*, pp. 303 sq.

[2] E. Holub, *Sieben Jahre in Süd-afrika* (Wien, 1881), i. 418. He calls the tribe *Marutse*.

[3] E. W. Smith and A. M. Dale, *op. cit.* i. 278.

[4] Adriani and Kruijt, *op. cit.* ii. 250.

CHAPTER XLV

MEN DRESSED AS WOMEN

ELSEWHERE I have noticed a practice prevalent among some
of the lower races in virtue of which certain men dress and
act as women throughout life.[1] There was a class of such
unsexed beings in Tahiti. They were called *Mawhoos* or
Mahoos. These mawhoos chose this mode of life in their
youth : putting on the dress of a woman, they followed the
occupations of women, such as making cloth, bonnets, and
mats. They were subject to the same prohibitions with
regard to food, and sought the courtship of men as women
do, being even more jealous of the men who cohabited with
them. In dress, appearance, and manners they were almost
indistinguishable from women ; but they were not numerous,
being almost wholly confined to the courts of chiefs, each of
whom might keep six or eight of them.[2]

[1] *Adonis, Attis, Osiris*, ii. 253.
[2] J. Wilson, *A Missionary Voyage
to the Southern Pacific Ocean* (London,
1799), pp. 200 *sq.* ; J. Turnbull, *A
Voyage Round the World* (London,
1813), p. 382.

CHAPTER XLVI

CHILDREN IN WINNOWING-FANS

ELSEWHERE I have referred to the custom of placing a child at birth in a winnowing-fan,[1] and have illustrated the custom by examples, to which I can now add a few more instances. In Greek mythology the new-born Hermes is said to have been laid by his mother Maia in swaddling bands on a winnowing-fan,[2] and the infant Zeus himself, according to Callimachus, was similarly deposited in a winnowing-fan of gold.[3]

Among the Chamars, a caste of tanners and labourers in northern India, it is customary to place a new-born child in a winnowing-fan upon a bed of rice.[4] Again among the Brahuis of Baluchistan, " most good parents keep their babe for the first six days in a *chaj* or winnowing-basket, that God may vouchsafe them full as many children as the basket can hold grain. . . . But some folk will have nothing to do with a winnowing-basket ; it harbours epilepsy, they say, though how or why I am at a loss to think. So they lay the child in a sieve, that good luck may pour upon him as abundantly as grain pours through a sieve." [5]

[1] *Spirits of the Corn and of the Wild*, i. 5 *sq.*

[2] Apollodorus, iii. 10. 2.

[3] Callimachus, *Hymn to Zeus*, 47.

[4] R. V. Russell, *Tribes and Castes of the Central Provinces*, ii. 413.

[5] Denys Bray, *The Life History of a Brahui*, p. 13.

CHAPTER XLVII

MAGICAL SIGNIFICANCE OF GAMES IN PRIMITIVE AGRICULTURE

ELSEWHERE I have discussed the magical significance of games in primitive agriculture.[1] Here I may cite a few more cases of them. Thus, for example, in Southern India " in villages in South Canara there are certain *rakshasas* (demons), called Kamble Asura, who preside over the fields. To propitiate them buffalo races, which are an exciting form of sport, are held, usually in October and November, before the second or sugge crop is sown. It is believed that, if the races are omitted, there will be a failure of the crop. . . . On the following day, the seedlings are planted. To propitiate various demons, the days following the races are devoted to cock-fighting, in which hundreds of birds may take part." [2] Among the Malays " in the ritual of the rice-field there is continual reference to ancestral spirits and goblins of the soil, the hill, the plain. Accordingly, every three or four years before clearing their fields for planting Malay husbandmen have a mock combat to expel evil spirits. Sometimes banana stems are the weapons wielded. Sometimes the two opposing parties hurl thin rods with pared flat ends like that of an old-fashioned stethoscope across a gully until a blow makes the face of one of the combatants bleed and ends the fray. It has been suggested that one of the parties in such mimic battles represented the forces of evil." [3] Among the Toradyas of Central Celebes on the day before the planting

---

[1] *The Spirits of the Corn and of the Wild*, i. 92 *sqq.*

[2] R. E. Thurston, *Omens and Super-*

stitions of Southern India, p. 299.

[3] R. O. Winstedt, *Shaman, Saiva, and Sufi*, p. 92.

of the rice begins, the villagers assemble in the rice-fields and spend the whole night in games and dances. One game that is always played on these occasions is " calf-kicking." The young men kick each others' calves. The game forms part of the ceremony of planting : if it were not played, they believe that the other plants in the field, maize, cucumbers, and so forth, would not grow well.[1] They think that the spirits love to witness the game of " calf-kicking " at the planting of the rice.[2] The magical or religious attitude of these Toradyas towards the spirit of the rice may here be further illustrated in passing by the rules of conduct which they impose at harvest upon the person whom they call the leader of the harvest. Every household chooses a woman from their number to be leader at the harvest : she is generally the housewife. The leader has to do all the work alone for the first three days. She must observe many taboos in order that the soul of the rice, which is in contact with her, may not go away. She may not bathe, nor drink running water. She may not change her clothes, for the soul of the rice might be clinging to them. She may not throw away the leaves from which she has eaten rice. She must sleep with her legs drawn up, to prevent the soul of the rice from leaving her. She may not look behind her, or see a bird flying, lest the soul of the rice should fly away ; she may not talk for fear of frightening the soul of the rice ; and if she speaks before or after harvest she must do so in a special form of speech.[3]

Among the Kiwai of British New Guinea " with the harvest begins the great festive season of the people. Two games, played as an introduction to one of the great ceremonies, seem to be particularly associated with the first cropping of the yam gardens, viz. the *aniopu* and the *paru*, which are rather alike. *Aniopu* (from which the name is derived) is the ball-like fruit of the *ani* tree. The game is played on the beach at low water, when patches of clay have been left on the beach by the falling tide. The players are divided into two sides. Each man picks up a lump of clay, forms it into a missile with his hands, and aims it at the

---

[1] N. Adriani and A. C. Kruijt, *op.*
cit. ii. 248 *sq.*

[2] *Ibid.* ii. 389.
[3] *Ibid.* ii. 272 *sq.*

aniopu, which is lying on the beach.   When properly hit the ball will fly a good distance, and each side tries to drive it as far as possible along the beach in their own direction.   The *aniopu* is generally played just before the harvest, and when the cropping of the yam gardens has actually begun, the people pass on to the *paru*, which is played with a ball cut from the hard root of the *sae* tree.   The paru is really a kind of native hockey, although hardly any kind of rules are followed, so far as I could note.   For sticks they use long very stout branches, and the violence of the game is evidenced by many severe wounds and much limping in the village the day after." [1]

Once more the Kiwai play the game of cat's-cradle as a mode of promoting the growth of the yams.   The custom is described and explained by Mr. Landtman as follows : " The first few yam stalks are usually tied up with strings which have been employed for cat's-cradles (*orova*).   This game may be played at any time, but is particularly common in the villages during the growing period of the yams, when almost everybody, adults as well, engages in it, the children copying their elders or being expressly taught, and afterwards handing over their strings to their parents.   The first pieces of strings with which the yams are tied up are generally treated with the usual medicine, fluid from the women's vulvae.   It is sometimes sufficient merely to hang pieces of these strings on the first few sticks, without actually tying the stalks with them, and some people just scatter pieces of cat's-cradle strings in their gardens.   In each case, however, the purpose is to ' help ' the yam stalks to grow well and twine in the right way." [2]   The custom is also described and still more fully explained by Mr. Riley, as follows : " Cat's-cradles—if such can be called a game—is played both inside and outside the house.   It is quite a usual thing to see a group of people, men, women, and children, young and old, sitting on the ground or on the floor of the house deeply engrossed in making cat's-cradles of an extraordinary character, with nothing more than a piece of string or cord.   It is very interesting to see the skilful manner, in which the hands, fingers, knees, feet, toes,

[1] G. Landtman, *The Kiwai Papuans of British New Guinea*, p. 81.   [2] G. Landtman, *op. cit.* pp. 78 *sq.*

and mouth are brought into operation.   There is one part of
the year when the making of cat's-cradles can hardly be called
a game, and that is when the yam gardens are finished being
planted.   It is much more than a game.   It is nothing less
than magic.   The object in making the cat's-cradles is to
ensure the yam shoots twining themselves round the sticks
put in the garden for this purpose.   In the Old Country you
would make cat's-cradles so that the sweet-peas would climb
round the twigs stuck in the soil.   Just as the string in the cat's
cradle is twined round the hands of the makers, it is desired
that the yam shoots shall imitate the string and climb round
the sticks.   There is a cat's-cradle time and there is a period
when they shall not be made.   At the commencement of the
turtle-fishing season cat's-cradles are prohibited.   This law is
strictly observed to-day in the coastal villages.   A person
making them would bring misfortune upon the turtle fishers."[1]
Similarly the natives of New Ireland play at cat's cradle,
especially during the bread-fruit season.   Some say that they
do so in order that the fruit may ripen, but others allege that
they play the game only as a sign of joy at the plentiful
harvest of bread-fruit.[2]

Among the peoples of Southern Nigeria the principal
sport is wrestling, " but with some of the Ibo sub-tribes, more
particularly the Ikwerri, it is practised as a religious ceremony, with the idea of strengthening the crops by sympathetic
magic.   The onlookers at once interfere should either wrestler
seem to be growing tired or angry—probably that no ill effect
should be produced on the reproductive forces of nature."[3]

---

[1] E. Baxter Riley, *Among Papuan
Head-Hunters*, pp. 162 *sq.*   For the
game of cat's-cradle in New Guinea,
see also W. N. Beaver, *Unexplored
New Guinea*, pp. 63 *sq.*; J. H. Holmes,
In Primitive New Guinea, pp. 279
sqq.; J. W. N. Saville, *In Unknown
New Guinea*, 102; H. Newton, *In
Far New Guinea*, pp. 63 *sq.*   As to the

game of cat's-cradle in general, see K.
Haddon (Mrs. Rishbeth), *Cat's Cradles
in Many Lands* (London, 1911).

[2] P. G. Bögerhausen, " Fadenspiele
in Matupit, Neupommern " in *Anthropos*, x.-xi. (1915–1916), 908 *sqq.*

[3] P. A. Talbot, *The Peoples of
Southern Nigeria*, iii. 816.

CHAPTER XLVIII

WOMAN'S PART IN PRIMITIVE AGRICULTURE

AMONG primitive peoples who practise agriculture the common rule is that men do the hard work of clearing the land for cultivation, while the lighter tasks of tillage, sowing, planting, and harvesting fall to the women. Thus among the Kpelle, a tribe of Liberia in West Africa, the men clear the waste land of trees and underwood, but leave all the rest of the agricultural work to the women, who do the sowing, planting and harvesting of the rice and the other field fruits. Accordingly the wife speaks of the farm as " her farm," and her husband says that he " makes the farm ready for his wife." [1] Among the Gagou, a tribe of the Ivory Coast in West Africa, the cultivation is migratory, a fresh patch of land being cleared every year from the forest. The clearing of the ground is done by the men alone; but they leave all the rest of the agricultural work to the women, who sow, weed, and harvest alone without help from their husbands. Each woman works in the field of her husband. When the husband has several wives they work together in the field. [2] Among the Gouro, another tribe of the Ivory Coast, it was formerly the women who did all the agricultural work except the clearing of the ground, which was reserved entirely for the men. But to-day the men begin to take a small part in field work in addition to the labour of clearing the ground. [3]

Among the peoples of Southern Nigeria " in the greater part of the country the men cut the bush, *i.e.* fell the small

---

[1] D. Westermann, *Die Kpelle*, pp. 68 *sq.*

[2] L. Tauxier, *Nègres Gouro et Gagou*, pp. 132, 134.

[3] L. Tauxier, *op. cit.* 165.

trees and burn down the larger ones ; clear the ground, dig it up into mounds or heaps, for the yams ; collect the sticks or props on which the vines of the yams, beans, etc. should climb, and cut the canes from which the tie-tie is made for fastening up the growing plants. They construct the racks in which the yams are stored and attach them to these ; they usually also do the rough work of preparing the ground for the women's crops. As a rule, the women and children do the rest—plant corn, yams, coco-yams, and all the lesser crops, as well as sometimes the plantains, and are solely responsible for the weeding. In some regions they are helped by slaves, in others these latter are confined to the men's work. Some parts of the farms, chiefly those containing coco-yams or corn, are accounted as the property of the women. On the whole, women do the least work among the Yoruba and Ibo— in the Ika country they hardly do any farming at all—and the most among the Semi-Bantu and Bantu. In some of these latter tribes they undertake the entire farm work except the clearing of the bush, and, in places, the construction of the yam heaps—a state of affairs no doubt mainly due to the fact that so much time was spent by the men in hunting and fighting." [1] Among the Baya, a tribe on the borders of the Cameroons, the parts which the men and women play in agricultural labour are quite distinct. The man creates the plantation by cutting down the trees of the forest, the woman turns the soil, prunes the plants, and gathers in the harvest.[2] In Loango, if a man is poor, he cuts down with his own hand the trees and bushes to make a farm for his wife ; but he thinks it beneath his dignity to turn up the soil or to carry water. These tasks he leaves to women or to slaves.[3]

Among the Lesa, a tribe of the Belgian Congo, when a man wishes to reclaim land for cultivation, he may clear a corner of the forest for the purpose. All the work done in felling the trees and cutting down the underwood is his. His wife cleans up and plants the ground thus regained from the forest. The plantations made in the plain are entirely the work of the women, and it is the women who maintain

---

[1] P. A. Talbot, *The Peoples of Southern Nigeria*, iii. 907.

[2] A. Poupon, " Étude ethnograph-

ique des Baya " in *L'Anthropologie*, xxvi. (1915), 110.

[3] *Die Loango-Expedition*, iii. 2, 213.

the fields and harvest the crops.[1] Among the Wangata, another tribe of the Belgian Congo, in agricultural work it is the man who fells the trees, lops off the branches, burns the heap of fallen branches, and trims the trunks of the larger trees that are left standing. When this has been done the women take possession of the land reclaimed by their husbands. They set to work, and clean the ground with the hoe and the knife and plant in it the little sticks of cassava. But when she has done so she has not finished her task. Round the sticks of cassava she digs up the soil, throwing it into a heap. And between the sticks of cassava she generally plants maize. The maintenance of the fields, like their establishment, is the work of the women. It is they who harvest the ripe maize and the cassava, according to the needs of their families. Besides this the Wangata plant banana trees : it is usually the men who establish the plantations but the women who maintain them.[2]

In the Embu, a Bantu tribe inhabiting the southern slopes of Mount Elgon in Kenya, many men are supposed to possess rights over large areas of forest, and any one who desires to clear a patch of the forest must first obtain leave from the owner which he generally does by a small payment, such as a large pot of beer. " The working tenant having thus acquired his land, it becomes necessary to clear it and bring it under cultivation. The heavier work of this, such as the felling of trees, the destruction of bush and the eradication of roots and stones, falls to the man, but once cleared and fit for cultivation it is the woman who begins to have an interest in it. The husband must clear and prepare the land, but it is the wife who sows and reaps the crop. She thus obtains a very definite right to the produce of the field, and this is generally recognized, though naturally the right is a short-lived one, depending upon the crop. Nevertheless the woman's right in any field is fully admitted, and she carries it with her in case of marriage or removal to another home." [3] Among the Ila-speaking tribes of Northern Rhodesia the present methods of cultivation are extremely wasteful, both of labour and land.

---

[1] M. Baeyens, *Les Lesa*, 23.

[2] Lieut. Engels, *Les Wangata* (Paris, 1912), pp. 29 *sq.*

[3] G. St. J. Orde Browne, *The Vanishing Tribes of Kenya*, 66.

When a man desires to reclaim a piece of land for cultivation he generally chooses a patch in the forest that commends itself to him and to his wife, arguing that if it grows timber it will also grow grain. Then he, " before winter is too far advanced, in order that the hot months before the rains may render the woods combustible, armed with a small hatchet, lops off all the branches of each tree in the field and then piles them carefully around the base. After allowing them to dry for two or three months he sets fire to the heaps, and the ground is free for the wife to commence her labours. The charred stumps of the trees are left standing. While the native is aware of the fertilizing power of the ash, it must be admitted that he utilizes fire as the readiest method of getting rid of the timber. When the sweet scent of the violet blossoms of the *mufufuma* tree fills the air and the Pleiades are visible in the East after sunset, the wife recognizes that the time has come for her to commence her labours. As-sisted by the members of her household she starts to hoe the ground, stacking the grass and rubbish in large heaps until dry enough to burn, her husband meanwhile hoeing his own little patch. As soon as the ground is hoed it is sown. The seed may lie in the ground two or three weeks waiting for rain, and as a result sprouts readily after a good shower." [1]

The Mambettu, a large tribe of Central Africa, " are more agricultural than warlike ; favoured as they are with a fertile soil, an extraordinary abundance of bananas, manioc, and sweet potatoes, the cultivation of which does not require much trouble. The women do all the field labour with the exception of the general preparation of the soil and the burn-ing of fallen trees and grass, which are done by the men." [2]

Among the Kiwai Papuans of British New Guinea " ac-cording to a direction given the people by one of their mythical heroes, as related in a folk-tale, it is the women's work to prepare a garden and the men's to plant it. But this rule is by no means strictly followed. The men, on the whole, do the heavier work—for instance, the fencing. The women dig the smaller ditches, directed by the men, who go behind and make them even and smooth. The planting is generally done

[1] E. W. Smith and A. M. Dale, *op. cit.* i. 136 *sq.*

[2] Major Casati, *Ten Years in Equatoria*, i. 127.

by both together, except that of the yam, which is regarded as principally the men's concern (being closely connected with certain secret myths and rites). The man wraps up the ripening banana bunches in leaves, but his wife may cut them (though not without his knowledge). Taro and sweet potatoes are dug by both men and women. For sago-making the men cut down the trunk of the palm and remove the upper part of the hard surface wood, whereas the women do the rest of the work." [1] Speaking of the same tribe, Mr. Beaver tells us that " as is the custom generally throughout New Guinea, garden work is women's work, that is, the lighter part of it, such as planting and digging with the digging stick or shell hoe, and weeding or gathering in the crop. Myself I have always thought it was the harder part. Once ground is cleared and fenced (they do not always fence in the Downs country) the man's job is practically over, while bending over taro beds in the heat of the sun all day is an everlasting task, to say nothing of dragging home heavy loads of food and firewood at dusk. The shell hoe is made of a piece of melon shell inserted into a wooden handle and kept there by wedges. It is now supplanted by the iron hoe or mattock." [2]

In Dobu, an island at the south-eastern extremity of British New Guinea, " the men clear the land for cultivation, and dig the ground for yam-planting. The women then plant the seed, and weed the garden. As the seeds sprout the men fix the poles for the vines to climb upon. The women harvest, store, and look after the supplies." [3] In the Murray Islands of the Torres Straits " the work of clearing the land (*itara*) and preparing it is divided between the two sexes. The women clear the undergrowth and cut down the small bushes ; the men cut down the big timber if necessary and do all the axe-work. Grass-land is generally cleaned by the women only, but Mr. Bruce notices that the men now begin to take a share in this work." [4] Among the natives of New Britain " the plantation work in the early stages is fairly divided

---

[1] G. Landtman, *op. cit.* 68.
[2] W. N. Beaver, *Unexplored New Guinea*, 90.
[3] W. E. Bromilow, " Some Manners and Customs of the Dobuans of South-East Papua," in the *Twelfth Report* of the *Australasian Association for the Advancement of Science*, 1909, p. 472.
[4] *Reports of the Cambridge Anthropological Expedition to Torres Straits*, iv. (Cambridge, 1912), 145.

between the men and women. The men clear the ground and burn off. They then turn up the clods and earth and other things. The women then go to work with short sticks, beating the clods into powder, passing the earth through their hands, gathering the grass, roots, etc., out of the soil to be burnt. This method of weeding is very effective. From that time forward the plantation comes principally under the care of the women." [1]

[1] Rev. B. Danks, " New Britain and its People," in the *Fourth Report of the* *Australasian Association for the Advancement of Science*, 1892, 618.

CHAPTER XLIX

PERSONIFICATION OF THE CORN-SPIRIT AT HARVEST

ELSEWHERE I have described the Irish custom of cutting the
last bunch of corn in a field, commonly called the *calacht*, by
throwing the sickles at it. The old custom was observed at
Toome, in County Antrim, as late as 1913. It is reported as
follows in the *Belfast Evening Telegraph*. " An old harvest
ceremony, ' Cutting the Calacht,' formerly largely practised
in Ireland, but now almost extinct, was observed at Toome,
County Antrim, about ten days ago. It consists in leaving
the last bunch of corn in the corner of the last field uncut.
This is plaited and called the *calacht*. The reapers provide
themselves with hooks (sickles) and standing back a reasonable
distance take turns to ' shy ' at it. The successful candidate
then places it round the neck of the master's wife (in this case
there was no master's wife, so it was placed round the master's
neck) and triumphantly leads her into the house, claiming the
first drink. After this it is hung up in the centre of the
kitchen, where a sufficient quantity of liquid refreshment is
provided for all, followed by a tea. and general jollification.
This is generally known as a ' churn.' ' Calacht ' in Irish
signifies an old woman, witch, or hag, who was considered
responsible for all the misfortunes from which the peasantry
suffered. She was represented by the upstanding plant of
corn, and in former times it was customary for the successful
reaper to bear it in triumph to the farmer's wife, telling her
that he has cut down the old witch who has caused her the
ill-luck from which she suffered, and that henceforth there is
nothing but good luck in store for her and her household.
While much of the reason of the ceremony may now be for-

gotten it is interesting to note that the important item, *i.e.* the liquid refreshment, still survives, ' churns ' as a wind-up to the harvest being held in much favour throughout the country." [1]

This report was sent to me by Mr. H. McNeile McCormick, of Cultra House, County Down, who in a letter to me writes that Toome, where the custom was observed in 1913, " is a district of the County of Antrim on the border of the County of Derry. It is about forty miles from Belfast and is one of two districts in Antrim where the basis of the population is Celtic." In this report of the custom the Irish name *calacht*, meaning old woman, is clearly identical with the Gaelic *cailleach*, old woman, which is similarly applied to the last corn cut in some parts of Scotland.[2] The reported custom of placing the last corn cut round the neck of the farmer's wife points to an identification of her with the Old Woman, or Mother of the Corn.

In India the Oraons of Chota Nagpur observe customs at harvesting the rice which closely resemble the harvest customs of Europe. Thus " at the rice harvest, the Oraon cultivator leaves unreaped on his last harvest-field a few stalks of paddy wherein apparently the corn-soul or corn-spirit is believed to reside. The Oraon calls this clump of rice-stalks the ' Field-Guard ' and believes that it keeps guard over the field until the next sowing or transplantation, as the case may be. Nowadays, however, this cluster of sheaves is, in many places, subsequently taken away by anybody who chooses—barring, of course, the owner of the field or any member of his family. Even this latter restriction is now disregarded in some places. In fact, in some Oraon villages, the owner himself subsequently brings home these sheaves on an auspicious day (preferably a Monday) and describes this proceeding as ' bringing the Bride home.' When the rest of the paddy (*i.e.* unhusked rice) has been threshed and garnered, these last-reaped sheaves are taken home and threshed, and the paddy grains are carefully set apart to serve as the seed-grain for the next sowing. Again, when an Oraon has threshed his rice and is carrying it home, he

---

[1] *Belfast Evening Telegraph*, Wednesday, October 15, 1913.

[2] *Spirits of the Corn and of the Wild*, i. 140.

leaves three or five handfuls of threshed rice on the threshing-floor. This paddy is called by the Oraon the ' Burhi Khes ' or ' Old (Mother) Rice.' It is said that this Corn-Mother keeps guard over the threshing-floor until the following harvest. This Corn-Mother is usually covered over with straw, probably to protect her from the evil eye or from evil spirits. Similarly to keep guard over his jack-fruit tree until the next fruiting season, the Oraon leaves on the tree the last jack-fruit of the season as *Mankha-page* or Tree Guard." [1]

Again, " the corn-baby is a general institution in India, and excepting Mohammedan farmers I suppose every farmer in this land would not dare to winnow without having first installed the corn-baby. I should have excepted the Christian farmers along with the Mohammedans. I understand on inquiry that the baby is made from the last corn reaped. It is tied to a bamboo pole and erected in the heap of corn ready for winnowing. The grain has been trodden out of the husk by the cattle and the mass heaped up in the threshing-floor. And on a favourable day when the wind is blowing strongly the mass is poured out before the wind, the chaff carried to a distance, and the clear grain falls at the winnowers' feet." [2]

Among the Palaungs of Burma, " while the paddy is growing, no offerings are made to the spirits ; but when the harvest is cut, a small quantity of grain is left standing till all the rest of the paddy is gathered in to be thrashed. This last sheaf is cut by the oldest man living in the house of the owner of the paddy-field, and from it a figure is made to represent a man. The inside of the figure is made of bananas, tea leaves, and flowers ; then water is sprinkled upon it. The outside of the figure is made of paddy-stalks, the ears being turned inwards ; it is then bound round with a wild creeper, or with strips of bamboo, in such a way as to represent head, body, arms, and legs. It is set up on the threshing-floor and the harvesters kneeling before it return thanks for the harvest. They then carry it to the house, and place it beside the images of the Buddha in the shrine on the verandah, or put it under the house. At the next harvest-time, if the figure is still in

---

[1] S. C. Roy, *The Oraons*, pp. 441 *sq.*
[2] T. Kilbey, in a letter dated Mission House, Sahagpur, Central Provinces, India, March 8, 1921, addressed to my friend Dr. Rendel Harris, who kindly sent the letter to me.

good condition, it may be carried once more to the threshing-floor, and again the prayer is said to it ; but if a new figure is made, the old one is carried to the harvest-field and thrown away there." [1]

Elsewhere I have discussed the custom of the " Barley Bride " as practised by the Berbers of Morocco. A more recent account of it has been given by M. E. Laoust, the eminent authority on Berber beliefs and usages. He tells us that at the time of the weeding of the fields, when the work is approaching an end, the women of a village take a stalk of daffodil (*asphodèle*) and dress it as a bride. They trace the eyes and mouth on a leaf of paper, and they put on it a sort of wig, made from the mane of a mare and covered with a silk handkerchief. This image they call *mata*. At first they merely play with it among themselves. Then they carry it round the fields in procession, repeating a particular song again and again. Soon they see coming to them the horsemen of the village, and among them the conqueror of the preceding year, to whom they confide the image. This horseman rides off with the doll, followed by almost all the others, who dispute the possession of it with him. It is part of the game for him who is in possession of the doll to give it up to any other who is quick enough to pass him. Then the conqueror of the preceding year himself takes part in the pursuit. Meanwhile the women cease not to call out " Here is Mata ! Here is Mata ! Her black eyes ablaze ! " The horsemen ride over the fields, trampling them down ruthlessly, till other bands of horsemen from other villages arrive on the scene and throw themselves into the struggle for the possession of the doll. After that the horsemen of the whole village unite in their efforts to retain the doll, and to prevent it from being carried off by a stranger horseman from another village. The racers redouble their efforts, encouraged by the acclamations of the women, who, from the heights of hills or perched on the roofs of their villages, follow with their eyes the passionate evolutions of the horsemen of which Mata is the prize. The confusion becomes complete and the contest only ends when the most adroit of the competitors succeeds in disentangling himself from the

[1] Mrs. L. Milne, *The Home of an Eastern Clan*, 224.

crowd and in carrying off the doll to his own village. The horsemen of the village who have lost the doll return crestfallen and shamefaced, admitting sadly that they will have no harvest that year. With regard to the explanation of the custom M. Laoust informs us that the natives agree in regarding the image of Mata as the Bride of the Fields and the ceremony as her marriage, but he himself is inclined to believe that in earlier times the Bride of the Fields was a real woman, and the Bridegroom a real man, who by their union were believed to fertilize the fields through sympathetic magic.[1]

Elsewhere I have described the Malay ritual of the rice-baby. A fuller account of it has since been published by Mr. Winstedt, from which I may extract some additional particulars. When the crop is ripe for harvest, a magician has to take the souls of the rice. For two evenings he walks round the edge of the field, coaxing and collecting them. On the third he enters the field to search for their host, looking about for ears of royal yellow, certain types of freak ear reminding one of a veiled or laughing princess, ears on stalks interlaced, ears from stalks with a lucky bird's nest at the root. When he has found a suitable host, he ties seven stalks with bark and fibre and many-coloured thread having a nail attached to it, and slips the nail into the middle of the bunch. Before cutting the selected seven stalks the magician walks thrice round them, bidding malicious earth-spirits avaunt. Next day at evening he cuts the seven stalks with a small knife which he cunningly conceals in his clenched hand ; but before cutting he prays to the spirit of the rice embodied in the seven ears, addressing the spirit as Princess Splendid in terms of fulsome flattery, and beseeching her to come, for all is ready. Then, holding his breath, shutting his eyes, and setting his teeth, he severs the ears from the seven stalks with one cut. Like a midwife holding a new-born child, he puts the ears in his lap and swaddles them in a white cloth. This rice-baby he hands to the owner of the land to hold. He cuts seven more clusters of grain from round the plant whence " she " was taken and puts them along with an egg and a golden banana into the basket prepared for the baby. The

---

[1] E. Laoust, *Mots et choses berbères*, pp. 332 *sqq.*

rice-baby is cradled among brinjal leaves, a stone and a piece of iron, and under a canopy of cool creepers and bark and fibre and coloured thread. The magician smears the seven stalks with clay, " as medicine for their hurt from the knife," and hides them under neighbour stalks that are whole. Then after praying to the ancestresses of the rice to establish their home in the field, the magician kisses the rice-stalks, and heads the procession carrying the rice-baby home. The farmer is addressed as the father of the baby and his wife as the mother. She and her children are waiting and, as she takes the basket from her husband, the woman exclaims : " Dear heart ! My life ! My child ! How I have longed for your return from your voyage ! Every day of your absence, every month, all the year, I've missed you ; now you've returned safe and sound ! Come ! Your room is ready ! " For three days thereafter the household must keep vigil, the fire may not be quenched, the food in the cooking-pots may not be finished ; no one may go down from the house or ascend to it. Thus all the precautions fitting for a new-born child must be observed. In Malacca the sheaf from which the rice-baby is cut is called the mother : it is treated like a woman after childbirth, and reaped by the farmer's wife.[1]

[1] R. O. Winstedt, *Shaman, Saiva, and Sufi*, pp. 83-91.

CHAPTER L

HUMAN SACRIFICES FOR THE CROPS

In Southern Nigeria down to recent times men and women used to be offered in sacrifices to the local fetish or juju both at planting the yams and at harvest.[1] The Yoruba of that region offered many human victims to make the fruits and crops plentiful, and at Ibadan many men and women were sacrificed before the kola trees.[2]

[1] P. A. Talbot, *Life in Southern Nigeria*, 257.

[2] P. A. Talbot, *The Peoples of Southern Nigeria*, iii. 859.

CHAPTER LI

THE CORN-SPIRIT AS AN ANIMAL

ELSEWHERE we have seen that in some parts of Europe the corn-spirit is supposed to take the form of a dog.[1] A correspondent, a native of Sanday in the Orkney Islands, writes to me as follows. " In Orkney in my childhood the harvest customs you mention still went on. There was some laughter over the last sheaf, and some attempt to avoid the job of tying it. More serious was the last load or sheaf to come into the stackyard : I have known young men almost at fists to avoid it. The last sheaf was the ' bitch.' When one farm had finished the ' leading-in ' before its neighbours, the lads would make a she-dog of straw and put it on the sly in a prominent position about the neighbouring steading, taking care not to be caught." [2]

[1] *Spirits of the Corn and of the Wild*, i. 271 *sqq.*
[2] Mr. J. A. Fotheringhame, in a letter to me dated So. School, Sandwick, Stromness, Orkney, April 20, 1919.

CHAPTER LII

THE PLEIADES IN PRIMITIVE CALENDARS

ELSEWHERE I have shown the importance which many primitive races attach to the observation of the rising and the setting of the Pleiades, especially for determining the beginning of the year and the seasons of planting and sowing.[1] To the examples which I have there adduced I may here add some fresh evidence.

Thus, for example, in the Shortlands Islands, a group of the Solomon Islands, " when the Pleiades appear on the horizon at the nutting season the houses are all hung with branches of nut leaves, having nuts on the branches. These are offerings to the spirits. They are also regarded as a preventive against accidents whilst collecting the nuts, and this time is regarded as the beginning of the new year. Should the nuts be ripe at an earlier period than that on which the Pleiades appear on the horizon they would not eat any of the nuts until this took place." [2] The natives of New Britain used to plant when the Pleiades appeared in a certain position in the sky.[3] To the natives of the D'Entrecasteaux archipelago, to the south-east of New Guinea, the best known of all the constellations is the Pleiades, which is called *yavunuga*. The natives often date their yam harvest from the time when the Pleiades appear in the east in the early evening till the time when they have moved over to the west.[4] With regard to the natives of the Marquesas Islands in the Pacific we are

---

[1] *Spirits of the Corn and of the Wild*, i. 307 *sqq.*

[2] G. Brown, *Melanesians and Polynesians*, pp. 210 *sq.*

[3] G. Brown, *op. cit.* 325.

[4] D. Jenness and Rev. A. Ballantyne, *The Northern D'Entrecasteaux* (Oxford, 1920), 161.

2 D

told that " the constellation of the Pleiades held an important place in the heathen mythology. Its appearance on the horizon at sunset, about the middle of December, determined the commencement of the new year. When at sunset the constellation was invisible, the second half of the year was supposed to have commenced. The reappearance of the Pleiades on the horizon at sunset was in many of the islands a season of extravagant rejoicing, and was welcomed with frantic dances and discordant shell-music." [1] In the Mandaya tribe of the Davao district of Mindanao, one of the Philippine Islands, " about November first, when a group of seven stars called *poyo poyo* appears in the west, it is a signal for all who expect to clear new land to begin their labours. By December first this constellation rises straight above and it is then time to plant. This is further confirmed by the appearance of a star known as *sabak*. If any have delayed their planting until the middle of December they are given a last warning when the stars forming *Bayatik* appear." [2] We may safely assume that the group of seven stars to which the writer refers is no other than the constellation of the Pleiades.

With regard to the natives of the Murray Islands in the Torres Straits we are informed that " there are various signs to indicate the beginning of the clearing season, such as the flowering of the *sobe*, *wiawi*, *meaur*, and *kud* trees, and the ascension in the north-east horizon of the stars *Usiam* (the Pleiades) and *Seg* (Belt of Orion). *Usiam* appears first, *Seg* a little later, as when it appears *Usiam* will be about nine degrees above the horizon ; they consider it time to prepare their gardens when *Seg* is first seen, but they term it ' *Usiam time*.' " [3] For the Eastern natives of Torres Straits " the Usiam constellation (Pleiades) indicates the beginning of the turtle season and of early food, and gardens are now prepared." [4]

In some districts in Celebes ploughing and harvest times are chiefly determined by observation of the Pleiades.[5] With regard to the Toradyas of Central Celebes we are told that the

---

[1] W. Wyatt Gill, *Life in the Southern Isles* (London, N.D.), 99 n.

[2] Fay-Cooper Cole, *The Wild Tribes of the Davao District, Mindanao*, 185.

[3] *Reports of the Cambridge Anthro-* *pological Expedition to Torres Straits*, iv. 145.

[4] *Ibid.* iv. 228.

[5] *Zeitschrift für Ethnologie*, iii. 404.

time for clearing the land for cultivation is determined by the position of a constellation called " The Cock," its head consisting of the Pleiades, its body of Orion's belt, and its tail of Sirius.   The constellation should be at evening just above the eastern horizon.   Some tribes observe the morning, not the evening, position of the Pleiades.   The constellation of the Cock used to be a real Cock and lived on earth.   To explain the origin of the Cock another story is told.   They say that a woman unwittingly married her own son.   A great drought followed the incest, so that all trees died.   The woman confessed the incest :   contrary to custom her life was spared ; and she foretold the chiefs that she would be turned into a white hen, visible in the sky, and that they were to regulate their agricultural labours with reference to her course in the sky.   Another story is told about " the Cock."   A man visited the nether world, and came to the village of Tamankapa (which is also the name of the constellation of the Cock). The people of the village initiated him in the secrets of agriculture, and told him how to determine the agricultural seasons by the position of the constellation in the sky.   When he returned home he imparted all that he had learned to his fellow villagers.[1]

Among the Malays of Perak and Kedah the time of planting the rice-seed is determined by observation of the Pleiades. " When at 4.30 A.M. or thereabouts a few grains of rice slip off the palm of the hand, the arm being outstretched and pointed at the constellation, or when, the arm being so directed, the bracelet slides down the wrist, it is considered to be time to put down the rice nursery." [2]

In Africa, among the tribes on the eastern shores of Lake Tanganyika, the constellation of the Pleiades bears the name of *Boulimiro*, from the verb *koulimira*, to cultivate, because its stars begin to appear in the east in the evening at the time of the first rains and the first agricultural work.   The same stars are at the zenith for the harvest of maize, and they set with the sun in the west as they harvest the sorghum or Indian millet, the last fruit of the year.[3]   We have already seen that

[1] Adriani and Kruijt, *op. cit.* ii. 234 *sqq.*

[2] R. O. Winstedt, *Shaman, Saiva,* and *Sufi*, pp. 77 *sq.*

[3] Mgr. Lechaptois, *Aux Rives du Tanganyika*, p. 213.

among the Ila-speaking tribes of Northern Rhodesia the appearance of the Pleiades in the east after sunset gives the signal for the women to begin their agricultural labours.[1] Among the Bakongo of the Lower Congo the Pleiades are regarded as " the caretakers who guard the rain " (*Ndunda-lunda zalunda mvula*). It is thought that the rain comes from the Pleiades, and if, at the beginning of the rainy season, this constellation is clearly seen, the natives expect a good rainy season, *i.e.* sufficient rain for their farms without a superabundance.[2] Among the Thonga or Ronga of South-east Africa the Pleiades are the only constellation that bears a native name. " They call it *shirimelo*, the one which announces the tilling season, because, in fact, in the lands situated in the Tropic of Cancer, it rises in July or August, when tilling is resumed." [3] " The Hottentots paid considerable attention to certain stars or groups of stars, and dated the seasons from the rising and setting of the Pleiades. Mothers would lift their babies up so that they might stretch their little hands to them. When the Pleiades appeared above the horizon they would begin to dance, and pray that they might give them abundance of food." [4]

In South America the Pleiades are known by all the natives of Guiana. They salute their return to the horizon with joy because it coincides with the beginning of the dry season. Their disappearance about the middle of May is accompanied by an outburst of rainy weather.[5] Among the heathen Guanas or Huanas of Albuquerque on the upper Paraguay river there is much respect shown for the god of the sun, but much more for a small constellation which they call the seven stars, and of which they celebrate the appearance at a certain part of the firmament by an annual festival.[6] These seven stars are no doubt the Pleiades.

Among the Chorotis, an Indian tribe of the Gran Chaco, the time of sowing begins after the appearance of the Pleiades.[7]

[1] See above, p. 382.

[2] J. H. Weeks, *Among the Primitive Bakongo*, p. 294.

[3] H. A. Junod, *The Life of a South African Tribe*, ii. 309.

[4] S. S. Dornan, *Pygmies and Bushmen of the Kalahari*, 215.

[5] J. Crevaux, *Voyages dans l'Amérique du Sud* (Paris, 1883), 215.

[6] F. de Castelnau, *Expédition dans les parties centrales de l'Amérique du Sud* (Paris, 1850–1851), ii. 398 *sq.*

[7] E. Nordenskiöld, *Indianerleben* (Leipzig, 1912), 52.

The Chiriguanos, another Indian tribe of the Gran Chaco, call the seven stars of the Pleiades *ychu*.   It is for them the most important constellation.   When they first become visible on the horizon in the early morning, it is the proper time for the sowing of maize.[1]   Among the Indians in the valley of the Amazon it is said that during the first few days of the appearance of the Pleiades, while they are still low, birds, and especially fowls, roost on low branches or beams, and that the higher the constellation rises, the higher the birds roost also.   These stars bring cold and rain : when they disappear the snakes lose their poison.   The canes used for arrows must be cut before their appearance, or else the arrows will be worm-eaten.   The Pleiades disappear, and appear again in June.   Their appearance coincides with the renewal of the vegetation and of animal life.   Hence the legend says that everything that has appeared before the constellation will be renewed, that is, its appearance marks the beginning of spring.[2]

[1] E. Nordenskiöld, *op. cit.* 183, 259.
[2] P. C. Teschauer, " Mythen und alte Volkssagen aus Brasilien," in *Anthropos*, i. (1906), 734 *sqq.*; and M. P. Nilsson, *Primitive Time-Reckoning* (Lund, 1920), p. 134. Much information on the subject has been gathered by Professor Nilsson in this book.

CHAPTER LIII

A PRIMITIVE FORM OF PURIFICATION

ELSEWHERE we have seen that among the Bechuanas custom requires every married man to cohabit with his wife as part of the ceremony of purification which he must undergo before partaking of the new fruits of the season.[1] We may compare a somewhat similar rule which requires cohabitation, apparently as a form of purification, in time of mourning. Thus among the Wajagga of Mount Kilimanjaro in East Africa when a married man dies a strange man is sought for his wife, who must sleep with her during the days of mourning.[2] Similarly among some tribes of Ruanda, a district to the west of Lake Victoria Nyanza, one or two months after the death of a husband his widow is obliged by ritual to cohabit with a stranger formally but not really at cock-crow in the morning. But the cohabitation is not complete ; if it were so they believe that the man would die.[3] We may conjecture, though we are not told, that the ceremony is intended to cleanse the widow from the pollution of death by finally severing her connection with her late husband.

[1] *Spirits of the Corn and of the Wild*, ii. 69 *sq.*

[2] B. Gutmann, *Dichten und Denken der Dschagganeger*, 135.

[3] P. P. Schumacher, " Die Tracht in Ruanda (Deutsch-Ostafrika)," in *Anthropos*, x.-xi. (1915–1916), 797.

CHAPTER LIV

THE MANIAE AT ARICIA

ELSEWHERE I have referred to the ancient custom of baking loaves called *Maniae* in human shape at Aricia, and I indicated that Mania, the name of one of these cakes, was also the name of the Mother or Grandmother of Ghosts.[1] I learn from a correspondent that a similar custom is still observed annually at Frascati, in the Alban Hills, not very far from Aricia. He writes : " During Lent the bakers of Frascati sell gingerbread cakes in the shape of human figures with three long horns, peppercorns for eyes, and a red riband around the neck. These, I was told, represent the Devil and are eaten as a symbolic renunciation of him and all his works. The custom, however, might well be pre-Christian, and the explanation a later addition." [2]

[1] *Spirits of the Corn and of the Wild*, ii. 94 *sqq.*

[2] Mr. John Rice Miner, in a letter to me dated : The Johns Hopkins University, Institute for Biological Research, Baltimore, Maryland, November 17, 1925.

CHAPTER LV

ATTEMPTS TO DECEIVE DEMONS

ELSEWHERE I have illustrated the primitive custom of attempting to deceive demons by mock burials.[1] To the examples there cited I may here add some other instances of the deceptions which primitive man attempts to practise on evil spirits for the purpose of evading their dangerous attentions. Thus, speaking of the spiritual dangers by which the Shans of Burma believe the life of a young child to be encompassed Mrs. Leslie Milne tells us that : " If he is a delicate baby, or meets with many accidents, his name may be changed more than once, to puzzle the evil spirits that are tormenting him ; all ills, sickness, and mischances come from them. Indirectly, the miseries of life are caused by bad thoughts or deeds in past lives, the merit acquired in former existences being insufficient to ward off the attacks of evil spirits. These spirits, fortunately, are easily deceived ; so if a little boy is very unlucky his mother may dress him as a girl, give him a girl's name, and call him ' Little daughter.' Perhaps the tormenting spirit is not deceived, and the child still continues to be unlucky ; so the mother takes him to the jungle and hides him under a bush. She leaves him there and tells a friend, who has followed her, where he is. She goes home and weeps and wails, and announces to all her friends that she is a miserable woman who has lost her baby. The father scolds her, and tells her that she has been very wicked ; and they all agree that a tiger has stolen the child, and has certainly eaten him. It is necessary to make a great noise for some time, as, if there is no baby to torment, the spirit will certainly

---

[1] *Spirits of the Corn and of the Wild*, ii. 104 *sqq.*

be deceived and leave the house. Towards nightfall the friend arrives, and says, ' See what luck I have had to-day ! I have found a baby.' She shows the child to the mother, who says, ' What an ugly baby ! How cross it looks ! How different from my beautiful lost baby ! ' The friend agrees : ' It is certainly ugly, but I shall keep it. To take a lost child into my home will give me much merit, and all men will say, " Well done." And my merit shall not die with me.' The mother answers that the mother has spoken wise words, and, after thinking over the matter, she says, ' Let *me* acquire the merit by taking the baby.' But the friend says : ' No ; your merit would be less than a sesamum-seed. Your house is empty and you want a child to fill it ; to take this little one would be a pleasure to you, but it would give you no merit. I shall keep the baby.' Then they change the subject, and begin to talk about their labours ; and probably the child begins to cry. So the friend says : ' What a cross baby ! If it pleases you, I shall sell it to you for one rupee.' So the baby is given to the mother, and is named ' Little Rupee,' or ' Little Found-in-the-Jungle.'

"Sometimes this elaborate acting is of no avail, and the baby is still unfortunate or ill ; so a last attempt is made to deceive the evil spirit. The father rolls his child in a mat, and carries him to the cemetery ; the mother follows, crying aloud ; they dig a little grave ; the child is laid in it ; the earth is heaped upon it—of course the father is very careful that the child's face is left uncovered—and passages from the sacred books are recited ; and now, as the baby is dead and buried, the evil spirit will surely depart. After a little while the baby is taken home, is again called by a new name, and has another chance to escape from the evil spirits." [1]

Similarly among the Toradyas of Central Celebes, when a man is at death's door, then as a last resort his friends make a coffin and stuff it with leaves. They say that the spirits which have come to carry off the soul will be deceived by this into thinking that the patient is already dead and coffined. [2]

[1] Mrs. L. Milne, *The Shans at Home*, pp. 38 *sq.*

[2] N. Adriani and A. C. Kruijt, *op. cit.* ii. 85.

CHAPTER LVI

THE SACRIFICE OF FIRST-FRUITS [1]

IN many primitive tribes it is often customary at harvest to offer the first-fruits to the gods, the spirits of the dead, or kings and chiefs, before any of the people are allowed to eat of the new crop. Thus among the Bagesu of Mount Elgon in Kenya at harvest, before any of the new corn is used for food, some of the first-fruits are gathered and sent with a little of the last year's corn and a fowl to the medicine-man, who offers them to the special deity before any one in the village may partake of the new corn. Such an offering frees the village from taboo and enables its members to begin eating the new crops of the year.[2] Among the Shilluk of the Upper Nile the first-fruits of the corn or maize are offered to the sacred king before the people may partake of the new crop.[3] So in Kiziba, a district to the west of Lake Victoria Nyanza, before a family may eat of the new crop they must send a portion of it to the king, that he may be the first to enjoy the new fruits.[4] Among the Wabende, a tribe of Tanganyika, at the harvest, when the maize is ripe, each family carries a basket of it to the chief, who uses it to brew beer for a general feast. These offerings made to the chief are regarded as made to the gods themselves.[5] Similarly among the Konde, a people inhabiting the territory at the northern extremity of Lake Nyasa, " the first maize cobs are taken to the chief ; then each head of a family presents a few cobs to his own

[1] *Spirits of the Corn and of the Wild*, ii. 109-137.
[2] J. Roscoe, *The Northern Bantu*, pp. 167 *sq.* ; *id. The Bagesu*, p. 14.
[3] W. Hofmayr, *Die Schilluk*, p. 312.
[4] H. Rehse, *Kiziba, Land und Leute*, 54.
[5] R. P. Avon, " Vie sociale des Wabende au Tanganyika," in *Anthropos*, x.-xi. (1915–1916), 104.

ancestors ; twins also must be presented with early cobs, and it is only then that common people are safe if they begin to eat the new season's crops. . . . In some districts a perhaps more primitive ceremony is observed. With a following of little children, the doctor goes to the grave of the chief's ancestors, and there roasts a few maize cobs, which he divides among the children ; on their return, intimation is made that all may now eat the new crops." [1]

The Bakongo of the Lower Congo offered the first-fruits of the harvest to the ancestral spirits, depositing them at the shrine. They believe that if they failed to offer the spirits the first-fruits, the earth would remain barren, as if it had not been sown.[2] In Klonu, a town in the south of Togoland, the people worship a certain great tree, which they believe to be inhabited by their principal god, *Azago*. The people believe that all that they possess—riches, children, field-fruits—are the gifts of the tree-god. He is also the dispenser of the yams, and when the new crop is ripe no one may eat of them until the priest gives his permission. They believe that if any one were secretly to eat of the new yams before the priest had given leave to do so, he and his whole family would die. They must wait for the day appointed by the priest, on which it is said : to-day the god *Azago* will eat the yams. As soon as they hear of it, everyone prepares for the day : the rich buy sheep, goats, and pigs, and the poor purchase hens. When the appointed day has come all the animals are slaughtered and the yams are cooked. Then everyone goes to the place where the tree stands. There the priest lays a piece of yam and a piece of flesh under the tree, and prays, saying : " *Azago* ! To-day thou has eaten of the yams, allow thy children to do so also." When the priest has himself first eaten of a new yam, all the people are free to follow his example. Then returning to the town they hold a great feast which is repeated every year when the new yams are ready.[3]

The Ila-speaking peoples of Northern Rhodesia have

[1] D. R. MacKenzie, *The Spirit-Ridden Konde* (London, 1925), 120.
[2] E. Torday, *On the Trail of the Bushongo*, 236.
[3] C. Spiess, " Beiträge zur Kenntnis der Religion und der Kultusformen in Süd-Togo," in *Baessler-Archiv*, ii. (1912), 64.

no such feasts of first-fruits as the Zulus and other southern tribes have, but before they partake of the new maize they offer some of the cobs to their ancestral spirits. " The man goes to the field and plucks a few ripe ears of the maize and takes them to the village. He strips off the husks and takes the cobs to the grave of a certain ancestor. He sweeps round the grave and then, kneeling before the grave, says, ' So-and-so, here is some of the maize which is ripe first and which I offer thee.' Having done this he returns to his home, and at the threshold of his hut makes another offering in the same way : afterwards hanging some of the cobs over the door or in the rafters." [1]

In the Ronga clans of the Thonga tribe of south-east Africa when the black Kafir corn is ripe the chief offers some of it to his ancestral spirits before he, or the people, may themselves partake of it. The great wife of the chief grinds the first grains of Kafir corn reaped in the fields. She cooks the flour in a pot and pours it into some of the royal powder kept in a calabash. The chief takes a little of the food and offers it to the spirits of his ancestors, at the main entrance of the royal kraal. He prays to them as follows : " Here has the new year come ! Precede us, you gods, and *luma*,[2] so that, for us also, Kafir corn may help our body, that we may become fat, not thin, that the witches may increase the corn, make it to be plentiful, so that, even if there is only a small field, big baskets may be filled." After this every-one is free to perform the *luma* ceremony, and to partake of the black Kafir corn, but they must do so in a certain order, the chief first, then the sub-chiefs, then the counsellors, then the warriors who have killed enemies in battle, then the headmen of the kraals who have all been summoned to the capital.[3]

In India the Birhors of Chota Nagpur abstain from eating the flower or the fruit of the *mohua* (*Bassia latifolia*) until they have offered the first-fruits to their ancestral spirits,[4] and they observe the same taboo for upland rice. Similarly

---

[1] E. W. Smith and A. M. Dale, *op. cit.* ii. 179 *sq.* ; i. 139 *sq.*

[2] *Luma*, a ceremony which removes the taboo on certain foods, including Kafir corn.

[3] H. A. Junod, *The Life of a South African Tribe*, i. 396.

[4] S. C. Roy, *The Birhors*, 112.

they abstain from eating honey from *Dhawai* flowers until a few drops of the first find of such honey in its season has been offered to the spirits.[1]   Among the Lushei Kuki tribes of Assam a little of the first-fruits of each crop is always placed on the wall under the eaves, above the spot where the water tubes are stacked, as an offering to the cultivator's parents.[2]

In Annam people offer the first-fruits of the rice to the ancestral spirits and the guardian spirits before they may themselves partake of the new crop.   The rice used in this ceremony is not the ordinary rice, but rice which has been specially planted and tended, that it may ripen for the day of the ceremony, which occurs twice a year, between the first and the fifth day of the fifth month and the first and tenth day of the tenth month.   On the day appointed for the presentation of the first-fruits to the spirit one or more pigs and sometimes several cocks are sacrificed, and their flesh is carried with the new rice to the communal temple, where both are laid on the altar.   The persons who are present at the ceremony are then free to take their share of the rice home with them and to distribute it to their families.[3]

In San Cristoval, one of the Solomon Islands, when nuts are gathered and yams dug, the first-fruits are taken and hung up in the gardens and in the houses ; part is allowed to remain there and part is sacrificed to Agunua, the great creator god, who is believed to have created all things, the sea, the land, men and animals, thunder, lightning, rain and storms, rivers, trees, and mountains.   When the time has arrived for the offerings of the first-fruits, the people place them ready, and wait for the signal from the priest at Haununu.   When the day has come a priest offers the first-fruits to a real snake called Kagauraha.   Then the people of Haununu perform the proper rites, and pass on the word to the next village by the sound of the drum.   So the news is passed on from village to village by beat of drum. Then the people of each village take dracaena leaves and go in procession to the sacred grove of Agunua.   As they go they indulge in sham fighting, and sing a song to the effect

[1] S. C. Roy, *op. cit.* 520.

[2] J. Shakespear, *The Lushei Kuki Clans*, 65.

[3] P. Giran, *Magie et religion Annamites*, pp. 300 *sqq.*

that the almonds shall ripen, the pig's tusks shall curl. When they come to the sacred grove, each person plants his dracaena leaf in the ground, and they stand round the central tree, and one of them builds a platform of twigs and burns sacrifices of pudding made from the first-fruits, and they all cry aloud praying that the taro when planted may thrive, and the banana may bear good fruit. Then they put a creeper by the tree, so that in that year all creepers by which men climb may be strong and hold them securely, being blessed by Agunua, and they put a stone to represent puddings so that Agunua may bless all the cooking in that year, and a crooked stick to represent adzes for cutting down trees, that wood-felling may prosper ; and they take a small stick and thrust it through a dracaena leaf, and bend the leaf over to represent a house that Agunua may bless all craftsmen who build houses in that year.[1]

At Sa'a in the south-east of the Solomon Islands the people keep skulls, jawbones, locks of hair, or teeth of the departed in a relic-case in the house. Each householder hangs up offerings of first-fruits alongside the relic cases, and at the offering of the first-fruits of the yam harvest he places food therein.[2] In the neighbouring island of Ulawa the offering of first-fruits is called *toliuhi*, where *toli* means to put, place, or lay. " The priest takes two yams which are dug for him, and ties them together with sprigs of dracaena and evodia laid on them. He ties a bunch of leaves on his back, and walks through the village about 4 P.M. down to the altar by the beach where he offers the yams. The people are all fasting, and they stay indoors and are quiet. The one offering suffices for the whole village." [3] In the Mortlock Islands of the Pacific when the bread-fruit ripens no one may partake of it until he has taken the first-fruits and offered them to the chief.[4]

In Europe the western Esthonians revere a certain deity called Tonn or Tonis, whom they regard as the protector or guardian of the house and household. A figure of him

[1] C. E. Fox, *The Threshold of the Pacific*, pp. 80 *sq.*

[2] W. G. Ivens, *Melanesians of the South-East Solomon Islands*, 178.

[3] W. G. Ivens, *op. cit.* 362.

[4] J. Kubary, " Die Bewohner der Mortlock-Inseln," in *Mittheilungen der Geographischen Gesellschaft in Hamburg* (1878–1879), 32.

made of rags and twigs is set up in the house and worshipped as the household god.   The first-fruits of every crop are brought to him as offerings, some beer of the new brew and blood of the slaughtered animals, small copper coins for new-born animals and some silver coins for a new-born child, some of the first milk of a cow after calving, and some of the wool of a sheep shorn for the first time.   A basket is used as a receptacle for the offerings to the god, and at a certain time every year it is emptied and cleaned, and the contents are immediately buried to leave room for the offerings of the next year.[1]

[1] Dr. F. J. Wiedemann, *Aus dem inneren und äusseren Leben der*   *Ehsten* (St. Petersburg, 1876), 443.

CHAPTER LVII

HOMOEOPATHIC MAGIC OF A FLESH DIET

THE savage commonly believes that by eating the flesh of a man or an animal he acquires the qualities and abilities of the animal or man. Thus with regard to the aborigines of Australia we are told that "it is the custom to cut portions from the soft parts of a dead warrior's body, whether he be friend or foe, and to eat them. The belief is that by so doing the brave qualities of the departed soldier will be kept among the tribe and will not all be taken away by the spirit when it migrates to the ancestral hunting grounds." [1] Similarly the Namau tribes of British New Guinea used to think that when a man killed another legitimately, that is, in warfare, and ate his flesh, the soul of the victim entered the body of the victor, thus enhancing his fighting qualities ; hence the need for cannibalism among them. [2] With regard to the Bagobo, a tribe of the Davao District in Mindanao, one of the Philippine Islands, it is said that when they have slain enemies in war it is customary for all the warriors to make at least one cut in the bodies, and to eat a portion of the livers of slain foes who have shown great bravery, for in this way it is thought they gain in that quality. This seems to be the only occasion when human flesh is tasted, despite the fact that the members of this tribe have been frequently referred to as cannibals. [3] The Indians of California assured the French voyager La Pérouse that they did not eat either their prisoners or their enemies who were killed in war ;

---

[1] H. Basedow, *The Australian Aborigine*, 189.

[2] J. H. Holmes, *In Primitive New Guinea*, 156.

[3] Fay-Cooper Cole, *The Wild Tribes of the Davao District, Mindanao*, 94.

but that when they had conquered and put to death on the field of battle chiefs or very courageous men they ate some parts of them, less as a sign of hatred and vengeance than as a homage which they rendered to their valour, and in the belief that this food would augment their courage.[1]

The Oraons of Chota Nagpur in India have a practice of eating certain things in order to imbibe their virtues. Thus an Oraon sometimes eats the eye of a hare to obtain keenness of vision, and the liver of a fox to acquire a musical voice.[2]

[1] *Voyage de La Pérouse autour du Monde*, ii. (Paris, 1797), 272 *sq.*

[2] S. C. Roy, " Magic and Witch-craft on the Chota Nagpur Plateau," in the *Journal of the Royal Anthropological Institute*, xliv. (1914), 32.

CHAPTER LVIII

THE PROPITIATION OF WILD ANIMALS BY HUNTERS [1]

BELIEVING that animals like men have souls that survive their
bodies, the savage hunter and fisher is careful to propitiate the
animals and fish which he kills and eats, lest the disembodied
souls of the creatures should take vengeance upon him, and
he treats the living animals or fish also with great respect in
the hope of thus alluring them to come and be killed.   Thus
among the Kassounas Bouras, a tribe of the Western or
French Sudan, when a man has killed a lion, or a panther, or
a buffalo, or an antelope, or a hyena the medicine-man tells
him that some misfortune will befall him.   Then the murderer
builds a small house about two feet high in front of his own
house to lodge the soul of the dead beast, and he offers a
sacrifice to this soul.   The bird called *kouma* in the native
language, which is probably the crested crane, may not be
killed at all.   But if a man should happen to kill it, he must
build a small house for it and offer it a sacrifice upon the
house.   If a man kills a red ape or a boar he builds a small
house and makes an offering to it if the medicine-man tells
him to do so.[2]   Again among the Gouros, a tribe of the Ivory
Coast, if a man has killed a hind, he hastens to take its skull
and to offer a small sacrifice over it, in order that the vengeful
soul of the dead animal may not pursue him.   The same
custom is followed by hunters who have killed an elephant or
a leopard.[3]   The Kwottos of Northern Nigeria fear lions,
leopards, and all the larger wild animals on account of the

[1] Compare, *Spirits of the Corn and
of the Wild*, ii. 204-273.
[2] L. Tauxier, *Le Noir du Soudan*,
p. 327.
[3] L. Tauxier, *Nègres Gouro et
Gagou*, p. 204.

spiritual power which they believe these creatures to possess. This fear, we are told, is at the base of all hunting and fishing magic whereby it is sought to propitiate the souls of animals slain, whether the animals are members of a totem species or not.

Captain Wilson-Haffenden received the following account of the procedure stated to be adopted at the present day when a hunter kills a lion at a place within the political jurisdiction of the chief of the lion clan. " After slaying the lion, the hunter, before taking any steps to remove it, reports the matter to the chief. At the same time he seeks to obtain the forgiveness of the latter for having slain his kinsman by the offer of presents, including a white cock and beer. The chief, on his part, rewards the successful hunter for his valour by gifts, usually including a gown and turban. These, incidentally, are among the traditional items of apparel with which a senior chief invests a junior on appointment, so that the gift may conceivably in origin be connected with the idea of hailing the hunter as ' chiefly,' owing to his having become impregnated with the royal spiritual influence of the lion. The chief then arranges for a bearer party to go and fetch the lion in order that it may be given ceremonial burial. . . . The skull of the dead lion is given to the hunter who killed it, to deposit on the lion-clan chief's grave, where he offers up sacrifice and prays before it. He beseeches the ghost (*ekiti*) of the lion not to harm him for his presumption in killing it, saying : ' O Lion, I give you refreshment to-day, let your spiritual power (*kofi*) not cause me to die.' After burying the lion and before returning to live in his village, the hunter retires to the bush for two days, where he performs certain further propitiatory and purificatory rites. These include the eating of a mixture containing atcha-millet, white beans, rice, seven ears of corn and seven ears of maize. To this is added palm-oil, and the whole boiled. Were the hunter to neglect to perform these rites it is believed he would go mad. His fellow-villagers will at any rate refuse to receive him into the village until he has purified himself from the *kofi* of the slain animal, conceived as still attaching to him. They fear that if they do so their houses, food, and all their belongings will become contaminated, and the remaining lions come and avenge their comrades by ' eating up ' the village." [1]

In Kiziba, a district to the west of Lake Victoria Nyanza, it is believed that the earth-spirit Irungu rules over the forest trees that grow on the edge of the banana groves, also over the rivers and the birds. The wild animals also are his, and when one of them is killed, either accidentally or in the chase, it is necessary to appease Irungu. All who took part in the killing, often hundreds of men, assemble round the dead beast, in front of the hut where the priest of the earth-spirit dwells. The priest appears with the cut blossom of a banana tree. He cuts it in two with a knife, and presses the two halves together, after inserting various kinds of wood in the blossom. Then he kills a fowl, sticks it and the banana-blossom on a spit, and carries the whole into the hut of the earth-spirit. As soon as the savour of the roasted flesh begins to ascend, the hunters arrange themselves in a line, and, headed by the priest, step over the dead animal. Thus the earth-spirit is appeased.[2] Among the Wandamba, a tribe of Tanganyika, when an elephant has been killed the chief medicine-man, or in his absence the man who has drawn first blood, cuts off the tail and the tip of the trunk, burying the latter, which is considered ugly and shameful and as unfitting to be seen by a woman as the nakedness of a man. Then he mounts the carcase and dances, singing, " He is dead, the rumbling one, he is dead." Then the others climb up and dance and sing, but a man who has not previously assisted at a death may not do so unless he is invited by the head medicine-man, who first binds a couple of hairs from the tail round his neck and washes him. Neglect of these precautions would result in the tyro being haunted by the spirit of the dead elephant and in fits of madness in which he would suffer from the illusion that the beast was pursuing him.[3]

Among the Ila-speaking peoples of Northern Rhodesia, when the hunters have killed an elephant they perform a ceremony, the object of which is said to be " to prevent the ghost of the deceased elephant from taking vengeance upon

[1] Captain J. R. Wilson-Haffenden, *The Red Men of Nigeria*, pp. 167 *sqq*.

[2] H. Rehse, *Kiziba, Land und Leute*, pp. 126 *sqq*.

[3] A. G. O. Hodgson, " Some Notes on the Hunting Customs of the Wandamba," in the *Journal of the Royal Anthropological Institute*, lvi. (1926), 63.

the hunters, and to induce it to assist them in bringing the same fate upon other elephants. When the elephant is dead the hunter runs off and is chased in mock resentment by his companions. Then he comes back and climbs upon the carcase, bearing ' medicine,' which, after chewing, he ejects into the wound and anus ; in doing this he crawls about over the body. He then stands up and executes a dance upon the carcase, his companions surrounding the elephant and clapping their hands in greeting and con-gratulation. They then proceed to cut up the carcase." [1]

At sacrificial festivals the Toradyas of Central Celebes spear buffaloes to death with many wounds. Buffalo hairs are put in a basket with betel, and moved seven times in a circle over the slaughtered animal's head, while words of excuse are spoken. This is said to be done to prevent the other buffaloes from dying.[2]

Speaking of the natives of Uvea, one of the Loyalty Islands, Mrs. Hadfield tells us that in the case of one particular kind of fish the Uveans use oratory instead of bait. " I have seen a shoal of about sixty large fish caught, as everyone assured me, by the persuasive arguments of one of their fisher-men. The circumstance and method were as follows. An Uvean walking along the sandy beach noticed a number of small objects bobbing about on the surface of the water, some distance from land. He pointed them out to a friend, who at once became greatly excited and exclaimed : ' I know something about these fish ; let us get a canoe as quickly as possible.' They were soon afloat, and paddled into the midst of a shoal of bottle-nosed porpoises. ' Now,' said he, ' do just what I tell you, and we will capture the lot. Paddle gently and slowly towards the shore, whilst I harangue the fish.' Then, standing up in the canoe, with many vehement gestures and persuasive native oratory he addressed the fish as follows : ' Oh fish, I am truly delighted to see you, and I sincerely hope you are coming to pay a visit to our island. If you intend to come ashore, you can't find a better place than this. There are many big chiefs living here. This is the home of Dauma, Nikelo, Beka—truly great men, who

---

[1] E. W. Smith and A. M. Dale, *op. cit.* i. 167.

[2] N. Adriani and A. C. Kruijt, *op. cit.* ii. 175.

rule many subjects and possess numerous coconut trees.   I beseech you come ashore here.'   Then, aside to the oarsman, ' Paddle very gently towards the shore.'   The fish, being persuaded by such eloquence, began to swim with the canoe until they reached rather shallow water.   Not for a moment had the orator stopped his harangue, but now he turned to his friend, saying, ' Do you see that small fish in the midst of the others ?   That is their king.   Jump into the water and throw him into the canoe.'   This was no sooner done than a great tumult arose amongst the other fishes.   They darted to and fro in search of their little one ;   many in their excitement stranded themselves on the sandy beach ;   whilst others were washed back into the shallow water.   These at once made off seaward, and the men thought they had lost them ;   but back they soon rushed, and stranded themselves as the others had done.   The men lost no time in dragging them to higher and drier ground.   A shoal has since been caught in exactly the same way at the north of Uvea ;   and I believe this also happens at times on the neighbouring islands of New Hebrides." [1]

Speaking of the Eskimo between Slave Lake and the Arctic Ocean, Mr. Stefansson, who lived amongst them, tells us :   " I learned also why it is that animals allow themselves to be killed by men.   The animals are much wiser than men, and know everything in the world, including the thoughts of men ;   but there are certain things which the animals need, and which they can only get from men.   The seals and whales live in the salt water, and are therefore continually thirsty.   They have no means of getting fresh water, except to come to men for it.   A seal will therefore allow himself to be killed by the hunter who will give him a drink of water in return :   that is why a dipperful of water is always poured into the mouth of a seal when he is brought ashore.   If a hunter neglects to do this, all the other seals know about it, and no other seal will ever allow himself to be killed by that hunter, because he knows he is not going to get a drink. Every man who gives a seal a drink of water, and keeps this implied promise, is known by the other seals as a depend-

[1] E. Hadfield, *Among the Natives of the Loyalty Group* (London, 1920), pp. 96 *sq.*

able person, and they will prefer to be killed by him.   There
are other things which a seal would like to have done for it
when it is dead, and some men are so careful to do everything
that seals want that the seals tumble over themselves in their
eagerness to be killed by that particular man.   The polar
bear does not suffer from thirst as much as the seal, for he
can eat the fresh snow on the top of the ice.   But polar bears
are unable to make for themselves certain tools which they
need.   What the male bears especially value are crooked
knives and bow-drills, and the female bears are especially
eager to get women's knives, skin scrapers, and needle-
cases ; consequently when a polar bear has been killed his
soul (*tatkok*) accompanies the skin into the man's house and
stays with the skin for several days (among most tribes, for
four days if it is a male bear, and for five days if it is a female).
The skin during this time is hung up at the rear end of the
house, and with the skin are hung up the tools which the
bear desires, according to the sex of the animal killed.   At
the end of the fourth or fifth day the soul of the bear is by a
magic formula driven out of the house ; and when it goes
away it takes with it the souls of the tools which have been
suspended with it and uses them thereafter." [1]

The Berbers of Morocco resort to various magical and
religious rites for the purpose of protecting their crops of
barley from the inroads of sparrows.   At Timgissin the
ceremony takes place towards the middle of February, because in that part of the country the barley ripens early.
The peasants collect offerings of wheat, barley, maize,
honey, butter, and oil, all in small quantities.   They place
these products on a plate which they give to an old woman,
round whom they group themselves.   Then they go in procession to the fields, the men firing salvos incessantly with their
muskets, the women singing, " May God preserve the fields
from all harm.   Here is your portion, O small birds, and
here is yours, O jinn ! "   Then they go to a thicket of palm-
trees.   There they deposit the grain at the foot of the trees,
saying, " Here is your part of the banquet, O jinn and small
birds."   Afterwards they go in procession round the fields,
the men still firing musket shots, and then return to the

[1] V. Stefansson, *My Life with the Eskimo* (London, 1913), pp. 56 *sq.*

village.   In another ceremony they carry one or two dolls in procession round the fields and then deposit them at the foot of a shrub.   At Tagadirt, when the time of the expulsion of the sparrows comes round, the young girls fashion an image with the help of a stalk of maize, or the axle of a mill-wheel, which they dress in the manner of a bride.   They call it " the bride of the other folk," a euphemism by which they avoid pronouncing the name of the jinn.   Decked out in this manner, the doll is carried round the barley, amidst the songs, the cries, and musket-shots of the procession, and is then deposited with a small cake at the foot of a tree. When their barley begins to ripen, the Ida Ou Zkri capture a small bird alive, which they release the following night in the middle of their fields, amidst a great din of singing, crying, and firing of muskets, just as is done at a wedding ; then, in the same attire, they return to the village.   They believe that next day all the sparrows will have fled the country, abandoning nests and nestlings, thus imitating the example set them by the bird that had been released the day before.   Among the Ait Hamed the bird captured by an old woman is put in a cage.   In a great procession they go and put it upon the stump of an old oleander at the boundary of their territory.   There the bird is stoned to death,[1] doubtless as an awful warning to the other sparrows not to trespass on the barley fields.

[1] E. Laoust, *Mots et choses berbères*, pp. 338 *sqq.*

CHAPTER LIX

THE TRANSMIGRATION OF HUMAN SOULS INTO ANIMALS [1]

ANOTHER reason which primitive man sometimes has for treating animals with respect and sparing their lives is a belief that they contain the souls of his dead kinsfolk, which have passed into the animals by transmigration at death. Thus for example, speaking of the natives of the Upper Zambesi in South Africa, Livingstone tells us that " The monkey is a sacred animal in this region, and is never molested or killed, because the people believe devoutly that the souls of their ancestors now occupy these degraded forms, and anticipate that they themselves must sooner or later be transformed in like manner." [2]   Again, with regard to the Malays of Perak, we are told that " the doctrine of metempsychosis has obtained some little hold upon the Malays, who consequently hesitate to slay the tiger, lest his body should be the tenement of some human being.   In fact they believe that, after the manner of the were-wolf of German romance, certain people have the power of occupying the body of the tiger by night, and transforming themselves at pleasure.   So great is considered the power and intelligence of this beast that the Malay will reluctantly mention its name in the jungle, lest evil should befall him ; and if asked if a tiger is nigh, will probably give his answer in the faintest whisper and in trembling voice." [3]

Once more a belief in the possible transmigration of

[1] *Spirits of the Corn and of the Wild*, ii. 285 *sqq.*

[2] D. and C. Livingstone, *Narrative of Expedition to the Zambesi* (London,

1865), pp. 160 *sq.*

[3] F. McNair, *Perak and the Malays* (London, 1878), 221.

human souls at death into animals is firmly held by the natives of San Cristoval, and has correspondingly influenced their treatment of the animals which they suppose to be tenanted by the spirits of their dead. The belief and the practice are well described as follows : " After death a great many ghosts become incarnate in animals. It may be wondered in what way the natives determine the particular animal into which the *ataro* (soul) of a dead relative has entered. It depends partly on where the man is buried. It is a common practice to bury in the sea both chiefs and common people, and their *ataro* naturally becomes incarnate in fish, especially in sharks. After his death his skull and other relics may be put into a wooden figure of a shark, which is then securely sealed with canoe gum, and allowed to float in the sea. Watch is kept, and the first thing seen to approach it is the future incarnation of the *ataro*. Usually a shark, it may also be an octopus, a skate, a turtle, or a crocodile. But all *ataro* have not a sea incarnation. When a man or woman grows old, natives watch to see whether any animal persistently associates itself with them. This is often a bird. The bird comes to the house and perches on the old man's shoulder. It must be a young bird. It is fed and treated respectfully as the future home of the man's soul. When he dies his soul is known to be in the bird. His children will not eat any bird of that sort. This taboo seems only to last for a generation. There is now a man living at Raumae whose father went into a hawk, *tehe*. This man cannot kill any hawks or eat them, though other people may do so quite freely. Birds into which the *ataro* may go are the hawk, the *afitaronga*, another kind of hawk, the *aususuwai*, a kingfisher, and the *waifirufiru*, a small black and white bird. Or again the *ataro* may go into a stone or a tree. This is known by dreams after a man's death. If in a dream the *ataro* of a man is seen at a stone, or by a tree, that is known to be its incarnation. Thus there is an *ataro* in a *topaga* tree near Rafurafu. The man's children will not cut down this tree, or any other *topaga* tree. Sacrifices are made there to the *ataro*." [1]

[1] C. E. Fox and F. H. Drew, " Beliefs and Tales of San Cristoval," in the *Journal of the Royal Anthropological Institute*, xlv. (1915), 161 *sq*.

CHAPTER LX

THE TRANSFERENCE OF EVIL

PRIMITIVE man often believes that he can rid himself of all his troubles by magically transferring them to other persons, or even to inanimate objects. Elsewhere I have given many examples of this belief, and of the practice which is based upon it.[1] Here I will give some fresh examples of this fruitful theme, beginning with the transference of evils to inanimate objects. Thus, for example, the Wajagga of Mount Kilimanjaro in East Africa think that they can transfer their bodily ailments to inanimate objects. If a man for instance is suffering from a pain in his neck he is recommended to rise early in the morning, go out, and walk several times round a certain tree, addressing it in an appropriate speech. By so doing he is believed to transfer the pain from his neck to the tree.[2] Among the Brahui of Baluchistan, when a man is suffering from tertian fever his friends will sometimes make a doll and dress it up in gaudy colours. " And early on the morrow when the fever is due, one of the kin rouses the sick man from his slumber, and making him take the doll and some parched wheat in his hand, he leads him to a lonely tree where none can see him, and there he leaves him. And beneath the tree the sick man seats the doll, and in her lap he pours the parched wheat, and says, ' Poor thing, keep my fever with you, I pray you.' And having so said, he hurries away with never a backward look, lest the fever come upon him again." [3]

Often the evil is thought to be transferred to stones or

[1] *The Golden Bough : The Scape-goat*, pp. 1 *sqq.*

[2] B. Gutmann, *Dichten und Denken der Dschagganeger*, pp. 161 *sq.*

[3] Denys Bray, *The Life-History of a Brahui*, 106.

sticks.   Thus for example the Berbers of Morocco think that there are certain ailments of which they can rid themselves by transferring them to stones which they deposit at certain spots.   At such spots large and imposing heaps of stones are gradually accumulated through the successive contributions of many sufferers.   Even to-day a man will go to such a heap, and, picking up one of the innumerable stones that lie about, he will lay it on the heap, saying as he does so : " Here is thy stone, O Sidi Boulkhef." [1]   Outside the caves of Imi n-Taq-qandut in Haha in Morocco " there are a multitude of small piles of stones, which have evidently been made by visitors not only as *ar* upon the saintly *jnun* inhabiting the caves, but also with a view to transferring their diseases to the stones ; for they rub the stones on the affected part of the body before they pile them up, and it is generally assumed that if anyone happens to overthrow one of these piles he will catch the disease of its maker." [2]

Among the Toradyas of Central Celebes, when a person is suffering from a certain inflammation of the skin he will sometimes take a stout stick, and press it against the affected part of his body, saying, " Go over into this." He believes that he thus transfers the inflammation to the stick, leaving his body whole.[3]

Again primitive peoples often attempt to transfer their troubles to animals.   Thus for example among the Banyoro of Uganda, " when a man of a pastoral clan fell ill a medicine-man was called in to transfer the sickness to some cow provided by the sick man's relatives.   The sick man was then taken by his wives and relatives to some place at a distance from the kraal, where the medicine-man rubbed him all over with herbs and then tied the herbs to the neck of the animal chosen, thus transferring the sickness to the animal.   The animal was killed, and its blood was caught in a vessel and smeared over the company, who then returned home leaving the medicine-man to dispose of the meat as he wished, either by eating it or by throwing it on to waste land.   Sometimes the medicine-man selected a sheep to which the sickness was

[1] E. Laoust, *Mots et choses ber-bères*, 154.
[2] E.   Westermarck, *The Moorish*

Conception of Holiness (*Baraka*), 96.
[3] N. Adriani and A. C. Kruijt, *op. cit.* i. 267.

to be transferred. He forced it to drink some fluid he had made from herbs into which the sick man had expectorated, and the sheep was then turned loose and driven into some uninhabited part of the country, carrying with it the man's sickness." [1]

Among the Basoga, another tribe of Uganda, " in certain cases the medicine-man will decide to transfer the illness to a goat or fowl or bunch of herbs, after consulting his oracle. The animal is brought into the sick man's presence and tied to him ; if it is a fowl or a bunch of herbs, the patient is brushed over with it and the sickness is commanded to leave him. The animal, bird, or bunch of herbs is taken to waste land, and is killed and left there, unless, in the case of an animal, the medicine-man takes the meat and eats it himself." [2] Among the Banyankole, " when a ghost had to be forcibly removed from a patient the diviner told the relatives what medicine-man to send for and what preparations to make. A goat of a particular colour, always either black or black and white, was tied to the head of the patient's bed during the night so that the ghost might pass from the patient into it. The medicine-man came in the morning, dancing and singing, and passed a bunch of sticks and herbs all round the house to sweep together all the evil influences into one place. He put the sticks at the head of the bed or outside the door and proceeded to kill the goat which had been tied to the bed, and which was now supposed to contain the ghost. He sprinkled some of the blood on the bed, the patient, and his family. A fowl was brought and passed round the body of the goat so that the ghost passed from the goat into it, and it was buried alive in the gateway through which the cows entered the kraal, thus preventing the ghost from returning." [3]

Among the Wajagga of Mount Kilimanjaro when a child is sick friends and neighbours assemble in the hut, and the child's uncle, the brother of the householder, brings a goat, and places it before the child, who is held up by its mother. With his open hand he strokes first the face of the goat and then the face of the child. By this action it is believed that

---

[1] J. Roscoe, *The Northern Bantu*, 55.

[2] J. Roscoe, *op. cit.* 223.

[3] J Roscoe, *The Banyankole*, 139.

he transfers the sickness from the child to the goat.   Next day the goat is killed, and some parts of the animal's peri-cardium are cut out.[1]   In Southern Nigeria " the principle of the scapegoat is known and acted upon throughout the country; a man often lays his hand on the animal and transfers to it his guilt or the fate or punishment which he fears is about to fall on himself.   Usually such a sacrifice is dragged round on the ground before relief comes from further suffer-ings by death." [2]

" In some villages in Gujerat, when there is an outbreak of a serious epidemic, it is customary to drive a goat, a ram, or a buffalo beyond the village boundary, with the disease on its back.   The back of the animal which is chosen for this purpose is marked with a trident in red lead and covered with a piece of black cloth, on which are laid a few grains of black gram and an iron nail.   Thus decorated, it is driven beyond the limits of the village.   It is believed that an animal driven in this way carries the disease wherever it goes.   Very often the animal used in this ceremony is kept tied to a post all its life, in the belief that by so doing, the disease remains enchained." [3]

Again, primitive man often imagines that he can magic-ally transfer his own troubles to other living persons.   Thus the Bagesu of Uganda think that illness may be transferred to other people by means of herbs.   " The medicine-man chooses his bunch of herbs from an uninhabited part of the country, ties them neatly into a bunch, brushes them over the patient, and then carries them to a distant path where by night he buries them, covering the spot in such a manner as not to attract attention.   The first unsuspecting person who passes contracts the disease and the patient recovers." [4]   Among the Basoga, another tribe of Uganda, when the mourning for a dead chief is over, next morning " the new chief shaves his head and puts aside his mourning garments, and all the people follow his example.   The chief's hair which was shaved off is made up into a small ball, wrapped in bark-

[1] B. Gutmann, *op. cit.* 146.
[2] P. G. Talbot, *The Peoples of Southern Nigeria*, iii. 858.
[3] R. E. Enthoven, *The Folklore of*

Bombay, 257.

[4] J. Roscoe, *The Northern Bantu*, 177.

cloth, and taken the following day by two or three warriors into the next district of Busoga. Here they lie in wait for some man to come along the road ; they first greet the man and then seize him, thrust the ball of hair into his mouth and strangle him ; the body is left in the road and the warriors escape back to their own chief. When the body of the murdered man is discovered by the relatives, they hasten to acquaint their chief with the outrage. This outrage leads to a tribal war, for the meaning of the ball in the man's mouth is well understood : it contains any evil which otherwise might befall the new chief, but which has now been transferred to the murdered man." [1]

Speaking of Southern Nigeria, Mr Talbot tells us that " among Yoruba and to some extent other tribes, particularly the Ijaw, a person about to act as scapegoat, take upon himself the sins of the people and bring them good-fortune, was usually treated with the greatest respect and indulgence by all and given the best of everything. When the time came for his death, the Oluwaw, as he was called—who might be either bond or free, rich or poor, and was chosen by the priest—was paraded through the streets, when many people took the opportunity of laying their hands on him and transferring their sins to him ; he was then led to the grove and executed—the people waiting outside to hear his last song, which was echoed by them." [2] " Among Ibo, as with Yoruba, human victims were in places offered up as scapegoats to purge the people of sin, bring good fortune for the coming year, and drive away all evil ghosts. At Onitsha, besides a special sacrifice for the king, two persons were annually put to death on behalf of the people. Each was decorated with palm leaves, and dragged with hands and feet tied, the two miles down the hill to the waterside, and then flung into the middle of the river. Great cruelty was displayed towards these unfortunates, one of whom was often a girl. As she passed by people pelted her with stones and sticks, while they prayed that their sins and misfortunes should be transferred to her." [3]

" In the Deccan it is believed that if a coconut is waved

[1] J. Roscoe, *op. cit.* 203.   *Southern Nigeria*, iii. 858.
[2] P. A. Talbot, *The Peoples of*   [3] P. A. Talbot, *op. cit.* iii. 865.

round a sick person and given to another to eat, the illness is transferred from the sufferer to the latter. . . . At Kolhapur the following ceremony is practised in the case of persons suffering from swollen glands. Rice, black gram, etc., are tied in a yellow cloth, and three knots are made in it. This is then kept for one night under the pillow of the diseased person. It is taken out the next morning and thrown away at a place where three roads meet. It is then supposed that the person who stepped on the bundle first is attacked by the disease, and the one for whom the rite is performed is cured. A similar rite prevails in the Deccan for the cure of boils, seven knots being made in the cloth, and millet being used in place of rice." [1]

[1] R. E. Enthoven, *Folklore of Bombay*, pp. 276 *sq*.

CHAPTER LXI

THE OMNIPRESENCE OF DEMONS [1]

SAVAGE man has everywhere a deep sense of the spiritual agencies by which he believes himself to be encompassed on every side. As a general rule these agencies are thought to be malignant and dangerous, and to them he attributes a great, perhaps the greatest, part of the evils which befall him in life. On this subject I will quote the account which an eminent Indian ethnographer gives of the Birhors, a primitive tribe of Chota Nagpur. What he says of them would be applicable to many other primitive races. " Of the Birhors, as of other tribes at a similar level of culture, Religion may very well be said to constitute almost their whole way of life. All the ills of life—and life to them is brimful of ills—are believed to be caused by supernatural agencies—either by spirits hovering about in earth, air, and water, hill and forest, river and spring, or by lesser powers and energies immanent in various animate beings as well as in certain inanimate objects and even in such immaterial things as a spoken word, an expressed wish, a passing thought or emotion, a passing glance, a magic formula or diagram, and certain names and numbers. And the problem of life which has ever presented itself to the tribal mind is how to protect the community and its members and their scanty earthly possessions from the evil attentions of spirits and the harmful influences of other mysterious powers and energies so as to make life worth living. The solution of the problem that the tribal mind appears to have arrived at is to seek to establish permanent friendly relations, through appropriate rites and sacrifices, with the more important spirits, powerful alike for good and

---

[1] Cf. *The Scapegoat*, pp. 72-108.

evil, and to drive off, control, scare away, neutralize, or avoid the lesser powers and energies by various rites and actions, spells and taboos, threats and tricks and thus to secure good luck and avoid bad luck to health, life, progeny, and food-supply.

" The Birhor's whole life—economic, domestic, social and socio-political—is pervaded by his religion (including that aspect of it which anthropologists generally term magic) ; and his religion consists in a haunting sense of ' sacred ' presences —a haunting fear of spirits and spiritual energies leading him to continuous endeavours, through appropriate rites and sacrifices, charms and spells, to conciliate them, when necessary, and control, avoid, or repel them, when possible.

" To the Birhor, everything above, below, or around him is animated either by a spirit or by a spiritual energy or power, as every living being is animated by a soul or souls." [1]

Again with regard to the Kiwai of British New Guinea, we are told that they " do not believe in the natural causes of misfortune, sickness or death. These are the work of evil spirits, who are ever striving to bring disaster upon them. Their souls are dominated by an awful overhanging fear of the unknown. This sense of fear, this something, they know not what, is a terrible reality and makes life a burden. Their one aim is to propitiate these unseen forces, to obtain their favours, that good crops may be produced, bumper harvests, and success in their fishing and hunting ventures ; and also that they may be kept free from sickness and disease." [2]

Again every native of Yap, an island of the Pacific, believes that he is surrounded at every step by maleficent spirits. These seek to baffle and defeat all his undertakings, hence he endeavours to forestall their attacks. He thinks that these uncanny beings have their hand in every misfortune that befalls him, especially in cases of illness. So when some mishap has overtaken him his first thought is to ascertain which of the spirits has done him this ill turn, and for this purpose he consults a diviner, whom he supposes to be in the secrets of the spirits. [3]

[1] S. C. Roy, *The Birhors*, pp. 284 *sqq.*
[2] E. Baxter Riley, *Among Papuan Head-Hunters*, 298.

[3] P. S. Walleser, " Religiöse Anschauungen der Bewohner von Jap," in *Anthropos*, viii. (1913), 1067.

CHAPTER LXII

THE PUBLIC EXPULSION OF EVILS [1]

SOMETIMES primitive man attempts to rid the whole community of their troubles by a general and public expulsion of evils. For this purpose the Kiwai of British New Guinea hold a great fire ceremony, which they call *mimia*. The men dance in the men's house, holding branches of croton in their hands. At the conclusion of the dance they all hasten out by the door, still holding the branches of croton in their hands. In doing this they are believed to drive all sickness before them. They run down to the shore, and stick the branches of croton in the beach. The high tide afterwards covers the branches, and sometimes drifts them away. According to the natives, the purpose of this ceremony is to drive away sickness from the people and the village. The north-west monsoon is supposed to carry the sickness away with it to the Torres Straits Islands, and when the news comes that a great illness has broken out there, the Kiwais know the cause of it, and feel glad at their own escape.[2] They imagine in fact that they have succeeded in transferring their own sicknesses to their neighbours in the islands.

When the Lakhers of Assam hear that sickness is rife in neighbouring villages they perform a ceremony called *Tlarai-pasi* for the purpose of preventing it from entering their own village, and of expelling it in case it should already have effected an entrance. The ceremony is as follows : " The inmates of each house make small bamboo baskets and fill them with samples of every kind of food. At one end of the

---

[1] Cf. *The Scapegoat*, pp. 109 *sqq.*

[2] G. Landtman, *The Kiwai Papuans of British New Guinea*, pp. 375 *sq.*

village a small bamboo fence is erected with a bamboo archway which spans the road. The baskets of food are placed outside this fence. The people then all go inside their houses and shut the doors. Meanwhile some of the young men have been sent out to shoot a gibbon (*Hylobates Hooluck*). As soon as they have bagged one they bring it to the village, and on the way they collect a quantity of pebbles. When they reach the village they sacrifice a fowl on the pebbles, and sprinkle the pebbles with its blood. Then one man carries in the gibbon and another man picks up the pebbles, and they enter the village, shouting out to the spirit of the disease, ' Go away, stranger.' The gibbon is carried right through the village, and the man with the pebbles throws a few of them against each house, in order to chase out the spirit of the disease. When they reach the farther end of the village, where the fence and arch have been erected over the road, the gibbon is hung up over the arch. The fowl that was sacrificed is placed beside the baskets of food, and the villagers all go and spit and blow their noses into the baskets. The village is *pana* (taboo) for the day of sacrifice, and no strangers may come in." We are told that the hanging up of the carcase of the gibbon at the entrance of the village is to frighten away the spirit of the disease, and that the spitting into the basket has the same object.[1]

The public expulsion of evils, from being occasional, tends to become periodic, and especially annual, the people thus hoping to make a fresh start in life, free from all the troubles which had beset them in the previous year. An annual expulsion of demons is carried out by the Oraons and Mundas of the Chota Nagpur plateau in India. Once in the year, in obedience to information sent from one village to another throughout the plateau, each village fixes its date for this ceremony of driving away the evil spirits that cause cattle-disease. At about midnight of the date so appointed, all the young bachelors of the village assemble at the village *akhra* or dancing-ground. Bachelors, who are supposed not to have any carnal knowledge, are, it may be noted, supposed to possess greater soul-power than married men. And that is why they are thus able to put disease-spirits to flight. At

[1] N. E. Parry, *The Lakhers*, pp. 455 *sq.*

the dancing-ground the *pahan* or village priest hands over to them a chicken and a few annas of drink-money. The village *Ahir* or Cattle-herd, too, comes there with a wooden cow-bell. The Cattle-herd and the young men all now strip themselves naked, and the Cattle-herd with his cow-bell hanging from the back of his waist, and the young Oraons and Mundas, each with a stick in his hand, proceed toward the boundary of an adjoining village. The Cattle-herd runs ahead, and the rest of the party run behind him as if chasing him. As the young men run, they go on uttering shouts of " *Hamba-hamba* " in imitation of cows, clapping their hands, and breaking to pieces with their sticks all the earthen pots, one or two of which every family has taken care to leave in front of their house. All the time every one else in the village must keep absolutely quiet, and as far as possible remain indoors. Should any person be heard talking or laughing, these young men would belabour such a person with their sticks, and the latter would have to submit to the flogging without protest. As soon as the Cattle-herd reaches the limits of the adjoining village, he silently drops his cow-bell and quickly retires. The young men then enter a few steps into the limits of the other village, and the fowl, on which marks of oil and vermilion are now put, and all the clubs, are left there, and the party return to the village, bathe in some tank or stream, and then put on their clothes, drink liquor, and return home. The village to which the disease-spirit is thus driven, in its turn performs the same ceremony, and transfers the spirit to the next village, and so on.[1]

Down to recent years the State of Perak, in the Malay Peninsula, " used to be ' cleansed ' periodically by the propitiation of friendly spirits and the expulsion of malignant influences. . . . The royal State shaman, his royal assistant, and the chief magicians from the river parishes assembled at a village at the foot of the rapids below which the habitations of the Perak Malays began. *Séances* occupied seven days. A pink buffalo was killed and a feast was held. The head and other pieces of the victim were piled on one of the rafts,

---

[1] S. C. Roy, "Magic and Witchcraft on the Chota Nagpur Plateau," in the *Journal of the Royal Anthropological Institute*, xliv. (1914), 344 *sq.* Cf. *id. The Oraons of Chota Nagpur*, pp. 253 *sq.*

which was then set out down-stream.   The four leading rafts were prepared for the four leading classes of spirits and were manned by their appropriate magicians.   The foremost raft carried a branching tree, erect and supported by stays, and was for the shaman's familiars.   The fifth raft bore Muslim elders.   Next came the royal band with its sacred drums and trumpets, and then the Raja Kechil Muda (the title of the assistant State shaman) and his followers.   As they floated down the river, the magicians waved white cloths and invoked the spirits of the districts passed to come aboard and consume the offerings.   Whenever they reached a mosque, they halted for one night while a *séance* was held and the villagers slaughtered a buffalo, placing its head on one of the spirit rafts and eating the rest of the carcase.   At the mouth of the river the rafts were abandoned and allowed to drift to sea. The State shaman did not accompany the procession downstream, leaving the escort of the spirit rafts with their grisly freight to his assistant.   So, too, the magicians of the different parishes of the river-banks stayed behind in turn, each of them supplying a substitute to go downstream with the assistant State shaman. . . . The ' cleansing ' of the States of Perak and Kelantan is said to have been triennial.   One account indeed states that Perak was cleansed once in seven years or once in a Sultan's reign, but this is probably a native explanation of the gradual lapse of the custom." [1]

Elsewhere I have referred to a certain ceremony which the Fijians performed every year, apparently for the purpose of expelling the accumulated evils of the community.   Its date was determined by the appearance in the sea of a certain annelid or sea-slug, *Palolo viridis*, which occurred only on a single day of the year.[2]   This curious slug appears in great swarms for one or two days in other parts of the Pacific, where it has been seen and described by several writers.   Thus with regard to Samoa we are told that " one other curious example of Samoan natural history remains to be noticed in a remarkable sea-worm, *Palolo*, of the natives. It is most singular in its habits and history, and is much prized by the natives as an article of food.   This remarkable

---

[1] R. O. Winstedt, *Shaman, Saiva. and Sufi*, pp. 113 *sqq.*
[2] *The Scapegoat*, pp. 141 *sqq.*

worm, *Palolo*, rises from the reefs at certain places of the islands in the early part of two days only—in the months of October and November in each year, and is never seen at any other time.   They appear with great regularity during the early mornings on two successive days of each of the two months mentioned, viz. the day before and the day of the moon's being in her last quarter, showing, however, much greater numbers on the second day than on the first.   After sporting on the surface for a few hours of each day, they disappear as mysteriously as they came, and none are ever seen until the return of the next season, when they repeat their visit under the same mysterious conditions.   In size they may be compared to small straws, and are of various colours and lengths, green, brown, white and spotted, whilst in appearance and mode of swimming they may be said to resemble small snakes.   They are brittle, and if broken each part swims off as though it were an entire worm." [1]

Again with regard to Aoba, an island of the New Hebrides, Professor Speiser tells us that " in this same place (in Aoba) I had occasion to observe an interesting zoological phenomenon, the appearance of the palolo-worm, which occurs almost all over the Pacific once a year, at a certain date after the October full moon.   The natives know the date exactly, which proves the accuracy of their chronology.   The palolo is a favourite delicacy, and they never fail to fish for it.   We went down to the shore on the first night; there were not many worms as yet, but the next evening the water was full of the greenish and brownish threads, wriggling about helplessly.   Each village had its traditional fishing-ground, and we could see the different fires all along the coast.   The worms were gathered by hand and thrown into baskets, and after midnight we went home with a rich harvest.   The palolo is mixed with pudding, and said to taste like fish." [2]

Speaking of Ulawa, one of the South-east Solomon Islands, Mr Ivens tells us that " when the annelid *palolo viridis* is caught, the first catch is given to the priest and eaten

---

[1] J. B. Stair, *Old Samoa*, pp. 208 *sqq.*

[2] F. Speiser, *Two Years with the*   *Natives in the Western Pacific* (London, 1913), p. 252.

by him in the canoe house.   The annelid attains a length of
six to eight inches, the colours being bright red or blueish
black or light yellow.   The day of the swarming is the
second night after the full moon in November.   The November moon is called Netting the Annelid ; the previous moon
is The Undersized Annelid ; the December moon is The
Full-grown Annelid ; this last is inedible.   In each case the
annelid appears on the same day of the month, two days after
the moon is full, but it is only in November that it is fit for
eating and appears in swarms.   During the rest of the year
the annelid lives in the coral rocks.

" At sunset a small yellow variety appears, at the moon-
rising the bigger red and black ones come out of the rocks
of the shore-reef.   The current carries it out to sea, and
every fish takes its share of the wriggling mass.   Countless
myriads perish, and the surface of the sea is white under
the moon with the dead bodies floating in the currents.
In anticipation of the swarming the people prepare small,
closely woven nets of fibre, shaped like trout landing nets.
Thirty miles down the coast at Aalai, the eastern entrance
to the dividing channel, the annelid swarms, curiously
enough, in October as it does in Samoa.   The success of the
season is judged by the report of how the fishing went at
Aalai.   Appearing only once a year, and being regarded as
a great delicacy, its failure to swarm properly would be a
great disappointment." [1]

---

[1] W. G. Ivens, *Melanesians of the South-east Solomon Islands*, pp. 313 *sq.*

CHAPTER LXIII

PUBLIC SCAPEGOATS [1]

SOMETIMES the evils which are publicly expelled from the community, either occasionally or periodically, are believed to be embodied in a material form, whether animate or inanimate. These we may call scapegoats, whether they are animal, human or inanimate. Thus among the Banyoro of Uganda "when famine appeared too imminent and the cattle were also suffering from lack of food, the medicine-men looked for the house of a poor man who had neither wife nor child. The door was taken from the house, and they also provided themselves with an empty milk-pot, an empty butter-dish, a potato, a few beans and some millet. These were then placed in front of the chief medicine-man with a bunch of herbs. A procession was next formed, headed by the medicine-man, who carried the door, with the various articles and herbs laid upon it, to some adjacent country in order to banish from the country hunger, famine and any cause that was bringing famine and want, and to cast them upon another nation." [2]

Some of the Kabyls of North Africa regard the jackal as an expiatory victim or scapegoat and heap curses upon it. Charged with the evils from which all are suffering, the animal is then solemnly killed, or chased from the territory of the tribe. [3]

Among the Ibo of Southern Nigeria in time of great public calamity when all other remedies had failed, recourse was had to the sacrifice of a human scapegoat, who was to bear away all the sins and misfortunes of the people. " The

---

[1] Cf. *The Scapegoat*, pp. 170 *sqq*.
[2] J. Roscoe, *The Northern Bantu*, 95.
[3] H. Basset, *Essai sur la littérature des Berbères*, pp. 107 *sq*.

victim was never a fellow-townsman—he was always a slave purchased specially for the purpose, or a captive of war. He must be a young man for choice, strong and vigorous, well able to bear the sins of those on whose behalf he was to die. He was known as *ónyé-ùmà*. It is difficult to render into English the word *ùmà*, but the underlying idea is exactly that of Deuteronomy xxi. 23 : ' He that is hanged is accursed of God.' The man was to die an ignominious death—he himself becoming an abomination—a cursed thing. Indeed the ceremony itself is called *ikpu-alu* (to carry away abomination). He was the sin-bearer, whether for the one or the many. The victim was conducted to an ebwo tree, to which he was bound after his arms and legs had been tied ; the king stepped forward and solemnly transferred first his own sins, then the sins of his household, and finally the sins of the community to the head of the sacrifice. The trespass-transfer being thus fulfilled, the man was loosed from the tree (his legs and arms remaining bound) and a rope was attached to his ankle and forthwith he was dragged round the town by two slaves appointed to the task. The whole populace treated the wretched creature as an accursed thing ; he was reviled, spat upon, kicked, stoned ; dust was thrown upon him, and in every form imaginable he was despitefully treated and denounced as an abomination. The slaves continued to drag him through the streets until life was extinct, and then the corpse was taken back to the king's quarters and cast away in the spot reserved for the bodies of human sacrifices. The victims were not buried ; they would have been left to rot but for the fact that the corpses were stolen during the succeeding night by the friends of the official executioners, who were not members of that community. The body was taken away to the native town of these officials and was there eaten. In towns adjacent to the river the corpses were sometimes cast into the water.

" Occasionally instead of dragging the man through the streets, after the ceremony at the ebwo tree, he was put upright in a hole and buried alive, his head being left above the ground. Here he was subject to all manner of abuse and ill-treatment, the sufferings of the unhappy creature evoking gross ridicule, but never a thought of pity. The corpse was left in this state, the memorial of an accursed thing to everyone that passed by. Again the form of death might be changed. After the initial ceremonies, the man, bound hand and foot as above, was placed on the ground and covered with grass and wood and burned to death. But what was considered, and undoubtedly was, the worst fate of all, was when, after the transfer of the sins to him, the victim was simply left bound to the tree. The tortures were not so painful at the beginning as any of the above described forms of death, but they were prolonged to a maddening length. The degrading insults of the mob continued longer and sometimes death was long delayed." [1]

In the Rathia section of the Bhil tribe of North-western India, " in casting out disease or an epidemic from a village, after a sacrifice to the principal deity, the *Badwa* (medicine-man) will visit all the sacred spots within the precincts of the village, chanting in a droning tone some invocation, followed by drummers clashing copper plates : at each spot he will offer up a little red ochre and a piece of cocoanut, while at the principal entrance into the village limits, he will show by various antics and rapid gestures of hand and body with back turned to the village, that the spirit to which the disease was due has been cast out into the adjoining territory. Another form of casting out an epidemic is to sling some baskets that have contained corn, and *gharas* (earthen pots) that have been used for water, on a bamboo or pole which is carried on the shoulders of men who run along the main road, shouting at the top of their voices *todkha, todkha*. On hearing the shouts the next village send out men to meet the boundary and these take over the burden and so the process is repeated. Thus the epidemic is carried away often to great distances, until eventually it is thrown into some stream or river which stretches across the path, or is deposited in the forest. If no one from the next village is present to meet the procession at the boundary, the bearers are at liberty to deposit their burden in the village precincts. Sometimes a young he-goat is similarly carried on the shoulders of men or tied on to a light bier." [2]

[1] G. T. Basden, *Among the Ibos of Nigeria*, pp. 231 *sqq.*

[2] C. E. Luard, *The Jungle Tribes of Malwa*, 62.

Such public expulsions of evils in the form of scapegoats, whether animate or inanimate, from being occasional tend to become periodic, and especially annual. Thus, for example, in Southern Nigeria " another way of driving out evil influences was practised among the Efik of Henshaw Town, Calabar. On the eve of the native New Year the townsfolk used to play the play called Edi Tuak 'Ndokk. In preparation for this, images formed of grass and bound round with mats of plaited rushes were prepared. These effigies were named 'Nabikum, and at least one of them was tied against every verandah. The Reverend Hope-Waddell, in describing the ceremony as performed in his day, states that the images were often in animal form. Chief Daniel Henshaw, on the contrary, has never seen any but what he calls ' Judases,' *i.e.* Guy Fawkes-like figures roughly resembling human beings. It is possible that the earlier effigies represented family ' affinities ' or totemistic animals. His account of the ceremony, which he had often witnessed, runs as follows :

" ' At about two o'clock on the last night of the old year the inhabitants of each compound ran round it, calling :

Ete mio !	*Eka mio !*
Father mine !	Mother mine !
Ekkpo yakk onyon !	
Devils must go !	

Gongs were played, " *Poom, poom.*" Torches were lighted and the burning wood knocked against the walls in every corner, while the cry, " Devils must go," was ceaselessly called. Each pot and pan was beaten that none of the spirits might find shelter behind it, but all the old year's evil ghosts should be driven forth to perish, and the whole town be freed from their influence, and remain quiet and prosperous throughout the new year.

" ' Next morning every scrap of cooked food or drop of drink left over from the night before had to be thrown away, together with any cracked or broken pans and the sticks used for driving forth the devils. The 'Nabikum were burnt, and their ashes strewn to the four winds. Then all the compounds were swept clean, the water jars refilled and a play given, in which the whole town joined. Next night a heavy rain was said to fall without fail, and this was called in the language of Calabar,

Ukpori ikpatt ekkpo.
Sweep feet devils.' " [1]

In the Nicobar Islands a ceremony of driving out devils from a village is performed twice a year, once in the south-west monsoon and once in the north-east monsoon.   The day for the observance is fixed by the people of Lapati, a large village on the east coast, who send notice of it to the neighbouring villages.   The men go and cut bamboos in the jungle, and bring them to the beach of the village, where they are decorated with certain leaves.   In the evening the bamboos are erected on the beach, and after sunset all the people assemble in the " village hall," and they all sing songs, and the witch-doctors spear the devils.   Whilst this last performance is going on the lights must be turned down, for the devils are afraid to come out, despite the charm of the singing, if there are many lights about.   The witch-doctors then spear the evil spirits with their magic spears, and when they have got hold of one in their hands the lay-folk will come forward to help them in their struggles.   They try to get the evil spirits down on the floor, when they jump upon them and shout in triumph.   This performance of catching and spearing the devils is carried on for three nights in succession.   On the third day the witch-doctors, with a great crowd following, go round the village to all the groups of houses, and flog and spear and catch the devils in every house.   Afterwards they spear the devils on the beach.   This time they go, not only into the village hall, but also into the " unclean " birth-huts and death houses, where naturally are the fiercest devils of all. When the struggle with the devils is over, and these are all safely bound with a kind of creeper, they are thrown into the sea.   But when the wind is suitable for the purpose—that is, during the south-west monsoon for the eastern villages—the people make a raft, and the witch-doctors put the devils on it. A doll of leaves about four feet in height, representing a beneficent spirit, is put on the raft to take charge of the devils. The raft has sails of palm leaves ; and torches of palm leaves

---

[1] P. A. Talbot, *Life in Southern Nigeria*, pp. 246 *sq.*

have been made and tied on to it, and will be lighted at night after it has been launched. Laymen then tow out the raft beyond the reef of rocks and on beyond where the surf breaks —they generally swim out to do this. While they are engaged in this doubly dangerous task, each of them keeps hold of some *to-ki-teuiny* leaves in his hand, as a protection against the evil spirits. After that all the people will watch with relief and pleasure the demon-laden raft drifting away with tide and breeze.[1]

At the end of the year the Chinese used to perform a ceremony for the purpose of dismissing, or rather expelling, the spirits of pestilence of the old year, and enthroning the better spirits of the new year. The essential part of the ceremony was a dance of the Twelve Animals. The ceremony was called Ta No. It was held for the purpose of expelling pestilences. It was performed in the Imperial Palace at Peking. Many persons took part in it. The principal performers were young boys. They had to be from ten to twelve years old. They wore red caps and black tunics, and carried large tambourines in their hands. The leader of the ceremony, called Fang-siang-che, had four eyes of yellow metal and wore a bear-skin. His upper clothes were black and his lower clothes red. He held a lance in his hand and brandished a buckler. There were besides twelve animals with feathers and horns. They were made to enter the throne-room, where a number of functionaries and guards were gathered, wearing red caps. The young boys first chanted an imprecation addressed to the Evil Things, then they executed the dance of Fang-siang-che and the Twelve Animals. They all, amid loud cries, marched thrice round the room in procession, and, carrying torches, left by the south door to lead the pestilences outside. There they were met by a troup of horsemen, who, taking the torches from their hands, carried them outside the precincts of the palace, where five squadrons of fresh horsemen met them, and taking the torches from them, rode with them to the river Lo, where they threw the torches into the water. According to one account of the ceremony the torches were passed on to three relays of horse-

---

[1] G. Whitehead, *In the Nicobar Islands*, pp. 153 *sqq.* Cp. *The Scapegoat*, pp. 201 *sq.*

men, the last of whom, after casting the torches into the water, cut the bridges in order that the pestilences which were thrown into the river with the torches might not return.[1]

In Ulawa, one of the Solomon Islands, once a year a live dog is driven from the brow of a cliff into the sea. The dog is supposed to be laden with all the sicknesses of the people. If it swims out to sea all is well : it will bear away from the people all the sicknesses of that year ; but if the dog turns back it is a bad sign.[2] Apparently the people imagine that with the return of the dog the sicknesses will return also.

Elsewhere we have seen that these annual expulsions of evil are commonly preceded or followed by a period of general licence or Saturnalia.[3] In Madagascar such a period of licence accompanies the New Year festival of the bath, to which the reader's attention has already been directed.[4] At this time in Madagascar unlimited licence was accorded to all. Everyone could do what he liked, he might commit all crimes, except that of high treason, with impunity. Many prisoners were set at liberty. Promiscuity reigned among all, without distinction of caste or class. A noble woman and a peasant, a slave woman and a powerful noble, might enjoy the most intimate relations without incurring blame. But the period of licence lasted only one day.[5]

Elsewhere I have conjectured that in ancient Rome the dances of the Salii, the dancing priests of Mars, in spring and autumn, may have been intended to quicken the growth of the corn sown at these seasons, by routing out and expelling the evil spirits which might retard or blight the crops, and in support of this conjecture I adduced some evidence of similar customs among savages.[6] To that evidence I would now add the following. When the Barundi of Central Africa begin to hoe their fields, on the first day a magician dances before them with cries and gesticulations, in order to ban evil spirits and to bless the seed.[7]

---

[1] M. Granet, *Danses et légendes de la Chine ancienne* (Paris, 1926), i. 299 *sqq.*

[2] C. E. Fox, *The Threshold of the Pacific*, 239 n.

[3] *The Scapegoat*, 225.

[4] See above, p. 370.

[5] A. and G. Grandidier, *op. cit.* pp. 357 *sq.*

[6] *The Scapegoat*, pp. 232 *sqq.*

[7] H. Meyer, *Die Barundi*, 57.

CHAPTER LXIV

THE SATURNALIA AND KINDRED FESTIVALS [1]

WITH the Roman Saturnalia we may compare a festival held by the Bagesu of Mount Elgon in Kenya. These savages are divided into clans, which used to be regularly at war with each other. But once a year, after harvest, when beer had been brewed, an armistice was declared between the clans. " At this time no man might carry any weapons ; spears and knives were carefully stowed away, and the people went about armed only with long bamboo staffs, inside which they carried beer tubes, sometimes as much as four feet long, with a cane-work filter in one end. As long as the beer lasted, people went from village to village drinking, dancing, and singing by day and by night. The beer was brought into open spaces in great pots, round which men and women sat in separate groups, each group having one pot in the centre into which all put their tubes. These gatherings became regular saturnalia, for men and women lived together regardless of marriage relationships. This was especially remarkable because at other times the women of the tribe were strictly chaste and the men guarded their own wives with jealous care." [2]

Elsewhere I have given some account of the Lord of Misrule in England, who may have been a distant successor of the King of the Saturnalia in ancient Rome.[3] A fuller account of this merry buffoon is given by Strutt in his work, *Sports and Pastimes of the People of England*, supported by

---

[1] Compare *The Scapegoat*, pp. 306 *sq.*

[2] J. Roscoe, *The Bagesu*, 4.

[3] *The Scapegoat*, pp. 331 *sqq.*

quotations from earlier writers, to which I must refer the reader for further details.[1]

Elsewhere I have referred to the unluckiness which is commonly ascribed to intercalary periods.   The Tigre people of Abyssinia appear to treat as intercalary (epagomenes) the five or six days which precede Midsummer Day (St. John's Day), for " in these days they do not move from their halting place, nor do they drive their cattle about ; they do not make the cattle urinate into a vessel,[2] and they do not churn their milk, but drink it sweet, and they do not send it away.   And in these days they do not look either on their fields, lest they be burned (by the sun and be lost) for them. Thereupon when these days are over they purify their cows (with holy water), and on the day of their purification they milk them ' for the church ' and give the milk to the priest. This they used always to do in the time of old ; and even now they keep some of these practices." [3]

Elsewhere I have referred to what has been called the Buddhist Lent, a period of three months annually observed with fasting and prayer by pious Buddhists.   On this subject I may cite the following account :   " The three months reckoning from the full of ' the beginning of Lent ' (*Waso*, June or July), to the full moon of ' the conclusion of religious duties ' (*Thadingyut*, September or October) constitute the Burmese Lent (*Wa*), a season regarded by devout and especially by elderly Buddhists as a peculiarly sacred season to be spent in fasting, in regular attendance at pagodas and shrines, and in careful observance of all the prescribed religious duties. During this Lenten period a monk, staying away from his monastery for a night loses his religious character through breach of monastic vows unless he continues repeating the prescribed formula for permission.   The pious layman suffering from sickness should, to be orthodox, request a dispensation (*Waban*) from the duties of Lent.   The esteem in which a *Pongyi* (the head of a monastery) is held is gauged, *ceteris paribus*, by the number of Lents he has kept uninter-

[1] J. Strutt, *The Sports and Pastimes of the Peoples of England*, edited by William Hone (London, 1834), pp. 339 *sqq.*

[2] " The urine of cattle is used in tanning."

[3] E. Littman, *Publications of the Princeton Expeditions to Abyssinia*, ii. 245.

2 G

ruptedly without severing his connection with the Assembly and mingling again with the laity. Even a superior or a bishop will pay respectful homage to a simple monk whose record in this respect excels his own.

" The fixation of Lent during the three months of summer, and not in spring, most probably has its origin in the fact that in Maghada (Behar or Nipal), where Buddhism was founded, these constituted the height of the rainy season, when the monks keep as much as possible to their monasteries ; and this would, of course, give them ample opportunities for studying the law and repeating it to the pious laymen who might flock there for instruction." [1]

Speaking of the Buddhist Lent in Burma another writer observes : " During Lent, marriages, feasts and public amusements are forbidden to the pious. Some of the monks retire into the forest, or into caves in the hills far from the haunts of men, to devote themselves to religious meditation ; and the people observe more strictly than usual the four duty-days which are prescribed in each lunar month, and in which all good Buddhists are expected to worship at the Pagodas. Only the most pious of the monks turn into recluses during Lent. The remainder return each night to their monasteries, and are not free to roam through the country until that season is over. In the Ping States, during Lent, lanterns are hung aloft to guide the spirits through the air, and thus leave no excuse for them to descend into the streets. The observance of this custom is general, and probably arises from the fact that the close of the rains is an unhealthy season, and that certain spirits are believed to bring disease." [2]

---

[1] J. Nisbet, *Burma under British Rule*, ii. 151 *sqq.*

[2] H. S. Hallett, *A Thousand Miles on an Elephant in the Shan States* (Edinburgh and London, 1890), 258.

CHAPTER LXV

NOT TO TOUCH THE EARTH

ELSEWHERE we have seen that certain sacred or tabooed persons and objects are not allowed to touch the ground, apparently because they are supposed to be charged with a magical virtue which would run to waste by contact with the earth.[1] Thus for example in India the feet of kings and holy men may not touch the earth.[2] Among the Bushongo, a tribe in the Belgian Congo, it was an ancient custom that the king was never allowed to touch the ground ; he was carried on men's shoulders when he had to change his place, and when he sat down it was on the back of a slave. In modern times the king of the Bushongo who visited Mr. Torday would have none of this custom, but at his interview with the traveller he so far complied with the old custom that he sat on a European chair with one leg curled up under him, the other foot resting on the leg of his friend and servant, Shamba Shamba, who sat on the ground.[3]

Among the Palaungs of Burma there is a priest who is charged with the worship of the spirits for the whole State. A house is set apart for his abode near the village of Namhsan. " He does not sit upon the floor, as it is the custom of his race to do, but upon a raised seat, and he is treated with considerable ceremony. He may not walk out of doors ; it would be a terrible catastrophe if his feet touched the earth ; there would certainly be a famine, and more cattle than usual would be carried off by tigers ; but he may walk in his house and come down the outside steps to the ground if a carpet or mat is placed there for his feet. If he should wish to go anywhere

[1] *Balder the Beautiful*, i. 1 *sqq.*
[2] R. E. Enthoven, *Folklore of Bombay*, 82.

[3] E. Torday, *On the Trail of the Bushongo*, 121.

—though as he is very old he seldom leaves the house—he is carried in a litter, with much care and ceremony, a white umbrella being held over his head." [1]

Among the Berbers of Morocco " bride and bridegroom must be protected from dangers not only from above but from below. In Morocco the bridegroom must avoid sitting on the ground. At the feast when he is painted with henna or, sometimes, has flour rubbed on his hand, he has underneath him a carpet and a sack or a saddle, and I was told that the object of this was to prevent his being affected by evil influences. After the ceremony he is in some tribes carried away by his best man or other bachelor friends ; and at Fez, on the great occasion when his head is ceremonially shaved, he is likewise carried by his friends, from the house where he has been sitting with them to ' the house of the wedding,' is there put down on a large chair, and is afterwards again carried away by the friends. Throughout the wedding he has in many tribes the backs of his slippers pulled up so as to prevent their falling off and his feet coming into contact with the ground, although there is also some fear that the slippers might fall into the hands of an enemy, who would harm him by working magic with them. Similar and still greater precautions are taken with regard to the bride ; as the Shereefa of Wazan writes, ' a bride would be unlucky to put her foot to earth at this period.' She too has the backs of her slippers pulled up. Sometimes she is carried to and from the place in the house where she is painted with henna. In country places she is carried to her new home on the back of an animal, on to which she is lifted sometimes from her bed, sometimes from the door of the house or the entrance of the tent, and sometimes after she has first taken a few steps on a blanket or cloak spread in front of her in order to prevent her stepping on the ground or the threshold. And when she arrives at the bridegroom's place she is carried to the nuptial bed or across the threshold. It may be asked why bride and bridegroom must not come into contact with the ground. In the first instance they have *baraka*, or ' holiness,' and persons or objects possessed of this delicate quality are in many cases not allowed to touch the ground. Moreover, the real native country of the

[1] Mrs. L. Milne. *The Home of an Eastern Clan.* 347

jnun is under the ground and they are always therefore liable to haunt its surface.   And as for the custom of carrying the bride through the entrance of the dwelling or otherwise preventing her touching the threshold, it is obviously connected with the idea that the threshold of a house and the entrance of a tent are much haunted by *jnun*.   The Moors say that ' the masters of the house,' that is, its jinn-owners, are walking out and in over the threshold.   Nobody is allowed to sit down on the threshold of a house or at the entrance of a tent ; should a person do so he would become ill himself or give *bas* to the house." [1]

Among the Banyankole of Uganda " during the first four months of a child's life it was kept lying upon its back and never allowed to touch the ground with the soles of its feet.   It was never carried about unless it was necessary to go on a journey, but it lay on a bark-cloth with another for covering." [2]

Among the Moï of Indo-China when a party of men is out hunting elephants the leader of the hunters is not allowed to touch the ground with his feet.   If he is obliged to leave his seat on the elephant, a carpet of leaves is spread beneath his feet, to prevent them from touching the earth. [3]

In British New Guinea, when Mr. Beaver was bringing back two Urio men to their home on the Fly River after a year's absence in a distant part of New Guinea, no sooner had the whale-boat grated on the beach than a mob of scantily clad women rushed down with green leaves which they placed on the sand, and they would not permit the men to land except on these, and then each of the two was lifted up shoulder-high and carried away by the women into the gloom of the Long House without being allowed to touch the earth.   Mr. Beaver could ascertain no reason for this procedure, except that if it were not adopted the two men would undoubtedly die. [4]

In San Cristoval, one of the Solomon Islands, the men who are engaged in fishing for bonito are secluded in the canoe-house for three months, during which they may have no intercourse with women.   At the end of that period a

[1] E Westermarck, *The History of Human Marriage* (Fifth edition, London, 1921), ii. 530 *sqq.*

[2] J. Roscoe, *The Banyankole*, 113.

[3] H. Baudesson, *Indo-China and its Primitive People*, pp. 135 *sq.*

[4] W. N. Beaver, *Unexplored New Guinea*, 148.

feast is given in the village, and the men return to the village. Mats are spread all the way from the canoe-house to the village, that the fishers may walk upon them, for they may not touch the ground with their feet.[1]

Among the Berbers of Morocco " neither the Koran, nor any other book containing the name of God, nor the writing-boards of schoolboys must be placed on the ground, at any rate if there can be the slightest suspicion about the cleanness of the place ; and even where the ground is clean a scribe would not leave on it the book which he consults when he writes a charm, for fear lest some person or animal should walk over it and thereby deprive the writing of its efficacy. If a written charm happens to fall on the ground it must at once be put in wheat or barley to be purified, but if anybody has trampled upon it its *baraka* (holiness) is irremediably lost. Bread must never be trod upon, nor exposed to the uncleanness of the ground." [2]

In Loango there is a small river called Nsongolo, which is crossed by a bridge formed by the trunks of oil-palms. This bridge is reserved for the exclusive use of the future king. When the trees are felled to form or repair the bridge they may not be allowed to touch the earth anywhere but at the point where they form the bridge. Hence when the trees are being felled the trunks are not permitted to touch the ground but must be received and carried by the hands of the woodmen. If one of them should chance to touch the ground it may not be used for the bridge.[3]

In the Bombay Presidency of India it is a rule that sacred books, cooked food, and many other things, such as conch shells, the blade of a sword, pearls, an image of the god Vishnu, the sacred thread of a Brahman, flowers intended for worship, and leaves of the holy basil may not be suffered to touch the earth.[4]   The Indians of Dutch Guiana (Surinam) in South America will not allow certain amulets to touch the ground, and they will not carry them at full moon.[5]

[1] C. E. Fox, *The Threshold of the Pacific*, 121.

[2] E. Westermarck, *The Moorish Conception of Holiness (Baraka)*, 132.

[3] *Die Loango Expedition*, iii. 2, 100.

[4] R. E. Enthoven, *Folklore of Bombay*, pp. 82, 87.

[5] F. P. and A. P. Penard, " Surinaamsch Bijgeloof," in *Bijdragen tot de Taal- Land- en Volkenkunde van Nederlandsch-Indie*, lxvii (1913), 179.

CHAPTER LXVI

NOT TO SEE THE SUN

ELSEWHERE we have seen that certain sacred or tabooed persons, and particularly women after child-bed, are not permitted to see the sun.[1] So in one family of the Mambila tribe of Northern Nigeria it is taboo for the woman to look upon the sun for ten days after having given birth to a child. " On the tenth day her father comes with a spear and a large string bag, and standing at the door of his daughter's hut presents the head of the spear to her. The woman grasps the spearhead and is then drawn by her father to the threshold. The father then spits a certain medicine on his daughter's temples and covers her eyes with his hands. Taking hold of her right hand he swings her round to the sun, at the same time uncovering her eyes. He then takes the infant, and places him in the string bag, which he fastens to the roof of the hut. At the same time he shouts out : ' Let any bird come and go.' He then whistles, and if a bird appears soon afterwards, it is a sign that the woman will bear another child. If no bird appears, she will never again become a mother." [2] In Sylt, one of the North Friesland Islands, it used to be deemed dangerous to allow the sun to shine upon a child before it had been baptized.[3]

---

[1] *Balder the Beautiful*, i. 18 *sqq.*

[2] C. K. Meek, *Tribal Studies in Northern Nigeria*, ii. 559.

[3] C. Jenssen, *Die nordfriesischen Inseln*, 221.

CHAPTER LXVII

THE SECLUSION OF GIRLS AT PUBERTY

ELSEWHERE I have described the custom of secluding girls at puberty, often conjoined with a prohibition to touch the earth or see the sun.[1] To the examples which I have there cited of the custom I may here add some further instances. Thus among the Bakongo of the Lower Congo girls at puberty are secluded for three months in a house built on a platform, because they are not permitted to touch the ground. During their seclusion they receive the instructions of a medicine-man.[2]

Among the Andaman Islanders on the first symptoms of puberty a girl informs her parents, who weep over her. She must then go and bathe in the sea by herself for an hour or two. After that she goes back to her parents' hut or to a special shelter that is put up for the occasion. All ornaments are removed from her except a belt and apron of leaves. But bands of leaves are tied round her arms and about her body. " Thus covered with leaves the girl must sit in the hut allotted to her, with her legs doubled up beneath her and her arms folded. A piece of wood or bamboo is placed at her back for her to lean against, as she may not lie down. If she is cramped she may stretch one of her legs or one of her arms, but not both legs or both arms at the same time. To relieve herself she may release one of her hands, but she must not take up the food with her fingers ; a skewer of *cainyo* wood is given her with which to feed herself. She may not eat nor sleep for twenty-four hours. Her wants are

[1] *Balder the Beautiful*, i. 22 *sqq.*
[2] J. H. Weeks, *Among the Primitive Bakongo*, 175.

attended to by her parents and their friends, who sit near her to keep her from falling asleep. The girl sits thus for three days. Early every morning she leaves the hut to bathe for an hour in the sea. At the end of the three days she resumes her life in the village." [1]

In the Gilbert Islands of the Pacific a girl's arrival at the age of puberty was a time of great anxiety to the parents, for then she was considered dangerously sensitive to enemy magic and especially to that sort which caused sterility. At her first monthly period she was made to sit, with her legs stretched straight before her and her knees closed, on a mat at the western side of a house set apart for her ; she faced west, that point of the compass being as important to a girl as was the east, apparently, to a boy undergoing his initiation rites. The hair of her father and mother and their male and female kin was cut to provide for her toilet, and if she were already betrothed, that of her future husband's relations was added. For three days she was obliged to remain in her place, moving as little as possible, and during that time her diet was very meagre, no cooked food at all being allowed her. The girl's father and mother made a great quantity of coconut oil, which was thickened by boiling to the consistency of a syrup and used day and night for the anointment of her body. It was applied by her adoptive grandmother, who had supervision of all the charms recited in this and other operations. Such charms were nearly all directed towards parts of the girl's body with the object of increasing her beauty and making her a mother of men. To protect her against enemy spells she wore a girdle of young coconut leaf, for the coconut leaf was much used by the natives in protective magic. After three days and three nights she was allowed to leave her place and was taken by her grandmother to a well of fresh water, where she performed her ablutions, the old woman meanwhile reciting over her a certain spell known as *the washing of blood*. Three further days of purification she must pass in her separate quarters and then might return to her family. [2]

[1] A. R. Brown, *The Andaman Islanders*, pp. 92 *sq.*
[2] A. Grimble, " From Birth to Death in the Gilbert Islands," in the *Journal of the Royal Anthropological Institute*, li. (1921), p. 42.

In the Marshall Islands of the Pacific the arrival of a chief's daughter at puberty used to be an important event. A hut for her occupation was built on the beach, one part of which she used, while another part was assigned to a female magician accompanied by a number of men and women, who were called "the servants of the anointing." The female magician brought coconut oil, with which she anointed the whole of the girl's body, and the women occupied themselves in making garlands of flowers, to make a sweet smell. After the anointing the girl went to the beach to bathe, and returned to the hut by the same path. The anointing and the bathing were repeated three times a day. At other times the girl was obliged to remain as motionless as possible, seated with her legs tucked under her. Her seclusion lasted from two to three weeks, and during all this time the whole population of the island, men, women, and children, were allowed to move only thrice a day, and that for the most necessary purposes of attending to the wants of nature. At the end of the period the girl was visited by a nobleman of high rank, who deflowered her. If on the island there was no one of sufficiently high rank to perform this ceremony, such a man had to be fetched from another island.[1]

In the Kakadu tribe of North Australia when a girl has her first menstrual flow she retires to a special bush shelter, a kind of rude hut, which has been prepared for her. There she remains sitting on grass cut for the purpose, and keeping her legs tightly closed. She may not eat any animal food, nor even smell the food that is being cooked in the camp. To prevent her from doing so, her nostrils are plugged. Her seclusion lasts till the flow has ceased. Then the mother breaks down the bush shelter and burns it with all its contents. During the time of her seclusion the girl may have a fire in her bush shelter, but the fire may not be brought from the tribal camp, nor may her food be cooked on the camp fire. After the hut has been burned down, the girl puts some of the hot ashes on her abdomen and makes a small heap of them and sits on it.[2]

---

[1] P. A. Erdland, *Die Marshall-Insulaner*, pp. 113 *sq.*

[2] Baldwin Spencer, *Native Tribes of the Northern Territory of Australia*, pp. 328 *sqq.*

CHAPTER LXVIII

THE FIRE FESTIVALS OF EUROPE

IN the islands of North Friesland there was formerly an old heathen festival on the evening of February 21, when sacrificial fires (*Biiken*) were kindled, and men and youths danced hand-in-hand with women and marriageable girls round the flames and invoked Woden in the words of a prayer which was still in use in the seventeenth century. In Christian times this festival was brought into connection with St. Peter's Day, February 22, on which St. Peter was supposed to come and throw a warm stone into the water. In Föhr the sacred fires (*Biiken*) are kindled on February 21, " to light St. Peter to bed, to singe off his beard." In Sylt the feast of St. Peter has sunk into a children's festival. For days and weeks before the festival boys go from house to house collecting fuel for the bonfire (*Biiken*). They receive bundles of straw and twigs, which they carry to " the holy hill." There they heap the fuel about a petroleum or tar barrel. At nightfall the bonfire is kindled and kept up as long as possible by means of bundles of straw cast into the flames. The children dance singing round the hill to the light of the bonfires, while some of the boys run up and down the slope with burning wisps of straw.[1]

In Savoy on the first day of Lent " the young men in many villages go round to every house, carrying an enormous straw figure, which they afterwards burn in the market-place. On the first Sunday in Lent, bonfires are lit, round which the young people dance and sing old songs. The children, in one very popular song, demand fritters, and the quaint refrain

[1] C. Jenssen, *Die nordfriesischen Inseln*, pp. 354 *sqq.*

runs thus : ' If my mother does not give me fritters, I shall set fire to her petticoats.' " [1]   In Savoy too " *the Calavrais*," the old fires of joy, are still lit by the children on the night of Easter Sunday.   As they dance round, they brandish torches and sing, and then they all throw their torches into the fire.[2]

In some districts of the Caucasus the Mountain Jews celebrate the beginning of spring as follows : Thus in the district of Kuba all the girls assemble and go out into the wood.   Here they seek to forecast the future in all sorts of ways, and weave crowns of snowdrops, violets, and other flowers.   Then they collect a quantity of brushwood and drag it with songs to the town, helped by the young men, who come at evening to the wood.   In the evening the brushwood is piled up and kindled, and the young men leap through the fire.   The same thing is done on the night before the Russian Easter.   For the Jews believe that Jesus Christ hovers over the earth, threatening them with misery and misfortune.   So they kindle the fires to keep him from their dwellings.   That is why on that night in all the villages you may see bonfires flaring.   The Jews settled in towns do not observe this last custom.[3]

Elsewhere I have referred to the custom of bathing in dew on the morning of St. John's Day (Midsummer).[4]   At Fenestralle in Piedmont " on the 24th June, St. John the Baptist's Day, the women hang out their linen and all their clothes on the balconies or else spread them out in the fields, for they believe that the dew on that day will preserve them from moths all the year.   Many people wash their eyes with dew that morning, as the effect, they say, is beneficial." [5]

In Mingrelia, on the evening of the day when the orthodox cult celebrates the Assumption (August 15), the people, throughout the country, light great fires near the churches on public places, through which everyone, great and small, leaps. They believe that in this way they frighten the devils, of which

[1] E. Canziani, *Costumes, Traditions, and Songs of Savoy* (London, 1911), p. 136.

[2] E. Canziani, *op. cit.* pp. 137 *sq.*

[3] C. Hahn, *Aus dem Kaukasus*, pp. 196 *sq.*

[4] *Balder the Beautiful*, i. 208 n.

[5] E. Canziani and E. Rohde, *Piedmont* (London, 1913), p. 57.

the most powerful resides at Tabakhela, a mountain situated near Martvili.   In Georgia the same custom is observed on the Thursday evening of the last week of the great Lent : the date alone differs.[1]

[1] J. Mourier, " L'État religieuse de la Mingrélie," in *Revue de l'Histoire*   *des Religions*, xvi. (Paris, 1887), pp. 85 *sq.*

CHAPTER LXIX

WERE-WOLVES

ELSEWHERE I have discussed the belief in were-wolves as it has been held in Europe and elsewhere. Such beliefs are still current among some tribes of the Western Sudan and the Ivory Coast in Africa, although there the animal into which the sorcerer transforms himself is not a wolf, but often a leopard or a lion, or some other creature. Thus among the Nounoumas of the Western Sudan sorcerers are believed to transform themselves into dogs or cats, and in this form they attack people and cattle. When the herdsman finds one of them molesting his beasts he tries to give it a cut with his knife. If he succeeds the cat or dog disappears, but at the same moment the sorcerer who was in the animal dies in his house from the wound.[1] The Koulangos, another tribe of the Western Sudan, believe that some men can transform themselves into certain animals, particularly into leopards and hyenas. But such men do this, not to attack or molest anyone, but purely for defensive purposes, for example to protect their plantations by night. To effect the transformation they bathe in water in which they have placed a certain medicine. Certain families have a speciality of changing into certain animals. Those who thus transform themselves may not eat of the flesh of the animals into which they change their human bodies. Thus those who change into leopards may not eat the flesh of leopards, those who change into lions may not eat the flesh of lions.[2] Among the Gouros of the Ivory Coast sorcerers are believed to transform themselves

[1] L. Tauxier, *Le Noir du Soudan*, 181.

[2] L. Tauxier, *Le Noir de Bondoukou*, pp. 197 *sq.*

454

into wild beasts, such as leopards and hyenas. Such transformed beasts are recognized by the sagacity with which they avoid the snares, and by their unprovoked attacks upon human beings. Man-leopards and man-panthers are particularly feared. Such men hide their leopard or panther skins in the trunks of trees, or in abandoned ant-hills. They return to the spot secretly, and donning the skins become leopards or panthers again. The Gouro hunters allege that they have witnessed such transformations with their own eyes. When they catch such fellows in the act they lead them to the village, and there execute them.[1]

The Bakongo of the Lower Congo believe that witches can transform themselves into insects, such as cockroaches and spiders, and in that form can inflict people with ailments of the chest and lungs. When a medicine-man decides that a patient is suffering from this cause he sets traps for insects at the door of the sufferer's house. Next morning if he finds a cockroach at the far end of one of the traps, he knows that the transformed witch belongs to a distant branch of the family, and crushes it without compunction, believing that the sickness will not pass from the patient to the witch represented by the cockroach, and the patient will now recover. If, however, the cockroach is only half way up the trap, he knows the witch is of very near kinship to his patient, and, as he does not want to pass the sickness on to a near relative, he warns the cockroach and lets it go. Should a cockroach be found in the trap next morning, he believes it is the same one (or, if it is a spider, that it has only changed its form) ; he will then either warn it and threaten it more strongly and let it go, or he will keep it shut up a few days without food, and will watch to see if a near relative of the patient becomes thin (that is, dying through having his soul so imprisoned in the trap that it cannot return to the body), and, if no one becomes thin and ill, he will vehemently threaten the witch in the insect and let it go. Should he find an insect in the trap on the third morning, he kills it at once, as it is evident that the witch is very persistent and should be punished. The writer who records these curious beliefs and customs

[1] L. Tauxier, *Les Nègres Gouro et Gagou*, 181.

adds that " it is interesting to note that witches can travel about disguised as insects, and that the folk they represent suffer in proportion to the suffering inflicted on the insects." [1]

[1] J. H. Weeks, *Among the Primitive Bakongo*, pp. 224 *sq.*

CHAPTER LXX

THE FIRE-WALK

ELSEWHERE I have described the custom of the Fire-walk, or religious rite of walking through fire or over red-hot stones.[1] Among the Oraons of Chota Nagpur in India, where a village happens to have a seat of the great god Mahadeo, the devotees (Bhagats) of the god, as an act of religious merit, ceremonially walk over burning charcoal on certain occasions. It is believed that on such occasions, by the grace of the god Mahadeo, his devotees pass unscathed over this burning charcoal although they actually stamp their feet on it.[2]

In India among the wild tribes of the Afghan Frontier Mr. Pennell met an itinerant fakir or Mohammedan holy man who sold charms for the cure of diseases. "One of his performances was to walk through fire, professedly by the power of the Mohammedan *Kalimah*.[3] A trench was dug in the ground, and filled with charcoal and wood, which was set alight. After the fire had somewhat died down, the still glowing embers were beaten down with sticks, and then the fakir, reciting the *Kalimah* with great zest, proceeded to deliberately walk across, after which he invited the more daring among the faithful to follow his example, assuring them that if they recited the creed in the same way and with sincerity, they would suffer no harm. Some went through the ordeal and showed no signs of having suffered from it;

---

[1] *Balder the Beautiful*, ii. 1 *sqq.*

[2] S. C. Roy, *The Oraons of Chota Nagpur*, 171.

[3] *Kalimah*, the Mohammedan confession of faith: "There is no God but God, and Mohammed is the prophet of God."

2 H

others came out with blistered and sore feet. These unfortunates were jeered at by the others as being no true Mohammedans." [1]

The Maoris have a legend of Te Hahae the fire-walker, who is said to have built a great oven of hot stones to cook taro for a feast: " When the fire had burned down to a fierce heated mass of glowing coals and the stones were red-hot, then it was that Te Hahae walked into the *umu* (oven) and stood upon those stones amid the fierce heat, clothed merely in a *maro* (girdle). . . . Though he stood for a long time in *umu* repeating *karakia* (spells), yet was he not burnt or in any way injured by the fire, and the green leaves of which his girdle was formed were not shrivelled or withered or affected in any way." [2]

In the Konkan, a district of the Bombay Presidency, cattle are worshipped by the Hindoos on the first day of *Kartik* (October-November), and they are made to pass over fire. [3]

Among the Tumbuka, a tribe of Nyasaland in Africa, when the mourners are returning from a funeral a medicine-man kindles a great fire in the path, and the mourners pass through it, doubtless to purify themselves from the pollution of death. [4]

---

[1] T. L. Pennell, *Among the Wild Tribes of the Afghan Frontier*, 37.

[2] Elsdon Best, " Notes on some customs and superstitions of the Maori," in the *Seventh Report of the Australasian Association for the Ad-*

vancement of Science (1898), p. 769.

[3] R. E. Enthoven, *Folklore of Bombay*, 221.

[4] D. Fraser, *Winning a Primitive People*, 159.

CHAPTER LXXI

THE MAGIC FLOWERS OF MIDSUMMER EVE

ELSEWHERE I have cited examples of the common European belief that plants acquire certain magical but transient virtues on a single night of the year, the magic eve of Midsummer or St. John.[1] In Savoy " there is a curious legend attached to the mountain ferns, which are said to flower luxuriantly with beautiful red blossoms on St. John's night only. The flowers are star-like in their brilliancy, and the devil always picks them immediately. Any one who wishes to secure them will have a terrible fight, but once he has obtained the flowers, or even their seeds, he can make himself invisible at any moment he wishes." [2]

We may compare a similar belief current among the Dyoula, a tribe of the French or Western Sudan. They believe that in order to secure the magical virtue of plants to be used as charms in ritual they must be gathered on the eve of the ninth day of the month Diomandé, which is the first month of their calendar. Everyone throughout the districts of Bondoukou and Kong knows that night to be of all the year the magic eve. On it a man need only go out into the forest and cut a bough at haphazard, and he will be sure that the ointments and beverages prepared from its leaves will possess a healing virtue.[3]

[1] *Balder the Beautiful*, ii. 45 *sqq.*
[2] E. Canziani, *Costumes, Traditions, and Songs of Savoy*, 14.
[3] L. Tauxier, *Le Noir de Bondoukou*, 392

CHAPTER LXXII

THE EXTERNAL SOUL IN FOLK-TALES

ELSEWHERE I have cited the popular Indian story of the warlock Punchkin, whose external soul was deposited for safety in the green parrot, and who could not be killed so long as the bird was safe.[1] A story of this type is told by the Korwas, a Kolarian tribe of the Chota Nagpur plateau in India. It runs as follows :

" A certain rich man, a banker and moneylender (Sahu), had twelve sons. He got them all married and they went out on a journey to trade. There came a holy mendicant to the house of the rich man and asked for alms. The banker was giving him alms, but the saint said he would only take them from his son or son's wife. As the sons were away the rich man called his daughter-in-law, and she began to give alms to the saint. But he caught her up and carried her off. Then her father-in-law went to search for her, saying that he would not return until he had found her. He came to the saint's house upon a mountain and said to him, ' Why did you carry off my son's wife ? ' The saint said to him, ' What can you do ? ' and turned him into stone by waving his hand. Then all the other brothers went in turn to search for her down to the youngest, and all were turned into stone. At last the youngest brother set out to search but he did not go to the saint, but travelled across the sea and sat under a tree on the other side. In that tree was the nest with young of Raigidan and Jatagidan [2] birds. A snake was climbing up the tree to eat the nestlings, and the brother saw the snake

---

[1] *Balder the Beautiful*, pp. 147 *sqq*   [2] Believed to be some kind of vulture

460

and killed it. When the parent birds returned the young birds said, ' We will not eat or drink till you have rewarded this boy who killed the snake which was climbing the tree to devour us.' Then the parent birds said to the boy, ' Ask of us whatever you will and we will give it to you.' And the boy said, ' I want only a gold parrot in a gold cage.' Then the parent birds said, ' You have asked nothing of us, ask for something more ; but if you will accept only a gold parrot in a gold cage wait here a little and we will fly across and get it for you.' So they brought the parrot and cage, and the youngest brother took them and went home. Immediately the saint came to him and asked him for the gold parrot and cage because the saint's soul was in that parrot. Then the youngest brother told him to dance and he would give him the parrot ; and the saint danced, and his legs and arms were broken one after the other, as often as he asked for the parrot and cage. Then the youngest brother buried the saint's body and went to his house and passed his hands before all the stone images and they all came to life again." [1]

Again, the Birhors, another tribe of the Chota Nagpur plateau in India, tell of a fierce battle between Ravan, the Rajah of Lanka, and the hero Lakshman, son of the Rajah Dasarath, assisted by the baboon Hanuman. In this battle all the people of Lanka were killed except Ravan and an old woman. As for Ravan, when his head was cut off twelve other heads sprang in its place, and again, as one of these was cut off, another would spring up by its side, and so on. Lakshman and Hanuman rested for a day after their strenuous labours, and then reported to Ram, the brother of Lakshman, the condition of affairs. Ram told them, " Leave the old woman for the present, and concentrate your efforts against Ravan." So they again proceeded to fight Ravan. Ravan told them, " You seek in vain to kill me : none but a person who has fasted twelve years will succeed in killing me." Hanuman assumed the shape of a *Suga* bird, and wheedled Ravan into divulging the secret as to where his life was secreted. Raven told him that his life was deposited in a small closet with golden walls inside the inner apartments of his brick-built palace Hanuman and Lakshman entered

[1] R. V. Russell, *Tribes and Castes of the Central Provinces*, iii. 579.

the palace and broke open the closet and freed Ravan's life from confinement. Then Lakshman and Hanuman went to fight Ravan, and as Lakshman had actually taken no food (except earth) for twelve years, he at length succeeded in killing Ravan. [1]

[1] S. C. Roy, *The Birhors*, pp. 422 *sqq.*

CHAPTER LXXIII

THE EXTERNAL SOUL IN FOLK-CUSTOM

ELSEWHERE I have argued that the widespread popular story of a warlock who kept his soul for safety in some external object, and therefore could not be killed in his own person, reflects a popular custom of depositing the soul for a similar reason in some external object, either temporarily or permanently.[1] Such a custom is still commonly practised by the Ila-speaking tribes of Northern Rhodesia. On this subject we are told that among them " one method of self-protection is, by means of a powerful charm, to put one's life into a hiding-place, whether into another person or into some object. This is *kudishita*, to shield, protect oneself. One chief, Mungaila, confided to us once that his life was hidden in the needle on a friend's head ; he was careful not to say which friend. Another told us that his was in a friend's finger-nail. One of the doctors gave us the following description of this part of his practice. The patient comes to him and says : ' *Ndeza kulanga mwin zobola luseba lwangu, ndaamba unkwatenkwate* ' (" I am come to seek a place wherein to keep my body, I mean that you should safeguard me "). If the doctor undertakes the case, the patient produces a hoe as a preliminary fee. The doctor then prepares *misamo* (medicines), and charms him (*wamwinda*) by giving him some to eat in porridge and others to rub on his body. And the doctor asks, ' Where is it you wish to hide ? Perhaps in the eye of some person ? ' ' Yes, I wish to hide in somebody's eye.' ' What person ? ' The patient thinks over the names of his relatives, and rejecting them says: ' I would hide in

---

[1] *Balder the Beautiful*, ii. 153 *sq.*

the eye of my servant.'   The doctor agrees and charms him
accordingly, giving him all the medicines necessary to enter
his servant's eye, whether it be man or woman.   So *wenjila
momo ulazuba momo mudinso* (' he enters and hides there in
the eye ').   He does not make the fact known to the servant,
but keeps the knowledge to himself.   He remains in the eye
all the days of his life.   Should he fall sick, he tells his chief
wife : ' Know, in case I should die, that I had certain medicines from So-and-So.'   This is because of the claims that
the doctor will make against his estate ; but even to his wife
he does not tell that he is in anyone's eye.   Should he die,
at the same moment that servant of his has his eye pierced
(*ulatuluka dinso*), that is, by his master coming out of it.
Then, seeing the man's eye burst, people know where the
master lay hidden.   And the converse is also true : should
the servant's eye be destroyed, the man would die.   Other
people are doctored so that they may hide (*zuba*) in a palm
tree.   When such a one dies, the palm falls ; and should
the palm fall first (a very unlikely event), the man would
die.   If he were not sick at the time, he would die suddenly
(*ulaanzuka budio*).   Others eat medicine for taking up their
abode (*kulala*) in a thorn tree (*mwihunga*).   On the death
of such a person the tree breaks and falls, and the man comes
out of it (*wavhwa mo*).   Others get medicines to enable them
to hide (*zuba*) in a cow or an ox.   When the beast dies the
person ' takes away his heart ' (*wakusha mozo*) and dies also.
Then the people know that he had hidden in the beast." [1]

Similarly in regard to the Kaonde tribe in the Kasempa
district of Northern Rhodesia we are told that " sometimes a
man, who wishes to live for a very long time, decides to
' bottle ' his shadow (*chimvule*) and takes it—I cannot discover how, but it does not need a witch-doctor's assistance :
either the man does it for himself, or asks the assistance of a
mulunda (blood-brother)—and puts it into an antelope-horn.
Then he hides it somewhere, *e.g.* in a hole in the ground,
believing that if his shadow be safe he cannot die.   This is a
risky undertaking, however, as, if the horn gets destroyed,
lost or stolen, the man has then lost his shadow, and will die

[1] E. W. Smith and A. M. Dale, *The Ila-speaking Peoples of Northern
Rhodesia*, ii. 255 *sqq.*

within the year." [1] The writer to whom we owe this account
tells us that in this passage he uses shadow in the sense of
soul or spirit. He adds that in the opinion of these people
" it is possible to *sweka wumi mu chitumbu* (to hide one's
' life ' in a medicine) so that one's enemies may not destroy it
by witchcraft or other means. Some ' doctors ' have a recipe
for this : the ' life ' is drawn from the body and placed in a
mbachi (shell, usually of a crab) and can be given to a dog or
other animal to eat, or can be hidden in a convenient spot." [2]

Similar beliefs and practices are current among the Gabin,
a tribe of the Adamawa Province of Northern Nigeria. On
this subject Mr. Meek tells us that " the conception that
disease may be transferred by magical means is the main-
spring of much of the religious ritual of the Gabin, Yungur,
Hona, and Longuda, all of whom employ pots for this purpose . . . When a person falls ill he goes to a maker of these
pieces of pottery, who takes some clay, circles it round the
patient's head, and then gives it the shape which the spirit
of the disease is supposed to possess. In this way the disease
is transferred to the pot, and if at any time the owner has a
relapse he can recover his health by a sacrifice offered to the
pot, this sacrifice being an inducement to the disease-causing
spirit to return once more to the pot. Similar ideas and
practices are also found among the Gabin. But on the other
hand, many Gabin seem to regard the pot as their own double,
the abode of a soul and not of a spirit. It is a common
practice, therefore, for a young man who has set up a home
of his own, to ask a friend to make a pot for him in order that
he may deposit his soul in the pot. The young man lies down
on the ground and the potter sits beside him shaping the clay
into what is supposed to be a likeness of the subject. Ears,
eyes, mouth and nose are indicated, and shoulders and arms
are represented by excrescences raised across the body of the
pot, which is supposed to represent the heart, *i.e.* the life.
There are no legs. When the pot has been fired, the owner
deposits it in some secret place in the bush, generally in a
small cave. He makes a small dolmen-like stone structure
for its reception, *i.e.* a circle of stones covered by a large

[1] H. E. Melland, *In Witch-Bound Africa*, 132
[2] H. E. Melland, *op. cit.* 165.

stone slab.   There is a doorway.   These stone circles closely resemble the shrines which the Yungur are accustomed to make for the corn-spirits.   If the owner ever feels ill he goes to his secret pottery symbol, smears it with red oil, takes a wisp of straw and transfers some of the oil to his left and right temple, his left and right shoulder, and to the abdomen. This causes his ' soul ' or ' heart ', as they say, to resume its former vigour.

" It is quite clear, therefore, that the Gabin regard these pots as soul-counterparts, just as the Kanakuru and Mbula believe that certain animals are their counterparts.   And just as an injury to the animal entails injury to the man, so among the Gabin injury to the pot entails illness or even death to the owner.   If, therefore, the owner finds that his pot has been broken or injured, he will become disturbed ; and after having had a new pot made will consult a diviner in order to discover the name of the individual who has designs on his soul.   The practice of depositing souls in pots is largely connected with witchcraft ideas, for it was stated that by relegating the soul to some secret place a sorcerer would be unable to capture it from his body, and could only injure the man if he happened to discover the hiding-place of the pot embodying the soul. . . . It is said among the Gabin that if a witch finds a man's pot and buries it the owner of the pot will die." [1]

The belief that human souls can be deposited in external objects was discovered by Mrs. Talbot in the Banana tribe of the Logone river, in French Central Africa.   There she found that for every female child born a long plaited bag was woven by her mother or grandmother, and with it the thread of the girl's life was thought to be mysteriously linked. " No bribe would induce a living woman to part with one, since with its departure her soul must leave her, but we were fortunate enough to purchase several which had belonged to dead members of the tribe." [2]

Often the external objects with which human lives are imagined to be inseparably bound up are plants or trees. Thus among the Kpelle of Liberia the lives of women are

---

[1] C. K. Meek, *Tribal Studies in Northern Nigeria*, ii. 374 *sqq.*

[2] P. A. Talbot, *Woman's Mysteries of a Primitive People*, 172.

thought to be closely bound up with banana trees. Soon after a girl is born a banana tree is planted for her, and is carefully tended, that the growth of the girl may go hand in hand with the growth of the tree. If the tree begins to wither, the girl falls ill.[1] Among the Toradyas of Central Celebes after a birth a coconut tree is planted on the spot where the after-birth is buried. Such a tree is regarded as the child's life-token. If the tree dies, then the child for whom it was planted dies also.[2] In the district of Seleo of Northern New Guinea there is an ancient tree with which the natives believe their lives to be inseparably bound up. When they sold to the Germans the ground on which the tree stands, they expressly stipulated that the tree should be carefully preserved, for if it were destroyed they would all die.[3] Among the Maoris of New Zealand the navel-string of a new-born child was buried in a sacred place (*urupa*) and over this a young tree was sometimes planted ; this tree was supposed to have some brotherhood with the child. A certain Maori chief asserted that he had a familiar spirit inhabiting a white-pine tree, which had sprung from his umbilical cord (*iho*), grew with his growth, and fell to decay as he became aged.[4]

Elsewhere I have described the custom of passing sick people through a cleft tree as a mode of cure.[5] Among the Ait Messat Berbers of Morocco there is a huge oak tree known by the name of *aseklu n-umudin*, that is to say, " the tree of the sick," because through a hole in its huge roots sick people pass as a mode of ridding themselves of their fever.[6] Near Eket, in Southern Nigeria, there is a sacred tree. Low down in the ancient trunk a great hole is to be seen through which sick folk creep, in the hope that their illness may be cured.[7] In Piedmont, " at Primolto, to know whether a child will recover, they split the trunk of a young walnut tree, and pass the child through the aperture. Then they fill up the hole with damp earth. If the tree thrives after

---

[1] D. Westermann, *Die Kpelle*, 221.
[2] N. Adriani and A. C. Kruijt, *op. cit.* ii. 49.
[3] R. Neuhauss, *Deutsch Neu-Guinea*, i. 411.
[4] E. Tregear, *The Maori Race*, 43. Cf. Elsdon Best, *The Maori* (Welling-ton, 1924), i. 21.
[5] *Balder the Beautiful*, ii. 170, *sqq.*
[6] E. Laoust, *Mots et choses ber-bères*, 151.
[7] P. A. Talbot, *Life in Southern Nigeria*, 111.

this, the child will recover, otherwise the child will die." [1] In all these and similar cases the notion probably is, not that the sick person by passing through a hole in the tree acquires a portion of the tree's life and vigour, but that by doing so he gives the slip to the ghost or evil spirit who is regarded as the real cause of his malady. Hence the hole through which the patient creeps need not be a hole in a tree : it may be a hole in a cleft stick or sapling or creeper ; indeed any hole will serve the purpose, provided only it be small and narrow. The smaller and narrower it is, the greater the chance of throwing the pursuing demon off the track.

Among the Wandamba, a tribe of Tanganyika, " when a Mndamba is killed by a lion, leopard, crocodile, buffalo, or any other wild animal, they first bury his remains on the spot, then his relations and all the people of his village assemble at the grave, strip off their clothes and don leaves or grass, and the principal hunter makes medicine and shaves their heads and pours the medicine over them ; after which he takes a *mlendi* sapling, splits it in two and sticks the pieces in the ground near the grave, and all the people walk between. Then he throws the pieces away and breaks the gourd in which he made the medicine by stamping on it. [2] Here the passage of the relations and mourners between the pieces of the cleft sapling at the grave is doubtless a mode of evading the dangerous ghost of the deceased, who having been done to death by a wild beast is likely to be very ill-humoured, and therefore formidable. We have already seen that among the Ila-speaking tribes of Northern Rhodesia, whoever has killed a person, whether in war or otherwise, must jump through a cleft stick three or four times, [3] no doubt in order to evade the victim's ghost.

Among the Kiwai of British New Guinea, " at the outset of each monsoon it is customary for a family to practise the following observance in order to keep off illness during the season just beginning. The parents take their children with them to the bush, where they split a creeper hanging down

---

[1] E. Canziani and E. Rohde, *Piedmont*, 143.

[2] A. G. O. Hodgson, " Some Notes on the Hunting Customs of the Wandamba of the Ulanga Valley, Tan-

ganyika Territory," in the *Journal of the Royal Anthropological Institute*, lvi. (1926), 69.

[3] See above, p. 240

from a tree, leaving the lower and upper parts of it intact. The mother places herself astride in front of the creeper facing the village, and the children, beginning from the eldest, crawl between her legs and through the opening in the creeper. The father spits *manababa* (a herb) at each child, and when they have passed through the creeper and stand up, he pushes them forward by lifting up their heels in turn, holding a *warakara* leaf in each hand ; this means that ' he shut him road behind piccaninny.' [1]   Then he, too, follows the children in the same way, and lastly the mother crawls through the creeper and, standing on the other side, draws her legs together, the two halves of the creeper closing themselves.   She places under her heels two pieces of *oivo* (fossil wood), which she leaves on the ground ; they too ' shut him road.'   Then they all bathe in the sea." [2]   Here the passage of the whole family through a cleft creeper, which closes behind them, is doubtless intended to bar the road to demons of sickness and misfortune in the new monsoon.

Among the Kiwai a man who has married a widow takes similar precautions against being pursued by the dangerous ghost of his wife's late husband.   Together the couple go to the place in the forest where the wife had connection with her former spouse for the last time.   There they have connection with each other, and before returning home they split the middle part of a certain creeper (*nu-rude*), leaving the base and top intact.   Then the man and woman crawl through the creeper, which closes behind them.   In this way, according to the natives, the couple shut the door against the ghost of the dead husband.   Similarly, when a man marries a widow whose husband had been killed by a snake they go together to the haunt of the snake and have connection there. Before returning they take a nipa leaflet and split it in the same manner as the creeper in the observance described above, and the two sides are kept apart by means of a transverse stick.   The man first crawls through the leaf, knocking down the stick, and after him the woman in the same way, the stick having been replaced.   On their return home the door is kept shut after them.   If the first husband has been

---

[1] That is, he shuts the road behind the child.

[2] G. Landtman, *The Kiwai Papuans of British New Guinea*, 222.

taken by a crocodile, the following rite is observed. The pair go to the place where the accident happened ; there the woman takes off her grass petticoat and breaks her *sogéré* (a plaited grass necklace, the last sign of her mourning), throwing them away into the water. After the two have had connection, the woman stands up astride with her back towards the water, and her husband crawls between her legs from behind. Then she puts on a new petticoat and walks home behind her husband. They keep the door of their house carefully closed till next morning.[1] In this last custom, when the widow closes her legs after the passage of her second husband between them, she is apparently supposed to bar the road against the pursuit of her first husband's ghost.

The same object, which some people seek to obtain by passing through cleft trees or sticks, others attempt to effect by passing through narrow openings between stones or through a cleft in a rock. Thus among the Berbers of Morocco Sidi Himmi is the name of a small dolmen-like structure built at Tanant. It is composed of two stones upon which rests a third in such a manner as to leave a passage similar to the entry to a room. This passage is sufficiently large to allow a child to enter. A mother brings her sick child to Sidi Himmi and passes her three times between the stones, at the same time pronouncing a vow to sacrifice a fowl if the child recovers.[2] Again, at a few miles distance from Demnat in Morocco there is a small rock projecting from the ground in the shape of the back and neck of a camel, with an opening underneath just large enough for a person to creep through. People who are suffering from some illness and women who are desirous of offspring crawl three times through the hole, from west to east ; but if they have been disobedient to their parents they are wedged in between the rock and the ground. Near the village Dar Fellaq, in the tribe Jbel la-Hbib, there is an isolated rock with a hole in its centre, through which sick children are dragged three times from west to east, in the hope of a cure.[3]

Many primitive peoples believe that their lives are so

[1] G. Landtman, *op. cit.* pp. 252 *sq.*

[2] E. Laoust, *op. cit.* 153.

[3] E. Westermarck, *The Moorish Conception of Holiness (Baraka)*, pp. 40 *sq.*

sympathetically bound up with those of animals that when the animal dies the man dies, and that conversely when the man expires the animal dies simultaneously. This belief is especially prevalent among the tribes of Western Africa, where the conception of a man's soul permanently or temporarily lodged in an animal is conveniently spoken of as a " bush-soul." Thus for example among the Nounoumas of the Western Sudan people do not sacrifice to crocodiles, because they say that crocodiles are not gods, but only their own human souls in animal form. The soul of every human being is at once in the man and in the crocodile. When the crocodile dies, the man dies the day after. If the crocodile loses an eye, the man loses an eye, and *vice versa*. If the crocodile loses a paw, the man becomes lame. The human crocodiles are of a small species, and each man knows the crocodile that corresponds to himself. When a crocodile is about to die, it comes into the village of the person whose soul is lodged in it. When it dies they wrap the carcase in white clothing and bury it, and sacrifice fowls to it. Then the man whose soul was in the crocodile dies in turn. The people of Leo believe that when one kills a crocodile in the river, one also kills a man in the village. This is because the soul of each inhabitant of the village is connected with that of a crocodile, and when the soul of the crocodile dies or leaves its material body, the same thing happens to the inhabitant of the village who corresponds to it.[1]

Similarly among the Kassounas-Fras, another tribe of the Western Sudan, most people believe that crocodiles are their souls, and that if they kill a crocodile the man who corresponds to it dies immediately. Thus they pay great respect to the reptiles, but do not offer them sacrifices. But at Pou it is not the crocodiles but the iguanas which are thus venerated and respected. Each iguana, it appears, possesses the soul of some person in the village. Hence if somebody kills an iguana, a man simultaneously dies in the village.[2] Again, among the Kassounas-Bouras, another tribe of the Western Sudan, it is believed that the souls of the living and of the dead inhabit crocodiles, and that when a crocodile dies

---

[1] L Tauxier, *Le Noir du Soudan*, pp. 192 *sq.*

[2] L. Tauxier, *op cit* pp. 238 *sq.*

in the river someone dies in the village.   In the country of
Kampala, each time that a man is about to die the people
know of it beforehand by the groanings and wailings of
the crocodiles.[1]   They often believe the same thing about
pythons.   At Gueunou, when a man is ill it is because his
serpent is ill (the serpent which corresponds to him as his
soul), and they treat the man with roots.[2]   The Mossis and
Foulses, two other tribes of the Western Sudan, do not make
sacrifices to crocodiles, but this does not prevent them from
recognising a relationship between the animals and themselves.   They are, they think, of the same family, the soul of
their grandfathers inhabiting the crocodiles.   Thus, when
they kill a crocodile they cause by a counterstroke the death
of someone in the village, and when they wound a crocodile
they wound at the same time the man who is attached to it
by a subtle, invisible, but real connection.[3]   Another account
of the creed of the Mossi, in respect of their external souls,
runs thus : every man has a soul which is called *siga*, and
kyma after death.   This soul, according to the Mossi, is an
animal, it may be a serpent, a crocodile, a goat or a hare.
The soul is related to this animal, it is of its family.   If somebody kills a serpent or a crocodile in a village where the souls
of the inhabitants are serpents or crocodiles, it is equivalent
to killing an inhabitant of the village, for every individual
related to the serpent or the crocodile has in this village a
serpent or a crocodile which represents him, and he will die
when his animal-soul dies.[4]

Similar beliefs as to human souls in animal bodies are
current among the natives in the interior of the Gold Coast
of West Africa.   We are told that among them " everyone
has some animal which is a species of *alter ego*—not to be
slain or eaten, an animal which is recognized as one's friend,
one's brother.   Most noteworthy of these animals is the
crocodile, which is called by the Paga people their soul.
The life of a man or woman is identical with that of his
crocodile, *alter ego*.   When he is born the crocodile is born ;
they are ill at the same time ; they die at the same time.   It

[1] L. Tauxier, *op. cit.* 325.
[2] L. Tauxier, *op. cit.* 326.
[3] L. Tauxier, *Le Noir du Yatenga,*

376.
[4] P. E. Mangin, " Les Mossi," in
Anthropos, x.-xi. (1915–16), 194 *sq.*

is said that when a man is at the point of death one can hear at night the groaning of his crocodile.[1] Beliefs of the same sort as to human souls in animal bodies are commonly held by the peoples of Southern Nigeria, and have been fully described by Mr. and Mrs. Talbot.[2] To quote a single example : " Not long ago a man of Usun Inyan town asserted that his wife, Esiet Idung by name, had told him that her soul sometimes left her and went to dwell in the body of a fish in the Kwa Ibo River. One day she came to her husband, crying : ' I am caught ! I am caught and must die ! for a fisherman has snared my soul in his trap by the waterside. Go therefore to the place of which I shall tell you and release me before it is too late ; for should the man come and kill my affinity, I must die also.' On this, in all haste, the husband took a canoe and went with his friends to the trap which his wife had described. They opened the door and let all the fish swim out into the river. Among the others they noticed one of great size, which plunged early out into the current. On their return they found that the woman had recovered ; but all believe that, had the fish been killed, she must have perished also." [3]

At Bia, in the island of San Cristoval, it is believed that the soul (*aunga*) of a living person may take the form of one of several species of animals, such as the shark, the hawk, the bonito, the skate, the green lizard, the yellow-breast bird, red and black snakes, the rat, the prawn, the hermit crab, and the millipede. Hence children at Bia are warned not to kill any of these animals, because the soul of a living man may take any one of these forms. If the green lizard is seen in a tree, the soul of a man may be in it, and if the lizard is killed, the man would die ; the souls of living men are supposed often to go about in the form of green lizards. A man may also send his soul into the yellow-breast, and the bird will fly off and tell the man's friends that he wants them to come to him.[4] Elsewhere in San Cristoval persons are sup-

---

[1] A. W. Cardinall, *The Natives of the Northern Territories of the Gold Coast* (London), 39.

[2] P. A. Talbot, *Life in Southern Nigeria*, pp. 81 *sqq.*; D. A. Talbot, *Woman's Mysteries of a Primitive People*, pp. 43 *sqq.*

[3] P. A. Talbot, *Life in Southern Nigeria*, 91.

[4] C. E. Fox, *The Threshold of the Pacific*, 271.

posed to have their souls in sharks. Such relations to sharks are hereditary, the descent being from father to son. When a shark-man has a son born to him he is initiated soon after birth into the mystery by his father, either in the house or at the shark-rock, Mr. Fox is not sure which. His father, the shark-man, takes the child in his arms and hugs him to his breast, and then crooks his left arm to represent a shark's fin, and puts the infant under his arm. Then at the shark-rock the child and his future familiar shark receive the same name. The child's soul (*aunga*) goes into the shark, and Mr. Fox thinks that the shark's soul is supposed to go into the child, or else the two become one so completely that they share the same soul. From that time the shark-child has his familiar at the shark-rock. If the child dies the shark will die, if the shark is injured the child will fall sick. The connection between the two is exceedingly close. Shark-boys have gone to Norfolk Island and their familiars have followed them and been seen on the fishing grounds. The shark-boy goes regularly to the shark-rock, and sacrifices yams, nuts, money, and betel to his shark-brother.[1]

Elsewhere we have seen that in the belief of some primitive peoples every human being possesses not one but several souls.[2] To the examples of this multiplicity of souls which I have there cited I may here add a few more instances. Thus among the peoples of Southern Nigeria there is a general belief that each person possesses four souls : first, an ethereal one, the double and inner frame of the physical form ; secondly, the soul proper, the consciousness, the thinking or mental body ; thirdly, the spiritual or minor Ego ; and fourthly, the Over-Soul, or Chi, the great Spirit, which often includes several lesser egos and always " stays with God." The shadow is considered the sign, usually of the ethereal, but sometimes of the mental body. The ethereal one dissolves with the physical structure, while the greater part of the soul is relatively immortal, and the third and fourth never perish.[3]

Again with regard to the Birhors of Chota Nagpur in

---

[1] C. E. Fox, *The Threshold of the Pacific*, 231.

[2] *Balder the Beautiful*, ii. 220 *sq.*

[3] P. A. Talbot. *The Peoples of Southern Nigeria*, ii. 259.

India, we are told that after a death the *umbul* or shade of the deceased is ceremonially taken to its old home, where it is enshrined as an ancestor spirit.   After a death among the Birhors a somewhat elaborate ceremony is performed to recover the shade (*umbul*) of the deceased and to bring it back to the house, and there install it among the ancestral spirits.   The friends go to the place outside the village where the corpse rested on its way to the burial-ground.   There they erect a miniature house, offer a sacrifice of a fowl at the spot, and call upon the spirit, saying, " Here we offer this fowl to you."   Saying this, the men strike one sickle against another and call out the name of their recently deceased relative, and set fire to the miniature hut.   Then they exclaim, " Come, so-and-so !   Look, thy house is burning ! " With repeated exclamations like this the party return home, followed, as they believe, by the shade of their dead relative. On entering the hut they ask with bated breath, " Has the shade come in yet ? "   The reply is always in the affirmative. A diviner is then called in, who, falling into a state of spirit-possession, ascertains whether the shade that has been brought home is really the shade of the deceased.   When that has been ascertained the spirit of the dead is questioned as to the evil spirit that caused his death, and when the evil spirit has been named sacrifices are offered to appease it. Afterwards at a feast the shade of the deceased is solemnly incorporated with the other ancestral spirits.   At this feast the headman of the village and another elder drop rice on the ground, by way of offering it to the ancestral spirits, and say : " Here we make rice offerings to ye in the name of so-and-so (naming the deceased).   Do ye incorporate him in your herd.   From to-day we shall offer rice and liquor to ye all."

In the opinion of the Birhors, besides this shade, which joins the invisible spirit world that interpenetrates this visible world of ours, a man has two souls—a male one and a female one.   These remain united in death as in life, and, when they finally lose their present body by death, are reincarnated together in a new body.   When a person dreams dreams, the male soul goes out of the body and visits different persons and places, while the female soul remains in charge of the body

" just as his wife is left in charge of the hut or encampment when a Birhor goes out to hunt." [1]

Among the Chams of Indo-China, at the initiation of a novice " some children carefully wipe his feet and march round him nineteen times in honour of the novice's nineteen souls. Throughout the East many souls are accredited to every human being. Of these, one alone is deemed immortal. The vital soul resides in the navel, the supreme soul in the bosom." [2]

The Trung Cha, a mountain tribe of Tonquin, believe that the human body is the seat of thirty-six vital spirits, which after death disperse in the tomb and on the altar of the ancestors. They believe, like the Annamites, that every human being possesses three souls, but instead of attributing, like these latter, nine vital spirits to the material soul, they attribute nine to each of the three souls.[3] Again, the Meo, another mountain tribe of Tonquin, believe that every human being has three souls, a belief which is said to be shared by all the peoples of the Far East.[4]

Thus the popular belief among the Chinese in the province of Kan-sou is that man has three souls : the soul in the highest sense of the word (*P'an chen hoen*), the second soul (*eul hoen*), and the terrestrial soul (*t'ou-hoen*), that is, the soul of earth. One of these souls, not yet reincarnated, wanders about the earth for a time, either for a punishment, or voluntarily to avenge itself upon its enemies. The terrestrial soul wanders round the tomb, and may go away : it is a vengeful soul. The soul in the supreme sense after death takes its place on the ancestral tablet set apart for it. It is the guardian spirit of the family, but may become terrible to strangers.[5]

Elsewhere I have suggested that totemism may be based on a belief that men and women keep their external souls for safety in their totems, whether these be animals, plants, or other inanimate objects.[6] Since then I have proposed two other alternative theories of totemism ; but the subject is too

---

[1] S. C. Roy, *The Birhors*, pp. 252 *sq.*

[2] H. Baudesson, *Indo-China and its Primitive People*, pp. 261 *sq.*

[3] Col. E. Diguet, *Les Montagnards du Tonkin*, 101.

[4] Diguet, *op. cit.* 144.

[5] P. J. Dols, " La Vie chinoise dans la province de Kan-sou (Chine)," in *Anthropos*, x.-xi. (1915–16), 727.

[6] *Balder the Beautiful*, ii. 228.

large to be discussed in this place.   For a full discussion I must refer the reader to another work of mine.[1]

Elsewhere I have referred to the ceremonial use among savages of the instrument called the bull-roarer.[2]   To the evidence which I have there cited I will here add some further references to the use of the instrument in Australia,[3] New Guinea,[4] the New Hebrides,[5] and Africa.[6]

[1] *Totemism and Exogamy* (London, 1910), iv. 40-71.

[2] *Balder the Beautiful*, ii. 228.

[3] Baldwin Spencer, *Native Tribes of the Northern Territory of Australia*, pp. 119 *sq.*, 154 *sqq.*, 161, 162, 164 *sqq.*, 211 *sqq.*; H. Basedow, *The Australian Aboriginal*, pp. 241, 270 *sq.*

[4] G. Landtman, *The Kiwai Papuans of British New Guinea*, pp. 75 *sq.*, 81 *sq.*; E. Baxter Riley, *Among Papuan Head-Hunters*, 94, 96, 98, 201 *sq.*

[5] F. Speiser, *Two Years with the Natives in the Western Pacific*, 211, 212.

[6] P. A. Talbot, *The Peoples of Southern Nigeria*, iii. 758 *sq.*; E. Torday, *On the Trail of the Bushongo*, pp. 87 *sq.*, 187; J. H. Weeks, *Among the Primitive Bakongo*, 126.

CHAPTER LXXIV

THE RITUAL OF DEATH AND RESURRECTION [1]

AMONG the Ibibio, a tribe of Southern Nigeria, there is a powerful secret society called the Idiong. A candidate, at being admitted to it, must undergo a rite of mimic death and resurrection. A goat is first sacrificed, and its flesh scattered about to attract the vultures. " While the birds are feeding, the aspirant's body is rubbed over with yellow powder. The head priest then stands forth, holding a yam-pounder in his right hand. With his left he takes the hand of the man and announces : ' I am about to kill you now ! ' Then with increased solemnity he continues : ' Close your eyes.' Next, amid breathless silence, slow-falling, come the words, ' Thou art dead '—upon which the neophyte staggers and appears about to fall. The other members seize the wrists of the supposed corpse, drag him to the local club-house and fling him to the ground, in a space marked off by a row of impaled tortoises, from end to end of which stretches a semicircle of plantain leaves. Over the body a cloth is laid, as with one prepared for burial, and all sit sadly around as though mourning the dead. After a while one of the number rises and goes out. He searches until a small plantain is found, which he then cuts down and bears back to the chamber of mourning. The head priest places native pepper in his mouth, chews it, and then ejects it over the tree, saying : ' This plantain has now power to revive our brother.' It is perhaps worth remarking that, according to general Ibibio belief, plantain trees, in the hands of powerful Juju men, have the power of recalling the dead to life. One near death too may sometimes

[1] *Balder the Beautiful,* ii. 225-278.

be revived if a very powerful magician climbs upon the roof of the house, as near as possible to the place beneath which the sick man lies. Seven strokes of the plantain stem must be struck against the roof, while after each the patient's name is called. To every call the sufferer must answer : ' Ekpenyon —O—! Ekpenyon—O—! '

" In Idiong rites also, the stem is beaten seven times against the ground at the feet of the supposed corpse. Immediately after the seventh stroke the man rises, whereon the chief whispers into his ear some prophecy supposed to have been learnt during his sojourn in the realm of the dead. This the neophyte carefully repeats. It is usually of a very vague nature. Next, all adjourn to the father's house, where a feast is spread, that the new-born may eat and be strengthened on his return to earth-life, after the strain of the terrible journey which he is supposed to have undergone." [1]

[1] P A. Talbot, *Life in Southern Nigeria*, pp. 174 *sq.*

CHAPTER LXXV

THE MISTLETOE

ELSEWHERE I have conjectured that the view that the mistletoe contains the life of the oak may have been suggested by the position of the plant among the boughs.[1] The Gallas of East Africa say that the mistletoe is grafted on a tree as the soul is grafted on the body. And they show their veneration for the plant by gathering it at a special ceremony and placing it in their houses to bring good luck.[2]

[1] *Balder the Beautiful*, ii. 279 *sq.*
[2] R. Chambard, " Croyances religieuses des Gallas," in *Revue d'ethnographie et des traditions populaires*, vii. (1926), 122.

INDEX

481

THE END

Printed in Great Britain by R. & R. CLARK, LIMITED, *Edinburgh.*

WORKS BY SIR J. G. FRAZER

THE GOLDEN BOUGH

A STUDY IN MAGIC AND RELIGION

Third Edition, revised and enlarged. 8vo.

Part I. THE MAGIC ART AND THE EVOLUTION OF KINGS. Two volumes. 25s. net.

II. TABOO AND THE PERILS OF THE SOUL. One volume. 12s. 6d. net.

III. THE DYING GOD. One volume. 12s. 6d. net.

IV. ADONIS, ATTIS, OSIRIS. Two volumes. 25s. net.

V. SPIRITS OF THE CORN AND OF THE WILD. Two volumes. 25s. net.

VI. THE SCAPEGOAT. One volume. 12s. 6d. net.

VII. BALDER THE BEAUTIFUL: THE FIRE-FESTIVALS OF EUROPE, AND THE DOCTRINE OF THE EXTERNAL SOUL. Two volumes. 25s. net.

VIII. (Vol. XII.) BIBLIOGRAPHY AND GENERAL INDEX. 25s. net.

The Complete Work. In 12 Volumes. £5 : 5s. net the Set.

AFTERMATH. A Supplement to " The Golden Bough."

THE GOLDEN BOUGH. A Study in Magic and Religion. Abridged Edition. 8vo. 18s. net.

LEAVES FROM "THE GOLDEN BOUGH." Culled by Lady FRAZER. With Illustrations by H. M. BROCK. 8vo. 10s. 6d. net.

TOTEMISM AND EXOGAMY. A Treatise on Certain EARLY FORMS OF SUPERSTITION AND SOCIETY. Four volumes. 8vo. 50s. net.

THE BELIEF IN IMMORTALITY AND THE WORSHIP OF THE DEAD. 8vo.

Vol. I. The Belief among the Aborigines of Australia, the Torres Straits Islands, New Guinea and Melanesia. 18s. net.

Vol. II. The Belief among the Polynesians. 18s. net.

Vol. III. The Belief among the Micronesians. 18s. net.

THE FEAR OF THE DEAD IN PRIMITIVE RELIGION. Three volumes. 8vo. 10s. 6d. net each.

CREATION AND EVOLUTION IN PRIMITIVE COSMOGONIES AND OTHER PIECES. 8vo. 8s. 6d. net.

THE WORSHIP OF NATURE: The Worship of the Sky, the Earth, and the Sun. 8vo. 25s. net.

MACMILLAN AND CO., LTD., LONDON

WORKS BY SIR J. G. FRAZER

MYTHS OF THE ORIGIN OF FIRE. An Essay. 8vo. 12s. 6d. net.

FOLK-LORE IN THE OLD TESTAMENT. Studies in Comparative Religion, Legend, and Law. Three vols. 8vo. 37s. 6d. net.

FOLK-LORE IN THE OLD TESTAMENT. Studies in Comparative Religion, Legend, and Law. Abridged Edition. 8vo. 18s. net.

MAN, GOD, AND IMMORTALITY. Thoughts on Human Progress. Passages chosen from the Writings of Sir JAMES GEORGE FRAZER. Revised and Edited by the Author. 8vo. 6s. net.

THE DEVIL'S ADVOCATE. A Plea for Superstition. Second Edition, revised and enlarged, of "Psyche's Task"; to which is added "The Scope of Social Anthropology." 8vo. 6s. 6d. net.

PAUSANIAS'S DESCRIPTION OF GREECE. Translated with a Commentary, Illustrations, and Maps. Second Edition. Six vols. 8vo. £6 : 6s. net.

STUDIES IN GREEK SCENERY, LEGEND AND HISTORY. Crown 8vo. 8s. 6d. net.

GRAECIA ANTIQUA. Maps and Plans to illustrate Pausanias's Description of Greece. Compiled by Sir J. G. FRAZER; with explanatory text by Professor A. W. VAN BUREN. 8vo. 25s. net.

THE FASTI OF OVID. Text, Translation, and Commentary. Five vols. Illustrated. 8vo. 20s. net each.

THE GROWTH OF PLATO'S IDEAL THEORY. An Essay. 8vo. 7s. 6d. net.

THE GORGON'S HEAD AND OTHER LITERARY PIECES. With a Preface by ANATOLE FRANCE and a Portrait of the Author from the Bust by ANTOINE BOURDELLE. 8vo. 7s. 6d. net

GARNERED SHEAVES: Essays, Addresses, and Reviews. 8vo. 21s. net.

LETTERS OF WILLIAM COWPER. Chosen and Edited, with a Memoir and a few Notes, by Sir J. G. FRAZER. Two vols. Globe 8vo. 3s. 6d. net each.

A BIBLIOGRAPHY OF SIR JAMES GEORGE FRAZER. Compiled by THEODORE BESTERMAN. 8vo. 12s. 6d. net.

MACMILLAN AND CO., LTD., LONDON

2

CPSIA information can be obtained
at www.ICGtesting.com
Printed in the USA
LVHW031809220222
711732LV00001B/51

9 781108 057509